MONTANA OUR LAND & PEOPLE

For Dad,
This is where I live now, and I'm hoping my wedding this summer is one of the best times we've had as a family — looking through this may add just a little to the visit.

Charlie

MONTANA

PRUETT PUBLISHING COMPANY
Boulder, Colorado

OUR LAND & PEOPLE

By
William L. Lang,
Montana Historical Society

Rex C. Myers,
Western Montana College

Bibliography prepared by David Walter, Montana Historical Society

Maps prepared by Robert L. Taylor, Montana State University

©1979 by William L. Lang and Rex C. Myers
All rights reserved, including those to reproduce this book, or parts thereof, in any form without permission in writing from the Publisher.

Library of Congress Number 79-2772

Trade Edition ISBN: 0-87108-586-0

First Edition
2 3 4 5 6 7 8 9

Printed in the United States of America

Unless otherwise noted, all photographs are courtesy of the Montana Historical Society. The abbreviation M.H.S. is used to indicate special collections which are property of the Montana Historical Society.

To
four special Montanans
Becky, Joel, Laura & Gary

Contents

Chapter I	The Land Forms, The People Arrive	1
	Montana's Buried Treasure	8
	A Special Buffalo Hunt	10
Chapter II	Explorers, Trappers and Priests	15
	St. Mary's Mission	20
	Pierre Chouteau, Jr.	23
	Lewis and Clark in Montana	26
Chapter III	Gold Lures Men	33
	Alder Gulch Becomes Virginia City	40
	Sam Hauser	45
Chapter IV	Politics in Montana Territory	51
	Governor Benjamin F. Potts	57
	Martin Maginnis in Washington	59
Chapter V	The Indians Lose Their Land	65
	Life in the Tribe	75
	With the Army at Fort Shaw	78
Chapter VI	Cowboys & Farmers Tame the Land	85
	Farmers Read the Rocky Mountain Husbandman	91
	Wanted: A Chinook—The Winter of 1886-1887	94
	At the Grant-Kohrs Ranch	97

Chapter VII	Social and Urban Development 103
	Montana's People Came from Someplace Else. 113
	Lizzie 116
	Fire! Fire! Fire! 119
Chapter VIII	Travel Across the Land 125
	Welcome Aboard a Steamboat 136
	Jim Hill Built a Railroad 141
Chapter IX	Industry Expands 147
	Hard Work Built Montana 157
	From Wheat to Flour 159
Chapter X	Land for Homesteads. 165
	You Need a Homestead in Teton County! 172
	Richland County is Born. 174
Chapter XI	Power Politics 179
	Senator Clark of Montana 188
	We Are at War 191
Chapter XII	Montana in the Twenties Was a Time of Trial 197
	A Governor Under Pressure 201
	Making Dry Farming Pay 204
Chapter XIII	Challenge of the Twentieth Century 209
	To Tame the Missouri. 216
	An Independent Man in Politics 220
Chapter XIV	Montana: Our Land and People. 227
Bibliography	 237
Index	 255

Preface

A preface is simply a two-fold introduction. In it the author, or authors, introduce readers to the book. They then introduce and thank everyone who helped with the book's preparation. This preface does no more.

As Montanans, we have seen the land. We have gazed across the endless sculptured beauty of eastern Montana where wind and water have crafted on the landscape. We have marveled at the touch added in modern times by fields of golden wheat and hillsides dotted with cattle. Equally impressive is the rugged grandeur of the western mountains. We have climbed its peaks, skied its snow, hiked its trails and fished its waters.

As Montanans we have also come to know many of our neighbors under the Big Sky. Each in his or her own way has shared the personality and heritage they give the state. Indian and white, student and pioneer, miner and rancher—each has been a teacher. We learn much from the stories of people—the history they leave. Some of those stories are recorded in books, others in photographs, still others only in the memories of Montanans.

This book attempts to do nothing more than tell the story—the history—of Montana's land and people. Our title suggests that approach. If the reader leaves this book with a better understanding of Montana, we have accomplished our purpose.

A word on organization may help as you wander the pages of this volume and Montana's past. The fourteen chapters are arranged by subject, within a loose chronological framework. They can be read separately for a study of a particular aspect of Montana history. They can be read in order as an historic narrative. More than a few stories or accounts appear in several chapters. This is deliberate. No event in Montana history took place as an isolated incident. A mining strike, a fire, winter weather or an election had some effect on the territory or state as a whole. In some cases the incident had national importance or national events had significant impacts on Montana. We have attempted to discuss those relationships.

Because of the large amount of history to be covered, it has been necessary to mention some items only briefly. Overviews provide the core of each chapter. There are specific details in them, but generally, they are very broad and filled with generalizations. To balance this approach, each chapter (except the last) has two or more vignettes—special stories. Here we have concentrated on one event, or one person, trying to provide deeper insights into the era we are discussing. We would be the first to admit we could have picked a different event or person to study. There is no claim that what or whom we have examined is the most important. We do think that these events and individuals are representative of the period discussed.

At the end of each chapter are two items designed to help the reader better understand the topic. The time-line places events in that chapter in a year-by-year sequence with other events. By taking two (or more) time-lines, it is possible to see quickly how subjects relate to one another. You can see how transportation developed in comparison with the livestock industry, for example. Finally, a brief list of suggested readings ends each chapter. These are not the only books available on a particular topic, but for anyone who wants to read more about the events and people discussed, they are a good starting point.

There is an index at the very end of the book to help readers locate a particular person or place. Between the last chapter and the index is yet another very important part of this book—the bibliography. Where the chapters discuss Montana by topic, the bibliography lists materials by area. General works on Montana are provided, to be sure, but the other histories may be the most important for a reader's use. *Montana: Our Land and People* is not the last word in the history of the state, nor of any particular county or community. Please use the bibliography to explore other books about Montana and the particular corner you call home.

We hope the chapters and bibliography of this book introduce you to Montana. We would also like to take the last part of this preface and introduce you to some of the people who helped us in researching and writing what you are about to read. Montana and the West are filled with friendly people; the list that follows more than proves that point.

When the idea of writing this book first came, we asked many individuals for their reaction to such a project. Among the first to respond enthusiastically was Ed Eschler, social studies and environmental consultant for the Office of the Superintendent of Public Instruction. His support and encouragement never faltered. Well beyond the professional requirements of his job, his optimism and assistance helped us keep going time and time again.

Good maps and a solid bibliography are essential in a book like this. We knew that and sought help from the best individuals we knew in those areas. Bob Taylor from the Department of Earth Sciences, Montana State University, graciously offered the use of maps he was preparing for an historic atlas of Montana. When what he had was not quite what we wanted, he drew just the right map. We are looking forward to the publication of his atlas, confident that it will become one of the essential tools for the study of Montana.

David Walter of Columbia Falls published one of the most thorough Montana bibliographies ever assembled in the May 1978 issue of *Montana Historian.* His bibliography at the end of this book is selected from that earlier research. If this volume is the start of your travels in Montana history, Dave Walter's bibliographies have to be the guides for the rest of your trip.

Photographs, like maps and bibliographies, are important. They illustrate in graphic terms what an author can never describe in words. Here we must thank the Montana Historical Society. With few exceptions, the photographs in this book come from their priceless collections. No one has a better understanding of those collections than the Society's photo archivist, Lory Morrow. When we had an idea, she found the photograph that best illustrated it.

There were other contributors. Bob Copely, plant manager of the General Mills operation in Great Falls, took time to explain how flour was made and provided a tour to illustrate. Michele Farmer, historian at the Grant-Kohrs Ranch National Historic Site in Deer Lodge, made sure that what we said about Conrad Kohrs and his ranching was correct. Jeannie Eder advised us on Indian traditions. Claire Rhein of the University of Montana Archives helped locate an H. G. Merriam photograph for us, and Jean Schmidt, archivist at Montana State University, did the same thing for pictures from that collection. The Minnesota Historical Society dug for a Hardy Campbell photo, too.

Obviously, book writing is not a solitary task. Polishing what is written also takes help, and we appreciate every bit of it. Barbara Rackley of the Montana Historical Society, and Michael Malone from the Department of History at MSU, read the manuscript and offered suggestions or criticism. Ed Eschler's name must come up again for doing likewise. Sharion Stark struggled through a collection of pencil marks and cryptic notes to type the final manuscript. The publisher should thank her more than we do. And speaking of publishers, Jerry Keenan of Pruett Publishing Company deserves a word of thanks for hustling the manuscript into type, and seeing the finished product off the presses into the hands of readers.

Before the list gets too long, let us hasten to say there are others. We have lost track of the names and the numbers of teachers who heard about this book and provided both support and suggestions. To each of you, many thanks. Finally, if this book is new to you, there are others who have seen it before. Our wives and families have heard and read the chapters over and over. They smiled when we worked late (or early) and missed doing something at home. If there is a last word in "Thank yous" it goes to our wives.

William L. Lang
Montana Historical Society

Rex C. Myers
Western Montana College

Indians used the travois for carrying their property and families when they moved.—*N. A. Forsyth photograph, M.H.S.*

Chapter I
The Land Forms, The People Arrive

Montana is land and people. Montana's history is the story of what land did to the people who lived on it, and what people did to the land. Writer Joseph Kinsey Howard called Montana high, wide and handsome. Historian K. Ross Toole called it an uncommon land. Pulitzer Prize-winner A. B. Guthrie looked at Montana and saw the big sky that covered it all. To each of these individuals and to all Montanans, the land is something special.

If you ask someone from Montana to describe where he or she lives you will discover an aspect of that closeness to the land. We think of our homes as geographic places: "up the Bitterroot," "along the Rosebud," "in the Little Rockies." More particularly, neighbors and friends live "downstream" or "over the ridge," or "in the next coulee." Montanans have a close relationship with the land and with their environment. The real history of the state begins with the land itself.

Three factors determine the environment in which Montanans live: water, elevation and soil. Water heads the list of important influences. Amounts of precipitation vary greatly. In the high western mountains, annual precipitation (much of it snow) may amount to sixty inches or more. On the plains—the "Great American Desert" early explorers called it—rainfall totals less than twenty inches each year. Because water is so scarce in many parts of the state, it is important for Montana ranchers and farmers to irrigate and time their crops to suit the rain.

Water that falls on Montana leaves the state along one of three courses. To the east, the vast Missouri and Yellowstone river drainages gather melting snows of winter and seasonal rains. Their waters serve residents as sources of irrigation, recreation and hydroelectric power. Then they flow to the Gulf of Mexico and the Atlantic Ocean. West of the Continental Divide, the Clark Fork and Kootenai serve the same collecting functions. They deliver their waters to the Columbia River and the Pacific Ocean. Because its waters also feed Hudson's Bay and the Arctic Ocean, Montana is unique among the United States. A portion of Sheridan County in northeastern Montana, and part of Glacier National Park feed the Saskatchewan and Belly rivers, which flow north. In Glacier National Park is an 8,011-foot tall monument to Montana's three watersheds: Triple Divide Peak.

Water is the first of the keys to understanding Montana's environment. Elevation is the second. Again, Montana is a state of extremes. The highest point in the state is the 12,850-foot Granite Peak, in the Beartooth Range just north of Yellowstone National Park. To the west and north, where the Kootenai River leaves the state, is Montana's lowest point—only 1,800 feet above sea level. Montana is a series of mountain ranges, broad valleys, and rolling prairies at an average height of 3,400 feet. Summer and winter temperatures are a product of this environment. Near the Continental Divide at the head of the Blackfoot River, over 5,000 feet high, a thermometer dipped to a record -70°F in 1954. At lower elevations, like 2,000-foot Glendive and Medicine Lake, temperatures have hit 117°F during July and August. This is a difference of almost 190°.

Between western mountains and eastern plains lies a central belt sometimes called the "chinook zone." Chinook is an Indian word meaning "snow eater." To resident and weatherman alike it means a warm wind along the eastern slope of the mountains. Chinooks may raise the mercury in a winter thermostat 50° or more in a few hours. In the path of these warm breezes, the deepest snow banks melt and winter's grip is temporarily broken.

Soil joins water and elevation as the third important factor in Montana's environment. Fertile soils on the broad plains and in the river valleys support a variety of agriculture and livestock. Rocky crags and barren ridges in the mountainous zones defy agricultural efforts. Residents there have turned to lumbering and mining.

It is possible to divide Montana in yet another way—geographically. People living outside Montana see a single, 147,138-square-mile state—fourth largest in the nation. Yet one part of Montana is as different from another as any two states.

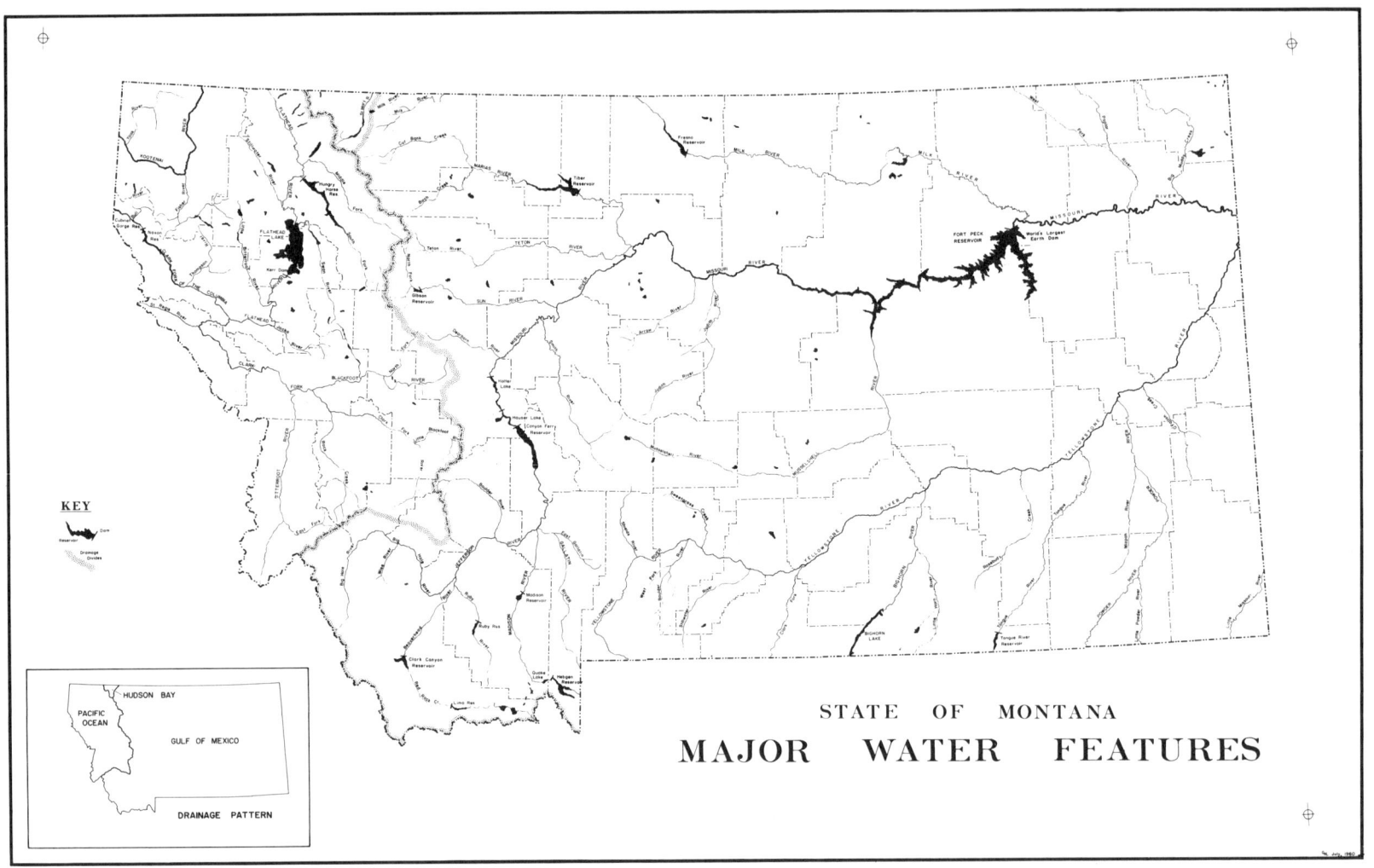

STATE OF MONTANA
MAJOR WATER FEATURES

Roughly the western third is filled with rugged terrain and large forests. It has tall mountain ranges, dividing the land into a series of north/south slices. Bitterroot, Mission, and Madison ranges are spectacular, lying at the northern end of the Rocky Mountains in the United States. Along the crests of these mountains runs the Continental Divide. Montana's western third is a region of heavy precipitation, dense forests, broad and fertile valleys. The land yields timber, gold, silver, copper and other metal ores.

A middle third of Montana forms a buffer zone between east and west. The climate here is drier than in the western portion. Broad benchlands and even broader valleys separate scattered mountain outcroppings. Isolated ranges like the Little Rockies, the Highwoods, Little Belts, Big Snowy Mountains, Crazy Mountains, and Pryor Mountains dot the land above the plains. Here, too, men found gold, silver and other metals. Here, as well, is more land for cattle and grain. Indeed, much of the golden harvest from this part of Montana has been in the form of wheat and other grains that thrive in the central region.

Eastern Montana—the remaining third—is drier still. The land is a vast rolling prairie, which supported first

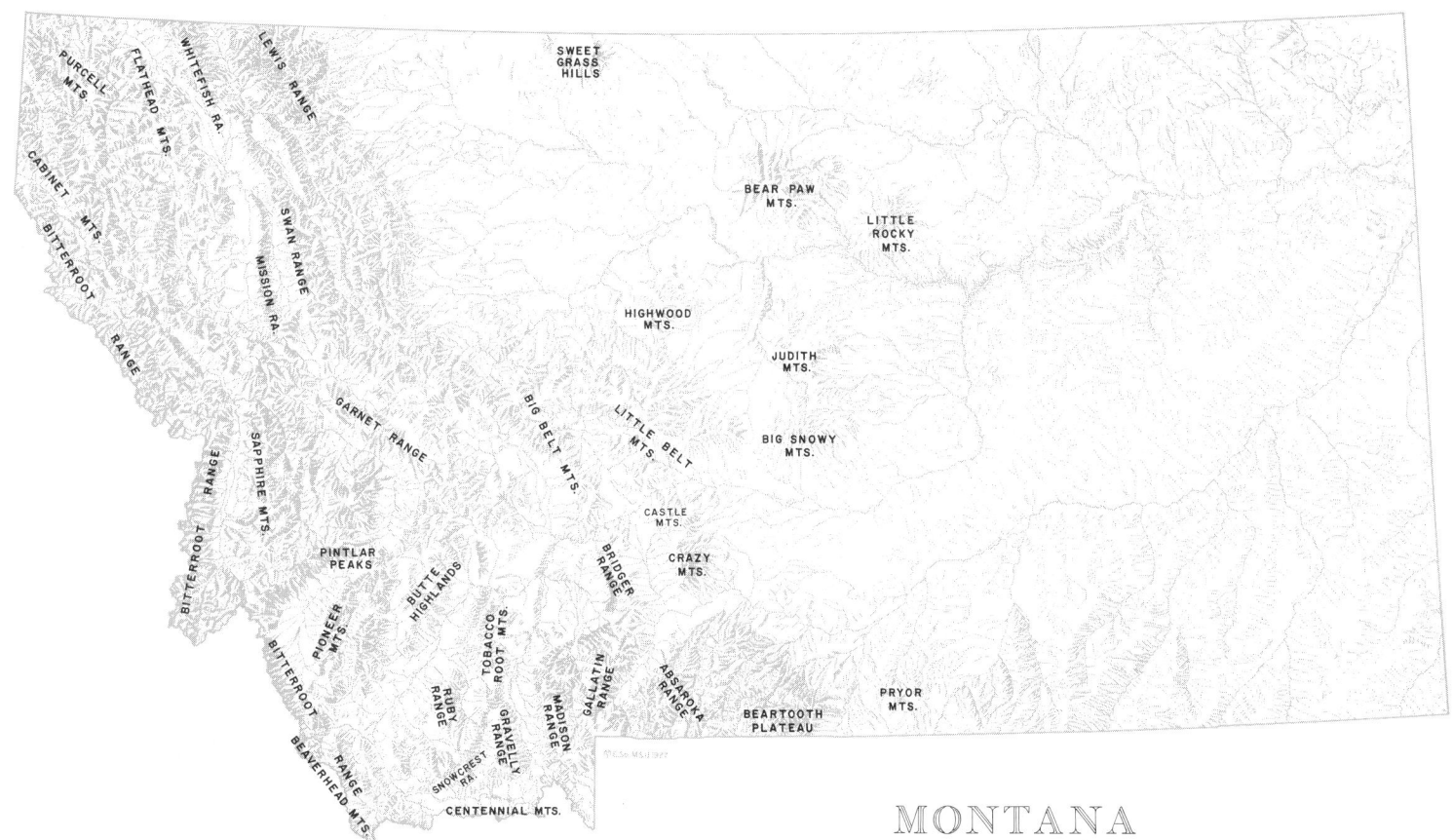

MONTANA

buffalo and then range cattle. Homesteaders discovered the land's fragile richness in dry land farming—wheat and cereal crops. More recent residents and visitors have found wealth below the surface in coal, oil, and natural gas. Over all is the big sky that seems never to end. It is a big sky to reflect the subtle contrasts and beauty of the plains. It is a big sky that seems to represent the vastness of all Montana.

The history of Montana is the story of people and land, but it is a story that begins long before the first early peoples arrived and long before Montana took the varied shapes we recognize today. It is a story told in the layers of rock below the surface of the land—a tale three billion years old.

Rocks in Montana are as old as rocks anywhere in the world. Geologists call the first layers of stone "basement rocks," because all other geological layers are built on this foundation. Basement rocks started as mud and sand, deposited on the bottom of early seas that once covered the region. This was during what is called the Precambrian Era. Over millions of years these sediments settled deep into the earth and cooked, all the while being squeezed under intense pressure. Basement rocks were formed. These are usually colorful combinations of glassy whites, pinks and reds, like quartz and feldspar, or the grays and black of mica and hornblende. To a geologist or rockhound, this super-cooked rock takes several forms: 1) gneiss—rock that looks streaky; 2) schist—rock with enough mica to make it actually flaky; and 3) granite—a blend of quartz, feldspar and mica without the streaky appearance. Sometimes we see granite outcroppings with ribbons of gneiss or schist running through them, looking something like ripple ice cream or a marble cake.

Basement rocks formed Montana's first mountains. Time and prehistoric weather gradually eroded them, changing it all into a broad, lifeless plain. The sediment from this erosion laid down the next layer of rock between one and one-half billion and 600 million years ago. In warm, shallow seas the first primitive plants developed, and fossil remains give us clues to the early life on the planet.

During the Paleozoic Era—600 million to 225 million years ago—and the Mesozoic Era—225 to about 60 million years ago—a shallow sea periodically flooded the region that includes Montana. Each flooding settled more and more sediment on the basement rock until it reached a depth of several thousand feet. Fossil remains tell us that plant forms continued to develop and thrive in these warm seas. Joining them were the first animals on earth—Paleozoic Trilobites and Brachiopods or primitive fishes and amphibians. Later came Mesozoic dinosaurs and reptiles.

As these plants and animals died and fell to the bottom of the seas, they were in turn covered by more sediment. Some went through periods of extreme pressure and heat to lie buried as fossil fuels—coal, oil and natural gas. Others left their imprint, or actual remains, imbedded in the rock as fossils. Among these early "Montanans" could be found the forty-seven-foot-long Tyrannosaurus Rex (a savage flesh eater) and the three-horned, thirty-foot long Triceratops. Fossils of these beasts and some of their contemporaries date back 155 million years. They have been found in several parts of the state, including Garfield and Carter counties.

More recent dinosaur finds—65 million years ago—include thirty-foot long Trachodons, a duckbilled fellow with over 2,000 teeth. One of his neighbors was twenty tons of swimming dinosaur called a Plesiosaur. Remains of these beasts have been found near Chinook, on the Custer Battlefield, and elsewhere. Interestingly, the Plesiosaur had a contemporary who still lives in Montana. Scientists tell us that the paddlefish, which inhabits the Yellowstone and Missouri rivers in northeastern Montana, began swimming about the time his larger neighbors sank into the Mesozoic muck and mud.

All this came to an end about 100 million years ago. At that time Montana got its present mountains. During this period, molten rock from deep in the earth began to heat and rise beneath western North America. It cracked and broke the twenty-five-mile thick crust of the earth. It lifted huge chunks of basement rock and Paleozoic or Mesozoic sedimentary rock. These formations broke into long, narrow blocks, running north to south. Those lifted highest became mountain ranges. Others became high, intermontane valleys.

Molten rocks broke through the surface in the form of granite or volcanic rock. The result of this violent action left Montana a hodgepodge of twisted, turned and scattered rock formations. Close examination of almost any major rock outcropping in western and central Montana reveals the varied forms and shapes resulting from this uplift. And it is a process that has not yet ended.

Earthquakes tell us that the earth is still moving. Mountains and valleys are still being created. Since 1864, over forty-seven major earthquakes have hit the belt of mountains from Kalispell to Yellowstone National Park. Among the worst were the 1935 quakes in Helena, and the 1959 Madison River earthquake. Scientists predict continued movements in the earth. This means future quakes.

Montana got her mountains as the earth aged through the Mesozoic Era and into the Cenozoic Era. Between 60 million and 3 million years back in time, the entire area went through the Tertiary Period. A desert-like climate replaced earlier warm seas. Infrequent rains washed away much of the mountain rock, depositing it thousands of feet deep in the valleys. It can be found today as multicolored muds and brown gravel.

Volcanos spurted forth here and there in western Montana. Across the land a variety of mammals roamed—elephants, camels, and primitive horses. Their fossils, and pieces of trees—petrified wood—can be found in the Tertiary deposits of almost any Montana valley.

A change in climate brought an end to the Tertiary Period and a start of the Ice Ages. Not really cold spells, the Ice Ages actually reflected very wet cycles. Mountain snowfalls accumulated to such depths that glaciers formed. Eventually these covered much of the northern part of Montana. Four separate glacial periods took place. During the runoff between each, rivers dug into the Tertiary valleys, digging them deeper, washing much of the mud and gravel downstream. Most western valleys have lost about one thousand feet of sediment to date. They have another two or three thousand feet left to go. Graphic illustrations of wind and water erosion are found today at Medicine Rocks and Makoshika State Park in eastern Montana.

One of the most impressive creations of the glacial period was a large lake in western Montana. Glaciers dammed the Clark Fork River and made Glacial Lake Missoula. This lake left shoreline marks on mountains in the region, but it vanished suddenly when the ice dam broke. What a tremendous flood it must have been!

Glaciers have all but disappeared in Montana, retreating to the high mountain valleys. Volcanos, too, have been inactive for at least 10,000 years. Elephants, camels, and primitive horses vanished in due time. Other mammals, large and small, replaced them: elk, deer, bears, bighorn sheep, foxes, skunks, rabbits, coyotes and so on. Some two hundred species of birds inhabit the mountains, valleys and plains. The state bird, Meadowlark, and the majestic Bald Eagle are among them. In the streams, the paddlefish now shares his space with trout, salmon, catfish, grayling and many others.

Humans joined the list of Montana's animal residents between 10,000 and 30,000 years ago. They followed what is sometimes called "The Great North Trail." The first groups came from Asia. They traveled across the Bering Strait on bridges of ice or land and moved down into Central and South America. They stopped along the way to hunt now-vanished mammals like the mammoth and the extinct bison. These early Montanans left skimpy evidence of their residence in places like the McHaffie Site east of Helena. A few broken projectile points, chippings, and primitive tools tell us early people hunted and lived in the region.

When a 1,000-year dry spell began about 5,000 B.C., the large animals disappeared. Early humans went with them. Then between 4000 and 1000 B.C. new residents moved in—plains archaic people, or "foragers." They migrated from the south, living on small animals, plants, and roots. Glaciers in western Montana had melted during the preceding 1,000 years, so these "foragers" moved into western Montana as well as the eastern plains.

A few centuries before or after Christ walked the earth, another group of prehistoric people came to live in what is now Montana. These late hunters perfected the use of the bow and arrow, the spear and atlatl (spear thrower). Unlike their eastern counterparts, Montana's late hunters did not engage in agriculture. They pursued buffalo herds, making their living by using every part of the large animals. In group hunts these horseless tribes often drove entire herds over buffalo jumps, or pishkuns, killing the surviving beasts at the bottom of the cliffs. Sometimes they used dead-end valleys or coulees to capture and kill a herd. Near these sites modern archeologists have found tipi rings. These are made of stones used to hold down the edges of the tents or lodges. These rings, arrowheads and the like, provide modern evidence of the life these late hunters led. They left their art on cliffs and cave walls throughout Montana, like Pictograph Cave near Billings.

These unmolested people ultimately experienced a tremendous shock. By 1500 A.D., Europeans had "discovered" the Western Hemisphere and North America. Europeans mistakenly dubbed the descendants of the late hunters "Indians," then moved into their lands from the east and south. With advanced technology and a never-satisfied hunger for land, the Europeans kept coming. They disrupted the Indians' culture and took his land.

As early as 1600, changes had already taken place in the lives of these late hunters. In a process of push and shove, whites displaced Indians in the south and east. These fleeing tribes acquired guns and horses and in turn pushed out their western and northern neighbors. Historians liken the effect to ripples in a pond, or falling dominoes. The results proved dramatic. Not one tribe that Lewis and Clark found in Montana east of the Continental Divide during the early 1800s had lived there before 1600.

Shoshoni Indians acquired the first horses in the region. Decked out in leather armor, with bows, arrows and spears, they swept into eastern and central Montana like fine cavalry troops. They drove everyone before them. Gradually, however, their enemies acquired horses and guns from eastern whites. In combination these two factors helped other tribes push back the Shoshoni.

Montana Indians adapted quickly to the horse and the gun. They became skilled at breeding and training the former, and proved always anxious to obtain more of the latter. The mounted, mobile plains Indian, which so captured the imagination of later Americans, came into being only during the 1700s. Nomadic, these groups packed belongings on horse-drawn travois and moved with the seasons and buffalo herds. Families, bands and larger tribes provided the organization for these groups. A tribe might contain only a few hundred Indians, or several thousand.

Socially, Indian men devoted their time to hunting, raiding (often for more horses), and war. Women took care of the household tasks. They tanned hides, raised the children, and did most of the camp labor. Leadership rested with the chief, a male who had usually distinguished himself in battle. A chief's authority was not absolute. Leadership changed depending on the "medicine" of one individual or another. Indians enjoyed a close relationship with nature, often seeking to communicate with supernatural forces—the Great Spirit—through visions or rituals. Symbolism and dancing became important parts of tribal and individual life.

West of the Continental Divide, separate culturally from plains tribes, lived plateau Indians like the Flathead, Kutenai, and Kalispel. Although these groups made seasonal treks to the plains to hunt buffalo, they were less nomadic than their eastern counterparts. They lived primarily on fish, roots (the bitterroot, for example), and berries.

Originally, Flatheads extended as far east as Three Forks. The invasion of the Shoshoni, then the fierce Blackfeet, later forced the Flatheads to retreat into western Montana. They took up residence in the beautiful Bitterroot Valley. Anxious to find allies against their enemies, Flatheads welcomed whites and accepted Christianity. Such "peacefulness" was not a sign of weakness, only an indication of competition among tribes.

Pend d'Oreille or Kalispel Indians shared the Salishan language and western Montana with the Flatheads. At one time these bands extended over the Divide into the Sun River Valley. Blackfeet and plains tribes forced them westward, too. Like the Flatheads, the Pend d'Oreille also saw allies in the first white settlers. Kutenai Indians joined the Flathead and Pend d'Oreille in the region. Although they had a different language, they faced the same Shoshoni and Blackfeet enemies. Now they share the same reservation in western Montana.

Blackfeet became the most feared of Montana's plains Indians. Like many of their neighbors, they did not originate in the region. Belonging to the Algonquin linguistic group, Blackfeet came from central and eastern Canada. As early as the middle of the seventeenth century, they began to retreat westward in the face of Cree and white encroachment.

The Blackfeet Nation included three groups. To the north were the Siksika; south of them, the Kainah, or Bloods; further south yet, the Piegans, or "Poor Robes." The Piegan were the only true Montana Blackfeet—fierce and feared by white man and Indian alike. Piegan males prided themselves in their ability as warriors. After acquiring horses, the Piegan drove the Shoshoni southwest, out of northern and central Montana. The Piegan also stopped white settlement in the area until disease hit the tribe in the late 1830s.

Along the Yellowstone River Valley in southeastern Montana lived the "Bird People"—Crows, or Absarokas. Originating in the upper Mississippi Valley, these people shared a Siouan language, but broke with the Sioux tribe very early. Under pressure from the Sioux and Cheyenne, they moved westward. Eventually they took up residence along the Yellowstone River.

Crows became nomadic plainsmen by the time they arrived in Montana during the early nineteenth century. They retained their eastern clan structure, but became true plains warriors. Crows broke into two subgroups—River Crows north of the Yellowstone, and Mountain Crows to the south. The tribe welcomed the white man as an ally against powerful Blackfeet and Sioux enemies who surrounded them.

East of the Blackfeet, and north of the Crows, two smaller Indian groups settled: the Atsina and the Assiniboine. With an Algonquin heritage, the Atsina originated in the Minnesota region, but fled before more powerful Cree and Sioux tribes. Early French trappers who encountered them misunderstood their sign language and called the Atsina "Gros Ventre," meaning "big bellies." The error only serves to confuse the Atsina with the Dakota Hidatsas, also known as "Gros Ventre." The Atsina allied with the Piegan and shared a reputation of war and hostility toward American settlers and explorers.

Assiniboine Indians also moved from the upper reaches

of the Mississippi River into the plains of Canada and the northeastern corner of Montana. Originally part of the Yanktonai branch of the Sioux Nation, the Assiniboine yielded to pressures from the Chippewa, Cree and Sioux. They left their homeland and moved west. Quickly the Assiniboine adapted to plains life and became good horsemen and mounted warriors. Only the smallpox epidemic of the 1830s broke their strength.

Additional groups of Indians inhabited or migrated through portions of Montana. In the southwest, remnants of the once powerful Shoshoni tribe crossed over the divide from Idaho near what is now Beaverhead County. Bannock and Sheepeater Indians likewise touched this portion of the state. Early miners named Montana's first capital after the Bannock tribe—misspelling the name in the process.

Far to the east, Cheyenne Indians vied for part of the Montana plains. Their original homeland included the Minnesota region, but like their Sioux allies, they moved west. Cheyenne warriors adapted superbly to plains warfare. Their Dog Soldiers earned respect from every Indian tribe or cavalry troop that encountered them. The Cheyenne split in the early 1800s. The northern segment remaining near Montana; the southern Cheyenne settling in Colorado or Oklahoma. Northern Cheyenne joined the Sioux in the climax of plains warfare during the summer of 1876. The alliance led to the defeat of General George A. Custer at the Battle of the Little Big Horn. Eventually whites gave the northern Cheyenne a reservation in eastern Montana near Tongue River.

Segments of two other tribes migrated into Montana late in the nineteenth century seeking better living conditions. Chippewas (Algonquin) and Crees (Athabaskan) both originated from the plains and northern portion of Canada. Associated with these two tribes were the Metis, a racial mixture of Cree, Chippewa, Assiniboine and French. The Metis spoke their own language and staged an unsuccessful rebellion against the Canadian government in 1885 under Louis Riel. His Metis followers fled to Montana joining the Chippewa and Cree as "Landless Indians." They roamed the state from Havre to Butte. Only in 1916 did the federal government agree to give them a small reservation near Box Elder.

Other tribes, among them the Nez Perce, Shoshoni, Bannock, Spokan and Sioux migrated with the seasons across portions of Montana in search of buffalo. Flathead, Kalispel, Kutenai, Blackfeet, Crow, Atsina, Assiniboine, Northern Cheyenne, Cree, and Chippewa became permanent parts of Montana when the federal government established a series of seven reservations. These reservations sought to preserve a portion of the vast land that the Indians once roamed.

During the nineteenth century, white men came to dominate Montana. They replaced the Indians who used the land before they did, just as the late hunters had replaced the foragers. Each group brought new cultures, new techniques, and new technology. Each touched the land that was Montana. Each used the water, crossed the land, experienced the climate. Before man, Montana grew and changed for millions of years. It had sediment, volcanos, earthquakes, glaciers and erosion. The people changed too. Montana's history began in the relationship between the land and the people who lived on it.

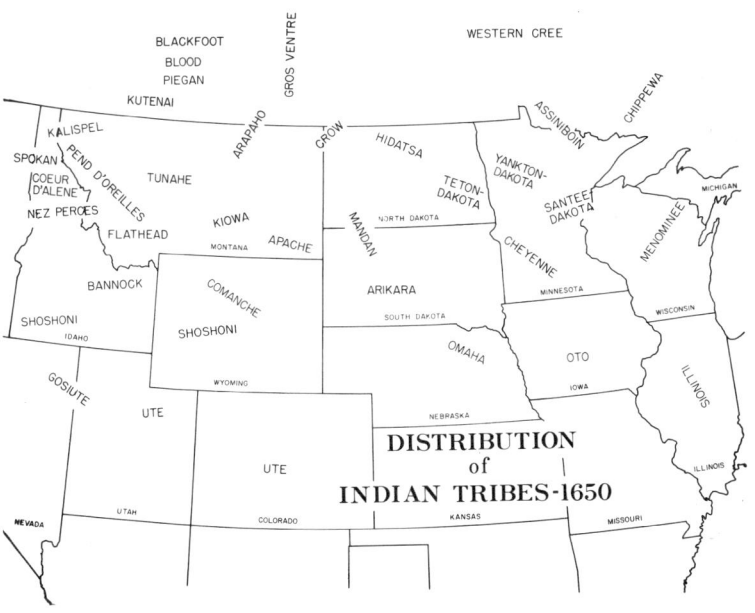

DISTRIBUTION of INDIAN TRIBES-1650

Montana's Buried Treasures

Gold is where you find it. Of course, the same thing can be said of silver, copper, coal, petroleum, and all other mineral deposits. Since the beginning of history, man made these minerals an important part of his life. Precious metals like gold and silver he used as money or decoration. Base (not precious) metals, like copper and lead, he fashioned into everyday utensils, swords and machines. Carbon fuels like coal, oil and natural gas have warmed, propelled and lubricated the world for centuries. All these minerals are found in Montana.

Gold, silver and copper deposits gave Montana its nickname, "The Treasure State." The first two metals appeared on the Territorial Seal designed in 1865. The motto "Oro y Plata" means "Gold and Silver" in Spanish. It indicates the early importance of these metals in Montana's history.

Deposits of gold, silver and copper share a common origin in geologic history. All three are found in veins (streaks of ore) in the central and western portions of the state. Scientists disagree on how these veins originated, but their appearance resembles the streaks of gneiss and schist that lace granite deposits everywhere.

During the middle of the Mesozoic Era and as late as the Tertiary Period volcanic activity abounded in the Rocky Mountains. One of the things this superheating did to rocks was to force water and dissolved chemicals upward. These solutions took routes of least resistance. They squeezed into cracks and crevasses where basement rock and sedimentary rock had settled or been split. Time and heat evaporated the water in these solutions. Only the chemicals remained. Depending on the nature of those chemicals, the results were cracks (veins) filled with minerals. Among them was a lot of quartz, and in combination, such metals as gold and silver. Copper deposits in Butte also exist primarily in veins caused by this process.

Of all metals, gold has attracted the lengthiest and most colorful attention. Early men undoubtedly knew of its existence, but did not prize it or mine it like European settlers. Gold mining in the United States dates back to 1799. The first Montana discoveries came in the 1850s and early 1860s.

As it does everywhere, Montana gold occurs in three forms: 1) primary deposits; 2) in combination with base-metal ores (like copper); and 3) in placers.

Primary gold deposits are veins of the precious metal wedged between other rock formations. Usually surrounded by quartz, this type of gold assumes a variety of beautiful forms: crystals, wires, and unusual shapes or designs. To mine it, a prospector had to chip, drill or blast loose the surrounding rock. He then recovered the gold physically, or through some type of chemical refining process.

Gold deposits that exist in combination with lead, zinc, or copper must be mined the same way. Pound for pound this ore does not have the same value as primary gold deposits.

Placer gold is the third form. Time, wind, and water eventually wore down many of the rocks that make up Montana's mountains and hills. This erosion broke up volcanic and sedimentary rock, forming gravel and dirt. As rock around a vein of gold broke away, the metal became exposed and washed downstream like any other stone. Gold, however, does not break and crumble as easily as most rocks. It is also heavier and sinks quickly to the bottom of a stream or river. Where the water moved rapidly, the gold tumbled along. In quiet water it settled and formed placer deposits. Such deposits first attracted miners to Gold Creek, Bannack, Alder Gulch, and similar mining districts. The presence of the placer gold, however, alerted prospectors to the primary gold buried somewhere in the mountains upstream.

Montana ranks seventh among gold-producing states, after California, Colorado, South Dakota, Alaska, Nevada, and Utah. As rich as gold deposits were in the Treasure State, Montanans are often surprised to learn that only Butte and Virginia City mining districts rank in the top twenty-five across the nation. Butte's production has come primarily as a by-product of copper mining. Virginia City's output came from placer deposits along Alder Gulch and neighboring streams.

Silver, like gold, occurs in three forms: 1) native silver; 2) silver-lead ores; 3) silver-copper ores. In rare deposits of native silver, the metal occurs in irregular threads, or branches—resembling ferns. Argentite is a form of native silver, and gave its name to one of Montana's early mining camps—Argenta.

Most Montana silver occurs in combination with lead or copper. Just a little silver can make the mining of copper or lead very profitable. Often silver (and gold) in these ores pay for the mining process, and the lead, zinc, or copper become the profit. Silver ores found near Elkhorn and Granite came in combination with lead and gold in an ore called galena. Butte's copper deposits also contain silver, which becomes a by-product of the refining process.

Copper worked its way into the rocks underlying Montana in the same manner as gold and silver. Hot, volcanic solutions squirting into the mountains around Butte contained a variety of mineral salts and chemicals. When the water disappeared, the residue included copper and a number of other minerals like sulphur. This resulted in Butte's copper sulphide ores. Veins of copper at Butte extend almost one mile below the surface of the ground, and run as wide as fifteen feet in some places. These large and valuable deposits earned Butte the nickname of the "Richest Hill on Earth."

Gold and silver sparkle to attract all the romantic attention of mining camps, dance hall girls, and outlaws. Copper and Butte shared their own unique place in Montana history, economics and politics. Yet, east and north of the gold, silver and copper, lie rich deposits of other minerals with a carbon base: coal and petroleum.

Beginning with the Precambrian and Paleozoic eras, plant life in the seas and oceans died and settled into sediment. The process continues even today, although it takes countless years to build up such deposits. Over millions of years this decaying material became compressed. For coal the process is easily traceable. Decomposing plant life forms peat. Time and pressure (like overlying sediment) pack the deposit tighter and tighter. Peat, first composed during the Tertiary Period, became a soft coal known as lignite. The longer the earth squeezed, the harder the coal became. Deposits from the Cretaceous and Jurassic Periods (late and middle Mesozoic Era) became sub-bituminous and bituminous coal. Going as far back as the Paleozoic Era, peat became the hardest type of coal—anthracite.

Montana's coal deposits are primarily bituminous and sub-bituminous. They stretch across much of the southeastern and eastern portions of the state. These are areas where large and lush swamps once existed. The sediment or rock on top of these deposits is not very deep in most places. Erosion removed some of it, exposing layers or seams of coal here and there. Because the coal burns well, it is an excellent source of energy. Because it is so close to the surface, it can be mined easily. The quickest method is to remove surface rock (overburden) and dig out the coal directly. The process is called strip mining. Modern mines at Colstrip, Decker, and elsewhere on the plains, use this technique. Where coal is buried deeper, underground mining is necessary. Red Lodge and Roundup coal mines have used these methods over the years.

Petroleum is the second type of carbon-based mineral in Montana. It exists in two forms: oil and natural gas. Both of these fuels owe their beginnings to the same plants and animals that preceded man in Montana. Like dinosaurs who "gave their all" to become coal, animals and plants from as far back as the Paleozoic or Precambrian eras died and formed layers of decomposing, organic material. Again, like coal, the process went on while Montana's rocks and mountains were being formed. Some petroleum deposits formed as recently as the Pleistocene epoch. Combinations of pressure and heat changed the remains of these beasts and bushes into oil or natural gas.

Petroleum products did not become truly important minerals until the late 1800s and early 1900s. During the last century, oil found use as a lubricant for machines. The automobile created the need for gasoline, which boomed the petroleum business. In response to this demand, exploration took place in Montana. Several important oil discoveries resulted. The Cut Bank, Kevin, and Sunburst fields along the Canadian border, and the Cat Creek field in central Montana are among them.

Natural gas has become an equally important fuel in recent decades. It is now essential for heating homes and firing the machines of industry. Montana has several natural gas deposits: the Cut Bank and Marias River field in the north central part of the state; the Bowdoin near Malta; and the Cedar Creek deposit along the North Dakota border. A series of pipelines links these fields with refineries and consumers.

Geological movements of molten rock during the Paleozoic Era left Montana with another unique mineral deposit. Considerable numbers of sapphires have been found in several parts of Montana. These light blue gemstones owe their origin to the hot molten rock that pushed toward the earth's surface about 300 million years ago. It came into contact with minerals in existing rock and created corundum deposits. These hard stones vary in quality from dull rocks to clear blue gems.

Montana sapphires are an official state gemstone and have attracted attention since the 1880s. They have been mined commercially in several locations. Of particular note have been mines near Rock Creek in western Montana; Eldorado Bar, American Bar, and neighboring placer deposits east of Helena; and extensive mines at Yogo, south and west of Lewistown. An estimated 30 million dollars in gem- and commercial-grade sapphires have been taken from Montana. The fun of digging for sapphires continues to attract rock hounds to Montana from across the nation.

Gold, silver, copper, coal, petroleum and sapphires are but a few of the many minerals found in Montana. A complete list is almost impossible. Among the other materials mined commercially during recent years, we find: antimony, clay, agate, iron, lead, lime, manganese, sand, building stone, zinc, cement, gypsum, fluorspar, phosphate, talc, vermiculite, tungsten, and chrome. The land contains many riches. Montana is, indeed, a Treasure State.

A Special Buffalo Hunt

Buffalo provided food, clothing, weapons, and tools for Montana's late hunters. Before the arrival of the horse and the white man's weapons, these wandering bands often used buffalo jumps or traps to hunt small herds of the shaggy animals. A jump consisted of a cliff or rimrock formation. Generally these are in the central portion of Montana where mountain gives way to plain. In more open areas, a cul-de-sac (a type of "box" canyon) was used. Other plains tribes resorted to a brush, branch and pole corral constructed at the head of a coulee or draw.

In the case of the "surround," a cul-de-sac or a corral, the animals milled about until the hunters had killed them. With a buffalo jump—sometimes called a pishkun—the animals died or received injuries in the fall. Hunters waiting below killed survivors.

There are at least seventeen known buffalo jumps in Montana today. In the case of all such locations, numerous tipi rings surround the sites, indicating repeated uses.

The story that follows describes the experiences of a young man, thirteen or fourteen, during this late hunter period. He joins in the excitement of his first buffalo hunt.

Running Wolf pulled his robe tighter about his shoulders and rolled over to get more sleep. Suddenly he remembered it was not just morning. It was the start of that special day when he could first take part in the buffalo hunt. He sat up and looked about the tipi. His mother's spot lay vacant. She had already gotten up and was outside tending the fire. His father and two younger sisters only now began to stir. Soon the entire camp would buzz with activity and anticipation.

Fires crackled about the cluster of tipis in the coulee. Eighteen buffalo skin lodges, each uniquely decorated, made up the camp. The support poles stuck out of the top of each tipi like the many feathers of a grouse's tail, Running Wolf thought to himself. He noticed one of the large rocks used to hold down the base of his family's tipi. It had slipped from the edge, and he replaced it. Hurriedly he joined his parents and sisters for breakfast. Too excited to eat much he only nibbled at the pemmican. The pounded and packed mixture of berries, moss, meat and fat felt dry in his mouth. Last summer's pemmican, he thought. If today's hunt succeeded, soon he would share in a feast of fresh meat. He sipped some water, then proudly joined his father and the other men of the band to plan the hunt.

Scouts had located a small herd of animals on the bench, several miles beyond the creek bed where the band had camped. The chief pointed to the rimrock formation above. There, at that point, the men would drive the animals over the cliffs. They would fall and be killed or wounded on the rocks below. Waiting hunters would kill the survivors and there would be fresh meat for all.

One by one, each man received his assignment. The fastest runners, the best hunters would circle the herd, working them ever closer to the jump. Before long the unwary bison would approach the "V" of rock piles extending back from the cliff. Young men would hide behind these. When they received the signal they were to jump up, yell, and wave robes or skins to frighten the herd. Running Wolf knew the importance of his assignment. If he sprang from his hiding place too soon, the buffalo might turn and avoid the pishkun altogether. He and the other young men must yell and scare the animals into a run—faster and faster toward the edge of the cliff.

Below the jump, his father and the other warriors would wait with spears, bows and arrows, and clubs to kill the wounded animals. Then the women would come from the camp to skin the bodies, tan the hides, and prepare the meat for the coming season.

All appeared in readiness. Running Wolf returned to the tipi for his robe. He watched his younger sisters muzzling the dogs to prevent their barking and alerting the buffalo to the danger awaiting them. Using a piece of tanned hide, with a hole cut large enough to pass over the dog's nose and well up on its jaws, the girls secured each animal. They tied the leather muzzle around each neck and secured the dogs to the tipi or nearby trees.

The runners and hunters had already left camp. Running Wolf hurriedly grabbed his robe and ran to catch up with the other young men as they climbed the trail toward the bench above the rimrock. As he reached the top of the cliff he looked out over the grassland, trying to catch a glimpse of the herd. They could not be seen.

Running Wolf took his place along the right side of the "V" that was to funnel the herd toward the jump. He lay his robe on the rock pile behind which he would hide. Into smaller, nearby piles he pressed sticks. On each he fastened a bit of hide, or a feather that would flutter in the wind and further scare the animals. Then he crouched behind his spot and waited.

The sun had risen to the middle of the sky before word came that the herd was approaching. They had wandered far during the night, and only through the skill of the best hunters had the animals been driven toward the desired site. Running Wolf peeked over the rocks. He could see them—twenty-five, maybe thirty-five animals. If his eyes did not play tricks on him a white buffalo mingled with the herd. He could not be sure. Perhaps the Great Spirit had honored his tribe and Running Wolf's first hunt this day.

It seemed like forever as the young man hid behind the rocks waiting for the sound of buffalo. He dared another look and watched the unsuspecting beasts enter the top of the "V" and move aimlessly on. Then the first figure jumped up, yelled and waved his robe; then another; and another. The herd began to jog, then run. Running Wolf leaped to his feet and added his cries to those of his companions. The herd was running now—the great White One among them—running toward the cliff.

Soon the lead bull realized his mistake. He hesitated, but those behind him pushed on, spurred by the running, screaming, waving band of young men. The animals rushed forward and almost as soon as it began, the drive ended.

Now the work of the day started in earnest. Running Wolf, his friends, and the skilled hunters who had first driven the animals, hurried down the trail. They joined others of their number below. By the time they arrived the last of the injured animals had been killed. Even now women, girls, older members of the tribe, and freed dogs rushed to the site, anxious to begin skinning and processing the buffalo.

Flint or obsidian knives and scrapers began their work in skillful hands. Preparing the food was woman's work, but in the big hunt, everyone joined to insure quick handling of the meat before it spoiled. Tribal members feasted on the raw meat as they cut it. Livers provided a special uncooked delicacy. Everyone ate his fill—dogs included—but the surplus would not spoil. Cut into strips it would dry in the sun on sticks and branches. Some they would smoke. Some would be pounded with other ingredients to make the pemmican that provided nourishment throughout the winter. Running Wolf knew the members of his band would be many days at their camp, preparing the food, tanning the hides, celebrating.

Success included the once-in-a-lifetime white buffalo. Running Wolf had no way of knowing albino bison occurred only once in five million, but even the band's oldest member could not remember ever killing one. Yet, the elders and the medicine man knew the ritual they must follow for this sacred event. The tribe would preserve the hide. It would bring power, "good medicine," and fame; but only if they took great care in its processing and protected it from all enemies.

The body of the animal lay among the others; no one touched it. Only a hunter who had killed a buffalo single-handedly could first touch the body. Black Eagle qualified and he respectfully propped up the white buffalo on its knees and belly facing east. Two Moons had actually killed the animal so the next duty was his. He ceremoniously pulled tufts of hair from the animal, right shoulder, right rump, left shoulder, left rump. He dropped each bit of hair to the ground and as he did so offered prayers to the Great Spirit.

With much ceremony everyone turned the animal on its back and disemboweled it before skinning. The man who skinned the head was a warrior who had touched an enemy in battle—counted coup—and taken his scalp. Hide removed, the meat and carcass went untouched. To eat the meat of a white buffalo would bring evil upon the entire clan.

Only the bravest warriors carried the hide to Two Moons' lodge. The man who carried it inside was one who had broken into an enemy's lodge during warfare. From outside, Running Wolf and the others watched. Only warriors who had counted coup on more than one enemy were permitted inside.

When all were seated about the hide, the woman who was to tan it came in. Pretty Weasel sat down beside the skin and lowered her dress to the waist. Two Moons painted the upper part of her body with a white paint, made of clay. On her chest he wiped away a circle to represent the sun. On her back near her right shoulder, he wiped away the paint in the shape of the moon. With his fingernails he scraped stripes from her neck to her waist. Behind Pretty Weasel's ears, over each hip, and from her waist in front, Two Moons carefully hung small bundles of sage. No woman would dare touch the skin of a white buffalo without proper prayers and purification. Even the knife she used received a ritual blessing.

Holding the knife upright, Pretty Weasel waited, as Two Moons told a story of his bravery in counting coup. When he finished, she cut a single hole in the edge of the hide for staking it out on the ground. In turn, all the warriors in the lodge told stories of their bravery. After each tale, Pretty Weasel cut another hole. When all the necessary holes were made, a warrior who had dragged an enemy from his tent received the honor of removing the hide from the tipi.

Outside, Pretty Weasel began staking out the hide—fur side down. As she drove each stake through the appropriate hole a warrior struck the hide at that point, as if counting coup. Completed, a warrior who had led a successful war party struck the hide an additional time. Only then did the tanning process begin, and for several days it would be Pretty Weasel's major concern.

With the hide staked and stretched, Pretty Weasel scraped away the remaining flesh using a chisel-like tool made from a buffalo leg bone. When the hide appeared clean, she left it in the sun to dry. Between the busy work of drying meat and tanning hides from the other buffalo, members of Running Wolf's band watched the solemn ceremony.

On the following day, Pretty Weasel returned to her important work. She spread an oily mixture of buffalo brains and liver over the hide, using a brush made of wild sage. Then she rubbed the concoction into the skin. Finished, she removed the hide from its stakes. Again, everyone supervised, and the bravest warriors offered prayers to the Great Spirit asking his blessing.

Pretty Weasel took the white robe to the creek near the camp. There she submerged it, placing several large stones on the robe to keep it from floating away. The next morning she removed it, wrung it out, stretched it on a square frame and pressed the remaining water from the hide. Once dry, it fell to the men to paint and decorate the robe with sacred symbols. These they applied carefully, respectfully, using bone brushes and paints made from the colors of clay and berries.

Tanning and decorating completed, the white buffalo robe became the tribe's most sacred possession. Other bands would learn of it and want its great powers. Running Wolf knew he would one day tell his children of the tribe's good fortune in getting it. One day he would join the warriors privileged to touch or wear it in ceremonies. For now he could anticipate many more visits to the pishkun. He could enjoy the meat he had helped get during his first hunt as an adult member of his tribe.

Suggested Readings

David D. Alt and Donald W. Hyndman. *Roadside Geology of the Northern Rockies.* Missoula: Mountain Press Publishing Co., 1972.

Dan Cushman. *The Great North Trail.* New York: McGraw Hill, 1966.

L. W. and A. R. Hagener. *Free For All, Edible and Useful Wild Plants.* Havre: The Authors, 1977.

L. W. and A. R. Hagener. *Common Fossils of North Central Montana.* Havre: The Authors, 1976.

Montana Superintendent of Public Instruction. *The Indian in the Classroom: Readings for the Teacher with Indian Students.* Helena: Montana Superintendent of Public Instruction, 1972.

David A. Walter. "Montana Regions: Space and Spirit." *Visual History of Montana,* Unit 4. Helena: Montana Superintendent of Public Instruction, 1977-78.

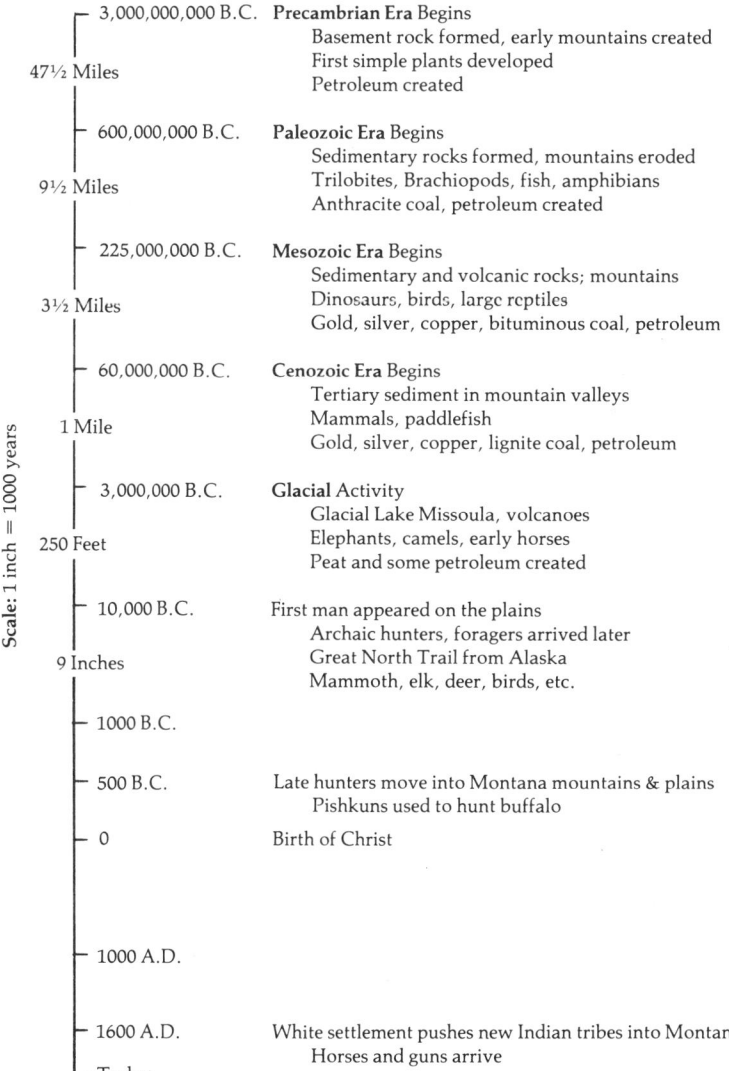

Scale: 1 inch = 1000 years

- 3,000,000,000 B.C. **Precambrian Era** Begins
  - Basement rock formed, early mountains created
  - First simple plants developed
  - Petroleum created

47½ Miles

- 600,000,000 B.C. **Paleozoic Era** Begins
  - Sedimentary rocks formed, mountains eroded
  - Trilobites, Brachiopods, fish, amphibians
  - Anthracite coal, petroleum created

9½ Miles

- 225,000,000 B.C. **Mesozoic Era** Begins
  - Sedimentary and volcanic rocks; mountains
  - Dinosaurs, birds, large reptiles
  - Gold, silver, copper, bituminous coal, petroleum

3½ Miles

- 60,000,000 B.C. **Cenozoic Era** Begins
  - Tertiary sediment in mountain valleys
  - Mammals, paddlefish
  - Gold, silver, copper, lignite coal, petroleum

1 Mile

- 3,000,000 B.C. **Glacial** Activity
  - Glacial Lake Missoula, volcanoes
  - Elephants, camels, early horses
  - Peat and some petroleum created

250 Feet

- 10,000 B.C. First man appeared on the plains
  - Archaic hunters, foragers arrived later
  - Great North Trail from Alaska
  - Mammoth, elk, deer, birds, etc.

9 Inches

- 1000 B.C.
- 500 B.C. Late hunters move into Montana mountains & plains
  - Pishkuns used to hunt buffalo
- 0 Birth of Christ

- 1000 A.D.

- 1600 A.D. White settlement pushes new Indian tribes into Montana
  - Horses and guns arrive
- Today

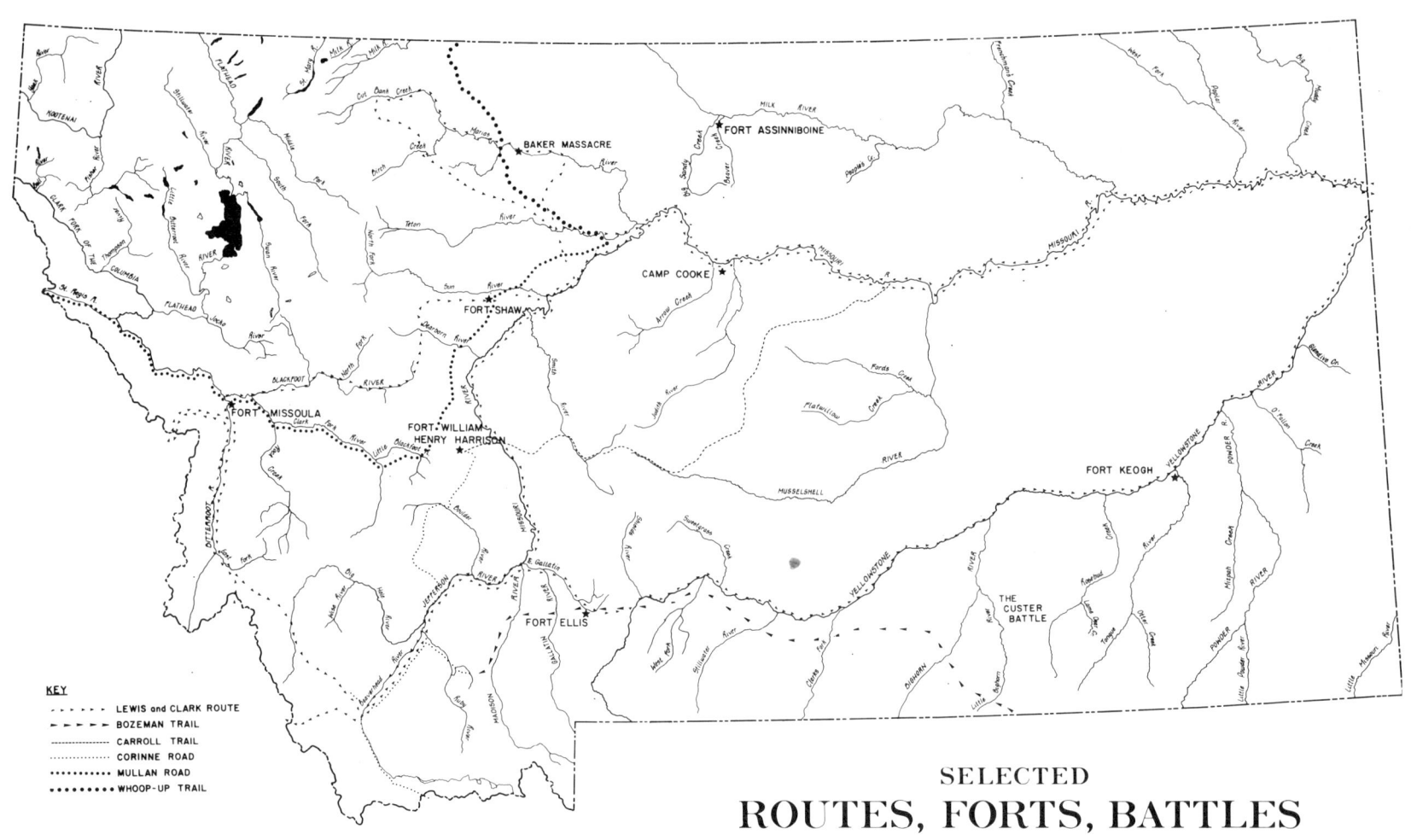

SELECTED
ROUTES, FORTS, BATTLES

Chapter II
Explorers, Trappers and Priests

No one will ever know who were the first whites to cross the land we now call Montana. Whatever their names or nationalities, it is likely that they were explorers pursuing western rivers beyond the Mississippi in search of furs and adventure. They were the advance guard of European civilization probing the wilderness. Just as Columbus, Hudson and LaSalle before them, they were discovering a new land. And like their predecessors, they claimed each new territory for their home nations. Since the discovery of the North American continent, European nations had vied with one another for dominance. So it was that these explorers went into the wilderness. It was history's highest adventure. One of its most exciting chapters was the exploration of the area we know as Montana.

Long before explorers actually reached Montana they had already mapped and described the territory between the Atlantic and the Mississippi. For over a century, Englishmen and Frenchmen fought for control of the land east of the Mississippi. Finally, after four imperial wars, England emerged the victor in 1763. The English, through their colonies, had control of the land east of the Mississippi. Before the conclusion of that international struggle, however, French traders and explorers pushed westward beyond the Mississippi. One family of French explorers, Louis and Francois de La Verendrye, may have been the first whites to stand on Montana soil. Searching for a large river Indians said flowed from great western mountains, the Verendrye brothers explored the western Dakotas in 1743. From their descriptions, it appears that they may have approached the Big Horn Mountains and visited with Crow Indians in southeastern Montana.

English control of the Mississippi frontier ended soon after they had achieved it. Within two decades after their great victory over the French on the American frontier, England lost her own colonies in a dramatic revolutionary war. A new and equally ambitious people, the Americans created their own nation firmly rooted in the new land. A little more than twenty years after their successful revolution, the young Americans joined their European rivals in a new contest for the lands beyond the Mississippi. During this time, at the beginning of the nineteenth century, the great exploration of Montana took place.

A stroke of fortune gave Americans their opportunity to be the ones to open the expansive western territories. From their historic base in New Orleans, seventeenth-century Spanish explorers and traders had investigated the southwestern portion of the continent. They claimed the area they called Louisiana for Spain. But maintaining such a large region became more than the Spanish could handle. After another imperial war erupted in Europe, Spain relinquished Louisiana to Napoleon and the French. The French, who had explored much of the Mississippi Valley too, soon faced the same difficulties. Burdened with a territory far from their native soil, the French decided to sell this immense property to the Americans in 1803. The misfortunes of warring European nations now gave America her opportunity to expand beyond the Mississippi.

The idea of American expansion was hardly new in 1800. Since the first days of colonization in the seventeenth century, Americans had steadily pushed their settlements westward. By the 1790s they had already added two new states to the original thirteen. In 1800 they elected a president who had long been an active supporter of expansion. Thomas Jefferson was a man whose accomplishments already included authorship of the Declaration of Independence, service as Governor of Virginia and as Secretary of State.

Jefferson had been interested in the trans-Mississippi region for decades. Twice in the 1790s he had tried unsuccessfully to organize expeditions to explore the area. For years, he had studied the reports of French, English and Spanish explorers who had floated the Mississippi and ventured westward up the mighty Missouri. At the time of his election, Jefferson probably knew more about the geography of Louisiana than any other American. He knew that if America delayed too long in claiming it, the British in

Canada would claim it first. When the opportunity came in 1803, Jefferson did not hesitate.

Even before the Louisiana Purchase, President Jefferson had already convinced Congress to appropriate funds for an exploration of the region. He told Congress it was essential for American defense and commercial interests to explore the territory. The United States must determine if, in fact, there was a navigable route across the continent—a Northwest Passage. If the passage existed, then America must claim it first. Once America purchased Louisiana in April 1803, the planned expedition became all the more important.

To lead what would become America's most impressive and exciting adventure in exploration, Jefferson selected his personal secretary, Meriwether Lewis. Lewis was no stranger to western exploration. He had studied the area and had applied to Jefferson several years earlier to accompany one of the president's planned expeditions. Since early 1801, Lewis had been with Jefferson, reading his extensive library on the western territories and generally preparing himself for the great adventure. As co-captain on the expedition, Lewis selected a fellow Virginian knowledgeable in exploration and frontier ways, William Clark.

The two leaders camped at the mouth of the Missouri River in 1804 preparing their crew for the journey. Lewis and Clark armed themselves with maps, descriptions of the region, trade goods for Indian tribes, and other essential provisions. Finally, in May they began their ascent of the Missouri. Sixteen hundred miles of travel brought them to the Mandan Villages where the Missouri makes a great turn heading due west. It had taken them longer to reach the Mandans than expected and the season was late. They decided to remain there for the winter.

After observing the countryside and learning as much about the Missouri as they could from the Mandan and Minnetaree Indians, they left the Indian villages in April 1805. They were confident that they understood what lay ahead. They also knew they were now alone. They left the Mandans with three new members of the expedition, one of whom proved to be very important later in the journey. Toussaint Charbonneau was a French trader and interpreter. His purchased wife, Sacagawea, and their newborn son joined Lewis and Clark, too. She was a Shoshoni Indian, captured years earlier by the Minnetarees.

As they left the Mandan Villages, everyone on the expedition knew that they were now venturing beyond the last point of safety. What lay ahead was only dimly known, and the prairies of Dakota seemed to stretch before them to eternity as they made their way up the Missouri. In six canoes and two pirogues, the corps paddled upriver, noting landmarks and carefully observing the countryside. Lewis recorded herds of bison, the abundance of antelope, and occasionally the fierce grizzly bear. The chief landmark they expected was the Great Falls of the Missouri. Once there, they hoped to cross the mountains in a short time and discover the Columbia River, their pathway to the Pacific.

It took them much longer to reach the Great Falls than they had expected. But finally on June 13 they arrived. After a portage around the falls, they proceeded up the Missouri into the mountains. Yet, two months later they still had not crossed the Continental Divide. Just as they were beginning to question their course, Sacagawea told Lewis and Clark that she knew where they were. It was territory that was often hunted by her people, the Shoshoni. As chance would have it, the expedition stumbled on a band of Shoshoni in early August. The coincidence was almost too good to be true. Sacagawea's brother was their chief and he gave the expedition horses and directions for the best passage through the mountains.

Lewis and Clark soon discovered that there were more mountains to cross. Following the Shoshoni's instructions, the expedition traveled over Lolo Pass, descended the Clearwater and Snake Rivers and finally struck the Columbia not far from Walla Walla, Washington. Once on the great River of the West, they made safe passage to the Pacific by November 1805. Resting on the coast, they built Fort Clatsop. Lewis and Clark felt satisfied with the first half of their journey. They had made their way across the plains, mapped the area, crossed the mountains and determined the exact distance from the Mississippi to the Pacific. They also found out that the fabled Northwest Passage simply did not exist. On their return to St. Louis they would learn even more about the land and people of Montana.

They left Fort Clatsop in April 1806. The winter had been wet and tedious. The entire expedition was eager to begin the return journey. They ascended the Columbia, made a reacquaintance with the friendly Nez Perce Indians, and headed east into Montana. Because they desired more knowledge of the geography, wildlife and Indian tribes of the region, Lewis and Clark split their forces and explored different regions. At Lolo the co-captains divided the men. Lewis headed north to the Marias River up to Cut Bank, while Clark took a larger group and explored the Yellowstone River valley.

Meriwether Lewis and his companions encountered the most serious trouble on the whole expedition as they explored the Marias. Coming upon a group of Piegan warriors, Lewis and his comrades soon found themselves in a desperate fight. With luck they escaped, but the incident alerted the Piegans that whites should be considered as dangerous intruders. This would prove to be one of the few negative results of the entire expedition.

William Clark and his contingent traveled overland from the Three Forks of the Missouri and began their descent of the Yellowstone River. While Lewis battled Piegans on the Marias, Clark found out how efficient Crow Indians were at stealing horses. Regardless of his brush with the Crows, Clark learned a great deal about the Yellowstone, especially how rich the region was in furs.

Finally, on August 12, 1806, Lewis and Clark joined up just below the mouth of the Yellowstone. All were safe, although Lewis had been wounded in a hunting accident. Now they drifted with the current down the Missouri to St. Louis, the conclusion of one of the greatest adventures in American history. They arrived on September 23, 1806, and were greeted by enthusiastic St. Louis residents. Lewis and Clark had trekked the wilds and could now report to Thomas Jefferson and all Americans. They reported the existence of great mountains, beautiful plains, fertile valleys, friendly and hostile Indians, and above all, an abundance of fur-bearing animals.

Lewis and Clark's description of the fur treasures on the upper Missouri stimulated great interest among St. Louis traders. For decades the French and English fur traders had skirted the upper Missouri region. Now with the purchase of Louisiana and the success of Lewis and Clark, American trappers looked enviously at the Missouri and Yellowstone river areas. Within four years after Lewis and Clark's return, American trappers reached the Rockies, while British traders descended into Montana on the western side of the Continental Divide on the Kootenai and Flathead rivers. The historic and intense competition between nations for the riches of furs and hides now flared anew in Montana.

Manuel Lisa was the first of the St. Louis traders to trap the upper Missouri area. In 1807 Lisa pushed up the Missouri and then the Yellowstone rivers where he found Lewis and Clark's descriptions of the abundant furs to be accurate. At the junction of the Big Horn and Yellowstone rivers, Lisa built the first fur post in Montana. Lisa's Fort was the base of operations for his expedition that winter, and he was able to make friendly contacts with Crow Indians. Returning to St. Louis in 1808, Lisa immediately organized an even larger expedition to return the following year. Organized as the Missouri Fur Company in 1809, Lisa, Auguste and Pierre Chouteau, Andrew Henry, and others expanded their operations in 1810 to the Three Forks of the Missouri. But at Three Forks Andrew Henry and his men engaged in a fierce battle with Blackfeet who were determined to frighten whites out of the region. Henry lost eight men to the Blackfeet and decided to withdraw from that advanced post.

Lisa's luck declined quickly after the Three Forks incident. Although there were plenty of furs lower down on the Missouri, additional business mishaps forced him to abandon Lisa's Fort and finally the company itself. Nonetheless, Lisa's penetration of the upper Missouri confirmed the riches of the area. After the War of 1812 more trappers invaded the homeland of the Crow, Blackfeet and Gros Ventre in search of furs.

British traders had also been busy. David Thompson of the North West Company first explored the Kootenai River area in 1807. By the following year he had erected a fur post near present-day Libby. In 1809 he developed another post, Saleesh House, in the Thompson Falls area. All the while Thompson built up a profitable trade with Flathead, Pend d'Oreille, and Kutenai Indians. He also mapped the entire region and thereby provided other trappers and explorers with the best geographical information on the area to date. The presence of Thompson and the North West Company on the west side of the Rockies only led to more concern on the part of American trappers. By the 1830s, however, the Hudson's Bay Company, which earlier had absorbed the North West Company, agreed with the challenging American Fur Company to stay clear of each other's trapping areas.

It was in the 1820s and 1830s that American trappers greatly expanded their operations in Montana. In 1819 Manuel Lisa brought the Missouri Fur Company back to life. The Missouri Fur Company headed upriver and built another fur post on the Big Horn River, Fort Benton. Within two years another group of St. Louis traders organized the Rocky Mountain Fur Company and headed into the wilderness. This latter outfit was headed by Andrew Henry and William Ashley. It was destined to be one of the most ambitious and innovative fur trapping concerns. After another costly scrape with Blackfeet in 1823, the Rocky Mountain trappers decided to move south into present-day Wyoming, away from the angry Blackfeet. It was in the Green River region that Jim Bridger, Jedediah Smith, Milton Sublette, Hugh Glass and other legendary "mountain men" carried out Henry and Ashley's plan to gather furs at annual meetings of trappers called the "rendezvous."

The mountain men who met each summer in rendezvous were heroic characters. They were men who seemed to crave the solitary life of the free trapper. They pursued all the major streams of southwest Montana and added greatly to the growing geographical knowledge of the region. By the early 1830s, however, the Rocky Mountain Fur Company faced its strongest competition for the upper Missouri trade. The end of the free trapper was in sight, for the control of the fur trade would soon be in the hands of a rich and powerful organization headquartered in St. Louis and New York.

Since its founding in 1808, John Jacob Astor's American Fur Company had grown yearly to become the largest of the American-based fur outfits. Astor's financial strength gave the company an advantage the others simply could not match. Under the leadership of Pierre Chouteau, Jr., the western unit of the company forced out the Columbia Fur Company in 1827. Then in 1828 Chouteau sent Kenneth McKenzie and James Kipp to the mouth of the Yellowstone to build an advance outpost to compete with the Rocky Mountain Fur Company trappers. This post, Fort Union, became the operational headquarters for the so-called Upper Missouri Outfit (*UMO*). By 1832 Chouteau brought a steamboat, the *Yellowstone*, to Fort Union's doorstep—the upper Missouri's first steamboat. Now, with improved transportation connections, the American Fur Company really put pressure on the free trappers. It took only two more years before the Rocky Mountain Fur Company sold out to Astor and Chouteau.

Pierre Chouteau's expert management of company operations on the Missouri encouraged him to send men into the dangerous Blackfeet territory in 1831. Free trappers had crisscrossed Blackfeet hunting grounds for several years, but Chouteau wanted a permanent outpost in Blackfeet country. Near the Marias River they built Fort Piegan and began to tap the region's fur riches. Predictably, soon there was trouble with the Blackfeet, but Kenneth McKenzie remained determined to establish a post. In 1832 he directed David Mitchell to erect an even stronger post near the battered Fort Piegan.

The new fort, named in honor of McKenzie, became a stronghold in the Blackfeet territory. Now the American Fur Company was supreme on the upper Missouri. McKenzie soon lost his position when the company came under fire for illegally producing and selling liquor to the Indians. It was then that Alexander Culbertson took over as head of the UMO. He soon expanded the fur trade even more on the upper Missouri.

The beaver trade was playing out. American and European fashions had changed and beaver was no longer considered stylish; the supply of beaver was dwindling. After a disastrous incident at Fort McKenzie in 1843 when twenty-one innocent Indians died at the hands of two UMO traders, Culbertson built what was to become the most important of all posts on the upper Missouri, Fort Benton. It was the second one to be named for Missouri's Senator Thomas Hart Benton.

Fort Benton was a massive structure with high adobe walls and the look of permanency. It would stand long after the fur trade had died in Montana. It was Fort Benton that became the terminus for Missouri River steamboats in the 1860s. It was from there that travelers to the gold fields would begin their overland trek.

The era of the fur trade was short. But it provided the first significant white penetration into Montana. Outposts were built, Indian tribes were contacted, and money was made. The overall effect of the trade is difficult to measure. It brought no permanent white settlements to the frontier. The trappers and traders were interested only in what they could take from the land. They did not venture into the wilderness to establish towns. The trade may have brought riches to some traders and their companies, but it had a negative effect on Indian culture. Traders used Indian people to aid in the trade. They introduced Indians to liquor, infected them with some diseases, and generally caused more conflict among Montana's tribes. Never again would Indian peoples be free of pressure from invading whites.

The demoralizing effects of the fur trade on Indian peoples is matched by the heroic images the "mountain men" left. These men were larger than life. Their feats defy belief. Stories about John Colter's discovery of the geysers of Yellowstone and his famous naked foot race for his life with the Blackfeet have been told and retold. Hugh Glass' incredible bout with a grizzly bear in 1823 and his overland trek to safety remains one of the great adventure tales of the mountains. How true some of these yarns are is not important. Worth remembering is the fact that mountain men were unique. Their exploits are part of our image of man in the wilderness.

The expansion of the fur trade also brought other whites to Montana. While fur traders pursued one kind of harvest among the Indian tribes, Jesuit priests pursued quite another. As early as 1830, some members of the Flathead nation learned of the existence of holy men among the whites. Perhaps French-Canadian trappers first introduced them to Christianity. In any event, in 1831 they sent a delegation east to find the priests, or Black Robes. After several attempts, Father Pierre Jean DeSmet came to the Flatheads in the Bitterroot Valley in 1841.

DeSmet's frontier parish was named St. Mary's. At St. Mary's a group of dedicated Jesuits ministered to the Indians for nearly a decade. In contrast to the demoralization among Indians created by the fur trade, the missionaries dedicated themselves to bettering the Indians' lives. DeSmet, Gregory Mengarini, Anthony Ravalli, and other priests built a small community around the mission. This included a sawmill, flourmill, and, of course, a chapel. More than that, the Jesuits expanded their influence in the region to include the Kalispel, Pend d'Oreille, Piegan, Spokan and other Indian tribes.

Jesuits were certain that bringing Christianity to Indian tribes in the Rockies would improve the Indians' lives. They soon found that introducing the Indians to Christianity was no magical cure for Indian problems. Whites still wanted Indian lands, for example. DeSmet's attempt to end inter-tribal warfare was equally doomed to defeat almost from the start. While they received Christianity willingly, the Indians had no intention of ceasing their traditional ways, including the art of warfare. White culture, in any form, threatened the Indians' traditional existence. But rather than the trappers' materialism, missionaries brought a new spiritual vision to Indian peoples. Their effect was benevolent.

Conditions at St. Mary's deteriorated in the late 1840s. By 1850 it was clear to the Jesuits that tensions among Indian tribes made the mission difficult to maintain. Accordingly, they sold the property to Major John Owen who turned it into a trading post.

After selling St. Mary's, the Jesuits left the Bitterroot. In 1854 they opened another mission, St. Ignatius, near Flathead Lake. Finally, in 1866, they reopened St. Mary's. Additional Catholic missions opened in Montana to minister to Crow, Gros Ventre, Cheyenne and other Indian tribes in following years. Their success is a testimonial to the benevolent effects of Christianity. It is also a tribute to the dedication of priests who braved wilderness conditions to bring the Christian word to Native Americans.

The coming of trappers and holy men was only the advance guard of white civilization. The lure of gain had brought fur traders to Montana, but it was nothing compared to the mining stampedes. Gold discoveries in the early 1860s transformed Montana almost overnight. Now native Indian peoples faced thousands of invading whites. It was the beginning of a new era in Montana's history.

St. Mary's Mission

Lewis and Clark were the first Americans to contact Indian tribes in the Rocky Mountains. C. M. Russell commemorated one of Lewis and Clark's meetings with Indians in a huge mural that now decorates the capitol building in Helena. Russell's choice was a good one. Lewis and Clark's contact with the Flathead people in September 1805 in Ross' Hole near the Bitterroot River began a history of friendly relations between whites and Flatheads.

Aside from fur trappers who established posts in the Flatheads' territory, the next significant contact they had with whites was the coming of Catholic missionaries. Flatheads probably learned of Christianity from Canadian fur trappers and Iroquois Indians who accompanied them to the Rockies. It was one of the Iroquois, Ignace La Mousse, or "Big Ignace," who told Flatheads of the existence of white holy men, the so-called "Black Robes."

The Flatheads and neighboring Nez Perce were eager to pursue Christianity. They undertook four separate journeys to St. Louis in the 1830s to find Black Robes. In St. Louis in 1831 the visiting Indians enlisted the support of William Clark, then Superintendent of Indian Affairs, the man who had first met them in 1805. At first the Flatheads got little response. Protestant missionaries went to the Oregon country in the 1830s, but no Black Robes came to the Flatheads. Finally, after Young Ignace led the fourth trip to St. Louis in 1839, Catholic missionaries came to the Bitterroot Valley.

Pierre Jean DeSmet, a native of Belgium, took up the Iroquois and Flatheads' request for a resident priest. DeSmet had come to America from Belgium. In 1837, at the age of thirty-six, he began missionary work among the Potowatomi Indians on the Missouri near Council Bluffs, Iowa. By chance the traveling Flatheads met DeSmet and impressed him with their pleas for Black Robes. DeSmet appealed to his superiors to establish a mission in the Rockies. They agreed, and on March 27, 1840, DeSmet left St. Louis to become the first priest in the northern Rockies. Young Ignace helped guide him west. At Pierre's Hole near the towering Tetons of Wyoming, DeSmet met with over fifteen hundred Flathead

Fr. Pierre Jean DeSmet, founder of St. Mary's Mission in the Bitterroot.—*Photograph by Keller, Helena, M.H.S.*

and Pend d'Oreille Indians who were there to lead him to Montana. After a month's travel, DeSmet said the first mass in Montana near Three Forks. After baptizing over three hundred Indians, DeSmet began his return trip to St. Louis, pledging his return.

DeSmet was determined to establish a mission among the Flatheads, but his superiors in St. Louis sadly informed him that there were no funds available for such a remote venture. With that news DeSmet resolved to raise the money himself. After a trip to new Orleans, he found the necessary monies and was able to enlist two other Jesuit priests and three Jesuit brothers in his Flathead mission. In 1841 DeSmet's party of eleven began their westward trek. The group included two priests, Nicholas Point and Gregory

Mengarini, and three brothers, William Claessens, Charles Huet, and Joseph Specht. After four months of travel, they reached the Bitterroot in October 1841. There they renewed contact with Young Ignace and other Flatheads who had been baptized the previous year.

After a hard winter, they began work on the St. Mary's mission buildings. Using cottonwood logs and hand-fashioned wooden pegs, they built a small chapel and two other structures. Since Claessens was a carpenter and Huet a blacksmith, the buildings were sturdy and designed for use. The chapel featured a shake roof, two galleries and a heavy wooden plank floor. Although it only measured twenty-five by thirty-three feet, it held over two hundred persons for prayer and worship.

With the chapel built, DeSmet soon had regular prayer meetings and religious instruction scheduled. Morning prayers were said each day followed by a Mass and religious instruction. In the afternoon Flathead children took classes, and in the evening another prayer session lasted over an hour. Fathers Mengarini and DeSmet also organized sports activities for Flathead youth and even introduced them to European musical instruments. The Jesuits hoped to make St. Mary's the focal point of Flathead life, but they soon realized that the semi-nomadic ways of the Indians were not so easily changed.

The Flatheads' principal food supply was the bison. Each year they took three or more extensive journeys over the mountains to the plains to hunt. They returned with enough meat to feed the tribe and hides to be sold to fur traders. Jesuits accompanied the hunters hoping to keep them true to the practice of Christianity. While the hunting parties were absent from the Bitterroot, the Flatheads who remained behind often had to exist on few provisions. Mengarini and Claessens remedied that by introducing the Flatheads to cultivated crops. The Indians were skeptical at first, but it was not long before they eagerly harvested carrots, beans and other vegetables.

In 1842 DeSmet realized that St. Mary's needed more funds and missionaries. He returned east to seek support. He traveled on to Europe and an audience with Pope Gregory XVI. He returned with over thirty thousand dollars and several new recruits for Catholic missions in the Northwest. Rather than travel overland to the Rockies, DeSmet sailed around Cape Horn and touched land in Oregon. From there he made his way to St. Mary's, arriving in the spring of 1845.

In DeSmet's absence Mengarini had managed St. Mary's very well. He had also aided in establishing other missions among the Coeur d'Alene Indians. In October 1845, Father Anthony Ravalli, an Italian Jesuit, came to St. Mary's. Ravalli was an exceptionally versatile man. He was a scholar, mechanic, artist and physician. His talents improved the mission considerably.

In addition to his own belongings, Ravalli brought millstones. It was not long before Ravalli designed and built a water-powered gristmill at St. Mary's. Ravalli's mill was the first of its kind in Montana. Now the Flatheads had flour, and with Father Mengarini's work the mission soon had abundant wheat, potatoes and even sugar refined from beets.

The gristmill was only the beginning of Ravalli's building projects. The priests needed lumber to construct the necessary additional buildings for themselves, livestock and grains. Using his engineering ability, Ravalli set to building a sawmill powered by water. He fabricated a saw blade and other mechanical parts from beaten and filed iron wagon tires. The additional buildings were soon constructed, including a new and larger chapel complete with a handsome bell steeple. The sawn lumber made fine interior carpentry possible. When completed the new chapel could vie with the best churches in white communities for beauty and utility.

Father Ravalli brought more than his engineering abilities to St. Mary's. Indian peoples historically had been very susceptible to white men's diseases. When Ravalli's small supply of medicines ran out he began distilling solutions, salves and lotions from local plants. He had also brought smallpox vaccine with him from Italy. He was careful to keep this vaccine active, and convinced Flathead chiefs to accept vaccination. There was great fear associated with smallpox, for once unleashed among Indian peoples there was little anyone could do. Ravalli's vaccination program was successful. When a small epidemic surfaced among non-vaccinated Nez Perce in 1852, the Flatheads escaped sickness.

DeSmet, Mengarini, Ravalli and the other Jesuits had been highly successful in their missionary work at St.

Fr. Anthony Ravalli came to St. Mary's Mission in 1845 and built a flour mill and sawmill. In 1866 Ravalli helped re-open St. Mary's.—*Photograph by A. J. Dusseau, Butte, M.H.S.*

Mary's. The Flatheads accepted Christianity easily and the future seemed assured in 1846. Nevertheless, serious problems remained. Historically the Flatheads had warred with the Blackfeet over prime bison hunting grounds east of the mountains. Battles between them flared each hunting season. DeSmet was determined to halt this warfare, and in this attempt he unknowingly jeopardized the entire mission.

In 1846 DeSmet made an heroic effort to Christianize the hostile Blackfeet. The Blackfeet looked with suspicion on the priests and their work. DeSmet journeyed to the Blackfeet encampment and persuaded some Blackfeet that Christianity was as good for them as it was for their enemies. He also accompanied the Flatheads' hunting expedition in August 1846 and witnessed a typical intertribal conflict.

The Crow people were at war with Blackfeet and Flatheads. DeSmet offered prayer before battle, and the success of the Flatheads against the Crows impressed the few Blackfeet warriors present. The Blackfeet now sought out DeSmet in the Flathead encampment. After the hunt, DeSmet appointed Father Nicholas Point to winter with the Blackfeet while he journeyed to St. Louis.

In DeSmet's absence the St. Mary's mission fell on bad times. Suddenly the Flatheads seemed to turn away from Christianity. It may be that they were angry at DeSmet's leaving, for they much preferred him to the stern Mengarini. It is more likely that the Flatheads disapproved of spreading Christianity to their enemies, the Blackfeet. There is also evidence that the Flatheads believed they had been cheated of promised gifts. Writing in 1847 after DeSmet's departure, Ravalli stated that DeSmet "had beguiled them (Indians) with promises and hopes of a village, animals, plows, etc." When all of this did not materialize, Ravalli wrote, the Flatheads "say now openly that the Black Robes are like other whites, that they are liars and are in league with their enemies."

What Ravalli feared was happening. Jesuits at St. Mary's were in jeopardy. Conditions deteriorated quickly after two visiting Blackfeet died at St. Mary's. After the summer hunt in 1850, it was clear to Fathers Mengarini and Ravalli that the Flathead people had begun to distrust the Black Robes' leadership. There were several disputes among the Flatheads in which the priests played a role, and in September the mission narrowly escaped destruction at the hands of an angry band of Blackfeet.

The Jesuits decided to close St. Mary's for a time, hoping that the Flatheads would plead with them to return. With the mission property put up for sale in 1850, Major John Owen negotiated for its purchase. Two years later the priests turned over St. Mary's to Owen. He rebuilt and expanded St. Mary's turning it into a trading post, which he named Fort Owen. Owen's outpost soon became a gathering place for travellers, Indians of several tribes, trappers, and new settlers coming to the Bitterroot.

The decision to vacate St. Mary's was not the end of Catholic missionary work in the Rockies. Within a few years a mission opened at the south end of Flathead Lake, named in honor of St. Ignatius. Today it stands as the oldest continuously operating mission in Montana. St. Mary's had proven its worth in its brief existence. DeSmet, Ravalli, Mengarini and the other Jesuits had begun the Christianization of the Flathead and Blackfeet peoples. They also helped open the area to larger white settlement.

In 1866 Father Ravalli and Father Joseph Giorda reopened St. Mary's on the old mission grounds close to Owen's outpost. They built the third chapel at St. Mary's and the mission again served the Flatheads. But the early strength of St. Mary's was not to return. It was only a matter of time before all of the Flatheads in the Bitterroot had to move north to the reservation in the Flathead Valley. By 1884, the year of Ravalli's death, most of the Flathead had moved onto the reservation. In 1891 Chief Charlot's band finally left the Bitterroot for the reservation.

St. Mary's remained a parish, first removed to Missoula and later to Stevensville. The buildings at the original site deteriorated over the years until interested people sought to preserve the area in the mid-twentieth century. Recently the chapel has been reconstructed for all to see. But it is not the physical presence of St. Mary's mission that is of importance. It is the courage of the Jesuits, the integrity of the Flathead people, and the opening of the Bitterroot that memorialize St. Mary's.

Pierre Chouteau, Jr.

Great fortunes were made in the fur trade. One of the most successful traders was Pierre Chouteau, Jr. of St. Louis. Heroic "mountain men" of the fur trade are familiar figures. They wandered the mountain West and told fantastic stories of their adventures. They were important, but the real story of the fur trade is to be found in the lives and exploits of men like Chouteau. His story is one of fortune, determination, a keen business sense, and a measure of luck.

To begin with, Pierre was fortunate to be a member of a prominent trading and business family in St. Louis. We might say that he began with an advantage. His grandfather was an early trader on the Mississippi and founded St. Louis. His father, Pierre Chouteau, Sr., and other relatives were all successful traders. This is significant because St. Louis soon became the most important trading city on the frontier, and the Chouteaus were its oldest and most powerful citizens.

Pierre was born in 1789. It was an exciting time to be in St. Louis. On the edge of the frontier, St. Louis was a new town populated by rivermen, adventurers, traders, and those eager to profit from the riches of the wilderness. Pierre was only fourteen when the United States purchased Louisiana Territory from France. The politics changed suddenly. There was confusion, but for the traders it meant greater opportunity to plunder the resources of the western region.

When he was fifteen, Pierre began his business career as a clerk in the family trading office in St. Louis. He learned quickly, and one year later he accompanied his father upriver to bargain for furs with the Osage Indians. Pierre learned the importance of keeping a careful accounting of the complicated aspects of the fur trade. Trade goods for bargaining with Indian tribes had to be purchased with care. Furs had to bring the highest prices from eastern buyers to realize a profit. With his father, Pierre saw firsthand the riskiness of the fur trading business. Everything depended upon acquiring the largest quantity of the best pelts and skins available.

By 1813 Pierre was able to begin his own business in St. Louis. In partnership with Bartholomew Berthould, he opened a mercantile store. This was the start of his career, but what made him so successful? If we follow his progress, it will be clear that to succeed in the St. Louis fur trade he had to be very competitive and take advantage of every opportunity. The first years, however, were anything but successful. After an initial fur trading expedition failed in 1815, Chouteau waited until he could finance another, larger expedition. It cost thousands of dollars to outfit trappers and traders to penetrate the wilderness in search of furs. Only if they returned laden with the best beaver, fox, wolf, and other furs could Chouteau realize a return on his investment.

A fur venture in 1819 also failed, but Chouteau did not give up. Competition from better financed rival companies was fierce. They could offer Indians better trade goods. Some companies had many more white trappers in the field, and some, like John Jacob Astor's huge American Fur Company, simply had more money. Yet Chouteau learned from his competitors, and soon he had a highly organized team of trappers, trading posts and traders. Chouteau drove hard bargains and before long he began to make great profits.

Chouteau realized that he could never hope to compete head-to-head with Astor's American Fur Company. He did the next best thing. In 1826, after making two trips east to New York, Chouteau signed an agreement with Astor. Chouteau became the sole western agent of the American Fur Company. This was the trading opportunity Pierre had hoped would come. After years of trading, he was now in the position to develop the rich upper Missouri River trapping region.

Beginning in 1827, Chouteau's concern in St. Louis promised to offer all of their furs for sale to Astor. In return Astor agreed to provide all trading supplies. Chouteau and Astor split the profits of the western trading evenly. Pierre himself received a salary of $2,000 per year and a liberal expense account. He must have been eager, for within several months the Columbia Fur Company sold out to Chouteau. They had been his last major competitor. Now the Missouri was to be the American Fur Company's backyard.

Chouteau immediately set to reorganizing the old Columbia Fur Company posts and traders. He called it the Upper Missouri Outfit—UMO for short. Kenneth McKenzie, James Kipp and other Columbia Fur owners joined Chouteau's organization and directed the actual trapping and

Pierre Chouteau, Jr. (1798-1865) was one of the most successful fur trade investors operating on the Upper Missouri.

trading of the UMO. This began the truly extensive development of fur trading on the upper Missouri. There were still competitors in the remote mountainous regions of the Rockies, but Chouteau came to terms with them as well.

William Ashley's successful "rendezvous" trapping system brought thousands of beaver pelts to market during the 1820s. Ashley was so successful that he was able to retire from the trade in 1826 a wealthy man. His successors, Jedediah Smith, Thomas Fitzpatrick, David Jackson, Jim Bridger, and several others, now called themselves the Rocky Mountain Fur Company. Chouteau, at the urging of Kenneth McKenzie, decided to compete with the Rocky Mountain boys in the field. It was frustrating, and Chouteau was never convinced that it was effort wisely expended.

Chouteau's UMO challenged the Rocky Mountain Fur Company trappers from an impressive outpost well up the Missouri. Headquartered at Fort Union, located at the mouth of the Yellowstone River, Kenneth McKenzie directed the UMO operations. Building Fort Union in 1828 was a risky venture, since it was so far removed from St. Louis, but it soon paid off handsomely. Fort Union was destined to be one of the most important fur posts in the entire West.

From Fort Union the UMO floated thousands of bundles of furs downriver by boat to St. Louis where Chouteau's company sold them to buyers. In 1830 McKenzie suggested Chouteau take an even greater risk and try to bring a steamboat from St. Louis all the way to Fort Union. It was not until 1832 that the *Yellowstone* made it to Fort Union, but it was a dramatic achievement. Now Chouteau could supply Fort Union more efficiently and bring many more furs to St. Louis.

Although Chouteau had mounted a well financed attack on the Rocky Mountain Fur Company, the rendezvous trapping system still dominated the Rockies region. The competition continued through the 1830s, but the UMO grew stronger each year. At Fort Union they maintained an efficient operation employing nearly five hundred persons in trapping, trading, craft-making and tending livestock.

One aspect of this competition was unsavory. Trade in liquor did great social damage to the native Indian tribes. Alcohol had been a mainstay in the fur trade from an early date until the United States government outlawed the trade in 1832. It had been lucrative since the traders often made their greatest profits by exchanging cheap whiskey for valuable furs. After the federal ban in 1832, McKenzie built a large still at Fort Union and continued to supply the Indians in violation of the law. Such was the competitive nature of the trade.

In 1834 John Jacob Astor quietly retired from the fur trade. This left Pierre Chouteau and his partners without the power of Astor's financial backing. Chouteau was confident all the same. He purchased the entire stock of the American Fur Company's western operations. The new firm, called Pratte, Chouteau and Company, now had to face the remaining competitors alone. This was to be Pierre Chouteau's stiffest challenge.

Chouteau had to attend to business on two fronts. While working hard to reorganize outposts, trappers, and traders in the interior, he could not ignore New York fur buyers, the impact of various Indian treaties, and the general finances of his company. The result forced Chouteau to spend nearly as much time in the East as in St. Louis. In 1837, for example, Chouteau traveled to Washington, D.C., and to New York four times.

Meanwhile, the powerful Hudson's Bay Company, an English fur trading concern, challenged the UMO on the upper reaches of the Missouri River. But Chouteau was fortunate to enlist the talents of Alexander Culbertson, who took over leadership of the UMO from Kenneth McKenzie. By the time Culbertson replaced McKenzie, Chouteau's men had already established two posts in Piegan country, far upriver from Fort Union. By 1840 Culbertson's men dominated the upper Missouri trade for Chouteau once again.

In 1843, however, a tragic incident at Fort McKenzie, located above the Marias River, turned Culbertson back from the upper Missouri. Angry at the Blackfeet, two of Culbertson's traders lay in ambush at Fort McKenzie and killed over twenty Indians. As might be imagined, this halted trade for a time and created danger for traders in Blackfeet country. It was not until 1845 that Chouteau convinced Culbertson to try once again. By 1846 Culbertson erected a formidable outpost that was named in honor of Senator Thomas H. Benton of Missouri, a staunch friend of Pierre Chouteau's in Washington, D.C.

Fort Benton was to be Pierre Chouteau's bastion of trading on the Missouri. By the 1840s the beaver pelt trade had given way to the lucrative trade in buffalo hides. Thousands of packs of buffalo hides left Fort Benton for St. Louis. Relative peace between the Piegan and the traders was affected by Culbertson himself, since Culbertson was trusted by the Indians and married to a Blackfeet, Natawista Ixsana.

It had taken nearly thirty years for Pierre Chouteau to erect his powerful fur trading company on the upper Missouri. By 1849 Pierre Chouteau gently eased himself out of the fur business and turned the operations over to his son, Charles Chouteau. Yet, Pierre Chouteau was far from retired.

He had been interested in railroad development as early

as 1835. Now with money to invest, Chouteau joined with others in building a railroad in southern Missouri to service iron mines. The railroad was completed in 1851 and seven years later Chouteau found himself involved in the iron mines as well. He made as much or more money from mining than he did in all his years of fur trading.

From an apprenticeship in the family trading business in St. Louis, Pierre Chouteau, Jr. had developed his business talents over the years. Now in the twilight years of his life he became a millionaire trader, railroad builder, and mine owner. It was a remarkable record of determined effort in the face of great competition. He was one of those adventurous types whose activities encouraged the opening of the West. He left behind a fortune when he died in 1865. He had left his mark on Montana and its native peoples. Pierre Chouteau, Jr. shaped Montana's early history.

Lewis and Clark in Montana

Spanish, French and English explorers of North America had looked in vain for the fabled Northwest Passage—that mythical all-water route connecting the Atlantic and Pacific oceans. By the beginning of the nineteenth century no one had yet found the Passage. Those who thought it might exist were certain that it might be in the northern Rocky Mountains below present-day Canada. Within a few years the great question was finally to be answered. In 1804, two courageous explorers led a modest band of thirty-one adventurers on a two-year expedition to the crest of the Rockies, on to the Pacific and back to their point of origin.

Meriwether Lewis and William Clark did not find the Northwest Passage, but their expedition proved to be the most important exploration in American history. They penetrated a vast unknown land without a supply line or safety line from civilization. They journeyed through a wilderness where no white man had set foot. They faced challenges from mountain weather to unpredictable Indian tribes. Their mission was awesome. President Thomas Jefferson directed them to chart the territory beyond the Mississippi, locate rivers and mountains, meet with Indian tribes, describe the land and its inhabitants, and search for the Northwest Passage. Their accomplishment remains a testament to their ingenuity, determination, and courage.

Meriwether Lewis was twenty-nine years old when President Jefferson selected him to lead the expedition. Lewis had already served in the militia and the regular army for several years. For co-captain of the expedition Lewis chose another militia veteran, thirty-three year old William Clark. So much happened to the co-captains and their cohorts that only a reading of their diaries and journals can do the expedition justice. But we can capture a glimpse of the excitement of the journey by pausing to investigate a few episodes of the trek in Montana.

Lewis and Clark began their journey up the Missouri River from St. Louis in the spring of 1804. By October 1804, they arrived at a group of Indian settlements called the Mandan Villages. They were 1,600 miles from their starting point on the Mississippi and winter was fast approaching.

Captain Meriwether Lewis, co-captain of the Lewis & Clark Expedition, as artist Charles Wilson Peale painted him in Philadelphia. —*Independence National Historic Park, Philadelphia, Pennsylvania.*

After spending the winter with the Mandan Indians, they began their westward travel on the Missouri in April 1805. By the end of the month they had arrived at the mouth of the Yellowstone River. They were now in Montana. It would be another four months of hard travel before they crested the Bitterroot Mountains and passed the boundaries of present-day Montana. They were following the mighty Missouri, a river that played many tricks on them and tested their strength and intelligence.

Minnetaree Indians had told Lewis and Clark a great deal about the Missouri. With this information, the expedition had a fair idea of what to expect. But they had to be cautious not to mistake a tributary of the Missouri for the river itself. A wrong turn could have sent them miles off course. As they ascended the river in their two pirogues and six canoes, Lewis and Clark marveled at the broad plains, the abundance of antelope, flocks of birds, herds of bison, and the fierce grizzly bears they encountered. They gained much respect for the grizzly bear when on May 5, 1805, they watched a 500-pound specimen take five direct rifle shots and swim half way across the river before dying on a sandbar. "It was a most tremendous looking animal," Lewis recorded, "and made the most tremendous roaring from the moment he was shot."

It was not the bears and wolves that worried Lewis and Clark. They were more concerned about how far they had traveled and how much distance lay between them and the mountains. A little over one week after they passed the Yellowstone, they saw the mouth of what the Indians called "the river that scolds all others." Because of its color, Lewis and Clark renamed it the Milk River. So far the information provided by the Minnetarees had been accurate, but the next large northern tributary encountered by the expedition proved confusing.

After they passed the Musselshell and Judith Rivers in late May, they came upon an imposing river flowing from the north. On June 2 Lewis and Clark began a week-long pause at the mouth of the Marias River while they tried to determine which watercourse was the true Missouri. For no apparent reason the Indians had not told them of this second large river. Now the co-captains had to take care in their choice of which to follow. Lewis trudged up the Marias, while Clark followed the Missouri to the south. They both concluded that the southern fork was the Missouri. It was an important decision and the leaders' correct choice testified to their knowledge of geography, their care in decision-making and their intuition. As they began to pursue the Missouri's course on June 8, Lewis named the northern river Maria's in honor of his cousin, Maria Wood.

If they had chosen the wrong river, the expedition almost certainly would have found themselves wintering in the mountains searching for a suitable pass. They would have been far off course for striking the Columbia River, the gateway to the Pacific. It was not long before they knew that their decision at the Marias was correct. On June 13 Lewis recorded his sighting of the Great Falls of the Missouri. Lewis and Clark now knew that they were pursuing the Missouri and would soon enter the mountains.

Negotiating around the Great Falls was no easy matter. It took them nearly a month to portage around the falls. Hauling canoes, supplies and equipment on the eighteen-mile portage was strenuous work in an area infested with grizzlies. Lewis' dog, Scannon, spent many a night barking at approaching bears, but the mosquitoes and gnats were nearly as bothersome. Finally, after preparing their canoes, they left the falls area and headed upriver. By July 19 they passed through a narrow gap in the limestone cliffs near present-day Helena; Lewis called them "gates of the mountains." They were now on the upper reaches of the river, and it was not long before Sacagawea recognized familiar countryside. She had been here before. It was the Three Forks of the Missouri where Sacagawea had been taken prisoner years earlier by the Minnetarees.

From Three Forks to their meeting with the Shoshoni Indians on August 17, Sacagawea proved to be a great help to Lewis and Clark. She spotted familiar landmarks, and the expedition was lucky enough to meet up with Sacagawea's own tribe. Even more fortunately, the chief turned out to be her own brother. Now Lewis and Clark had the allies they needed to point a safe way through the mountains to the Columbia River. More importantly, they were able to purchase horses to carry them over the rough terrain. This chance meeting saved the expedition many precious days searching for a way through the mountain barrier.

The Indians advised the expedition to go north into the Bitterroot Valley and cross the mountains over Lolo Pass. Following this advice, Lewis and Clark met Flathead Indians in Ross' Hole and finally made their way over Lolo Pass in September. On November 7, 1805, after two months' travel down the Columbia River, the expedition camped on the shore of the Pacific at a place they called Fort Clatsop. The first half of the journey was now behind them. In the spring they would begin the return to St. Louis.

On the return, begun in March 1806, Lewis and Clark decided to split their corps and explore the area east of the Continental Divide. Lewis was particularly interested in exploring the Marias River. After Nez Perce guides took them through the Bitterroots, they were again in the Bitterroot Valley by July 1806. Lewis took nine men and headed north to the Marias, while Clark returned to Three Forks and took another small group east through the Gallatin Valley and down the Yellowstone River. It was Lewis who was to experience the most danger.

Lewis took the advice of the Nez Perce guides and crossed the Divide over Lewis and Clark's Pass and then dropped down to the Missouri above the falls. Proceeding downriver, Lewis reached the Marias and began ascending it in hopes he might find a waterway into Canadian territory. By July 26 the search seemed fruitless and Lewis resolved to turn back. "I now call (this) camp disappointment," Lewis wrote in his journal.

The next day the Lewis party chanced upon eight mounted Indians. Lewis did not know it, but they were Blackfeet, a tribe feared by most other tribes. Lewis met them and learned that they were part of a large Indian camp. Fearing the worst from these Indians, Lewis decided to camp with them but watch them carefully. He was not alert enough and morning brought conflict. Lewis recorded the action: "This morning at daylight the Indians got up and crowded around the fire, J. Fields, who was on post had carelessly laid his gun down behind him near where his brother was sleeping, one of the Indians the fellow to whom I had given the medal last evening slipped behind him and took his gun and that of his brother unperceived by him, at the same instant two others advanced and seized the guns of Drewyer and myself."

Now Lewis faced his most severe test. Awakening to the scuffle that ensued between his men and the Indians, Lewis cautioned his men only to retrieve their weapons and protect their horses. But bloodshed was not avoided. One Indian was killed by a knife thrust and Lewis himself was forced to shoot another dead before the party made their escape. Riding like the wind, Lewis and his men covered nearly one hundred miles on horseback to the Missouri, where they met up with other members of the expedition.

While Lewis met Blackfeet in less than ideal circumstances, Clark was exploring the Yellowstone River. Clark's side trip was not as eventful as his partner's, but the information he gained was to be one of the most important results of the entire expedition. Clark was exploring one of the prime fur trapping areas of the West.

After recovering the stashed supplies and canoes they had left the previous August, Clark's group proceeded beyond Three Forks, by the towering Bridger Mountains and finally over present-day Bozeman Pass on July 15, 1806. Now they descended to the Yellowstone, noting the abundant wildlife. Then Clark ran into Indian troubles of his own. A band of Crows stole half of the party's horses. Clark had been the first American victim of the most expert horse stealers on the plains.

In newly fashioned dugout canoes made of cottonwood trunks, Clark and his men floated down the Yellowstone passing the Big Horn River and finally arriving at a most "remarkable rock," which rose some 200 feet high. There, on July 25, Clark inscribed his signature on "Pompey's Pillar," which was named in honor of Sacagawea's son Baptiste, whom Clark had taken to calling "Pomp." From here Clark's group floated to the Missouri and looked for signs of Lewis and the rest of the expedition.

It was many days, on August 12, before Lewis overtook Clark on the Missouri. They were nearly to Fort Mandan when they were reunited. Much to his embarrassment, Lewis was recovering from a gunshot wound he received when one-eyed Pete Cruzatte mistook him for an elk. Nonetheless, the reunion was joyous. All that was left of the grand expedition was to drift home to St. Louis.

When they arrived in St. Louis on September 23, 1806, they were greeted by the town's surprised citizenry. Most had given them up for lost or worse. They talked with traders, wrote to government officials informing them of their safe return and then rested. The greatest of American explorations and adventures was now history. Meriwether Lewis and William Clark had given President Jefferson what he desired. They had penetrated the vast land and introduced Americans to mountains, plains, rivers, and native peoples of Montana.

Lewis and Clark Meeting the Flatheads at Ross' Hole, painted by Charles M. Russell (1864-1926) in 1912 expressly for the Montana House of Representatives. The heroic-size painting (26' x 12') hangs in the House chambers in the State Capitol building in Helena.

Timeline

1713: Earliest possible evidence of whites in Montana, a carved rock found near Chester, Montana.

1743: Verendrye Brothers see "shining mountains" in Montana.

1789: Pierre Chouteau, Jr., born in St. Louis.

1790s: Hudson's Bay Company explorers come near Montana.

1800: Thomas Jefferson elected President.

1803: France sells Louisiana to United States; William Clark and Meriwether Lewis selected to explore Louisiana Territory and beyond to the Pacific.

1804: Lewis and Clark begin expedition near St. Louis; spend winter at Mandan Villages.

1805: Lewis and Clark enter Montana heading west in April and leave Montana in September.

1806: Lewis and Clark enter Montana heading east in July and leave Montana down the Missouri in August.

1807: Manuel Lisa builds fur post at mouth of Big Horn River.

1808: David Thompson begins exploration of northwest Montana; American Fur Company organized in New York; Missouri Fur Company organized in St. Louis.

1809: Thompson builds Saleesh House fur post at Thompson Falls.

1810: Fur trappers attacked by Blackfeet at Three Forks.

1819: Missouri Fur Company reorganized by Lisa.

1821: Fort Benton on Big Horn River built.

1822: Rocky Mountain Fur Company organized.

1824: "Rendezvous System" developed by Rocky Mountain Fur Company.

1826: Pierre Chouteau becomes western agent for American Fur Company; Upper Missouri Outfit (U.M.O.) created.

1828: Fort Union construction begun near mouth of Yellowstone River.

1831: Flathead delegation travels to St. Louis in search of priests.

1832: *Yellowstone* steamboat arrives at Fort Union.

1833: Alexander Culbertson arrives at Fort Union.

1840: Fr. Pierre Jean deSmet comes to Montana.

1841: St. Mary's built in Bitterroot.

1842: deSmet travels to Europe.

1845: Fr. Anthony Ravalli arrives at St. Mary's.

1846: Fort Benton built on Missouri by Culbertson.

1850: John Owen buys St. Mary's Mission.

Suggested Readings:

John Bakeless. *Lewis and Clark: Partners in Discovery.* NY: Wm. Morrow, 1947.

Bernard DeVoto. *The Journals of Lewis and Clark.* Boston: Houghton, Mifflin, 1953.

Lucylle H. Evans. *St. Mary's in the Rocky Mountains.* Stevensville, Mont.: Montana Creative Consultants, 1976.

A. B. Guthrie, Jr. *The Big Sky.* NY: Wm. Sloane, 1947.

John U. Terrell. *Black Robe: The Life of Pierre-Jean deSmet.* Garden City, NY: Doubleday, 1964.

David Walter. "Lewis and Clark: The Course of Empire," *Visual History of Montana.* Helena: Superintendent of Public Instruction, 1976.

Granville Stuart discovered gold at Gold Creek in 1858. It was not long before he invested in cattle and became one of Montana's pioneer cattlemen.

Chapter III
Gold Lures Men

Montana's gold had been there for millions of years before it was first discovered in the 1850s. It could have been found much earlier. But gold was not the chief interest of the men who chased beaver pelts. Indians seemed to have had little or no interest in it. The great discoveries would have to wait until improved transportation brought more wilderness travellers to Montana. The first serious mining activity came after there were already a few scattered white settlements.

In the late 1850s Fort Benton on the Missouri was the most significant outpost of white civilization on the Montana frontier. Fort Benton was a sizeable and prosperous trading post when frontier surveyor and explorer Isaac I. Stevens arrived in 1853 with an expedition of over 250 people.

Stevens, newly appointed governor of Washington Territory, was given the task of exploring the Missouri River region. He was to determine the best route possible for a transcontinental railroad across the high plains and Rockies. Fort Benton stood as the lone settlement along Stevens' route above the Missouri River. Oregon and California had already attracted many settlers in the 1840s. By 1846 the United States had acquired Oregon from the British, and after California's gold rush that region had enough population to become a state in 1850. Montana had been passed over. Stevens was looking for a way to pass through Montana as efficiently as possible.

After a short visit at Fort Benton, Stevens took his expeditionary force to the Bitterroot Valley where John Owen's trading post was a solitary settlement. From Fort Owen, Stevens sent John Mullan on mission after mission to find a quick and safe route through the Rockies for the iron horse. Back and forth across the mountains Mullan trekked until he finally found a broad and low pass just north of present-day Helena—Mullan's Pass.

A few years later, Mullan got the job of building a road over the route he and Stevens had surveyed. Construction began in 1858, and by 1862 a very rough and sometimes unusable road joined Walulah Gap on the Columbia River with Fort Benton on the Missouri River.

About the same time, steamboats began arriving at Fort Benton during the spring and summer months. With more travellers crisscrossing Montana small settlements developed. One on the Hell Gate River near present-day Missoula began with a small trading post under the ownership of Christopher P. Higgins and Frank L. Worden. Other small settlements, a few farms, and ranches began to dot the Deer Lodge and Beaverhead valleys.

Two of the early settlers in Montana were James and Granville Stuart. From Iowa they went to California, then drifted north into Montana. In 1858 the Stuart brothers moved to the Deer Lodge Valley and settled near the Little Blackfoot River crossing on the Mullan Road. There was some activity in the area and talk of gold in a nearby creek. The Stuarts, who had learned placer mining techniques in California, made their first gold discovery at Gold Creek in 1858. Whether this was the first genuine strike in Montana will never be known, but Gold Creek was the site of the first true mining rush.

Francois Finlay, sometimes called Benetsee, may have been the discoverer of gold at Gold Creek in 1852. It was storied that Finlay, a Hudson's Bay Company employee, found quite a bit of gold but kept it a secret. This may be, but one of the most difficult secrets to keep on the frontier was the existence of gold. There has also been the suggestion that Hudson's Bay Company officials told Finlay to say nothing of the discovery for fear it would generate a stampede to the area and ruin the remaining fur trapping.

All the same, by 1860, there was quite a bit of mining activity at Gold Creek. It drew notice from the travellers on the new Mullan Road, but these diggings were paltry. Not until John White's discovery of great placer deposits at Grasshopper Creek in July 1862 was there a major strike. The Grasshopper diggings attracted wide attention, and before long a ramshackle mining camp, Bannack, became a new Montana settlement. Miners came to Bannack from Idaho, California, and Colorado goldfields. The rush was on and hundreds seeking riches swelled Bannack's population within months.

Sluice boxes and tailings piles represented the placer mining period in Montana history.

Mining camps seemed to grow up overnight. Everything centered on the mining activity itself. Typical camps had only one main street lined with hastily constructed buildings. Sluice boxes were more important than homes. At the sluices gold-bearing gravel was dumped and washed. It took the labor of many men working long hours to recover the gold particles. Placer mining, characterized by sluices, rocker boxes, and gold pans, required a minimal investment and often yielded quick profits. The camps, however, were populated by many people other than miners.

Miners were not hunters, farmers, freighters, or carpenters. There existed an immediate need in mining camps to provide food, housing, and entertainment. The business of freighting groceries from Salt Lake City and nearer points meant wagons, teams of oxen, and the men to drive them. Housing needs meant logs and lumber to build small shacks, boarding houses, and business structures. Saloons for entertainment, general stores for provisions and implements, blacksmiths, bakeries, and all manner of other businesses appeared to serve the miners' needs. Mining camps soon took on the look of settled towns, including newspapers and hotels. If the strike lasted long enough, the camp might become a sizeable frontier community. Montana's gold strikes created both varieties of mining camps. Some died as soon as the gold played out. Others survived the initial rush to become genuine frontier towns.

The Bannack rush brought enough prospectors and settlers to create a strong little community, but it would be dwarfed by the greatest of Montana's gold rushes the following year. In the spring of 1863 a group of prospectors who had tried and failed to overtake James Stuart's Yellowstone Expedition stumbled on to a small creek near the Madison River valley. There Bill Fairweather, Henry Edgar, and several others, tired from their journey, took time to look for gold. Their first panning on May 26, 1863, yielded $2.40. The following day they panned $150. After staking twelve claims in the gulch, Fairweather and his companions returned to Bannack for supplies.

The news of the strike touched off a stampede to Alder Gulch. "I never saw anything like it," Edgar commented when he witnessed the rush. By June 17 a mining district had been organized, including a miner's court and townsite company. Originally named after Confederate President Jefferson Davis' wife, Varina, the new settlement took the name Virginia City. Within one year Virginia City boasted 10,000 residents. Nearby Nevada City qualified as Montana's second largest town.

In rapid succession strikes were made at other locations in western Montana. In July 1864, the so-called "Four Georgians" prospected one last time before giving up. They hit a rich placer deposit. Reginald "Bob" Stanley, John Crab, D. J. Miller, and Thomas "John" Cowan named their strike Last

Chance Gulch. The familiar rush brought gold-seekers to the area. Helena was born. At nearly the same time other miners struck gold twenty miles northeast of Helena at Confederate Gulch. Before long news of a large new mining region near Helena had spread throughout the West.

Those who rushed to Virginia City, Helena, Confederate Gulch, Silver Bow, Butte and other camps came overland on the Mullan Road. They came up from the Oregon Trail through the Beaverhead Valley and across the plains on the Minnesota Wagon Road, pioneered by the Fisk brothers in the 1860s. Others took steamboats up the Missouri to Fort Benton, then travelled overland to Helena. From Helena wagon roads fanned to other mining areas. Helena's central location, plus the nearly twenty million dollars in gold mined there, made it the most important transportation center. Freighting companies and large mercantile firms in Helena supplied Montana towns and made Helena Montana's financial center by the early 1870s.

Placer mining camps quickly expired unless significant quartz deposits were found. Extracting gold locked in underground quartz formations required heavy equipment and large investments. Huge stamp mills to crush and process the gold-bearing ore had to be erected on solid foundations as permanent structures. The mines themselves required stout timbers to prevent cave-ins. An entirely different set of tools was necessary to dig gold from underground veins. In short, quartz mining was a much more extensive operation.

Quartz mining by the early 1870s began a second phase of Montana's gold boom. At the height of the placer mining days in the 1860s, Montana's mines produced between ten and twenty million dollars per year. Some later quartz operations, such as the famous Drumlummon mine in Marysville, were nearly as rich. The result of this second phase encouraged the growth of stable communities and improved transportation routes.

The image of mining towns in Montana suggests a wild atmosphere dominated by rough, hard drinking men, women of little virtue, gamblers, robbers, and vigilantes. While these people certainly existed, popular fiction, movies, and television have exaggerated conditions. Mining towns attracted all types of people: all social backgrounds and all races. Their lives, outside of frontier mining and business opportunities, reflected this diversity.

Virginia City, for example, boasted a dramatic society, literary reading group, a polite social club, and a men's singing society in 1865. Horse racing, baseball games, and tests of strength were popular amusements, but culture and fine arts attracted a fair share of the population. Theatrical groups could be found in nearly every mining town, while travelling dramatic troupes played regularly in towns like Helena and Virginia City. Masons and other fraternal orders were also formed in these mining communities.

Education was a priority. In Bannack, Lucia Darling opened one of Montana's first schools. By 1866, Virginia City had organized the first public school district in Montana. Mining town residents, and frontier people in general, greatly valued books. As early as 1868 a group of Helenans organized a library, and the first territorial legislature incorporated the Montana Historical Society in 1865. If anything, mining communities were overly concerned about their isolation and lack of refined culture.

There is no denying that violence and vice were part of life in Montana mining towns. The gold rush brought too many people to the diggings for hastily organized miner's courts to handle. Miner's courts could deal with claim disputes, but robbery, murder, and other violent crimes demanded established courts and judges. In some communities, the residents turned to vigilante law for relief.

Vigilantes are greatly misunderstood. They are often pictured as impulsive men who were little more than a mob. In Bannack and Virginia City there was a burst of criminal activity and violence in 1863-1864 that would have shocked people in any city or town in the nation. The condition warranted action of some kind. Henry Plummer, who was elected sheriff of Bannack in 1863, led a particularly brutal gang of road agents and thieves. Plummer's gang went unchecked until a number of killings aroused a general anger among Bannack's residents. The bandits killed Deputy Sheriff D. B. Dillingham, allegedly to prevent him from ending their game. At the trial the killers escaped conviction. Then one gang member, George Ives, killed a young man named Nicholas Tbalt and faced trial in late 1863. This time the prosecuting attorney, Wilbur Fisk Sanders, determined that Ives would not escape punishment.

The Bi-Metallic Mill near Granite, Montana, in 1888. The Bi-Metallic was one of Montana's more important silver producers in the 1880s.

Sanders got his conviction on December 19, 1863, and, before any leniency could surface, he moved the crowd to execute Ives. After Ives' hanging, the vigilante mood gained favor. A vigilance committee was formed and moved quickly in 1864 to destroy Plummer's gang. In one month they caught and hanged twenty-four men, including Plummer. Other vigilante committees in Helena and elsewhere took similar actions in the 1860s. The mysterious symbol 3-7-77 became a warning of swift and final vigilante action. Only the establishment of a territorial judicial system in 1864-1865 quieted vigilante justice. It was not a pleasant chapter in Montana's history, but conditions seemed to warrant some dramatic action to end a potential reign of terror.

For good or ill, the great gold rush to Montana brought the population needed to qualify the area for territorial status. On May 26, 1864, Montana became a territory. With this distinction came regular justice, political districts, an elected legislature, and appointed executive officers, including a governor and a secretary. On the strength of gold mining and related business the territory continued to grow in the 1870s and 1880s.

Part of the reason for Montana's continued growth was additional mining discoveries and the construction of more sophisticated mills for processing ore. One of the best examples was the Marysville district just north and west of Helena. Although placer deposits were located there in the mid-1860s, it was not until 1876 that Thomas Cruse discovered the fabulous Drumlummon deposits. The ore was rich and Cruse wasted little time in constructing a large stamp mill at the site of the mine.

Cruse named it Drumlummon in honor of his native parish in Ireland. By the mid-1880s two mills operated. One fifty-stamp mill featured 900-pound stamps (or hammers) that dropped ninety-six times per minute and crushed over 150 tons of ore per day. Cruse sold the property to an English mining syndicate, the Montana Company Limited, in 1883. By 1891, the mine had produced $5.6 million in gold and $3.5 million in silver. Near the mines Marysville developed with an opera house, a newspaper, hotels, and a variety of businesses to serve the population.

Discoveries such as the Drumlummon fueled Montana's mining growth. The biggest boom in the 1880s, however, came in silver and copper. Silver, lead, and copper often occur in the same type of geological formation. Where you find one, the other minerals are often nearby. Processing silver, however, was more complicated than gold. Silver ore was usually a combination of several minerals, and separating them required special processes. Silver was also more abundant and, therefore, brought a lower price.

The first silver smelter was erected at Argenta near Bannack in 1866. A review of the silver mines and smelters in Montana two decades later indicated how important the metal was to Montana's economy. By then Montana was the second largest producer of silver in the nation. Mines and smelters operated in Butte, Philipsburg, Elkhorn, Wickes, Glendale, and the Castle Mountains.

Samuel T. Hauser built the Argenta smelter in 1866, and it was Hauser who first invested heavily in Montana silver mining. By 1867 he had investments in Philipsburg, and in the 1880s he organized silver operations in Wickes, and finally a huge smelter works just east of Helena. According to James Stuart, Hauser suffered from "a severe attack of quartz on the brain," but he was a sharp capitalist who took hold of opportunities and became the territory's most important financial figure. He was destined to be governor of the territory from 1885 to 1887.

In the mid-1870s a nationwide financial depression stalled business. It halted Northern Pacific Railroad construction in the Dakotas, and otherwise made silver production uneconomical. Yet, in the face of hard times, significant new discoveries were made on Big Butte's slopes near the old placer camp on Silver Bow Creek. William L. Farlin developed the Travona mine in 1875 and built the Dexter Mill. Although the ore was rich, Farlin mismanaged the operation and lost it in 1876 to his banker, William Andrews Clark.

The Alice Mine and Mill in Butte about the time Marcus Daly came to manage it for the Walker Brothers.

W. A. Clark was a native of Pennsylvania who had rushed to Bannack in 1863, taking up the business of merchandising. He later moved to Deer Lodge and entered the banking field. By 1872 Clark had invested in Butte mining properties including the Original, Colusa, and Mountain Chief mines. In 1876, when Clark took over Farlin's interests, the Butte mining district was already attracting many investors. The Walker Brothers of Salt Lake City purchased the Alice mine in 1876. Activity was furious, and it was clear to all that the Butte Hill was one of the richest finds in the Rockies.

When they purchased the Alice, the Walker Brothers sent a manager to Butte named Marcus Daly. An Irish immigrant with mining experience in California and Nevada, Daly proved to be an ambitious mine operator. He later became one of Butte's famed "Copper Kings." Clark, Daly, and others increased silver production in Butte to nearly $15 million in 1891 alone. But Butte's future lay in copper, not silver. Copper had always been considered an obstacle by miners. It was a mineral with little use; it was just in the way. With the coming of the railroad in the 1880s and the development of the electrical industry, however, the demand for copper suddenly increased. Great copper deposits in Michigan met much of the demand, but there was room for competitors, and it was Butte that challenged the Michigan copper interests.

In 1882 wily Marcus Daly discovered one of the richest copper deposits in the nation. After purchasing the Anaconda mine from its original developer, Michael Hickey, Daly improved the property and then looked for financial backers. He found three powerful allies in George Hearst, Lloyd Tevis, and James Ben Ali Haggin, all important capitalists from San Francisco. With their support, Daly then took the risk that brought them millions. In 1884 Daly located and built the world's largest copper smelter along Warm Springs Creek in the Deer Lodge Valley, twenty-six miles west of Butte. Alongside the giant smelter, Marcus Daly's own city, Anaconda, grew rapidly according to his own plans.

Daly and his backers had tapped one of the greatest copper deposits in the world. The Butte Hill was a mountain of rich copper sulphide ores—up to 12 percent copper. Centuries of geological actions created the complex and broken vein system that constitutes the Butte Hill. It took skill and ingenuity to mine and then smelt the copper ore.

The first copper ore bodies were discovered 300 to 400 feet below ground level. Before long, Daly's miners were blasting ore at the 1,000-foot level, then 3,000 feet, and eventually more than a mile underground. To insure what safety they could, the shafts and horizontal passages—called drifts—were braced with stout timbers. Using the square-set method of timbering, heavy wooden arches were constructed to shore up ceilings where miners chipped and blasted away the copper veins. Above ground wooden and steel hoists—gallows frames—marked the shaft entrances where the ore was hoisted to the surface.

Using horse-pulled and later electric-powered carts, the miners moved the ore to the vertical shafts where it was raised to the surface. From there Anaconda's ore was hauled to the smelter in Anaconda on Daly's own railroad. At the smelter, mechanical ore crushing and concentrating prepared the ore for a chemical and electrical process that separated copper from the other minerals. By 1891 the Anaconda smelter was producing pure copper ingots. In the following year Butte's copper production topped the great Michigan producers for the first time.

There is an interesting story behind the competition between Michigan and Butte. Just as the demand for copper was on the increase, Michigan interests lowered their price in an attempt to drive the Butte mines out of business. It was a classic struggle. Haggin and Daly refused to give up. They finished the Anaconda smelter and upped their own production. By mining more copper ore than any other mine in the nation and smelting it in their huge smelter, Anaconda remained competitive. By 1888 the price of copper was so low that only Anaconda was still making a profit at ten cents per pound.

Additional interests in Europe took this opportunity to enter the copper business. Realizing that copper prices could be manipulated by controlling the world's supply, a group of investors formed a syndicate to do just that. Their plan was to control all of the world's copper production and set their own price. The plan worked for less than one year. In 1889 the syndicate collapsed. In the meantime, however, the Anaconda along with Butte's other copper mines had become the nation's leading producers. Butte truly had become the "richest hill on earth."

The great burst of production in the 1880s required more miners and smeltermen than anyone could have predicted a decade earlier. To meet the need, Clark, Daly, and other mine operators imported thousands of workers to Butte and Anaconda. Populations swelled in both cities. Miners, smeltermen, engineers, carpenters, machinists, and dozens of other craftsmen came. They were Irish, Cornish, German, Finnish, Scandinavian, Slavic, and many other nationalities. Butte quickly became a city of smaller ethnic cities. Dublin Gulch, Finntown, Chinatown, and other districts created an international mining city a mile high in the Rockies.

Butte was a boom town. Just as thousands had crowded into Alder Gulch in 1863-1864, now Butte's population seemed to double every three or four years. By 1890 there were 45,000 residents. And, like other mining boom towns, it was a rough environment. The clash of nationalities and the furious activity in Butte soon made it notorious as the toughest mining town in the West. Liquor flowed plentifully, gambling was wide open. Prostitutes abounded in a town populated by many single miners. Generally Butte reflected how dangerous and tough hardrock mining was. It was a unique place.

"The Richest Hill on Earth"—Butte in the heyday of copper mining.—*N. A. Forsyth photo, M.H.S.*

The influx of population helped justify Montana's bid for statehood in the 1880s. Finally, after a lengthy political struggle in Congress, Montana became a state in 1889. It was due, at least in part, to the advent of copper mining in Butte. More to the point, the wealth created by mining development in Montana provided the new state with the financial strength it needed to develop a dynamic economy.

Montana's mining industry included gold, silver, copper, zinc, lead, and coal. Smelter and reduction works were operating in Butte, Anaconda, East Helena, Philipsburg, Great Falls, Neihart, and several other locations. In 1891 the Boston and Montana Copper Company built the first electrolytic copper refining facility at Black Eagle near Great Falls. Four years earlier Sam Hauser's Helena & Livingston Smelting and Reduction Company built the state's first custom refining smelter at East Helena. In short, mining was the backbone of Montana's economy.

Because mining was so essential to the new state, the fortunes of mining in the nation affected Montana directly. The first years of the 1890s were energetic and bountiful, but in the spring of 1893 a nationwise financial panic threatened Montana's security. Eastern banks failed by the dozens. Thousands of people lost their jobs. Business and industry slowed to a crawl. Montana's copper and silver mining industry could not escape the consequences.

Poor business conditions throughout the nation decreased the demand for copper. Butte suffered terribly in 1893-1894. Hundreds of people were out of work. Then in the summer of 1893 Congress decided to halt any further U.S. government purchases and minting of silver. They believed that the minting of silver coins had something to do with the financial depression. The result for Montana and other silver-producing states was disastrous. Montana's silver mines suddenly lost their best customer. It was nearly a deathblow to small silver camps such as Elkhorn, Wickes, and Neihart.

The financial depression of the 1890s halted Montana's economy. It demonstrated how important mining was to the young state. But more than just mines and miners were affected. All business conditions worsened. In Helena, for example, five banks failed. All of the state's railroads declared bankruptcy. And, of course, there was significant unemployment. Mining was Montana's strength, but it depended upon a healthy national economy. The depression in the 1890s was the first time Montanans were to learn this fundamental lesson. Montanans also learned how much they depended on the land for their wealth.

Alder Gulch Becomes Virginia City

In the 1860s just the suggestion of a gold strike prompted pioneers to stampede to the area with pick and pan in hand. In the summer of 1863 Bill Fairweather, Henry Edgar, Tom Cover, Barney Hughes, Mike Sweeney, and Harry Rodgers returned to Bannack, Idaho Territory, after prospecting. They created more interest than they desired. As they purchased materials and provisions, paying for it in gold, word circulated that a new discovery had been made. Bannack buzzed with the news. Leaving town was easy for the prospectors, but shaking the gold-hungry mob following them proved impossible. Fairweather and Edgar realized the situation was hopeless, so as they neared the Alder Gulch diggings they called a miners' meeting and laid down a few bare regulations. With their own claims guaranteed, the leaders went on until Henry Edgar announced to all: "This is the place."

"I never saw anything like it," Edgar commented later. A full-scale stampede brought hundreds and later thousands of fortune-seekers into the gulch. Within eighteen months there would be over ten thousand people in a mining area twelve miles long. Two towns, Virginia City and Nevada City, seemed to grow up overnight. The excitement was justified. In five years the area produced over $40 million in gold, making it one of the richest finds in the West. The wealth brought miners, speculators, gamblers, storekeepers, freighters, and practically every other variety of tradesman and craftsman to Virginia City. By 1865 Virginia City was easily the largest settlement in the new Montana Territory, and it had become its official capital.

It all started quite accidentally. James Stuart, the energetic and adventuresome brother of Granville Stuart, organized a prospecting expedition to the Yellowstone country in 1863. Gold had been rumored there, but Stuart was fearful of conflicts with Indians in the area. He reasoned that there was strength in numbers. Fairweather, Edgar, and others in their party tried to join the Stuart expedition, but somehow missed connections and pursued Stuart's group in haste. All they found was a disagreeable band of Crow Indians who captured the entire lot of them. Luckily, one of the prospectors, Lew Simmons, had lived with the Crows and knew their language. For two days in early May 1863 the Crows kept them prisoners and seemed to threaten their lives. Simmons convinced the Crows to let them go upon the promise that they would not return to prospect. Fairweather, Edgar, and the others headed back to Bannack, disappointed at their luck but thankful they escaped harm.

Rather than travel by way of Three Forks, they decided to cut across the Madison River and then to Bannack. It was on the divide between the Madison and the Stinking Water (Ruby) River that they made the great discovery on May 26. Seeing a little color in an outcropping near their camp, they prospected and turned up well over one hundred dollars in two days of panning. Naming the gulch for the numerous alder trees growing in the area, they staked several claims and set out for Bannack. And then the rush began.

Miners learned early that one of the first priorities when a new strike was discovered was the creation of mining districts and regulations. In the case of Alder Gulch, the first miner's meeting took place before the boomers even knew its location. On June 7 and 9, 1863, two additional meetings wrote and adopted rules for the Fairweather Mining District. Dr. William Steele served as district president. Dr. G. G. Bissell was selected as judge, and James Fergus, later a wealthy cattle rancher, took responsibility for recording all claims. These officers and the miner's court had to suffice as the only authority at Alder Gulch. Judge Bissell, in fact, changed the proposed name of the camp from Varina, the name of Confederate President Jefferson Davis' wife, to Virginia. Bissell was a staunch Unionist and refused to give the camp any Confederate name.

The rules the miners established were simple enough. No one could file more than two claims and each claim was limited to one hundred feet along the lode. To maintain a claim it had to be worked at least three full days per week, and no claim could use creek water more than ten inches in depth for sluice boxes. The miner's court handled civil and criminal cases. Jury trials were to be granted upon request. The townsite itself was limited to 320 acres along Daylight Creek, a tributary to Alder Creek. There was no plan to the town, although the first buildings lined Wallace Street. Before long four or five other camps popped up along Alder

Virginia City in the 1860s looking northeast from the corner of Van Buren and Wallace Streets.

Gulch, but Virginia City remained the most important.

As a rough mining camp, Virginia City was no different than others that had preceded it. The prospectors who choked the gulch in 1863-1864 were mostly young, single, and male. They came from nearly every state in the union. Many of them had served in the Civil War, which still dominated politics and discussion. There were foreign tongues heard in the gulch as well. Germans, Chinese, and other nationalities made Virginia City a genuine melting pot. Those who came to mine the gulch worked long hours hoping for riches, but only a small percentage became truly wealthy—it was hard work without shortcuts.

Alder Gulch in the summer and fall of 1863 was a beehive of activity. It seemed that everyone pursuing gold was digging, washing, and inspecting piles of dirt and gravel. Getting the gold was no easy matter. Alder Creek's deposits were buried and required miners to penetrate several feet to get at the gold-bearing gravel. This meant hard labor digging a shaft, erecting a windlass hoist, constructing long sluice boxes to wash the gravel, building flumes to carry water from the creek to each claim, and hiring laborers to help with all of this work. Working several feet down was dangerous. Cave-ins were a regular occurrence. And it took a skilled diplomat to build flumes across other claims to bring water to a particular digging—disagreements and worse were common. Most of their work was tough manual labor.

There were several methods used to extract gold from the gulch dirt. Since gold is a heavy mineral, placer mining used water as a solvent to wash away lighter material. Panning for gold was prospecting; mining meant processing tons of material to retrieve ounces of gold. Miners dumped gravel into rocker boxes or long sluice boxes and watched for gold nuggets, flakes, and dust. From seven or more feet down in their shaft hole, they hoisted a mucky gravel and dirt mixture to the sluice where water moved the muck down the box over the wooden riffle bars to catch the gold. Again and again they dumped, washed, and watched, working ten hours or more each day.

They were always eager to make the big strike and dig into the "mother lode." Few did. It is, however, interesting to note just how much gold they left behind for others. Mollie Sheehan, a twelve-year-old in Virginia City, remembered taking air-blowers and brushes to get abandoned gold dust from sluices. "Sometimes our gold dust weighed to the amount of a dollar or more. It was," Mollie wrote, "the only kind of money I ever saw in Virginia City."

The Chinese were famous and notorious for how much gold they extracted from the abandoned tailings of other miners. They were very efficient miners and were despised by whites who never tried to understand Chinese customs and ways. In 1872 the territorial legislature passed a statute forbidding Chinese to own mining property. The law was declared unconstitutional in 1874. As late as 1900 there were still two hundred or so Chinese in Virginia City working over old claims.

As the miners dug for riches until the ground was literally "turned inside out," a town of some permanence grew up on Wallace, Jackson, Idaho, and other streets alongside Daylight Creek. It was not a polished town. Freight wagons hauling in goods from Fort Benton or Salt Lake City turned the streets into mud flats in the spring and dust bins in the summer. Garbage, manure, dead animals, and worse littered the streets. There was no time or money to worry about cleanliness or street repairs. Virginia City was a place of furious activity.

From one end of Virginia City to the other there was evidence of industry. Bakeries, breweries, saloons, blacksmiths, hurdy-gurdy houses, general stores, banks and assay offices and so many other businesses catered to the miner's needs. The basic fact of life in Virginia City was its isolation. That meant paying high freight bills for imported goods and supplies, whether they came from Portland, Salt Lake City, or upriver from St. Louis. Freight costs were as high as twenty cents per pound, and that often equalled the values of the goods hauled. The solution was local manufacturing. Within a year of the gold discovery residents could find everything from leather goods, to whiskey, to gold jewelry being made in Virginia City.

Timothy Luce's bakery was probably the first actual business building in town. That stands to reason, for bread was as much the staff of life then as it is now. Soon crude log structures gave way to frame buildings and later buildings made of native stone or locally made brick. Virginia City was alive with merchants, tradesmen, and opportunists eager to make a dollar selling their products at competitive prices. Contrary to what we might expect, people could live in Virginia City fairly reasonably in the 1860s. Wages ranged from three to five times higher than in the States, while commodity prices were only twice as high. While the gold boom continued, jobs were plentiful and nearly everyone found a way to make ends meet.

There was plenty to do in Virginia City, even during the freezing winter months when mining activity practically halted and seasonal miners evacuated the town. Rough entertainment could be found at the city's numerous saloons. Locally distilled whiskey flowed at Con Orem's Melodeon on Jackson Street, and you could always find a billiard game at the Idaho Billiard Hall or at John Ming's fancy parlor. Those with spare gold dust could buy a $2.50 dance at one of the "hurdy-gurdy" houses. And if you wanted to gamble there were card games, Chinese games of chance, and sporting events. Con Orem's heroic 193-round prizefight against Hugh O'Neill on January 3, 1865, drew thousands.

There was a softer side to Virginia City's social life. Music, dancing, and singing were favorites. A woman could expect plenty of attention at dances, for as late as 1870 men still outnumbered women eight to one. You could dance to DeWitt Waugh's band in the early years, and later to the Virginia City Orchestra. By 1864 miners could take dancing and singing lessons, and in 1865 a group of them formed the Amphion Serenaders to entertain ladies at their doorsteps. Even theater was there. Everyone eagerly awaited travelling dramatic troupes and minstrel shows at Jack Langrishe's the People's Theatre. And then there were picnics, baseball games, and enthusiastic celebrations of Independence Day, St. Patrick's Day, and any other day that provided an excuse for fun and revelry.

Besides Walter Dance and James Stuart's general store and other Wallace Street gathering spots, Virginia City's churches served as meeting places for some. Father Joseph Giorda said the first Catholic Mass in Virginia City at Peter Ronan's cabin in November 1863. One year later the Reverend A. M. Hough dedicated a small log building on Jackson Street as a Methodist church. In 1868 Daniel S. Tuttle dedicated St. Paul's Episcopal church on Idaho Street. Unfortunately, church services never quite competed with hurdy-gurdy houses, billiards, saloons, and the like. The congregations were never large, but they were very important to the many families in town.

To serve the people's need for news Thomas J. Dimsdale's *The Montana Post,* the territory's first newspaper, began publication in late 1864. Virginia City's population was literate, and education was not neglected. Concerned over the number of children who seemed to run wild, Dimsdale and two other teachers established private schools in 1864-1865. Dimsdale charged two dollars per pupil per week. By 1866 the first public school opened, but it was not until the 1870s that a majority of the children attended with any regularity.

Gold dust, business affairs, and social happenings were not the only source of excitement in Virginia City—there was politics. The first who rushed to Alder Gulch came to Idaho Territory, but in May of 1864 President Lincoln signed legislation creating Montana Territory. Sidney Edgerton, who had come to Bannack in 1863 as an Idaho territorial justice, was appointed Montana's first governor and held the first official meetings of the new territory in Bannack. But Virginia City was already larger than Bannack in 1864, and it took only a few months of persuasion to move the capital to Virginia City.

Edgerton and his small territorial administration moved to Virginia City in 1865 and rented what office space was available. For the next ten years the town's residents would be treated or plagued, depending on their viewpoints, to a lively political atmosphere. It was difficult to remain politically neutral in the 1860s. The population of Virginia City and the territory generally were Democrats. Federally-appointed executive and judicial officers were Republicans. And there were many miners who had fought for the Confederacy. They did not like Republicans, and Republicans did not like them. The story of these political battles stretched across the territorial era and into the first years of statehood.

Equally as important and interesting was the establishment of law and order in Virginia City. There had been entirely too much mayhem and vigilante justice. Gangs of thieves, particularly in the summer and fall of 1863, struck at will, waylaying miners and merchants on the roads around Bannack and Virginia City. Miner's courts were ineffective in these matters. Peace officers were even worse, for it turned out that the sheriff of Bannack and Virginia City was the gang's leader.

Henry Plummer had lived a life of violence before he arrived in Bannack in 1862. He had murdered a man in California. But he was an attractive character with a smooth manner and confident style. Somehow he was elected sheriff of Bannack and Virginia City. It did not take him long to organize a gang of road agents. Robbing coach passengers and miners was one thing, but murdering men in cold blood and plain sight was too much for the citizens to endure. The tide was turned and the vigilantes formed after the trial of George Ives in December 1863.

Governor Edgerton's nephew, Wilbur Fisk Sanders, was just short of thirty years old when several citizens pleaded with him to prosecute George Ives, supposed murderer of a German miner named Nicholas Tbalt. Sanders realized that someone had to see justice done. Thanks to Sanders' fortitude, Ives was convicted and summarily hanged on December 21, 1863. Soon thereafter, either in Bannack or Virginia City, Sanders and several others, including Don Byam and James Williams, formed a vigilance committee and pledged themselves to rid the area of thieves and murderers. They were unaware that Plummer was the gang's leader.

The vigilance committee was sworn to secrecy, and all agreed that "the only punishment that shall be inflicted by this committee is death." In late December Williams and others cornered a gang member, Red Yeager, who told them that Plummer was their leader. On January 10, 1864, Plummer and two of his men were hanged at Bannack. Four days later five more died by execution in Virginia City. "People were gathered in front on Wallace Street," Mollie Sheehan remembered. "The air was charged with excitement. I looked. The bodies of five men with ropes around their necks hung limp from a roof beam."

Virginia City's vigilantes had done their job. Counting those captured and hanged elsewhere, twenty-four desperadoes were executed. Thomas J. Dimsdale, writing of the whole affair in *The Vigilantes of Montana,* called their record a "proud one." But there have been many commentators who did not agree. Truly it is difficult for us well over a century later to sit and pass judgment on the actions of Vir-

Corner of Jackson and Idaho Streets in Virginia City when placer mining was at its height.—A. C. Carter photo, M.H.S.

ginia City's famous vigilance committee.

Disorder of a far less menacing type also afflicted Virginia City before the coming of territorial law. It all started with the unpredictable nature of freight shipments to Virginia City. At times freight wagons could not negotiate roads for months. Flour, an essential commodity, had to be freighted from distant points and its price often increased as supplies dwindled. In late 1864 Dimsdale's *Post* warned residents that the supply might be short during the winter. He was right. Speculators in flour sat back and watched the prices rise when freight trains struggled and failed to reach Virginia City.

A sack of flour weighing one hundred pounds cost $20 in early October 1864. Two weeks later it cost $26, then $28 in late November, and over $40 in April 1865. Those who had flour hoarded it, stretched it, and hoped a shipment would arrive soon. Merchants with flour remaining kept increasing the price until it hit over $90 per sack on April 17. The next day a group of so-called "Regulators" announced that they would liberate the flour for the good of the community. Dimsdale's *Post* was alarmed, but the speculators had simply pushed the price too high. The flour "Regulators" met armed guards at several stores, but when nearly five hundred men began confiscating the flour there was little the merchants could do. Sheriff Neil Howie watched for violence, but none occurred. Mayor Paris Pfouts sighed relief for himself and everyone else when the first shipments arrived a few days later. The so-called "flour riots" were not riots at all, but they do point up Virginia City's isolation and the self-reliance that was necessary to live on the frontier.

Virginia City was a typical mining boom town in most ways, but it was also the territorial capital and the home of Montana's famous vigilantes. Its population declined when the gold played out. By 1870 only a few hundred of the 10,000 remained, the capital relocated in Helena in 1875, but Virginia City refused to become a ghost town even into the twentieth century. Now, through the foresight and devotion of the late Charles M. Bovey, modern tourists can stroll down Wallace Street and marvel at a magnificently restored Virginia City—Montana's greatest gold camp.

Sam Hauser

On May 14, 1862, the steamboat *Emilie* slipped away from the dock in St. Louis. It began that sometimes perilous passage up the Missouri River to Fort Benton, Dakota Territory. Among the 136 passengers that day was an adventuresome young man of twenty-nine who hoped to strike a bonanza at the gold diggings in Idaho. When he arrived at Fort Benton, 2,500 miles upriver from St. Louis, it was June 17, 1862, a little less than two years before the birth of Montana Territory. Samuel T. Hauser's life, his accomplishments in mining, banking, business, and politics, was to be tied directly with the growth and development of Montana Territory. In the next three decades, Sam Hauser became one of the three or four most successful and influential men in Montana. His biography is the story of a masterful enterpriser on a frontier full of opportunity.

Sam Hauser was born in 1833 in Falmouth, Kentucky, to a slaveholding family. His father was a successful lawyer, gentleman, and politician. Young Sam took his first steps toward a career by studying surveying and engineering in Cincinnati, Ohio. In the early 1850s he moved west to Missouri where his cousins held positions of some importance. In Missouri he worked as a surveyor and construction inspector for the Pacific Railroad Company and later the Lexington and St. Louis Railroad.

By 1860 Hauser had worked for eight years around locomotives, iron rails, and trestles. He learned a great deal about the importance of dependable transportation on the frontier, knowledge he would use later in Montana. But by the time he was twenty-nine, Hauser had tired of the Civil War tensions that dominated Missouri politics and life. He was quietly in favor of the rebels' cause, yet loyalties were divided in Missouri. Even in Hauser's own family there was strong disagreement. Perhaps to escape all that, or just to seek a fortune, Sam Hauser decided to move west again; so he boarded the *Emilie*.

When he arrived at Fort Benton, Hauser was eager to get to the Idaho mines. Rustling up a group of travellers, he set out on the Mullan Road not realizing just how sparsely populated the area was. On June 29, 1862, the party was re-

Samuel T. Hauser came to Montana in the 1860s to find a fortune. He became one of Montana's most successful businessmen, and was already a prominent banker when this picture was taken in the late 1870s.

lieved when they made Gold Creek without encountering hostile Indians or some other calamity. James and Granville Stuart, Walter B. Dance, A. Sterne Blake, Christopher P. Higgins, and a couple of dozen other miners were prospecting Gold Creek for what they could find. Hauser, still impatient to get to the Salmon River diggings, pushed on with a few men, but he returned to Gold Creek just in time to join the general rush to the big strike at Grasshopper Creek.

It was late July and Hauser was still anxious to strike paydirt. He did not find it in Bannack. After a winter there, he joined a prospecting expedition to the Yellowstone country. It was a disappointing trip. They found no gold but plenty of hostile Indians. When they returned to Bannack the town was in a turmoil over the bonanza discovery at Alder Gulch. Hauser could not resist the pull. By August he had staked a claim on Bivan's Gulch, about fifteen miles from

Virginia City. But again Hauser missed his chance to "strike it rich."

He was only able to scratch enough from his claim to survive. His real talents, however, seemed to be his knack for making friends easily and involving himself in promotional schemes. Wilbur Fisk Sanders came to Virginia City during the summer of 1863. He was drumming up gold dust to finance Sidney Edgerton's proposed trip to Washington, D.C. Edgerton wanted Congress to approve a new territory in the mining region. Sam Hauser offered to help. Although Hauser was a Democrat, he left political bickering in Missouri, striking up friendships with Edgerton, Sanders, and Nathaniel P. Langford, all staunch Republicans. They collected $2,500 and in November 1863, Edgerton, Langford, and Hauser made their fateful trip to lobby Congress for a new territory.

Hauser and Edgerton sensed something disturbing about Sheriff Henry Plummer as they planned to leave. Was Plummer scheming to rob them? Hauser worried. Boldly, Sam publicly entrusted the sheriff with $1,400 in gold the day before Hauser's planned departure from Bannack. The gold was returned safely the next day with Plummer's advice that Hauser wear a gift scarf to protect himself from the cold. He had foiled Plummer. The sheriff's scarf now marked him as off-limits to road agents. It was a clever move and typical of Hauser's political ability, an ability he used often in his career.

Sam Hauser was an organizer. Edgerton, Langford, and Hauser were successful in Washington. On May 26, 1864, President Abraham Lincoln signed legislation creating Montana Territory. Although Hauser did not return to Bannack until December, he was already busy getting his friends in the upcoming First Territorial Legislature to pass legislation favoring his interests. Langford, Walter Dance, James Stuart, and others joined Hauser in several of his schemes, including an irrigation company and a gas company. These plans did not amount to much, but they indicate Hauser's ambition and enterprise.

Sam returned to St. Louis in February 1865, seeking additional financial aid in his true interest in Montana—gold and silver quartz mining. He realized that the great bonanzas were to be made in quartz not placer mining. What Sam had in mind was buying up quartz claims and developing them with investors' capital. By 1866 he had formed the St. Louis and Montana Mining Company to do just that.

It did not take Hauser long to locate a promising property some fifteen miles from present-day Dillon. There he built the Argenta silver smelter—Montana's first. Shipping the mining machinery up the Missouri to Fort Benton and freighting it overland was expensive, but Hauser paid out freely. August Steitz and Philip Deidesheimer, two mining engineers hired by Hauser, built the smelter in October 1866. Hauser had great expectations, but smelting the silver ore was difficult, and Sam's poor management convinced St. Louis backers to cease operations in 1867. They had invested $150,000 at Argenta, and the smelter returned less than $18,000. This first effort was a flop.

Hauser was not discouraged. As the Argenta mill began to fail, Hauser invested more money in new silver discoveries in the Flint Creek Mountains. At Philipsburg, named for Philip Deidesheimer, Hauser built a new and more sophisticated smelter. The mill, called the James Stuart, was initially a success. But problems soon developed, and in late 1868 the mill closed. Operations at Philipsburg continued later under a new company, the Hope Mining Company, but Hauser played less and less of a role in the operations. He simply was not a good business manager, but he was a superb promoter—a man who always had another enterprising plan in mind.

From his first days in the gold fields, Sam had been interested in the business of buying and selling gold. There was great excitement in assaying gold specimens, exchanging gold for paper money, and financing mining operations. This was an ideal business for someone like Hauser. He worked easily with people, and he was always eager to invest in mining properties. In December 1864, Sam and Nathaniel P. Langford established a partnership under the name of "S. T. Hauser and Co." Their business was exchanging gold for paper money. But Hauser was already thinking of establishing a national bank in Montana. After getting Langford, a German immigrant named Theodore H. Kleinschmidt, and several Missouri investors involved, Sam Hauser organized the First National Bank of Helena, Montana Territory, on March 17, 1868.

When Hauser located his new bank in Helena, the rich little town on Last Chance Gulch already was becoming the banking capital of the territory. There were four private banks in operation in 1868, but Hauser's First National was easily the largest. Sam was shrewd. He took advantage of the mining boom by dealing in gold and silver bouillion directly with eastern bankers. They wanted gold and silver, and in return Hauser was able to get more money in the First National to lend to Montana businesses. In 1873 he was doing well enough to open another bank, the Missoula National Bank, with Daniel C. Corbin and Christopher P. Higgins as partners. Four years later Hauser and Andrew J. Davis opened a third national bank in Butte, and by 1880 he had opened a fourth in Fort Benton. By the early 1880s, there was no question that Sam Hauser was the most important banker in the territory.

Because Hauser's banks lent a great deal of money to Montana businesses, he knew that the territory desperately needed better transportation. Montana needed railroads. Sam Hauser was ready to help. In 1869 the first transcontinental railroad was completed, but it was far to the south of Montana. The Northern Pacific interested everyone most, for it would cut across the whole territory from east to west. Montanans waited anxiously for the railroad's completion, but the national financial depression of the 1870s halted the Northern Pacific's construction in the middle of Dakota. Hauser now tried to get the Utah and Northern Railroad to build a line from Salt Lake City to Helena, but it only built as far as Butte in 1881. Finally, the Northern Pacific reached Helena in 1883, and Sam Hauser began planning branch lines to serve nearby communities and mining districts.

Hauser wasted no time in organizing branch railroad companies. From the Northern Pacific line at Livingston, rails went to Yellowstone Park. Another line connected Helena with mines at Wickes in Jefferson County. But by 1887 Hauser was in competition with other railroad interests. James J. Hill and his Helena associate Charles A. Broadwater entered the railroad business in Montana. They laid tracks north, west, and south from Helena, competing with Hauser for the best roadbeds and locations. Hauser was not always successful in these railroad schemes, but his activities were very important in improving Montana's rail connections.

Hauser wanted to build a branch railroad south of Helena into the Boulder Valley. He had heavy investments in Jefferson County silver mines. In 1877 he and William Wickes of Philadelphia developed a profitable silver mine a few miles south of Helena on the slopes of Alta Mountain. There they erected a large smelter and the town of Wickes. The mines and smelter prospered. By the mid-1880s Hauser, A. M. Holter, Daniel Corbin, and others involved in Hauser's Helena Mining and Reduction Company realized that they had to build a new smelter to remain competitive. In 1887 Hauser began his most ambitious mining and smelting project, building the Helena and Livingston smelting works just east of Helena. By 1891 the new smelter employed over three hundred workers and paid daily wages of $10,000.

As if mining and railroading were not enough, Sam Hauser also invested in cattle. Hauser was never as interested in cattle ranching as his other investments, but his partnership with Granville Stuart and A. J. Davis created a huge cattle company—the famous DHS Ranch. Hauser and Stuart ran the company, but it was Stuart who took care of the actual ranch operations. They located their home ranch in 1880 at the base of the Judith Mountains in central Montana.

These were the days of the open range. Herds roamed the prairies, and only the huge roundups kept everyone's cattle branded and under control. But in the 1880s the lush Montana range had too many cattle competing for the grass. There were rustlers, too. Granville Stuart helped organize a vigilante committee in 1884 that took care of the rustlers on the DHS range, but there were still too many cattle. Some larger organization was needed to control the numbers and preserve what grass was left. In 1885, Hauser, Stuart, Conrad Kohrs, and others formed the gigantic Pioneer Cattle Company. It was successful in organizing the Judith Mountain range area. Also in 1885, Hauser's partners were instrumental in organizing the Montana Stockgrowers Association. Montana's cattle industry was changing to meet the times, but it was the end of Hauser's brief career as a cattleman. By the early 1890s he had sold most of his cattle interests.

Sam Hauser's life was complicated, yet he seems to have had the energy of several men. In the midst of all this activity, he involved himself in politics. Sam had been a Democrat since he came to Montana in 1862. He was loyal to his party, and by the early 1880s he stood with three other men as the "Big Four" of the party in Montana. Helena freighter Charles A. Broadwater and copper barons William A. Clark and Marcus Daly were Hauser's Democratic colleagues. In 1885 Democratic President Grover Cleveland appointed Hauser governor of Montana. It was the first time a resident Montanan had been appointed governor.

When Hauser took office he worried about how he could juggle his new responsibilities with his business interests. It did not take him long to realize that he could not do both. His business took him to New York and elsewhere too frequently. In 1886 his silver mines and smelters needed more attention than he could give. Finally, in 1887, he decided to step down as governor.

For most men holding the top political office in a state or territory would cap their careers. But Sam Hauser remained an organizer and promoter right up to his death in 1914 at the age of eighty-one. In 1893 when the great silver panic struck the United States and closed most silver mines, Hauser suffered a tremendous economic blow. His bank closed its doors for six months in 1893 and then for good in 1896. He overcame this setback and continued to function as a trustee for more than one hundred and thirty companies. In his last years he dedicated himself to the new age of electricity. He risked nearly all his wealth building Hauser and Holter Dams on the Missouri River near Helena. When high water destroyed Hauser Dam in 1908, his business empire tottered. Bankruptcy came in 1910. At his death four years later, Hauser left a relatively small estate of $140,000.

Sam Hauser had helped develop Montana perhaps more than anyone else. His interests touched nearly every business activity in the territory. His prominence was justified. His rewards were both financial and personal, for he was a man who accomplished what he set out to do. He stood solidly as a respected leader. Most of all, Hauser's biography demonstrated what an intelligent and energetic man could do on the frontier. It was an era of unlimited opportunities, and men like Samuel T. Hauser took full advantage of them. He came to Montana in 1862 with the desire to "strike it rich." He died not with moneyed riches but with riches in accomplishments for Montana.

Timeline

1850: John Owen purchases St. Mary's Mission in Bitterroot Valley.

1852: Francois Finlay (Benetsee) may have discovered gold at Gold Creek.

1853: Isaac Stevens' survey party explores Montana.

1854: Lt. John Mullan searches Continental Divide for easy route across mountains; St. Ignatius Mission established.

1855: Stevens negotiates treaties with Flatheads and Blackfeet.

1858: James and Granville Stuart discover gold at Gold Creek.

1859: Steamboat *Chippewa* makes it to Marias River; John Mullan begins construction of Mullan Road.

1860: Steamboats *Chippewa* and *Key West* make it to Fort Benton.

1861: Eastern Montana becomes part of Dakota Territory.

1862: Sam Hauser arrives at Fort Benton; John White discovers gold at Grasshopper Creek (Bannack); gold discovered in Prickly Pear Valley (near Helena).

1863: Henry Edgar and others discover gold at Alder Gulch (Virginia City); western Montana becomes part of Idaho Territory.

1864: Montana Territory created; "Four Georgians" discover gold at Last Chance Gulch (Helena); *Montana Post* published in Virginia City; vigilantes formed and hang road agent Henry Plummer; gold discovered at Confederate Gulch.

1865: Montana Historical Society founded; Virginia City made Territorial Capital; "flour riots" in Virginia City.

1866: Gold discovered at Copperopolis (Musselshell River); Sam Hauser builds Argenta Smelter; first public school in Montana opens in Virginia City.

1868: Gold discovered near Cooke City; Hauser founds First National Bank of Helena.

1869: Gold discovered near Superior at Cedar Creek; transcontinental railroad completed in Utah.

1874: William Farlin mines silver in Butte.

1876: Marcus Daly comes to Butte to manage the Alice Mine; Thomas Cruse discovers Drumlummon Mine near Marysville.

1877: Hauser and William Wickes develop silver mines south of Helena.

1878: Butte Workingmen's Union organized by miners.

1882: Marcus Daly discovers copper in Anaconda mine.

1883: Northern Pacific Railroad completed; Cruse sells Drumlummon to English syndicate.

1884: Anaconda builds huge copper smelter on Warm Springs Creek.

1885: Sam Hauser becomes governor of Montana; Castle mining district discovered near White Sulphur Springs.

1887: Hauser builds Helena and Livingston Smelter east of Helena.

Suggested Readings

Larry Barsness, *Gold Camp: Alder Gulch and Virginia City, Montana*, NY: Hastings House, 1962.

Merrill Burlingame, "Montana's Righteous Hangmen: A Reconsideration," *Montana the Magazine of Western History* Vol. 28 (October 1978)

Dorothy M. Johnson, "Flour Famine & Alder Gulch, 1864," *Montana the Magazine of Western History* Vol. 7 (January 1957).

Muriel Wolle, *Montana Pay Dirt*, Chicago: Sage Books, 1963.

Otis E. Young, Jr., "The Craft of the Prospector," *Montana the Magazine of Western History* Vol. 20 (Winter 1970).

Territorial capital Virginia City in 1866. It was an established town in the most populous county in the Territory.

Chapter IV
Politics in Montana Territory

On May 26, 1864, President Abraham Lincoln signed the Organic Act giving Montana Territory political life. For the next twenty-five years Montana Territory grew rapidly and matured. Statehood came finally in 1889. Montana's territorial experience was similar to all of the other western territories. But there were many unusual twists—many strange political happenings. These unique aspects make Montana's territorial history one of the most interesting episodes in our past.

What were territories? Why did they exist? Americans learned a valuable lesson from their British rulers before the Revolution of 1776. They learned that building empires and ruling colonies brought nothing but trouble. Instead of establishing colonies in new areas, Americans created a territorial apprenticeship system. The plan made it possible for territories to become states on an equal basis with the original thirteen.

Any legally annexed area could apply to Congress for territorial status. Once the territory's population reached 5,000 it could hold elections for a legislature. The legislature had authority to pass laws and generally govern the territory. Congress could veto actions of territorial legislatures, but for the most part, there was local rule. The governor, a secretary and three justices were all federally appointed positions. Local residents elected a territorial delegate to Congress. He could speak for the territory but had no vote. When the territorial population topped 60,000, it could apply for statehood.

The process appeared simple and logical. But the history of territories is also the history of political problems. Congress created territories and also decided on the final admission to statehood. Because of this, political battles between Republicans and Democrats in Congress played a large role in each territory's history. Montana was no exception.

Montana was actually part of several territories before becoming a territory itself in 1864. The western part belonged first to Oregon Territory, then Washington Territory, and finally Idaho Territory. The eastern plains section had been part of many territories: Louisiana, Missouri, Nebraska, and then Dakota. The great gold rush of 1862 and 1863 brought the first significant settlement into Montana's western mining camps. From this region came Montana's demand for territorial recognition.

The first territorial official to live in Montana was Sidney Edgerton. A former Republican congressman from Ohio, Edgerton was chief justice of Idaho Territory. That territory had been in existence only six months when he arrived in Bannack during the fall of 1863. It was the seat of Idaho's third judicial district and a booming mining camp.

Bannack and an even newer gold strike at Alder Gulch attracted thousands of fortune-seekers. The eastern portion of Idaho Territory grew so quickly that territorial government was soon inadequate. Lewiston, capital of Idaho, was hundreds of miles and two mountain ranges distant from Bannack and Virginia City. In 1863 gangs of thieves robbed citizens at will. Nothing seemed to be done about it. Before long a vigilante organization appeared and took the law into its own hands. In 1863-1864 vigilantes executed nearly two dozen desperadoes. The crime rate dropped sharply.

There was little that Sidney Edgerton could do. The government's weakness was apparent to everyone. Edgerton, his nephew Wilbur Fisk Sanders, along with Samuel T. Hauser, Nathaniel P. Langford, and other men realized the need for a new territory. It was the only way law and order might come permanently to the mining camps.

A committee collected $2,500 in gold and cash to send Edgerton to Washington, D.C., in 1864. In the nation's capital Edgerton asked Congress for a new territory. Even before he arrived a bill to create Montana Territory was introduced. Congressman James M. Ashley of Ohio, chairman of the House Committee on Territories, strongly supported the new territory. In fact, it was Ashley who named Montana—from a Latin word meaning "mountainous."

Congress created Montana Territory with very little debate. They included more than the mining regions within its borders. The largest portion of Montana actually came from western Dakota Territory. The boundaries established in 1864 have remained unaltered to the present. In May 1864, President Lincoln signed the Montana bill. Sidney Edgerton had accomplished his mission. On his return trip to Bannack, he received word that Lincoln had appointed him Montana's first governor.

Edgerton had a difficult job. Montana's population included individuals holding nearly every social and political belief. Most of them were Democrats. Edgerton and the national administration were Republicans. This political difference was important, for the nation was still fighting the Civil War. Some Republicans actually blamed the Democrats for beginning the war. And there were Democrats who countered that Republicans only wanted to rule the entire nation. Montanans continued these political debates for years. Despite politics, Edgerton's prime challenge was to organize Montana's first government. As provided by law, a territorial legislature and numerous officials had to be elected by the people. They set the election for October 1864.

Territorial government was a combination of appointed and elected officials. Each had specific duties. The governor was the chief executive. He could veto territorial legislation. He also served as commander-in-chief of the militia and the superintendent of Indian affairs. The secretary had responsibility for all federal monies and served as governor when the actual governor was absent. The justices, a chief and two associate justices, carried the burden of court business for the entire territory. Each justice was assigned to a specific district.

The territorial legislature consisted of a seven-member council and a house of representatives numbering thirteen. Council members served for two years. Representatives had one-year terms. The first legislature met on December 4, 1864, in Bannack, Madison County, the most populous county in the territory with the largest representation. The legislators' first order of business was to write a code of laws. They created nine counties, enacted a property tax, and passed numerous laws establishing schools, business licenses, and regulations for mining and agricultural activities. In sixty days they accomplished a great deal.

Throughout the first half of 1865, however, Montana

Organizer of vigilantes in Bannack in the 1860s, Wilbur Fisk Sanders was active in politics all of his life. He became one of Montana's first U.S. Senators in 1890.

was without an essential territorial officer, the secretary. Only the secretary could sign warrants for payment of federal monies. The president could not find anyone to take the post. Finally, Thomas Francis Meagher accepted the position as secretary of Montana Territory in August 1865. Edgerton eagerly awaited Meagher's arrival, then promptly left Montana to enroll his daughter in an eastern school. Edgerton evidently disliked being governor for he left without a word of when he might return. Montana was in Meagher's hands.

Meagher's background did not prepare him for executive leadership. A Civil War veteran on the Union side, Meagher was a Democrat and a native of Ireland. By the time he was twenty-five, Meagher had established a reputation as a political activist. He fought to free Ireland from British rule. He had been found guilty of treason in 1848 and banished to a British penal colony in Tasmania. After a successful escape in 1851 he came to New York City. He continued agitating for the Irish cause in New York until he volunteered for Civil War service. He was an impulsive man with a fiery spirit. As acting governor of Montana, Meagher created more problems than he solved.

Montana politics were confusing when Meagher arrived. Democrats were unhappy with federally appointed Republicans. Edgerton failed to get the first legislature to establish procedures for electing a new one. Republicans wanted new elections, hoping to defeat Democrats. Democrats wanted to keep the membership of the first legislature. First Meagher sided with the Republicans. Then he changed his mind and supported the Democrats. Neither side trusted him. His impulsive nature got him in more trouble. He suddenly called a territorial convention to seek statehood in February 1866. Montana had nowhere near the necessary population to justify statehood. Republicans thought that Meagher and the Democrats were only trying to "steal" the territory.

In March Meagher called the old legislature back into session. Republicans objected again. This second legislature was a fiasco. Republicans appealed to Congress for an official ruling on the legislature's legality. In May Congress declared all laws passed by the second legislature null and void. This was unfortunate. Not only did the young territory have an "acting" governor and no secretary, but now its laws were in complete chaos.

A new governor arrived in October of 1866 and promised to bring some order to territorial politics. Governor Green Clay Smith was a native of Kentucky, a Union officer in the Civil War, and a former congressman. A fair man, Smith was still unable to quell Montana political disputes. The third legislature met in November 1866. Democrats and Republicans fought again. Governor Smith went to Washington to justify this legislature. Congress, however, did not agree with Smith or Territorial Delegate Samuel McLean. Congress declared the third legislature illegal, too. New elections were held in October 1867 for a fourth legislature.

Democrats swept the election. Only one Republican was elected to the assembly. Democrat James Cavanaugh won election as territorial delegate. Republican leaders, Wilbur Fisk Sanders and *Helena Herald* editor Robert E. Fisk, shuddered at what might come next. The fourth legislature simply approved all of the laws previously passed by the second and third legislatures. So much had to be done that Governor Smith called a special session of the legislature in December 1867. One of the most pressing issues in this special session was the territory's Indian policy.

When Smith had journeyed to Washington in early 1867, his absence left Meagher as acting governor once again. Meagher, still overeager, took advantage of a few Indian raids to call up the militia. He asked for federal arms and money. Meagher's war never materialized. In the excitement, however, Camp Cooke was established at the mouth of the Judith River, Fort Ellis was begun in the Gallatin Valley, and Fort Shaw was established on the Sun River. Meagher himself died during the Indian war preparations. He drowned in the Missouri at Fort Benton on July 1, 1867.

The Indian war never took place, although Meagher had certainly tried hard to create it. Nevertheless, there were serious problems concerning Indian lands. Settlers urged reduction of the huge Flathead and Blackfeet reservations. Piegans harassed whites who seemed to threaten their land. Ultimately these small conflicts led to the Baker Massacre in 1870. The only warfare between Indians and whites during these years took place on the Bozeman Trail far to the east of Montana's mining camps.

Governor Smith did not like Montana any more than Sidney Edgerton. He left Montana and resigned the governorship in early 1869. Secretary James Tufts became acting governor. Montanans anxiously waited to see if President Grant would send another eastern politician as governor. Many hoped he would pick a Montana resident. Several Montana Republicans, including W. F. Sanders and Nathaniel Langford, wanted to be governor. Instead, Grant selected James M. Ashley. As chairman of the House Committee on Territories, Ashley knew more about territorial government than any other congressman. Despite his knowledge, he turned out to be a poor governor.

Ashley was a strong Republican and a constant critic of Democrats. When Montana Democrats heard Ashley was to be their new governor, they predicted the worst. A Democratic newspaper called him "a broken down political hack." Another pleaded "Angels and Ministers of grace defend us." Ashley was in for a short and difficult time as governor of Montana.

President Grant suddenly removed James Ashley in mid-December of 1869. Ashley had been governor less than ten months and in Montana less than six. But in those six months he had thoroughly antagonized the Democratic legislature. He tried to appoint loyal Republicans to offices held by Democrats. Legislators objected. They passed laws limiting Ashley's powers, but he vetoed them. He was an inflexible man, and Democrats in the legislature were determined to block his actions. The result was a stalemate that President Grant finally broke by removing Ashley. Once again Montanans were without a governor.

Montana's new governor in 1870 was Benjamin Franklin Potts. He remained territorial governor for thirteen years—longer than anyone else. The secret to his longevity was political ability. Potts avoided destructive political battles. He did this by gaining support from politicians in both parties.

Potts was a Republican from Ohio, like Edgerton and Ashley before him. Unlike them, he was not determined to fight with Democrats. A Civil War veteran, lawyer, and experienced Ohio state legislator, Potts was careful to gain the support of powerful Montana Democrats. He allied himself with Samuel T. Hauser, Charles A. Broadwater, and Martin Maginnis. Some Montana Republicans objected to this. Wilbur F. Sanders and Robert E. Fisk, for example, were horrified. Nevertheless, it was a successful alliance.

Benjamin Potts had been governor only a few years when Montanans began to argue again about the location of the territorial capital. Potts tried to stay neutral. The capital was Bannack for less than a year before it was moved to Virginia City in 1865. Other cities soon tried to move the capital again. By the time Potts became governor, Helena had enough power to try to become the new capital. Helena tried in 1869, but Virginia City held on. In 1874 voters had another chance to decide the issue. This time Helena seemed to be the choice. At the last moment some of the election returns were questioned. There was great confusion. After a court battle, Helena emerged the victor. In 1875, the capital moved from Virginia City to Helena.

Potts had remained as neutral as possible on the capital issue, but he was not inactive. Montana faced a huge territorial debt. The governor resolved to do something about it. He forced the legislature to revise tax laws. He cut waste in government. In the end he brought territorial finances under control. It was the major accomplishment of his administration.

Territorial governors were at the mercy of the federal government. Large decisions affecting territories remained in the hands of Congress. Because of this, each territory's future often depended on the ability of their territorial delegate in Congress. Although delegates could not vote, they could and did influence legislation. Montana was fortunate while Benjamin Potts was governor. During all but two years of his term as governor, Potts had an aggressive ally in Washington, Martin Maginnis. Maginnis was territorial delegate from 1872 to 1883.

Maginnis came to Montana from Minnesota. A Civil War veteran and newspaperman, he founded the *Rocky Mountain Gazette* in Helena in 1867. In 1872 he was elected territorial delegate. He was reelected five times. He worked closely with other Democrats, including Sam Hauser and Charles Broadwater. He also worked well with Governor Potts. Maginnis was able to get Congress to build additional military posts in Montana and to decrease the size of Indian reservations. He also kept watch on the interests of individual Montanans by helping them in Washington. His success as territorial delegate was very helpful to Potts.

Benjamin Potts left office in 1883. Martin Maginnis did the same. Their partnership had stabilized Montana's territorial government. They were from opposite political parties, but they worked jointly for Montana. In fact, that was the measure of Potts' success as governor. He was able to work with Democrats and Republicans. He left office knowing that his administrations had greatly improved the territory.

Montana's new governor in 1883 was John Schuyler Crosby of New York. He was born into an aristocratic eastern family and was accustomed to living in style. A Civil War veteran, Crosby came to Helena with intentions of restoring the strength of the Republican party. He spent money lavishly, investing in a ranch, expensive horses, and even a steamboat. Crosby was governor a little less than two years. During that time he angered Democrat and Republican alike. He carried an attitude of superiority. In November 1884, Crosby took a position at the Post Office Department in Washington and resigned as governor of Montana.

Another New Yorker, B. Platt Carpenter, became Montana's next governor in January 1885. Carpenter's career as governor was doomed from the start. Democrat Grover Cleveland had won election as president in November 1884. As soon as he moved into the White House in March 1885, it was certain that he would name a Democrat to replace the Republican Carpenter. Both Martin Maginnis and Sam Hauser wanted the job. And there were many Montanans who thought it was time that a resident of the territory be made governor.

Martin Maginnis had many friends in Washington, but Sam Hauser must have had more. President Cleveland selected Hauser as Montana's governor in 1885. Finally Montana had a resident governor. Hauser was a powerful Democrat. He had been active in nearly every aspect of Montana's economic and political development. He was one of a handful of men—including copper barons Marcus Daly and William A. Clark—who directed the activities of the Democratic party in Montana. Hauser seemed ideally suited to the job, at least in the eyes of Montana Democrats.

Sam Hauser was not happy as governor. His business interests kept him so busy that he could not give the governor's job his full attention. He was absent from the territory for several months in 1885-1886. By December 1886, Hauser had decided to resign. Hauser was a popular man. When he resigned, many Montanans agreed with the *Helena Herald's* comment that he was "the most popular and satisfactory governor Montana has ever had. . . ."

The next governor was a complete contrast to Hauser. A Democrat and lawyer, Preston Leslie worked practically without a break. He remained governor for two years. These were the great boom years in Montana's territorial history. The Butte mines had grown enormously. Cattle ranchers had opened the central range, even if they experienced a setback in the horrible winter of 1886-1887. Marcus Daly had built a huge copper smelter at Anaconda. Political power shifted to the booming mining regions in Silver Bow and Deer Lodge counties. Copper barons Marcus Daly and William A. Clark took the lead in Democratic politics. Leslie did not disrupt this growth, nor did he meddle in state Democratic politics. He did his job efficiently and without controversy.

The election of 1888 was a political turning point in Montana. First, a Republican, Benjamin Harrison, was elected president. That meant a change in the federal administration. It also meant another change in Montana's governorship, since Preston Leslie was a Democrat. In the 1888 election for territorial delegate Republican Thomas H. Carter surprisingly defeated Democrat William A. Clark. Clark felt certain he would win in heavily Democratic Montana. He lost the election in precincts he should have won—precincts controlled by Marcus Daly's political followers. Clark blamed Daly for his loss. It was the beginning of a long feud between the two copper barons.

Benjamin F. White, formerly mayor of Dillon, became Montana's last territorial governor in April 1889. A merchant and banker, White came to Montana in 1878. He helped organize the town of Dillon. Although he had ability, White did little more than take care of the territory until statehood came in November 1889.

Montana tried for statehood three times. The first attempt in 1866, under the direction of Acting Governor Thomas F. Meagher, was hopeless. Montana did not have sufficient population to qualify, and Meagher only had support from Democrats. A constitutional convention met in Helena in 1866, but the constitution itself was lost. No one truly knows what happened. One story has it that the document was lost when it was taken to St. Louis to be printed.

The second attempt at statehood came in 1884. Montana's population was still below the required 60,000, but many were optimistic about the chances for success. Forty-five elected delegates met in Helena during January and February 1884. William A. Clark served as convention president. Convention delegates represented many interests. Lawyers were the largest group. The mining industry had the second largest number of delegates.

Montanans voted in favor of the constitution in November 1884 by a margin of almost four-to-one. Unfortunately, Congress was in no mood to create new states in 1885 when they considered Montana's application. The senate was Republican. The house was Democrat. The new president, Grover Cleveland, was the first Democrat in the White House since 1860. The instability of the new administration and Congress did not work in favor of statehood. Territorial Delegate Joseph K. Toole argued at length in Congress for statehood. Nevertheless, Congress rejected Montana's bid.

By 1889 the prospects for statehood had improved considerably. Montana's population continued to grow. Congressional politicians had worked a series of compromises to provide for the admission of several states at once. They tried to pair prospective states having Democratic populations with those having Republican populations. In that way neither party would gain over the other in Congress. On February 22, 1889, just before the new Congress met and a new president was sworn in, President Cleveland signed the Omnibus Bill. It allowed Montana, Washington, North Dakota, and South Dakota to enter the Union.

Montanans elected constitutional convention delegates in May 1889. They met on July 4 in Helena. As in 1884, the delegates represented a variety of interests. Again lawyers and mining industry representatives dominated. Again William A. Clark was elected president of the convention. Delegates split up into two dozen committees to complete the work of writing the document. They used the 1884 constitution as a general model. Several sections of the 1889 constitution, in fact, were copied directly from the 1884 document.

Most of the delegates were politically experienced men. Joseph K. Toole and Martin Maginnis were former territorial delegates. James E. Callaway had been territorial secretary, and B. Platt Carpenter had been governor. There were thirty-nine Democrats and thirty-six Republicans.

Two issues generated considerable debate. One was political, the other was economic. The committee on the legislative branch of government recommended that there be no more than sixteen state senators and that no county could have more than one. Those delegates representing the more populous counties thought this was unfair. They tried to amend it. Joseph K. Toole said it was ridiculous to give a county with less than 1,000 people the same representation as a county ten times its size. Defenders of the plan noted that the state house of representatives was to be based on population. The plan was accepted.

The economic issue involved taxation. How could mining property be taxed? Should the state tax the minerals in the ground or only the net proceeds from mining ore? The committee on taxation recommended that only surface machinery and the net proceeds of mining be taxed. This was a tremendous tax break for the mining industry. Delegates from the mining areas, of course, defended this special treatment. Montana was built on mining, they argued. Convention delegates agreed. After a series of debates, the measure was accepted.

There were many other discussions over controversial questions. Delegates debated women's suffrage. Those who wanted women to get the vote argued that they were just as capable as men in deciding political issues. Those opposed to women's suffrage claimed that women did not want to vote. Some even argued that voting would injure women, psychologically and emotionally. Women's suffrage was not included in the constitution. The vote would not come for women in Montana until 1914. A few delegates representing laborers and labor unions tried and failed to prohibit employment of Chinese workers.

On October 1, 1889, Montanans approved the constitution by a vote of 26,950 in favor to 2,274 opposed. Montana became a state on November 8, 1889. The long territorial apprenticeship was over. As a full and equal participant with other states in the Union, Montana began its new political life with great optimism. Some of that optimism would be blunted when the first state legislature became entangled in disputes. Nonetheless, Montana had weathered the storms of its territorial period as well as most. The future was bright. Montana now belonged to its people.

Governor Benjamin F. Potts

President Ulysses S. Grant surprised Montanans in December 1869. Less than a year earlier he had appointed James M. Ashley of Ohio as governor of Montana Territory. Suddenly Grant removed him from office. Ashley was a "radical" Republican. He blamed Democrats for the Civil War and wanted to punish them. In Montana, where the Democrats outnumbered Republicans, Ashley's views were not well received. Ashley made matters worse. He attempted to help Republicans and hurt Democrats. It caused a terrible political battle. The legislature fought Ashley. The strong-willed governor persisted. The conflict politically paralyzed Montana. Whether these problems or other factors angered President Grant is not known. By late 1869, however, Grant had decided to replace Ashley.

Ashley said his removal was "the hardest blow I ever received." It was. For years a powerful congressman from Ohio and chairman of the House Committee on Territories, he would never again hold elective office. It was a hard blow to Montanans, too. They had suffered through one poor governor after another. Although some Montana Republicans tried to save Ashley, most wondered anxiously who Grant would choose as their new governor. Would the new governor be a political adventurer? Would he bring more problems? Would the new governor last long?

Happily for Montana, Grant chose a man of moderate temperament and genuine ability. It was "a startling surprise," Benjamin Franklin Potts remarked when he was chosen to succeed Ashley in Montana. At the time of his selection Potts was serving in the Ohio state senate. Although Montana Republicans had mentioned him previously as a prime candidate for governor, Potts did not lobby for the job.

Potts was born in Carrollton, Ohio, on January 29, 1836, into a farming family of moderate means. He attended local schools and worked in a retail business until 1854. In that year he pursued his schooling at Westminster College in Pennsylvania. Lack of funds forced him to drop out and return to Ohio the following year. After several years of study, Potts became a lawyer in Carrollton in 1859. When

As governor of Montana Territory in the 1870s, Benjamin F. Potts stabilized a politically-divided territory.

the Civil War began, Potts switched from Democratic to Republican parties and enlisted to fight for the Union.

In the Civil War he served bravely and was commended several times for valor. He served under Generals Grant and William T. Sherman. After the war, Potts returned to Carrollton and his law practice. He was active in Republican politics and was elected to the Ohio state senate. He was a moderate Republican, not a "radical" like Ashley. It was his moderate politics that allowed him to remain governor of Montana Territory longer than anyone else. Potts was governor for thirteen years, from 1870 to 1883.

Potts arrived in Virginia City in August 1870. He knew that Ashley's administration had created political havoc. He hoped Montana Republicans would help him calm the situation and begin solving Montana's political problems. But he did not get unanimous support from fellow Republicans. Wilbur Fisk Sanders and *Helena Herald* editor Robert E. Fisk had been angry when Ashley was removed. They attacked Potts rather than helped him. They feared that he would make political "deals" with Democrats. Potts soon realized that he almost had to make some peace with Montana Democrats. Since they outnumbered Republicans, he genuinely needed their support. If Benjamin F. Potts knew anything about politics, he knew that success demanded compromise and cooperation.

He enlisted Democratic support. Samuel T. Hauser, Charles A. Broadwater, and Martin Maginnis were three important Democrats who helped Potts. Hauser was one of the most influential men in the territory. His mining and banking investments made him one of the wealthiest, too. Charles A. Broadwater was also a banker and wealthy. Martin Maginnis was Montana's territorial delegate to Washington longer than anyone else. Gaining their support was crucial to Potts. They gave him the added strength he needed.

Potts did not inherit an easy job. Territorial finances were in terrible shape. Counties and the territory itself were in debt. He went to the legislature in 1871 and again in 1873 urging that waste in government be eliminated and that spending be held to a minimum. He vetoed bills that he thought were too extravagant. Potts improved the territory's tax system. Slowly at first, he improved Montana's finances. By 1883 the territory was free of debt. Former Territorial Delegate William Clagett remarked that Governor Potts "probably saved it (Montana) from the verge of bankruptcy."

As governor of an expansive territory, Potts recognized how important it was to improve transportation. Roads became quagmires of mud during spring thaw. Ice and snow made them impassable in winter. Rivers froze for months. The railroad, as everyone realized, was the only answer. Two railroads planned to enter Montana. From the east the Northern Pacific was building through Dakota when Potts became governor. In 1869 the first transcontinental was completed to the south of Montana. From Corinne, Utah, on the transcontinental line the Utah and Northern planned to build into Montana. For his part, Benjamin Potts favored the Northern Pacific. By 1873, however, a nationwide financial panic had stalled construction of the Northern Pacific in Dakota.

There was quite a struggle over the railroad issue. Governor Potts was right in the middle of it. The north-south railroad faction battled with the east-west group. Both suggested that the legislature approve payment of construction costs to encourage railroad construction. Potts was against any subsidies. In 1873, when the legislature passed a railroad subsidy bill, he vetoed it. His action angered many. Some of his opponents yelled for his removal—they even sent complaints to Washington. Potts remained firm on the issue. Yet he, too, grew anxious in the late 1870s. When would the railroads build into Montana? By 1879 he was ready to support Sam Hauser and agree to exempt a north-south railroad line from taxation in Montana. But the action was not needed. In 1880 the Utah and Northern finally entered Montana from the south and the Northern Pacific came in from the east.

Governor Potts also had to contend with Indian affairs. Although Montana had a separate official to deal with Indian affairs by the time Potts became governor, he still had charge of the territorial militia. In the event of Indian-white conflict, the governor might have to call out troops. It was a heavy responsibility. Potts, unlike Acting Governor Meagher before him, did not sound false alarms to increase the militia. But Potts was no different from other Montanans. He wanted hostile Indians punished and removed as obstacles to white settlement.

Sioux on the Yellowstone worried Potts in 1875 and 1876. He warned Washington that something had to be done. They had to be "whipped," Potts told them, or there would never be peace in Montana. He tried but failed to get approval to raise troops under his command to battle the Sioux on the plains. When the Nez Perce fled through Montana in 1877, Potts was ready to institute a very harsh policy. He favored punishing the Nez Perce. Potts consistently pressed for expanding white settlement and for the reduction of the size of Indian reservations.

Throughout his years as governor, Benjamin F. Potts walked a political tightrope. He worked hard to improve territorial finances. He forced legislators to make hard decisions. He fought waste in government by watching salaries and expenses closely. He did all of this with the benefit of Montana in mind. But he was still faced with a split Republican party. Sanders, Fisk, and other strong-minded Republicans disliked Potts. They distrusted his easy alliance with

Democrats like Hauser and Maginnis. They wanted him to use his powers as governor to benefit Republicans, not Democrats. A genuine feud developed.

As 1878 drew near and Potts considered an appointment for a third term as governor, his opponents organized to block his chances. Potts liked being governor. He enjoyed the challenges. The truth is that Benjamin F. Potts became very attached to Montana, its land and people. In 1877, however, he faced serious opposition.

Sanders and Fisk were joined by Territorial Secretary James E. Callaway. Potts and Callaway had experienced some disagreements, but the governor thought them to be minor. In 1876, however, Potts had complained about Callaway's performance in office. He accused Callaway of favoring friends with territorial contracts—contracts that brought them money. Callaway denied these charges. But now, in league with Sanders and Fisk, Callaway drew up his own list of charges against Potts. He accused Potts of mismanaging territorial funds, of giving the mail contract to a favored company, and of being allied with Democrats. Callaway included these charges in a formal letter to Secretary of Interior Carl Schurz. The feud had heated up.

The anti-Potts group hoped Callaway's charges would bring action from Washington. Surely, they thought, Potts would be replaced by a governor who would support the Republican party in Montana. In Montana words flew back and forth between Potts and his opponents. Each called the other names. Sanders at one point called Potts an "arrogant piece of executive stupidity." The *Helena Independent*, a Democratic newspaper, defended Potts. Robert Fisk's *Helena Herald*, of course, blasted Potts at every opportunity. Finally the duel ended. Potts was reappointed governor and Callaway lost his post as territorial secretary. Potts won the battle, but it took a great deal out of him.

Benjamin Potts served out his third term but was not reappointed. He probably wanted it that way, for he knew his opponents would not rest until he was gone from office. He was satisfied with his performance. He loved Montana and decided to remain. After leaving the governorship in 1883, he lived out the rest of his life on a farm near Townsend. In 1885 he was elected to the state legislature. Two years later he died.

Martin Maginnis in Washington

Martin Maginnis was Montana territorial delegate to Congress from 1872 to 1883. Six times Montanans sent him to Washington as their only representative. Although territorial delegates had no votes in Congress, Maginnis fought as hard as any congressman to protect his territory's interests. It was a frustrating job. Territorial delegates often felt powerless, and often they were. Maginnis himself once called the territorial system the worst kind of "colonial government that was ever seen on the face of the globe." Yet he continued to seek election and to represent Montana's interests.

Martin Maginnis was born in New York in 1841 to Irish immigrant parents. Martin lived in New York until his family moved to Illinois in 1852. After one year there, the family moved again to Red Wing, Minnesota. Martin was above average in school and entered Hamline University just before the outbreak of the Civil War. Once the war erupted, he volunteered to fight for the Union and joined a Minnesota regiment. He fought in some of the war's bloodiest battles. Promoted several times for bravery, he left the military with the rank of major. After the war he returned to Red Wing, where he helped edit a local newspaper.

Evidently he found Red Wing dull or without opportunity. In 1866 he helped organize a wagon train to travel the northern overland route to Montana. He came to Helena in September. At first he tried mining. By 1867, however, Martin went back to journalism. In that year he founded the *Rocky Mountain Gazette* in Helena. He was an active Democrat, and his paper reflected his political beliefs. In 1872 he challenged Territorial Delegate William Clagett and won.

He was thirty-one when he went to Washington, making Maginnis the youngest of Montana's territorial delegates. He was also the only delegate who was not a lawyer. A man of strong beliefs, Martin's greatest asset was his ability to work with other men toward a common goal. In Helena he allied himself with other Democrats. With Samuel T. Hauser and Charles A. Broadwater, he played a powerful role in shaping Montana's politics. Once in Washington he proved his ability to work with other territorial delegates, regardless of party label. This was to Montana's advantage, for Maginnis was able to gain many favors for the territory.

Territorial Delegate Maginnis worked energetically for those who elected him. He paid close attention to their requests. Montanans who visited Washington were often amazed at how much influence he seemed to have. By 1876, in fact, Martin had become president of an association of territorial delegates in Congress. He impressed presidents Ulysses S. Grant, Rutherford B. Hayes, and James Garfield as one of the best at his job. He was especially good at getting benefits from the federal government for Montana.

He succeeded in getting the government to build more forts and spend more money in the territory. He worked closely with the War Department. In 1877 he got approval for Fort Missoula, Fort Custer on the Big Horn River, and Fort Keogh at the mouth of the Tongue River. Two years later Fort Assiniboine was built on the Milk River thanks to his efforts. Finally, in 1880, he even got a fort named after himself, Fort Maginnis in the Judith Basin. There had been Indian war scares after the great battle on the Little Big Horn in 1876, but these additional forts are really a testament to Martin Maginnis' political abilities. Montanans, of course, welcomed the forts. They meant security, but they also meant gain for local farmers and merchants who sold their produce and wares to the forts.

Because of his close relationship with Montana politicians, Martin Maginnis also helped specific individuals by influencing federal legislation. Samuel T. Hauser, for example, got the benefit of Maginnis' efforts when his bank was named to receive soldiers' payrolls. T. C. Power, the great merchant at Fort Benton and Helena, received contracts with army posts while his friend Maginnis was territorial delegate. And Martin personally took claims from Montana friends through the bureaucracy in Washington. In one instance he argued a case for Charles Broadwater all the way to the cabinet and won the issue. Even staunch Republicans like Robert Fisk had to admit that Maginnis was a remarkable politician.

The work of a territorial delegate was difficult. He had to be aware of much legislation. If a bill came before Congress that might have an effect on Montana, Maginnis had to be sure that key congressmen understood why the bill should or should not be passed. There was a great deal of informal

Martin Maginnis while he was in Washington, D.C., as Montana's Territorial Delegate in the late 1870s.—*Burgess & Co., photographers, Washington, D.C. Copy courtesy M.H.S.*

political maneuvering. In the end, the territorial delegate had to convince congressmen of his point of view. Even after getting a favorable vote in Congress the delegate might have to appeal to the president. In 1873, for example, Maginnis convinced Congress to approve a federal assay office in Helena, but President Grant would not sign the bill. Maginnis did not give up. In 1874, after lobbying the president himself, the assay office became a reality.

Under the territorial system each territory depended to a

large extent on federal monies. All federally appointed officials were paid from Washington. Even the salaries and expenses of territorial legislators came from federal funds. Because of this, the territorial delegate's role was a crucial one. Whenever Montanans wanted something they really could not afford through local taxation, they tried to get the federal government to pay for it. They asked Martin Maginnis to enter a bill in Congress for this or that new item. For several years he introduced bills to fund a territorial insane asylum, but he failed. Maginnis was more successful in getting federal funds for a territorial penitentiary. Each year he tried to get Congress to put more money into the Deer Lodge prison. He was successful, but the funds were never sufficient.

Martin Maginnis did not seem to tire of his duties. He must have enjoyed being Montana's man in Washington. When he came up for election in 1874 he faced a strong opponent, Superintendent of Public Instruction Cornelius Hedges. Hedges was a well-known lawyer and cultured man. He ran as a Republican, and some thought he had a good chance to defeat Maginnis. Hedges lost by a sizeable margin. Erasmus D. Leavitt challenged Maginnis in 1876. It was at the height of the Indian war fears. Voters stayed with Maginnis.

It was in 1880 that Maginnis had a significant Republican opponent. Wilbur Fisk Sanders, who had run for the office twice before, decided it was time to retire Maginnis. Sanders waged a hard-hitting campaign. He charged that Maginnis was too close to Hauser and Broadwater, that he did their bidding in Washington. Maginnis stood on his record. He reminded voters how much he had done for the territory. On election day the voters remembered and returned Martin Maginnis to Congress.

In 1882 it appeared that Maginnis would not run for reelection. It would mean a sixth term and some criticized Maginnis' domination of the office. His supporters finally convinced him to run. The Republican candidate was Alexander Botkin. Formerly a U. S. Marshal and a graduate of the University of Wisconsin, Botkin was paralyzed and confined to a wheelchair. Botkin hurled the same charges at Maginnis as had Sanders. This time Maginnis won, but not without protest. Republicans claimed that ballot boxes were stuffed and that deceased voters had miraculously cast votes.

Montana Territorial Council (Senate) Eleventh Session, January-February 1879.

One Republican charged that names from Cleveland and Cincinnati city directories provided voters in one precinct. Despite these claims, Congress seated Maginnis.

By 1884 he had tired of being territorial delegate. He chose not to run for reelection. Maginnis supported a young lawyer, Joseph K. Toole. Toole defeated his Republican opponent, Hiram Knowles, in a very close election. Maginnis returned to Montana in time to seek the governorship. For the first time in over two decades a Democrat, Grover Cleveland, had been elected President of the United States. A Democrat would certainly be appointed as the new governor of Montana. Democrats were hopeful that a Montana resident would be chosen. Two men seemed likely candidates: Martin Maginnis and Sam Hauser.

Hauser and Maginnis had been political allies for years. Republicans had consistently charged that Maginnis was only Hauser's "tool" in Washington. Now lines were drawn between them. Maginnis received support from Irish Democrats. Hauser, however, had a broader appeal. Even Republicans lined up for him. It may have been Hauser's financial power, but whatever it was, President Cleveland selected him as governor in 1885.

That was not the political end of Martin Maginnis. He remained active in the Democratic party. In 1889 he served as a delegate to the Constitutional Convention. In the same year he ran for Congress and was defeated. The following year he was elected U.S. Senator by the Democrats in the legislature. He never took his seat, however, because the first state legislature sent two senatorial delegations to Washington. The Republicans were seated. It was an incredible turn of events and had nothing to do with Maginnis. Nevertheless, he lost his chance to represent Montana in the U.S. Senate.

Martin Maginnis served his territory and state over many years. Montana voters showed their confidence in him six times. As territorial delegate he worked under pressure and played a hard-nosed political game. It was almost as though he had served out his usefulness. He was never again successful in his bids for public office. Governor Joseph Toole appointed him land commissioner in 1890. That was his last public position. He moved to California later and lived there until his death in 1919.

Timeline

1861: Civil War begins; eastern Montana part of Dakota Territory.

1863: Western Montana part of Idaho Territory; gold discovered at Alder Gulch.

1864: Montana Territory created; Sidney Edgerton becomes governor; gold discovered at Last Chance Gulch.

1865: Territorial capital moved from Bannack to Virginia City; Thomas F. Meagher is "acting governor."

1866: First Constitutional Convention meets in Helena; Green Clay Smith becomes governor.

1867: Meagher drowns in Missouri; Forts Shaw and Ellis built; Martin Maginnis founds *Rocky Mountain Gazette* in Helena.

1868: Military abandons forts on Bozeman Trail.

1869: James M. Ashley becomes governor, transcontinental railroad completed in Utah.

1870: Benjamin F. Potts becomes governor.

1872: Martin Maginnis elected territorial delegate.

1875: Territorial capital moved from Virginia City to Helena.

1876: Custer battle.

1880: Northern Pacific Railroad enters Montana from east; Utah & Northern Railroad enters Montana from south.

1883: John Schuyler Crosby becomes governor; Northern Pacific Railroad completed.

1884: Second Constitutional Convention meets; Joseph K. Toole elected territorial delegate.

1885: B. Platt Carpenter becomes governor; Samuel T. Hauser succeeds Carpenter as governor.

1886: Hard winter, severe stock loss.

1887: Preston Leslie becomes governor; Benjamin F. Potts dies.

1888: Thomas H. Carter defeats W. A. Clark for territorial delegate.

1889: Benjamin F. White becomes governor; Montana admitted to the Union.

Suggested Readings

Robert G. Athearn, *Thomas F. Meagher: An Irish Revolutionary in America.* Boulder, Colorado: University of Colorado Press, 1949.

Stanley R. Davison & Dale Tash, "Confederate Backwash in Montana Territory," *Montana the Magazine of Western History* Vol. 17 (October 1967).

James M. Hamilton, *History of Montana,* Chapter VII. Portland: Binfords & Mort, 1957.

Clark C. Spence, "Beggars to Washington: Montana's Territorial Delegates," *Montana the Magazine of Western History* Vol. 24 (January 1974).

———, "Spoilsman in Montana: James M. Ashley," *Montana the Magazine of Western History* Vol. 18 (April 1968).

Chief Joseph of the Nez Perce was the spiritual leader of his people during their panicked flight across Montana in 1877.

Chapter V
The Indians Lose Their Land

Westward up the Missouri River, Lewis and Clark, traders, miners, and settlers traveled across the high plains—an inland sea of grass. As far as the eye could see lay an endless expanse of rolling hills, high grasses, and prairie animals. Some plains travelers were frightened by a feeling of loneliness and isolation. It was a new environment. It was the domain of the bison, antelope, eagle, and also the Plains Indians. For hundreds of years Indian peoples had lived out their lives on the high plains and in the mountains beyond. They lived in harmony with their natural surroundings; they became part of the environment itself. When the whites came in large numbers during the nineteenth century, they entered the region as strangers. They had reason to be frightened.

If it had been just a case of initial fright or uneasiness for whites on the western frontier, much of what happened between them and the native Indian people might have been much different. But there was more to it than that. At the heart of the problem was the reason for whites moving westward. They came for what the land could provide. They came for furs, gold, and silver. They came to settle the land and raise crops. In the end it totally disrupted the Indians' pattern of life. It meant conflict between white men and red men, and it ended in tragedy for both.

To understand what happened we need to know who the Indian peoples were and how they lived. The earliest evidence of man in Montana stretches back 12,000 years, but modern man is a much more recent resident. All of Montana's Indian tribes migrated into the region, some of them within the last three hundred years. They came from the north, south, and east. Most tribes came to Montana either in search of new territory, or they were pushed here by other Indian tribes in conflicts over land and resources. Once in Montana the tribes continued to fight over territory, although by the time of Lewis and Clark's visit each tribe had its own area. Their wars continued because as semi-nomadic people, who followed herds of game animals and moved with the season, tribal territories often overlapped and created reasons for war. War itself was central to their lives.

By the early nineteenth century, the Kutenai, Kalispel, Pend d'Oreille, and Salish (Flathead) tribes claimed the northwest corner of Montana. Directly to the east were the Pikuni (Piegan), Kainah (Blood), and Siksika (Blackfeet), the three confederated tribes of the Blackfeet nation. They roamed central Montana. Their neighbors to the east were the Atsina (Gros Ventre), and further east lived the Assiniboine. Along the southern boundary of Montana lived the Absaroka (Crow) in the Yellowstone country. In the southeast corner the Cheyenne and Teton Dakota (Sioux) resided.

The boundaries between tribes were not fixed. No tribe owned the land, but each claimed its use and a specific hunting territory. Stronger tribes, such as the Piegan and the Sioux, dominated their neighbors and wars often flared. Sometime in the eighteenth century, all of these tribes had acquired horses, probably from the Spanish territories to the south. With horses they became mobile, more efficient hunters, and even more effective warriors. The mounted Plains Indian was one of history's greatest light cavalry.

Equipped with a quiver of one hundred or more arrows, a bison hide shield, and a long lance, there was no other fighting force on the western plains who could match them man for man. They fought from horseback or foot. They were truly awesome when mounted and firing several arrows in succession, each with enough force to penetrate completely man or beast. As horsemen they learned feats that amazed American cavalrymen. Riding at full speed, Indian warriors could sling themselves alongside their horses for protection and suddenly rise and fire arrows with deadly accuracy.

The way of warfare for Plains Indians, however, was much more than fighting an enemy. The act of war was the way young men proved their worth, established respect, and acquired wealth by stealing horses and enemy goods. Although warfare among Indians often took many lives, killing was not the primary object. They fought to protect themselves and their territory. Their daring raids struck fear in the enemy. Once they established their supremacy in battle, they retreated before too many lives were lost. This hit-and-run strategy, developed over decades of intertribal warfare, later frustrated the American army's attempts to defeat Indian forces on the warpath.

To be brave in the face of the enemy was all important. The ultimate demonstration of bravery was to approach an enemy close enough to touch him and return unharmed. The warrior who accomplished this feat had "counted coup," and he was honored. More than once American soldiers watched in amazement as an unarmed warrior rode directly into their guns tempting them to fire at him only to turn suddenly and retreat. Stealing horses from an enemy's camp without flinging an arrow or firing a shot was more impressive than engaging in an all-out fight.

The bloodiest encounters were usually reprisal raids when a tribal warrior or chief had been killed by the enemy. In these battles the dead were often mutilated and scalped, for Indians believed that the dead entered the afterlife in the same exact condition they left this life. War had religious significance, too. Before going into battle, warriors looked for signs of "good medicine," indications that the Great Spirit was with them. They often prayed for aid, decorating themselves with feathers and paint, singing a war song. Warriors were organized into animal cults, such as the Assiniboine Bear Cult, in which the members wore special garments, carried decorated weapons, and held elaborate ceremonies on the eve or morning of battle.

Plains Indians were nomadic. Their villages were portable, and they moved in fairly regular patterns often following the great bison herds. Except for the village tribes of the Mandan and Hidatsa along the Missouri River in Dakota, hunting was the mainstay for plains tribes. They hunted many animals, from deer and elk to squirrels. The bison, however, provided them with most of their meat and a great variety of products, from clothing to utensils. In the warm months they moved freely hunting bison. In the winter months they selected a protected area for an extended encampment, living on dried meat, collected roots, and preserved vegetables.

This pattern of life could exist only so long as there was abundant game and the freedom to move from camp to camp across the high plains. The coming of the white man threatened all this. Here lay the primary reason for Indian-white conflict. It was not the ownership of the land that created conflict. It was the nearly total disruption of the Indian's use of the land, his ability to take from nature what he needed, and to live in harmony with the spirits. If we wonder why Indians fought so fiercely, it is easily understood. We must recognize that they were fighting to protect their way of life—their bison hunts, their relationships with religious spirits, and ultimately their freedom.

The first conflicts between whites and Indians on the western plains came with the expansion of British, French, and Spanish fur trading in the eighteenth century.

Lewis and Clark's experience with Indians in the upper Missouri region had been favorable. Except for Lewis' unfortunate scrape with eight Piegans at Two Medicine River in 1806, the expedition made friendly contact with most tribes. The next four decades, however, would be far different. Fur trappers and traders created problems. Too often these traders cheated Indians of furs and took advantage of the Indians' friendship. Traders introduced upper Missouri tribes to whiskey and carried disease to their villages. Increasingly Indians began to see all whites as greedy. Although they welcomed the goods, metal utensils, and guns they received from the traders, many tribes recognized what the coming of the whites meant.

By the 1850s a second wave of whites came west and brought a larger threat to Indian life. The Oregon country had drawn emigrants in the 1840s. Then the gold discoveries in the 1850s drew even more whites to California, Colorado, and by the 1860s to Montana. In 1853 Isaac Stevens brought an expedition to Montana searching for a favorable railroad route to connect the Mississippi Valley with the Pacific Coast through the heart of Indian lands. Stevens knew that an agreement with upper Missouri tribes was essential to this project. He was an unusually good negotiator. What Stevens accomplished in two treaties in 1855 changed Indian-white relations in Montana forever.

The first treaty with Plains Indians, at Fort Laramie on the Oregon Trail in 1851, established precedents for all subsequent Indian-U.S. government treaties. Although no Indian land was ceded to the government at Fort Laramie, each Indian tribe was assigned territorial limits, and they agreed to allow the government to build military posts and roads on their land in return for annual payments of livestock and supplies. Stevens met with Flathead, Kutenai, and Pend d'Oreille chiefs in July of 1855. The chiefs agreed to live on a large reservation—the Jocko reservation—near Flathead Lake. In the fall Stevens went east of the divide and concluded a similar treaty with the Blackfeet that restricted them to an enormous area north of the Missouri and east of the divide.

These treaties, and others like them, were made in good faith, but events quickly changed conditions and threatened these understandings. Gold changed everything in Montana. The great stampede to Bannack, Virginia City, and Helena made clashes between whites and Indians inevitable. By 1867 the government had established military outposts at Fort Shaw on the Mullan Road and Fort Ellis in the Gallatin Valley. These two posts were meant to protect travellers to the goldfields. The Bozeman Road, a shortcut to the goldfields cutting across Wyoming from the Oregon Trail, was the scene of the first significant Indian-white conflict in Montana.

Cutting off at Fort Laramie on the Oregon Trail, John Bozeman's road blazed a trail through the prime hunting lands of the Cheyenne and Sioux in the Powder River country. The Sioux particularly were determined to block the use of the road. Travellers demanded government protection in 1865, and a fruitless campaign against the Sioux followed. It was clear to Chief Red Cloud of the Oglala Sioux that the government meant to defend the road at all costs. When a peace conference was called at Fort Laramie in 1866, Red Cloud scolded government officials. "The Great Father sends us presents and wants us to sell him the road, but White Chief goes with soldiers to steal the road before Indians say Yes or No!"

Fighting Sioux chiefs, Red Cloud, Crazy Horse, and Hump, led the resistance, and the government responded by building Forts Phil Kearny and C. F. Smith in 1866 and Fort Fetterman in 1867. Indian raids continued as the few hundred soldiers stationed to protect travellers battled thousands of hostile Sioux, Cheyenne, and Arapahoe. On December 21, 1866, Captain William J. Fetterman foolishly exposed eighty men to a carefully laid ambush. Fetterman's force died to a man, and their scalped corpses shocked the nation and made

The Indian warrior Red Cloud, leader of Sioux Indians, who closed the Bozeman Trail in 1868.

it clear that the Sioux meant to drive off all soldiers in the Powder River country. After another year of fighting, the government decided to seek peace. In March 1868, another peace conference convened at Fort Laramie. There the Sioux and other tribes accepted a huge reservation (all of present-day South Dakota) and a promise that soldiers would evacuate the hated forts as the reward for their resistance. Red Cloud did not sign. He waited until the soldiers left, then destroyed the forts. He finally signed the Laramie Treaty in November 1868.

It was a great triumph for Red Cloud and the Sioux, but the central problem remained unsolved. As long as Sioux, Assiniboine, Gros Ventre, and Cheyenne tribes in Montana could not hunt bison at will, there would be more conflict.

Blackfeet lands were also in the path of miners and overland travellers. In 1865 they were persuaded to leave the area south of the Missouri in return for annual payments and other rewards. The treaty seemed to solve the problem, but Congress failed to ratify it. When the annual payments did not come, Piegans, Blood, Blackfeet, and Gros Ventre Indians began to fight among themselves over their restricted hunting grounds. They also occasionally raided whites. The so-called "Blackfoot War" frightened Montanans and provided Acting Governor Thomas F. Meagher the best reasons for demanding that the military be built up in the territory. The army built Camp Cooke at the mouth of the Judith River in 1866 and in the following year established Forts Shaw and Ellis. But this did not frighten the Blackfeet. Occasional raids continued. The government negotiated yet another treaty in 1868, and again Congress refused to ratify it.

It is hard to tell how long the situation might have continued, for in August 1869, Piegan warriors shocked Montanans into action when they killed Malcolm Clarke, a popular rancher who lived north of Helena. Citizens demanded a major military campaign against the Blackfeet. In January 1870, Colonel E. M. Baker led his men north from Fort Ellis to punish Mountain Chief's band of Piegans. With a fury Baker followed his superiors' orders to "strike them hard." Baker's troops descended on the unsuspecting Indians and left 173 Piegans dead. Tragically, they had attacked the wrong camp! Instead of Mountain Chief's camp, Baker had destroyed that of Heavy Runner, a friendly chief. This shocking incident convinced Blackfeet that white vengeance could be swift and complete. Blackfeet resistance ended that day in 1870.

Montanans had not seen the last of the Indian wars. In the 1870s, as the Northern Pacific pushed westward across Dakota, whites tangled again with the Sioux. The Laramie Treaty of 1868 had created a huge reservation, but many chiefs preferred living in the Powder River country. At first there were few problems, but soon whites invaded their reservation. When George Armstrong Custer entered the Black Hills on the reservation in 1874 to build a new outpost to protect Northern Pacific survey crews, Sioux leaders objected. They were even more furious when gold was discovered in the Black Hills and a genuine rush developed. Reservation and nonreservation Sioux realized that no

General George Armstrong Custer as he looked not long before he fought his last battle at the Little Big Horn in 1876.

ground was safe. Many now left the reservation and decided to defend their Powder River hunting grounds to the end.

Only a revision of the 1868 treaty allowing sale of the Black Hills to the government could avert disaster. Sioux leaders said "No" to the government's offer to purchase. In response the government ordered all nonreservation Indians to report to the Indian agency on the reservation by January 31, 1876, or suffer the consequences. It was bitterly cold that winter. It was a demand the Sioux could not and would not satisfy. In the spring plans were made to begin a general campaign against the Sioux in the Powder River country.

At Fort Abraham Lincoln in Dakota, General Alfred H.

Terry and Lieutenant Colonel George Armstrong Custer prepared to lead their column west to the Big Horn Mountains in search of the hostile Sioux. From Fort Shaw in Montana, Colonel John Gibbon led another column, and General George Crook's force had already moved north from Fort Fetterman in Wyoming. The chilly spring turned to summer as they searched for the main Sioux camp. Indian scouts thought they could be found on the Little Big Horn or the Rosebud drainages. By now, however, the Sioux had been joined by angry Northern Cheyenne. The Cheyenne had been relatively peaceful until Two Moons' camp had been suddenly attacked for no reason. After the generals met aboard the steamboat *Far West* on the Yellowstone, General Terry sent Custer up Rosebud Creek on June 22, 1876, to find the Sioux and wait for support.

No one will ever know precisely what happened. Custer had orders to be cautious, but he rashly disobeyed them and struck the Sioux camp on the Little Big Horn, June 25, 1876. Custer, Major Marcus Reno, Captain Frederick Benteen, and the remainder of his column, totalling some six hundred men, would have been no match for the four thousand to five thousand warriors who waited on the Little Big Horn. But Custer, for reasons unknown, divided his regiment into battalions. With just over one hundred men, he marched on his own course taking all to their deaths. Reno and Benteen's force stumbled on the huge Indian encampment first. They fought furiously and soon had to take defensive positions. Meanwhile, Custer rode directly into the trap laid by Crazy Horse, Gall, and Two Moons on the rough terrain above the Little Big Horn. Fighting on foot and at close range, Custer's men had no chance against such superior numbers. In very short order, Custer and the entire battalion was wiped out.

On the following day, June 26, Colonel Gibbon's troops came upon the battle scene. Many of the dead had been scalped, but few were mutilated. Custer had been stripped naked, but he had not been scalped, perhaps because he had cut his famous long hair very short just before the campaign had begun. Word of the battle soon flashed over telegraph wires and made newspapers across the nation. The largest force of Plains Indian warriors ever assembled had stung the most celebrated cavalry unit on the frontier. Congress, the public, and of course, the army, were all angry and

Col. John Gibbon led one column to the Battle of the Little Big Horn in 1876 and fought the Big Hole Battle against the Nez Perce in 1877.—*Matthew Brady photograph, M.H.S.*

demanded an end to Indian warfare.

It would take another year to pursue, persuade, or force Indians back to the reservations. Sitting Bull, Gall, and their followers went north to Canada, hoping for better treatment. By 1881 all, including Sitting Bull, had returned. The Northern Cheyenne were sent to Indian Territory (Oklahoma), but their desire to return north was so strong that three hundred men, women, and children marched heroically to the Yellowstone in 1878. By the early 1880s the Sioux and the Cheyenne had agreed to live in peace on reservations. They said goodbye to the life they had known. The buffalo herds had dwindled to nearly nothing due to a greatly restricted range and the marksmanship of buffalo hunters. In truth, the life of the nomadic Plains Indian was no longer possible. The entire environment had changed too much.

Sitting Bull, chief of Hunkpapa Sioux and one of the leaders of the forces against Custer in 1876. This photo was taken by D. F. Barry in 1885, after Sitting Bull returned from exile in Canada. —*Smithsonian Institution*

Whites in Montana, however, experienced one other great campaign against Indians in the 1870s. After rejecting life on their reservation in Idaho, several hundred Nez Perce undertook a desperate journey through Montana in the summer of 1877. Led by warrior chiefs White Bird, Looking Glass, and Toohoolhoolzote and spiritual leader Chief Joseph, the Nez Perce were pursued by some four hundred soldiers under the command of General Oliver Otis Howard. For three months Howard chased Chief Joseph's Nez Perce, ending in early October 1877, in the Bear Paws Mountains in north-central Montana. It was an odd campaign. There were few battles and the Nez Perce truly desired only one thing— to be allowed to live in their home territory in northeastern Oregon.

Howard's pursuit of the Nez Perce began after a few skirmishes in Idaho in July 1877. The Nez Perce fled eastward over Lolo Pass and then down the Bitterroot Valley in Montana. The Indians wanted no confrontations, and in one instance, at the mouth of Lolo Canyon near Missoula, they rode around a hastily constructed fort—appropriately named Fort Fizzle. From the Bitterroot the Nez Perce trekked over the divide to recently created Yellowstone National Park, where they frightened a few tourists. Howard's troops were in pursuit, but they were unable to corner the Nez Perce until they reached the Bear Paws. There, with the aid of General Nelson A. Miles, Howard forced Joseph to surrender. Joseph had little choice, for too many warriors had been killed in the final battle. The women, old men, and children were hungry and ill-prepared to last the winter.

Chief Joseph's surrender, memorialized in the famous line: "From where the sun now stands, I will fight no more forever," ended a tragic and heroic story. Joseph and the Nez Perce did not want to fight whites. Since Lewis and Clark's first meeting with the Nez Perce, they had been friendly. But there was little choice in 1877, and the warrior chiefs like Looking Glass decided to flee and fight if necessary. They travelled over one thousand miles with women, children, and livestock through some of the roughest terrain in the West. Yet they managed to stay ahead of the pursuing soldiers. The army was frustrated. As one soldier wrote: "I wish they (Nez Perce) would go to the buffalo country and be done with it, and let us go home." In the end, of course, the Nez Perce lost and their future was to be on the reservation. It was the future of all the Plains Indians.

The Indian wars of the 1870s ended the warfare of the Blackfeet, Cheyenne, and Sioux. Now the Indians of Montana moved onto reservations. Eventually there would be seven Indian reservations in Montana. Reservation life meant dependence. The buffalo herds were practically gone. Whites wanted more land, and even the reservations lost additional land after they were formally established. In 1887 Congress passed a law that changed things even more. The General Allotment Law, usually called the Dawes Act, affected nearly every aspect of Indian life. Indians became U.S. citizens. Each head of family was to be given 160 acres of reservation land. The legal authority of the tribe was practically destroyed. Congress wanted Indians to cultivate crops, reside on a homestead, and generally live like whites. Just two decades before they had roamed Montana almost at will; now their lives were turned upside down. The reservation life would not be easy.

The first reservations in Montana resulted from Isaac Stevens' negotiations in the 1850s. The federated tribes of the Salish (Flathead) and Kutenai were the first to agree to a reservation in 1855. The huge reserve in the Jocko Valley south of Flathead Lake was acceptable to the Pend d'Oreilles and Kutenai, but the Flatheads wanted to stay in the Bitterroot. By the early 1870s, however, the government decided that they should move to the Jocko. Charlot, chief of the tribe, said no, although other chiefs, Arlee and Adolph, agreed to move. Twenty years later, in 1891, Charlot finally agreed to join the rest of the Flatheads on the Jocko Reservation.

The Blackfeet also agreed to a reservation in the 1850s, but its size was so large and the boundaries so confusing that no one really knew where it started and stopped. In 1874 the reservation extended from the divide to the Dakota line above the Missouri. Indian agencies were established at Fort Peck in the east, Fort Belknap in central Montana, and at Blackfoot Agency on the Teton River in the west. Piegans, Blackfeet, and Blood Indians lived in the western area. Gros Ventre and Assiniboines lived at Fort Belknap, and some Sioux and Assiniboines were attached to the Fort Peck agency. But with the coming of the railroad and the disturbances of the 1870s something had to change.

In 1886 new arrangements were made through the secretary of the interior and formalized by law in 1887. The Blackfoot Reservation in the west was home for Piegans, Blood, and Blackfeet Indians and encompassed an area east

Little Dog of the Blackfeet.—N. A. Forsyth photo. M.H.S.

of present-day Glacier National Park. The Fort Belknap Reservation for Gros Ventre and Assiniboines originally included land between the Little Rockies and the Milk River, but in 1895 it shrunk to just over 600,000 acres. The Fort Peck Reservation in northeastern Montana became home for Sioux and Assiniboines.

The Crow Indians, a tribe that had been friendly to whites, originally had a large area south of the Yellowstone River established as their reservation in 1868. Gold discoveries in the western portion of the Crow reserve and pressure from stockmen in the Yellowstone Valley forced the government to rearrange the Crow Reservation in the early 1880s. In 1884 the Crow Agency moved into the Little Big Horn Valley after ceding much of their original reserve, some of it to make way for the Northern Pacific Railway along the Yellowstone River.

The story behind the creation of the Northern Cheyenne Reservation on the Tongue River is dramatic. Two great

Crow Indian musicians preparing for a dance on the Crow Reservation in 1890.

leaders of the Cheyenne, Dull Knife and Little Wolf, led their people from Oklahoma back to Montana in 1878. Only Little Wolf's band made the complete journey. After surrendering to soldiers under Lieutenant William P. Clark, they were sent to Fort Keogh on the Tongue River where Little Wolf and other Cheyennes performed exceptionally as army scouts. But their final home had not yet been established. They had risked everything in their daring outbreak from Oklahoma, and still they were not assured a place in Montana. Finally, in 1884, when General Nelson Miles and other high-ranking officers supported them, the Northern Cheyenne were given a reservation on the Tongue River.

The last of Montana's Indian reservations was established in 1916 after years of controversy. The Rocky Boy's Reservation in north-central Montana is the home of the Chippewa-Cree people. These Indians were granted no legal status under the Dawes Act in 1887 and were forced to live in Montana without a landed home. These "landless Indians," as they are sometimes called, came to Montana from Canada after the failure of Louis Riel's rebellion against the Canadian

Rocky Boy, chief of the Crees. —*N. A. Forsyth photo, M.H.S.*

The Second Infantry out of Fort Keogh takes a break after marching across the plains.

government. From the mid-1880s until Rocky Boy's Reservation was established, there was conflict between the wandering Crees and white residents. The Indians were despised and treated very roughly by Montana whites. Finally, with the support of Frank Linderman, a longtime friend of Indian people, the Chippewa and Cree tribes gained legal status and a homeland, named after Rocky Boy, a Wisconsin-born leader of the Chippewas.

Montana's Indians had lost their lands. In 1900 there were just over 11,000 Indians in the state. Most lived on reservations. There was no danger of war, but the military maintained Forts Assiniboine, Custer, Maginnis, Missoula, and Harrison. They were reminders of the seriousness of the conflict between Indian and white. Nothing could be done to undo the harm both peoples had endured. For Indians it meant an end to the old life. Life on the reservations offered no real opportunities to be part of the white man's civilization. If Indian agents on the reservation were capable and sympathetic, such as Peter Ronan on the Flathead Reservation, then the times were less harsh. But even a good agent could not alter the failure of the Dawes Act. The land allotment program and the destruction of tribal authority made Indian adjustment even more difficult. Unfortunately, many

Morning inspection of the Guard Mount at Fort Assinniboine near Havre, Montana. Fort Assinniboine was one of the last forts constructed in Montana.

of the problems first encountered by Indians in the 1880s on reservations remain unsolved.

The Indians lost their land in less than a century. It is difficult to see how they could have maintained the nomadic life. American westward expansion was powerful. Whites were determined to conquer the land and turn it to their own uses. Nothing would stand in the way of what whites called progress. Beginning with fur trapping and overland trails, it was gold and the railroad that finally brought thousands to Montana. The buffalo—the Indian's staff of life—lost its range. With the near extinction of the buffalo in the 1880s, the days of freedom for Plains Indians were numbered. They were the first Montanans, and today in a new culture they remain Montanans—people with a special reverence for the land they lost.

Life in the Tribe

Over a century ago Plains Indians freely roamed Montana and buffalo were plentiful. That life is only a dim memory. No Indian alive today can remember life before the reservations. But Indian oral tradition—stories told by one generation to another—and written observations of whites tell us of a magnificent life on the plains. Life was not identical for each Indian tribe, but they all faced the same brazen environment. They all depended on their hunting and gathering skills to provide them with food, clothing, and shelter. Everything an Indian child or adult owned or used came from nature. Even after whites invaded the plains, Indians traded the rewards of their hunts for manufactured articles from white traders. They lived a nomadic life, moving from camp to camp. All of their possessions were portable and functional. Life itself had a natural rhythm, from season to season.

The rhythm of life beat in the heart of the tribe—the family. Tribes themselves were really groups of large extended families. That meant living with your aunts, uncles, grandparents, and cousins as well as parents, brothers, and sisters. As children grew up in the family they learned that love and respect were the cement of family and tribe. Children learned a special name of endearment for each family member they addressed. Your father and mother were special, of course, but you had many "fathers" and "mothers" in the family. Crow people call aunts and uncles mother and father; cousins were called brothers and sisters. Because of this closeness, orphans were almost unheard of, even when both parents were dead. An uncle or aunt naturally took the children in as their own.

Life itself was school for children in the tribe. Playtime was practically anytime, but even in play Indian children learned and prepared for life as an adult. Sioux and Crow boys played with bows and arrows from an early age. They spent hours shooting at targets and judging who was best among them. Blackfeet boys tested themselves against moving targets, such as a buffalo chip flung in the air. Girls played household games with dolls made from cottonwood or birch tree limbs. Girls imitated their mothers, playing house, preparing to move camp, or pretending to tan buffalo hides. In wintertime boys and girls made sleds of buffalo ribs and hides and slid down steep gully sides. On ice-covered streams they "skated" on moccasined feet to see who could glide the farthest.

Adults also played games, engaged in sports, and generally had fun. One of the most popular games among all plains tribes was the "handgame." It was a guessing game where opponents tried to pick in which hand his opponent concealed a special bone, elk tooth, or other ornament. Everyone crowded around the players and bet on the outcome. Men played a fast-paced outdoor game resembling field hockey. Two teams armed with sticks battled over a small hide-covered ball. The object was to knock the ball into the opponent's tipi at the end of the playing field. It was exciting and bets were waged on the game by each side. Crow women played a type of dice game. Specially marked bones or wooden buttons were thrown from a bowl onto a playing surface and scores were calculated according to how the bones and buttons landed. Again, all kinds of articles were bet on the outcome.

Sports and games, of course, did not feed or clothe the tribe. Plains Indians waged a constant struggle with nature to kill enough game and gather enough roots, vegetables, and fruit to sustain life. Hunting was the man's role. Western Montana tribes also fished, but hunting buffalo, elk, and deer was common to Sioux, Blackfeet, Crow, and other plains tribes. They hunted individually and in small groups, both mounted on their favorite horses and on foot. In other cases, especially on buffalo hunts, they hunted in large groups with nearly the whole tribe involved.

Among the Sioux, for example, the communal buffalo hunt involved moving camp and following the directions of a "Buffalo Dreamer" who prayed to the Great Spirit for guidance and success. Scouts found the herd and small hunting parties surrounded it. At a signal from experienced hunters, the attack began. The best hunters actually killed the buffalo. Each hunter chased down his prey. Behind them older men and young boys brought pack horses and helped butcher and pack up the kill. Regardless of who killed the buffalo, no family in the tribe went without meat. Some of the better hunters could claim the fattest animals as their own, but the purpose of the hunt was to provide meat for the entire tribe.

After the kill the meat, hides, hooves, and other parts of the buffalo were brought into camp. Now the women began the work of cooking the fresh meat, preparing dried foods and working the hides. Nothing was wasted. Fresh steaks were cooked. Sausage was made from the intestines. Bone marrow was boiled for fat. Buffalo meat was dried in the sun for storage, and in the fall it was cut and mixed with fat and berries to make pemmican. Pemmican often carried Indian families through the winter when fresh meat was unavailable.

Buffalo hides, which were tanned by the women using buffalo brains and liver, were used in a thousand ways. Hides were used for tipi coverings, shirts, dresses, leggings, heavy-duty moccasins, war shields, and saddles. Hides with the hair left on were used in winter for fur-lined moccasins, warm bed robes, winter caps, and mittens. Rawhide became a universal tie material for travois, pack saddles, horse bridles, and picket lines. Other parts of the buffalo were used to produce sewing thread, pouches and bags, bow strings, and even paint. It is no exaggeration to say that Plains Indians survived because of the buffalo.

The large spring and fall hunts provided families with much of their meat and raw materials, but women also were experts at finding and preparing edible plants. All kinds of berries were gathered and some were dried and preserved in a mash-like mixture. Wild onions and turnips were favorites. Turnips were preserved for winter eating by boiling them in buffalo fat after drying in the sun. Indian women also dug potatoes and picked cherries, plums, and other native fruits. In the spring, men and women tapped box elder trees for a sugar sap to sweeten dried foods.

Women did almost all of the domestic labor in camp, including building the tipi. In fact, the tipi was considered by many tribes to be the woman's property. But the men were not idle. When they were not hunting, Indian men manufactured and maintained their weapons, trained their buffalo horses, or made religious items. From an early age, Indian men learned how to fashion bows, arrowheads, arrows, and shields. Arrow shafts were usually made from gooseberry or cherry wood. They were smoothed with stones. Arrow points were tied and glued in place, and each warrior marked his arrows with decorative bands near the feathers. Stone arrowheads gave way to metal ones once the whites came.

Making bows and bowstrings took great patience and knowledge. Ash was the best wood for bows, but the wood had to be cut when green and carefully dried and shaped if the warrior expected to have a reliable weapon. Bowstrings were made from buffalo sinew. First the sinew was stretched and dried, then twisted in a triple braid and stretched a second time. A completed bow and string was the warrior's single most important manufactured item.

The one thing that determined life in the tribe more than anything else was its mobility. Tribes divided themselves into bands, usually a group of several families. Each band was nearly self-sufficient. It was a group large enough to kill buffaloes, but small enough not to go hungry. Bands were always on the move; their life was nomadic. The direction and distance of each move was determined by the location of buffalo herds and other game. Just about everything they owned was portable. Tipis, clothing, cooking utensils, weapons, toys, and every other item was packed up on travois to be dragged behind the strong horses when the camp moved. Sioux and Blackfeet roamed more than Crows, for example, but all plains tribes followed the buffalo.

On a hunt the Indian band might spend several weeks in a specific camp before moving. They did not camp just anywhere. There were favorite camping spots for each season of the year. Sometimes they left caches—hidden reserves—of food and other essentials near these campsites. Water, wood, good grazing areas, protection from the weather, and safety from enemies were all considered when choosing a camp. Choosing a camp location was the job of a specially appointed individual or group of men in the tribe. Like wagonmasters, they directed the village's movement. Once at the new location, each family knew where to place their tipis, wickiups, and gear. Tipi placement, for example, kept families close together and gave the preferred camp spots to special individuals in the tribe. It was all very well disciplined.

In the village the daily routine revolved around the tasks at hand. Women and children made sure that the water bags —usually made of buffalo rawhide—were full. Meals were served in wooden bowls. Plains Indians did not use much pottery, for it was too heavy and fragile to be portable. Spoons and cups were made of buffalo or mountain sheep horn. In the autumn camp activity was furious. Men hunted daily to provide food for the coming winter, and women worked tirelessly to tan hides and prepare pemmican.

Religion was a daily experience for Plains Indians. It was not assigned to a special day or activity; religion was a natural part of their lives. The universe, Indians believed, consisted of a harmonious nature where all life was directly connected. Life itself was precious and revered. Plants, animals, and man used the land, water, and air given them by the Great Spirit. When Indians prayed they prayed to the Great Spirit—a supreme power and life-provider. The Sioux called him Wakan Tanka. In their dreams and visions Sioux asked Wakan Tanka for guidance and aid. Before a hunt or a battle, Plains Indians celebrated special dances and prayers to bring "good medicine"—the best luck or the most strength. But central to Plains Indian religions was belief in the harmony of nature. They respected and honored the buffalo because it was his sacrifice that made life possible for Indian people.

They honored the sun, too. Indians recognized the sun as the source of infinite energy. They looked to the sun for renewal of strength. Each summer Blackfeet, Crow, Gros Ventre, and other plains tribes celebrated the Sun Dance—a long celebration of spiritual and physical renewal and sacrifice. The Sioux ceremony, for example, lasted twelve days. Usually a family who wished to celebrate a personal triumph or gain strength after a tragedy offered to sponsor the Sun Dance. They organized everything. They directed the building of the Sun Dance lodge, the arbor overhead, the cutting and placement of the center pole, and other events.

Men, women, and children participated in the Sun Dance. Its theme was always renewal and sacrifice. Indians knew that nothing in life was achieved without personal sacrifice. In the Sun Dance a few brave men even tortured themselves to test their own strength of purpose. These men punctured their chests with skewers that dangled by rawhide ropes from the center pole. Dancing away from the pole or actually hanging from the pole, the men who dared to "Gaze at the Sun Suspended" pulled until the skewers broke free from their skin. To accomplish this without fainting was impressive and demonstrated the power of the man's vision or dream. More importantly, the Sun Dance was a celebration for the entire tribe. "Give-aways"—free gift giving among the tribe—were popular. Individuals renewed their own beliefs and their harmony with the tribe and nature.

The fall brought hunting, and finally the winter forced the tribe to find a camp protected from the harsh plains weather. From December until April they remained in the same place. Tipi coverings were heavier, buffalo robes and heavy furred clothing kept families warm. Food was rationed carefully, and water could be drawn from streams only after holes were cut in the ice. It was a time when starvation threatened, and many times fallen horses were eaten and even hide scrapings provided nutrition.

Although life in the tribe meant a constant struggle to extract what nature could provide, Plains Indians had time for art. In fact, art could be seen everywhere in camp. Clothing, tipi coverings, weapons, ceremonial pipes, utensils and even toys were decorated. Plains Indian art was composed of three basic forms: quillwork consisting of porcupine quills sewn onto hides; beadwork using glass trade beads manufactured in Europe and acquired from whites; and painting on tipis, shields, travois, and utensils.

Quillwork was a highly developed art form among many Indian tribes. Blackfeet women, for example, took great care in selecting only the most pliable quills from the back and sides of young porcupines. They chewed the quills until they were flat and even more pliable, then colored them with natural dyes. After laying out a design, the quill-worker attached each quill separately to the garment with deer sinew thread. The result was a beautiful multicolored design that might tell a story, express an individual's dreams, or simply give the wearer pleasure.

Once glass beads came into their hands, Plains Indians adapted their geometric designs to beadwork. Each tribe used different and distinctive color combinations, and there were several different methods used to stitch the beads to garments. The bright glass beads gave Indian artists a much greater range of colors for their designs. Beadwork could be startlingly vivid in color or quietly soft. Sioux designs used white beads for backgrounds. Crow beadwork usually had soft pink or blue backgrounds.

Geometric designs were painted on tipis in bands at the bottom. Bold paintings of animals, battle scenes, or an individual's heroic deeds dominated tipi coverings. In some tribes one or two men specialized as tipi artists. When a tipi owner wanted an important picture painted, he called a tribal artist and carefully explained just how he wanted it done. Indians also used furs, particularly ermine, for decoration on ceremonial shirts. Women often adorned dresses with elk teeth. Feathers, animal horns, bird talons, and dyed animal skins were also used. Art brightened life. It expressed the Plains Indians' belief in the harmony of nature. It tells us that Indian artists had great imagination, a sense of abstract design, and a brilliant manner of creating beauty.

Life in the tribe changed little over the centuries before the coming of the whites. Then a whole range of new materials became available. Stone arrowheads were replaced by metal ones. Knives, scrapers, bowls, axes, and many other metal tools made Indian men and women even more efficient in their work. Trade blankets took the place of buffalo robes, and trade beads made of glass brightened Indian art. But even after trade with whites, the essential rhythm of life in the tribe remained much the same. As long as the buffalo were plentiful the nomadic life functioned. What the Plains Indians could not foresee was the end of the great herds. It happened in the 1870s and 1880s. From that time on, the Indian family's fate was to live on reservations. Life in the tribe was never to be the same again. The harmony between men, animals, and all of nature had been shattered. There was no way to retrieve it.

With the Army at Fort Shaw

The guns of the Union and Confederate armies had barely cooled. Officers and army regulars headed west as frontier guardians of the newly planted white settlements beyond the Mississippi. It must have been a welcome change for soldiers who had experienced over four years of bloody fighting. But life on an isolated frontier post was also lonely, boring, and frustrating. Plains Indians were elusive enemies. They preferred striking and retreating rather than engaging in continuous combat. Frontier soldiers also had to contend with lawless western settlers. The frontier army protected Indians from land-hungry whites almost as much as protecting the settlers from hostile Indian warriors.

The first military outposts in Montana were temporary. In 1866 the army built Fort C. F. Smith to protect the Bozeman Road in southeast Montana. The fort lasted only as long as the soldiers garrisoned the Bozeman Road. By 1868 all the posts were evacuated as a result of the treaty ending the Powder River War. North of the Bozeman Road, in central Montana, the military built another temporary post in 1866 at the mouth of the Judith River. Montana residents appealed for militia to protect them from raiding Blackfeet. Acting Governor Thomas Francis Meagher became excited. He demanded that the army establish a separate military district in Montana. There were many incidents along the Missouri, so in 1866 a battalion of the Thirteenth Infantry established Camp Cooke.

The infantry had been at Camp Cooke just one year when the proposed Military District of Montana became a reality. In the summer of 1867, a major post, Fort Shaw, was built at the Sun River crossing on the Mullan Road between Fort Benton and Helena. Fort Shaw's soldiers were there initially to protect travellers on the Mullan Road. To protect settlers, travellers, and miners in southeastern Montana from Cheyenne and Sioux raiders, the army established a second major post in 1867. Fort Ellis sat just west of Bozeman Pass, the gateway to the Gallatin Valley. The Military District of Montana suddenly had two garrisoned forts. Their soldiers would engage in significant combat against Indian warriors in the 1870s.

Fort Shaw was regimental headquarters—the more important of the two forts. Named after the commander of a black regiment in the Civil War, Robert G. Shaw of Massachusetts, the fort was typical of other frontier outposts. Fort buildings were arranged in a hollow square measuring 600 feet on a side. Surrounding this was a 160,000-square-foot parade ground. It took two years to complete all the fort's buildings. They were constructed of adobe brick reinforced with straw. Walls were over one foot thick, providing excellent insulation in winter and summer. Wooden siding covered the exterior walls, while lath and plaster were used to finish interior walls. Fort buildings housed four hundred men. There were officers' quarters, a house for the commander, a large hospital, a guardhouse, and a prison. Outbuildings included a sawmill, bakery, stable, and a granary.

Soldiers lived in four barracks of identical size and design. Each contained dormitories, sergeant's quarters, messroom, kitchen, laundress' quarters, and a storeroom. The barracks each held one hundred and twenty men comfortably. The regimental band had its own barracks. The hospital featured two wards with beds for over twenty patients, a dispensary, kitchen, and a large dining room. All post buildings were finished with wood floors and glass windows.

Soldiers at Fort Shaw came from nearly every state in the Union and several foreign countries. Men born in Canada, Sweden, Germany, Ireland, Scotland, Prussia, Switzerland, and even India were on company rolls in 1880. Irishmen and Germans predominated among the foreign-born. A few soldiers had families at Fort Shaw. Judging from the birthplaces of their children they were probably career soldiers who moved often from post to post. Two soldiers had taken Indian wives after coming to Montana. Some of these women worked as laundresses. Civilians also lived at Fort Shaw. The 1880 census listed a butcher, blacksmith, carpenter, painter, stonemason, teacher, two cooks, and several teamsters. Several of the officers also had Chinese or black servants attached to their families.

Supplying Fort Shaw with essentials meant freighting commodities by wagon from Fort Benton. Locally-grown vegetables in season and locally-slaughtered beef supplied the best of the fort's provisions. For the most part, they lived

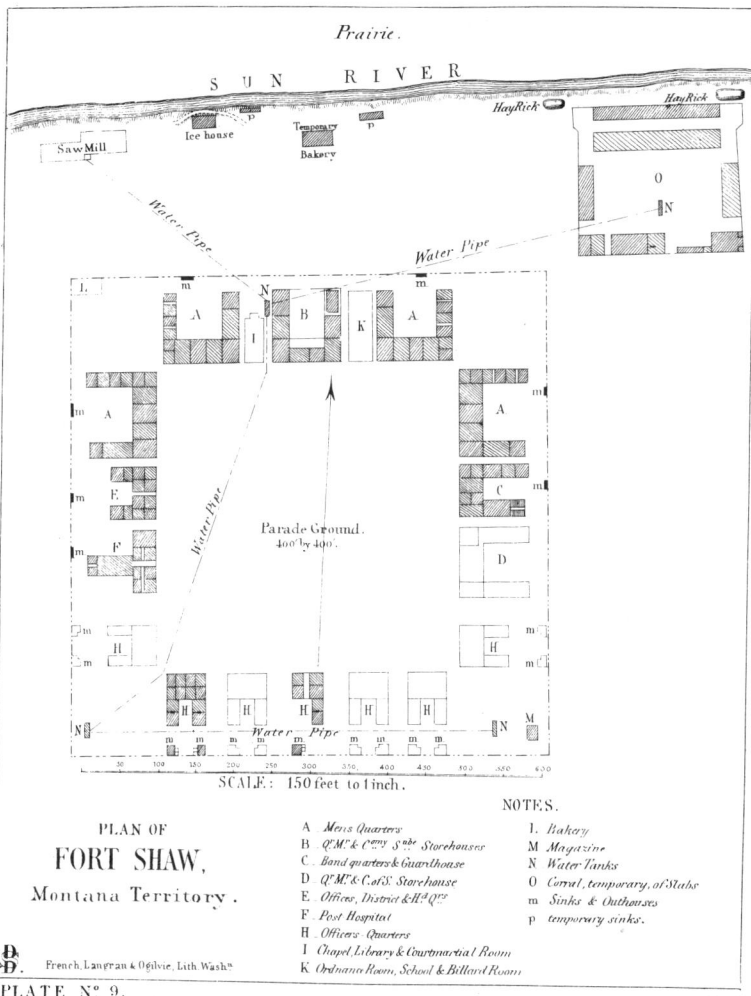

Diagram of Fort Shaw buildings, parade ground and other particulars as published in a War Department report in 1870.

on beans, bread, salt pork, and dried fruits. The fort's water supply was another matter. Initially they drew water directly from the Sun River by bucket and barrels. In the second year, a system of pipes brought river water to the fort compound. Even so, river water was often gritty, muddied from spring runoff, or brackish to the taste. Nevertheless, compared to other frontier posts, Fort Shaw was moderately well-equipped and situated.

Fort Shaw's troops did see action in the Indian campaigns in the 1870s. The majority of their military activity,

Interior of enlisted men's barracks at Fort Shaw.—*C. Eugene LeMunyon, photographer, M.H.S.*

however, involved serving on police, patrol, and escort duty. A primary responsibility of the command was to protect settlers from Blackfeet Indian raiders along the Mullan Road and in the Sun or Marias River areas. More commonly, however, their police duties meant pursuing and capturing whites who were trading guns and whiskey illegally with Indians.

Territorial police forces were so minimal that Fort Shaw's soldiers constituted the only effective policemen between the Missouri and the Canadian line. But they were not very successful in capturing illegal traders. Traders knew the terrain too well and were very resourceful. Colonel John Gibbon, commanding officer at Fort Shaw from 1870 to 1878, suspected that the large Fort Benton mercantile firms, such as T. C. Power and I. G. Baker, participated in the illegal trade. Proof was difficult to obtain. Power and Baker always denied these allegations, claiming they never violated trading regulations.

Patrol and escort duties also kept Gibbon's men busy. On patrol, soldiers often spent days helping repair telegraph lines. This was unexciting work and hardly fits the romantic image of army duty during the Indian wars period. On escort duty, however, there was plenty of action.

When the Northern Pacific Railroad's survey crews entered Montana in 1872-1873, Colonel Gibbon was obliged to send his men to protect surveyors. The Sioux in southeastern Montana were the greatest threat. Gibbon sent four companies from Fort Shaw to aid soldiers from Fort Ellis as the surveyors worked in the dangerous Yellowstone River country. In the summer of 1872 and again in 1873 they had several fights with Sioux and Cheyenne war parties. These were not large battles, but one man was lost and several wounded in 1872. Gibbon's troops also escorted army supply wagon trains. These travelled as far west as Fort Colville, Washington Territory, and eastward to Forts Belknap and Peck.

The majority of army routine, of course, did not entail patrol, escort, or battle duty. Soldiers spent the first two years completing the fort itself. Manual labor, the most disagreeable activity for soldiers, took up most of their time. Carpentry work, painting, and general maintenance brought continual complaints from enlisted men. They did keep themselves in readiness for action by drilling, cleaning weapons, and looking after their horses. Discipline was rigid and followed standard military practice. At dawn companies formed on the parade ground for inspection and the flag raising. In the evening they formed again for the lowering of the flag.

The bright spot at Fort Shaw was the regimental band. Led by professional musicians, they performed at concerts, dances, celebrations, and whenever an excuse could be found. In fact, Fort Shaw became something of a social center for settlers in the area. Concerts were so popular that printed programs were circulated announcing the time and musical selections. Birthdays, holidays, and occasional weddings were always celebrated. The officers and their wives, of course, had the best life at the fort. There was even a "society circle" of sorts among the women. They gave teas, dinners, and dances. The fort also sported a baseball team, held other athletic contests, and organized horse races. There was also a dramatic society that performed and attracted professional touring minstrel shows. For the single enlisted men, of course, gambling and drinking provided the bulk of entertainment.

The first major campaign involving troops from Fort

Shaw was a foray against a band of Blackfeet camped along the Marias River. In August 1869, Malcolm Clarke, a rancher in the Little Prickly Pear Valley near Helena, was murdered. Clarke had a Blackfeet wife and had the reputation of friendliness toward Indians. Whites were outraged, and a grand jury was called to charge his murderers. U. S. Marshal William F. Wheeler claimed that fifty-six settlers had been murdered by Blackfeet—a charge that was never substantiated. The jury charged five Blackfeet with Clarke's murder. Blackfeet chiefs were given time to turn these warriors over to civilian authorities. When they refused and raids continued, the army decided to act.

It was believed that Mountain Chief's band of Blackfeet was responsible. They had to be punished, at least that is how the army's high command saw it. In January, General Philip Sheridan at division headquarters in St. Louis wired Fort Shaw's commander, General Philippe de Trobriand, "Tell Baker to strike them hard." From Fort Ellis Major Eugene M. Baker led a column in below-zero weather to Fort Shaw. There he added more troops. Five companies of men left for the Marias with orders to strike Mountain Chief's camp and leave friendly Heavy Runner's people unmolested. At daybreak on January 23, 1879, Baker hit the quiet Blackfeet camp with everything he had. Losing one man, Baker left 173 Indians dead, including 50 women and children.

It was a horrible scene, but even more tragically Major Baker had struck the wrong camp—he had killed Heavy Runner and his people by mistake. The event created great controversy, particularly among eastern defenders of Indian rights. Exactly why Baker attacked the wrong camp will probably never be known. Soldiers at Fort Shaw, however, thought it was a bold stroke that would keep Blackfeet raids to a minimum. In fact, the Blackfeet never again waged war on the army.

The largest military operations for soldiers at Fort Shaw, however, were yet to come. In 1876, when the army decided to corner the Sioux and Cheyenne in the Big Horn Mountains in Montana and Wyoming, Fort Shaw's troops were involved.

Colonel Gibbon led a column from Fort Shaw in March 1876, to the Yellowstone River. There he was to join with General Alfred H. Terry and General George Crook in a three-pronged attack on the Sioux. It was the campaign that cost George Custer his life. Gibbon commanded over four hundred men and several Crow scouts. Joining with Terry's troops, the "Montana Column" moved up the Little Big Horn, while Custer descended the stream. Gibbon and Terry camped nine miles from the scene of Custer's battle, and it was Gibbon's men who first discovered the battle scene two days after the famous disaster. Gibbon took the remnant of Custer's Seventh Cavalry and headed back to Fort Shaw, while Crook and Terry pursued the Sioux.

The following year Colonel Gibbon's troops were again called into a major action. This time it was the threat of the Nez Perce. They had fled from Idaho into Montana with General O. O. Howard's troops in hot pursuit. Montana citizens panicked and demanded army protection. As Chief Joseph's Nez Perce pushed south up the Bitterroot Valley, Gibbon left Fort Shaw with 146 men moving fast to overtake the Indians. They marched swiftly for five days and caught the Nez Perce in the Big Hole Valley on August 9, 1877. Gibbon attacked, expecting an easy victory, but the Nez Perce stood their ground. After a day's fighting and much loss of life on both sides, the Nez Perce retreated as Howard's troops neared. Gibbon lost nearly thirty men. The Nez Perce counted eighty-nine dead, including women and children.

Fort Shaw's involvement in Indian campaigns was brief. The fort was probably more important as a security measure for the settlers and ranchers who developed the Sun River area in the 1870s and 1880s. It was in these years that Robert Ford, Conrad Kohrs, and John Bielenberg brought the first large cattle herds into the region. Fort Shaw was also noteworthy because black troops of the Twenty-fifth Infantry were stationed there for several years in the 1880s. By 1890, however, the post had served its purpose. In September of 1891 the last troops left Fort Shaw for other assignments on the frontier. The military reservation became the property of the Department of the Interior in 1893. Later an industrial school for Indians was established there. Today only a few of the original buildings remain and are being restored by local historical societies.

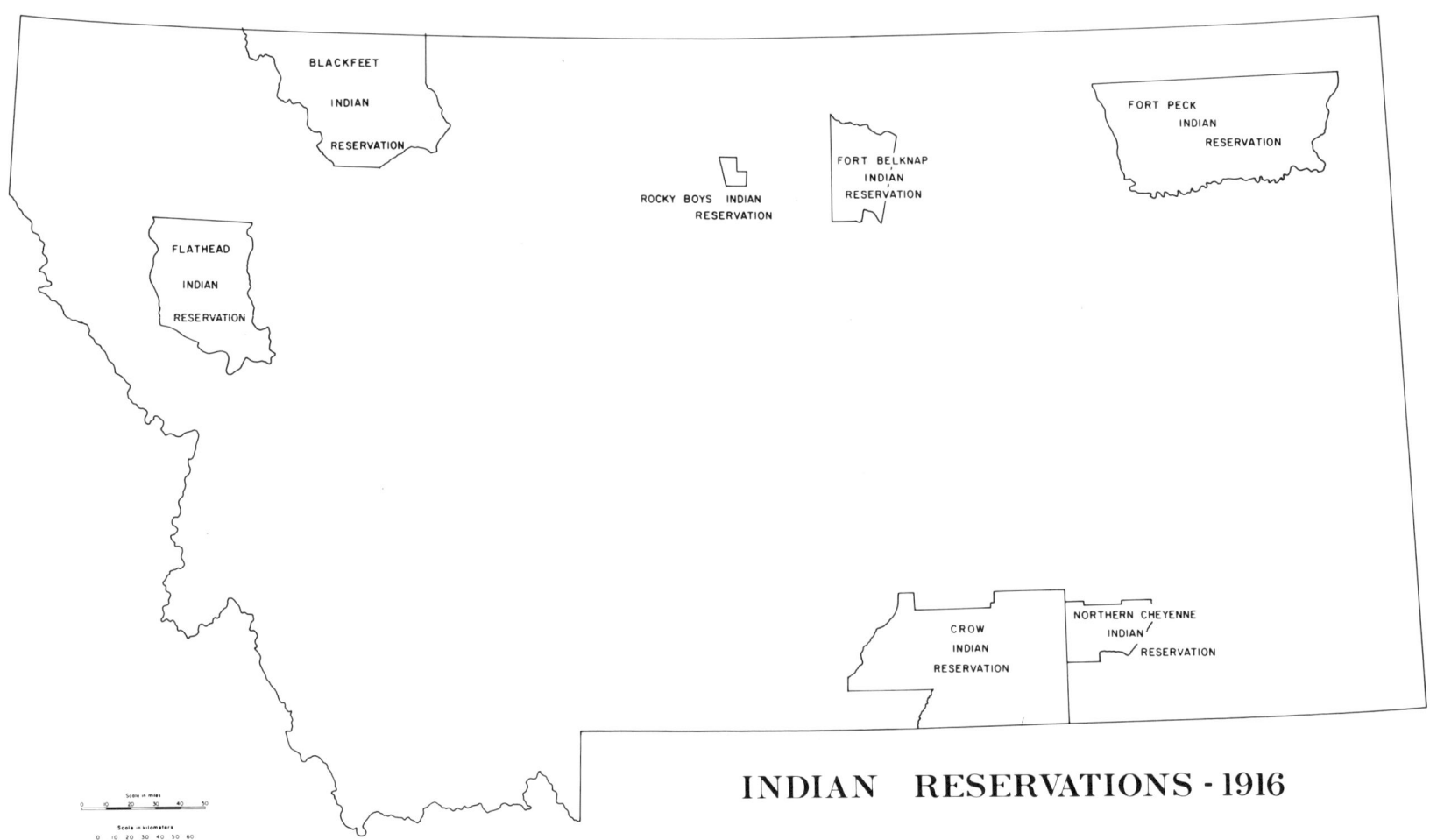

Timeline

1805: Lewis and Clark make contact with Sacagawea's Shoshone relatives.

1806: Lewis battles with Blackfeet at Two Medicine River.

1810: Missouri Fur Company trappers attacked by Indians at Three Forks.

1831: Flathead "delegation" sent to St. Louis to find priests.

1840: Fr. Pierre Jean de Smet arrives in Bitterroot Valley.

1841: St. Mary's Mission established.

1851: Fort Laramie Treaty.

1854: St. Ignatius Mission established.

1855: Isaac I. Stevens negotiates treaties with Flatheads and Blackfeet; Jocko Indian Agency established.

1866: Fetterman Massacre; Camp Cooke built.

1867: Forts Ellis and Shaw built.

1868: Fort Laramie Treaty; military abandons Bozeman Trail forts.

1869: Malcolm Clarke murdered by Blackfeet.

1870: Baker Massacre.

1871: Fort Belknap Indian Agency established.

1873: Baker Battle against Sioux; Fort Peck Indian Agency established.

1876: Custer battle at Little Big Horn.

1877: Forts Custer, Missoula, and Logan established; Nez Perce flee through Montana.

1878: Northern Cheyenne under Little Wolf and Dull Knife flee from Oklahoma to Montana.

1881: Sitting Bull surrenders.

1882: Crow Indians establish final reservation boundaries.

1884: Northern Cheyenne Reservation established.

1886: Blackfeet Reservation reduced in size.

1887: Dawes Act.

1891: Charlot's band of Flatheads journeys to Jocko Reservation.

1895: Fort Peck Indian Reservation reduced in size.

1916: Rocky Boy's Indian Reservation established.

Suggested Readings

Merrill Beal, "I Will Fight No More Forever": Chief Joseph and the Nez Perce War. Seattle: University of Washington Press, 1963.

John Fahey, The Flathead Indians. Norman: University of Oklahoma Press, 1974.

John S. Gray, Centennial Campaign. Fort Collins, Colorado: The Old Army Press, 1977.

Dorothy M. Johnson, The Bloody Bozeman. New York: McGraw-Hill, 1971.

Alvin M. Josephy, The Indian Heritage of America. New York: Alfred A. Knopf, 1969.

Edgar I. Stewart, Custer's Luck. Norman: University of Oklahoma Press, 1955.

Miles City cowboy Ed Ranine—dressed to look the part.

Chapter VI:
Cowboys and Farmers Tame the Land

Francis M. Thompson served as Montana's commissioner of emigration in 1865. His job was to promote the territory. He did not mince words. In addition to all the gold and silver mines, the territory had potential as the finest farming and ranching domain in the nation. In the long run (although Thompson had no way of knowing it) farming and ranching, not mining, would provide better and more renewable returns from the land.

For most of Montana's Indians, agriculture was not important. Yet for tribes living near the Bitterroot Valley, there had long been an annual crop to be harvested. Each spring the delicate pink petals of the bitter root dotted the valley. The Indians dug up the turnip-like roots. Then they boiled, pounded, and dried them into a nutritious supplement for their diets. Lewis and Clark "discovered" the plant and made note of its longstanding use in 1805.

As fur trappers and missionaries penetrated the region, they too began to farm. In small plots around their cabins, trading posts, or churches, they planted vegetables. They raised and milked a few cows. Perhaps they planted some grain. Father Anthony Ravalli even established a small mill for grinding flour. As military posts and Indian agencies came into being, they too augmented bland, all-meat diets with vegetables, poultry, and grain crops. One of General John Gibbon's first acts when he came to Fort Shaw in the early 1870s was to construct an irrigation ditch and raise potatoes for his troops.

Settlers around Fort Owen, Hellgate and Fort Benton planted small subsistence crops to keep themselves going. Gold strikes at Grasshopper Creek, Alder Gulch and elsewhere changed the nature of agriculture in 1863 and 1864. In the booming mining camps were ready markets for vegetables, grain, potatoes, and meat. Crop planting could be expanded and profits realized.

Before long, many farms flourished in western Montana river valleys. The soil was fertile. Mountains sheltered the farms from severe weather. Nearby rivers provided irrigation water. Forests provided building materials for cabins and barns. Neighboring mining camps became profitable markets.

A farmer could secure 160 acres for almost nothing under the provisions of the 1841 Preemption Act or the 1862 Homestead Act. With little mechanical equipment, 160 acres was about all a farmer could handle. He had a field or two of grain, another of hay for his few horses and cows and a garden or orchard for personal use. A plot of potatoes and a few chickens or hogs added variety. Farms looked very much like eastern or midwestern farms. Indeed, many of their owners had come from these regions.

Irrigation through a crude ditch from the river might provide relief from drought if the season proved dry. Relief from grasshoppers or crickets was not as easy to obtain. Year after year, the pests appeared. Farmers tried to burn them, mash them, and scare them. Finally they had to endure them and hope the hordes did not prove too devastating.

To help one another with these and other problems, farmers across the nation began to come together under the banner of the Patrons of Husbandry—or Grangers. Founded in 1867, this group soon became nationwide. By the mid-1870s it had spread to Montana. Grangers worked to further the cause of the farmer. They met socially for dances and recreation, which helped relieve the monotony of everyday life. Granger newspapers—like the *Rocky Mountain Husbandman*—educated farmers on new agricultural methods, as well. The Patrons of Husbandry also attempted to organize for political purposes, seeking beneficial legislation and prices.

During the same years the Grangers expanded, Montana's farms grew, too. Under three acts—Timber Culture Act (1873), Desert Land Act (1877), and Timber and Stone Act (1878)—farmers could obtain additional plots of 160 or 320 acres. Combining entries under more than one act, they might increase the size of their farms to 640 acres (one mile square) or more.

With a growing population in Montana plus ever-increasing numbers of military forts and Indian agencies, farmers found good markets. Agriculture expanded eastward into the Yellowstone, Musselshell, and Missouri valleys. Some specialization took place. The Missouri and Gallatin valleys became well-known for their wheat; the Bitterroot Valley produced vegetables and, later, fruit.

The career of James Fergus reflected the eastward movement of Montana agriculture. Fergus first came to Montana in 1862. He tried mining, then settled on a 160-acre farm in the Prickly Pear Valley in 1866. For the next fourteen years he ran a diversified operation. At one time or another he raised cattle for meat, milk, butter and cheese. He kept chickens for eggs and meat. He bred hogs for pork and bacon. And he sold miners and Helena residents potatoes, wheat, oats, peas, carrots, rutabagas, corn and salad vegetables. By 1880, Fergus thought his range was too crowded. He moved east to a spot on Armells and Box Elder creeks, north of the Judith Mountains. Soon he was supplying produce and beef to Fort Maginnis and the growing mining communities in that region.

When the Utah and Northern Railroad arrived from the south in 1880 and the Northern Pacific was completed three years later, farmers found even greater markets in eastern cities. Agriculture continued to expand in Montana through the 1890s. Still, it existed primarily in the central and western parts of the state. Agriculture continued to prosper in river valleys where irrigation water was available.

Livestock development followed much the same patterns as farming. Francis Thompson had observed Montana's grazing potential. Vast herds of buffalo—Charlie Russell called them "Nature's Cattle"—lived on the rich grasses of central and eastern Montana. When the first white settlers came to Montana, however, they—and the cattle or sheep with them—took up residence in the western valleys. By the 1850s, the Bitterroot and Flathead valleys had several hundred head of cattle.

Late in the 1850s and early in the 1860s, livestock raising changed. Men like Johnny Grant in the Deer Lodge Valley exchanged cattle and oxen with emigrants on the Oregon Trail. At Fort Hall, in Idaho, Grant often traded one healthy animal for two travel- and trail-worn cattle. Then, slowly he drove the weakened animals back to the Deer Lodge Valley. There he fattened them, and returned the next spring and summer to Fort Hall to trade once again. Soon his herd included several thousand cattle and oxen.

Grant was not alone. Conrad Kohrs and John Bielenberg joined him in the Deer Lodge Valley. They bought him out in 1866 and set up headquarters on what is today the Grant-Kohrs Ranch National Historic Site. Philip Poindexter and William C. Orr established a similar operation in the Beaverhead Valley near present-day Dillon. These men brought in cattle from Utah, California and Oregon over the Corinne and Mullan Roads. They introduced good breeding stock (not just range cattle) to strengthen their herds. Ranchers also included a few sheep and horses in their growing livestock business.

These early ranchers, like the farmers, found their markets limited until the gold rush. Soon Bannack, Virginia City, Butte, and Helena had meat markets. Business boomed. A growing number of military posts provided another outlet for beef. At the same time, federal authorities worked to confine Indians on reservations and prevent them from roaming in their traditional search for buffalo. To achieve this, the government contracted to have cattle provided as a source of food.

Growing markets produced two changes in the livestock business. More cattle came into Montana, and the industry moved east into the central valleys and plains. In 1866 Nelson Story brought in the first trail herd of Texas cattle, six hundred in all. Many thousands more would follow over the years.

East of the mountains lay forty million acres of free grazing land. Native bunchgrass (gramma), which had sustained the buffalo, could do the same for cattle. Nutritious in the spring and summer, the grass "cured" and provided a good source of feed even in the winter. Like the fur trade, mining and agriculture, a new business developed using the land: ranching.

Conrad Kohrs was one of the first to move cattle east out of the western valleys. In 1869 he drove one thousand head from the Deer Lodge to the Sun River Valley. Shortly, Granville Stuart moved cattle into the Judith Basin. By the middle 1870s, central Montana was range country. By the end of the decade, Sioux and Cheyenne Indians had been removed from eastern portions of Montana. The range cattle

Typical of ranches along river bottoms in Central Montana in the 1880s.

industry expanded there.

Eastward expansion pushed white settlers to the borders of Montana's Indian reservations. In short order, pressure developed to restrict the size of these preserves. Blackfeet, Gros Ventre, Assiniboine and Crow reservations occupied most of the region north of the Missouri, south of the Yellowstone and east of the mountains in the 1860s. As agriculture and livestock ranges expanded, Indian lands shrank.

Sheep also joined cattle on Montana's ranges. The first sizeable herd entered the territory in 1865 under the care of Major G. G. Kimball. He had driven them all the way from Red Bluff, California. In Virginia City he sold them to local meat markets. Two years later Jesuit fathers at St. Peter's Mission brought in three hundred sheep and raised them commercially.

Others soon joined the field. J. F. Bishop and Richard Reynolds brought 1,500 sheep in from The Dalles, Oregon, in 1869, and established a ranch in the Beaverhead Valley. Poindexter and Orr did likewise in the same area the next year. They drove 2,467 rams and ewes in from California. The great pioneer Montana sheepman, Henry Sieben, began his operations in central Montana in 1872. Within eight years, the number of sheep in the territory increased sixfold to 385,000. Sheep men faced the same opportunities and hardships as cattlemen. Wintering, watering and feeding stock was hard work. The same profits or bankruptcy awaited their efforts.

As Montana's ranges opened, southern ranges in Colorado, Kansas, and Oklahoma became depleted. More beef moved north. They came up the Goodnight-Loving Trail to Cheyenne, then the Western Trail to Miles City. With a bandanna across his face to keep out the choking dust, a wide-brimmed hat to protect his head, chaps to save his legs from the sting of sage and brush, and a yellow slicker tied on behind the saddle, the cowboy came, too. He trailed longhorns up from Texas. He watched over them on their new range. The cowboy became a part of the business, and slowly worked his way into the American mind as a new "hero."

E. C. "Teddy Blue" Abbott was among those trail drive cowboys. He arrived in Montana during October of 1883. His "ticket" north was a herd of New England-owned FUF cattle from Texas, bound for Forsyth. In his book, *We Pointed Them North*, Abbott tells of the hardships and hard work cowboys faced. He remembered rubbing tobacco juice in his eyes to stay awake on night guard. He also recalled riding the last bit of trail flat on his back in a wagon—sick from drinking alkali water.

Cowboys watched the cows. Investors watched profits. The whole business looked like a good way to get rich quick. For some it was. In 1881, James S. Brisbin published a book entitled *The Beef Bonanza, Or How To Get Rich On the Plains*. For a while it appeared as if Brisbin knew what he was talking about. With a small investment cattlemen made great profits.

Granville Stuart ran the DHS ranch near present-day Lewistown in 1884. His annual report to his bosses showed how little it took to run 15,000 or 16,000 cattle. Stuart's inventory included only four wagons, two mowing machines, one horse rake, five saddles, three stoves, and six Winchester rifles.

Cattle could be purchased in Texas for $4 or $5 per head. Cowboys got $1 per day plus room and board. On the Chicago market a cow or steer brought from $32 to $50 per head. Everyone could see the logic in Brisbin's mathematics. True, a company might lose ten percent of its cattle during the winter, but, on the bottom line, they could expect annual profits of fifteen to forty percent. Brisbin had to be right!

Speculators—absentee owners—soon flooded the range with their cattle. From Texas the XIT outfit brought up herds. The Matador and Swan River Cattle companies owned by Scots also ran cattle in Montana. The Powder River Cattle Company was English. On the eastern border, Pierre Wibaux and the Marquis de Mores ranged French-bought cattle. As the Northern Pacific pushed into Montana during 1881 and 1882, eastern markets became more accessible. Miles City became the "Cow Capital of the World."

Ranch life developed a hard-working routine. During the spring and fall, representatives ("reps") from the various companies combed the open range for stock. After sorting, branding and ear notching, the steers, cows and new calves could be tallied. To facilitate the work and the all-important recording of brands (the sign of ownership), regional range associations soon formed. The Shonkin Pool near Fort Benton was among the first. Ultimately, the Montana Stockgrowers Association was organized in July of 1884. It served as a clearing house for brands and information on the range cattle industry.

Expansion brought more cattle and more profits. It also generated problems. The first problem was rustling. Central Montana cattlemen reckoned their losses to rustlers at about three percent in 1883. During the summer of the next year they organized a vigilante group to lessen the "competition."

The second problem was overcrowding on the range. By 1885 and 1886 there were 700,000 cattle grazing on the Montana plains. Perhaps there were more. Overcrowding brought overgrazing. Dry years in 1885 and 1886, and a poor cattle market, had the entire industry teetering on the edge of financial disaster. The winter of 1886-1887 pushed it over the brink.

When the cold temperatures finally moderated, when chinook winds finally came, when snow actually melted in 1887, cattlemen went out to discover losses ranging from fifty to ninety-nine percent. Of the 220 separate cattle operations in Montana in 1886, only 120 survived bankruptcy in 1887. Cattlemen had abused the range. They had asked more of the land and the climate than it could give. They paid dearly for their mistake.

After 1887, the livestock industry in Montana changed. Speculators from Chicago and Europe deserted the field. The

At a range camp of the XIT Cattle Company near Fallon.—*Evelyn Cameron photo, M.H.S.*

open range became the closed range. Barbed wire fences marked first one grazing area, then another. This type of fencing proved ideal for a region where wooden fence posts were hard to acquire. Fencing made it possible for ranchers to set aside hay pastures and regular watering spots.

In short, ranchers became conservationists—protectors of Montana's precious grasslands. They bought or leased land and water rights. They dug wells and used windmills rather than depend on unpredictable stream flows through summer and fall. Here and there they built crude shelters for their stock rather than counting on chinook winds. In the river bottoms they grew, cut and stacked hay for winter feed. Statistics reflect the change. In 1880, 56,801 acres of land was in hay. By 1890 the total had risen to 300,033 acres. By 1900 it was 712,048. The mowing machine and hay rake became as important to the cattle business as the lariat and chuck wagon.

Cattlemen returned to earlier practices begun in the

1860s. They bred their stock for quality rather than quantity. Hereford, Angus, Shorthorn and Durham breeds were mixed with the range cattle survivors of 1886-1887. Ranchers also diversified. They added sheep and sometimes farming to their operations.

Almost immediately, the Montana livestock industry began to recover from the 1886-1887 disaster. The next spring and summer more than 100,000 head of cattle entered Montana from the south. Ranchers who had not been wiped out took advantage of low prices. They began to restock at minimal expense. By 1893 Montana had 100,000 more cattle on its ranges than it did in the fall of 1886. They were not grouped in big herds as before. Now on smaller ranges, with feed and shelter provided, Montana's cattle flourished and business prospered.

Less than a decade after the hard winter, one of the largest roundups of all time took place in the still largely unfenced region near the Montana/North Dakota/Canada border. Nearly one thousand cowboys participated, representing twenty companies.

Montana's winters became no milder with passing years. Some ranchers who experienced the 1886-1887 winter claimed that the winter of 1906-1907 was far worse. Railroad tracks snapped in the bitter cold. Starving cattle invaded eastern Montana towns in search of something to eat. But livestock losses averaged only twelve to thirteen percent. They would have been worse had ranchers not relied on winter feed and protective shelters.

For the cowboy, the change in the industry also marked a change in life-style. His days were still long and hard, but ranch chores were monotonous compared to the excitement of a trail drive. Instead of an open range, trail driving hero, he became a fence builder, a hay cutter, a range manager. More and more, the reckless, devil-may-care cowboy became a myth and not an actual resident of the Montana plains. Owen Wister's novel, *The Virginian: A Horseman of the Plains* (1902), became a model for the mythical cowboy—the hero of the plains—who survives today on movie and television screens.

Agriculture and livestock interest in Montana during the 1890s and 1900s followed the same lines established in the late 1880s. Diversified operations, with a good water supply, had the best chances for economic survival. The cattle industry had been the first to use eastern ranges commercially. It had also been the first to abuse them and discover the consequences. Managing the land and its resources proved to be the solution.

As Montana communities grew, new rail lines entered the state. The agricultural and livestock industry had also grown. It had grown out of the western river valleys eastward to the plains. It had grown to be a diversified, well-rounded industry with markets outside the state. Bustling mining towns no longer absorbed the produce of Montana's farms and ranches. Now places like Chicago and Minneapolis carried all-important quotations. Output of the livestock and agricultural industries went beyond the value of gold and silver produced in the state. Francis Thompson would have been surprised.

Farmers Read the
Rocky Mountain Husbandman

Robert N. Sutherlin believed in agriculture. He believed in Montana. From his arrival in the Missouri Valley in 1865 until his death in 1926, his faith in Montana's agriculture never wavered. During his sixty-one years in Montana he served as the spokesman for farmers and ranchers. For over fifty of those years he spoke as editor and publisher of Montana's first agricultural newspaper, the *Rocky Mountain Husbandman*.

Many men came to Montana in the mid-1860s in search of gold. When they failed to strike it rich, some turned to farming as a substitute. Robert Sutherlin was different. He came to Montana to farm. Northeast of present-day Townsend he laid out his farm. He called it the "Raven's Roost Ranch." For ten years he farmed and freighted between Fort Benton and Virginia City. Everywhere that he took his ox-drawn freight wagons, he saw potential for farming and ranching. He knew that agriculture would be a vital part of the territory's economy. Miners needed food to support their work, and farmers needed miners as markets for their produce.

When the Patrons of Husbandry organized in Washington, D.C., in 1867, Sutherlin watched with interest. As they spread nationally, and as farm prices dropped during the national financial depression of 1873, he came to believe there was strength in organization. That year he organized the Star of the West Grange in the Missouri Valley near his home. In short order twenty more branches formed throughout central and western Montana.

Two years later the Territorial Grange met in Gallatin City to discuss the past year and plan for the future. Several people approached Sutherlin and suggested he start a newspaper to extoll the unbounded agricultural resources of Montana. These men also felt the journal should spread information about new techniques and developments in farming. They wanted it to be a source of information all farmers and ranchers could trust.

With his brother William, Robert Sutherlin considered the possibilities. Montana had a population of little more

Robert N. Sutherlin was an influential voice among stockmen and farmers as editor of the *Rocky Mountain Husbandman*.

than 20,000. Only 2,000 of these were farmers. Yet the Sutherlins believed the need existed. An amazed crowd gathered about the Good Templar's Hall in Diamond City on Thanksgiving Day, 1875. They watched Robert crank out the first issue of the weekly *Rocky Mountain Husbandman*. It was a gamble.

No paid advertisements appeared in the first issue. Robert figured the newspaper cost about fifty dollars to print, and one week later William had been able to round up only three hundred subscribers at four dollars per year.

Single copies went for ten cents. It did not look good, but they pressed on. Robert did the editing and actual printing. William travelled the territory. He got subscribers, advertisements and sent back regular detailed letters on agricultural and mining developments throughout Montana.

By the end of the first year's publication, the *Husbandman* had assembled thirty-nine paid advertisers. These came from as far away as Augusta, Maine, and Corinne, Utah. They also included a wide variety of businesses in Diamond City and Helena. Soon they had over eight hundred subscribers.

Robert Sutherlin did what he promised to do. Each week the eight-page newspaper carried a wide cross-section of agricultural news. At least one full page carried Grange news. It had a list of all national and territorial officers, and had anything else of interest to Grange members. "Our friends throughout the Territory," Sutherlin reminded his readers, "are requested to send us short, pointed accounts of conditions of crops, items in regard to stock, the grange, news, or anything which they think would be of interest." Anything that came in, he tried to print.

The *Rocky Mountain Husbandman* covered the spectrum of agricultural news. Agriculture, Floriculture, Live Stock, Poultry, and Dairying were regular columns. From a wide variety of territorial and national newspapers Sutherlin gathered items of interest. From Connecticut came word that a farmer was using a flock of fifty guinea hens to keep his fields free of potato bugs. "They do the work in a very thorough manner," the farmer reported. From elsewhere came a note that meadowlarks ate more insects than grain and were an asset to any farm.

A weekly feature on page one was the "Domestic Economy" section with current recipes and helpful hints for the kitchen. How about potato pudding for dessert tonight?

> Beat well together 41 ounces of mashed potatoes (free from lumps), four ounces of butter, four of sugar, five eggs, a grated rind of a small lemon, a pinch of salt; add a small teacup of sweet milk; pour the mixture into a well buttered pudding dish; pour a little clarified butter on the top, and then sift plenty of white sugar over it. Bake in a moderate oven three-quarters of an hour.

On pages two and three, Sutherlin addressed local issues. As the only newspaper in Diamond City and all Meagher County during its first years, the *Husbandman* carried much local and territorial news: Mr. & Mrs. James Grubb and Mr. & Mrs. William Hortop had new baby boys. Smallpox had been reported near Pleasant Valley on the road up from Corinne, Utah—stay clean, get plenty of fresh air, and perhaps you will not catch the disease. Felix Poznainsky who operated the Mountain Lode near Butte, announced plans to install a five-stamp mill. Diamond's Jacob Magle got kicked by one of his oxen last week. I. O. Proctor's cheese factory on the Smith River turned out three tons of "as good cheese as was ever manufactured in the Rocky Mountains." Ed Brassey would teach school in Diamond City for the 1876-1877 term. Classes started on November 28 and ran for five months. No one had to go to school, of course, but Mr. Brassey was highly spoken of. Most parents will want to send their children.

Sutherlin used every page as an editorial forum when he had something to say. He did not hesitate to express his views on any subject. He felt strongly that Montana needed a railroad. Yet, he did not think the state should subsidize it with money nor give it free land. He opposed the Northern Pacific land grant because it removed much property from private ownership. Equal taxation of mines and farms was another issue Sutherlin advocated. Taxes on a mine producing $1000 in ore should be the same as that on a ranch with $1000 in cattle.

There were other issues. When grasshoppers returned year after year to damage Montana crops, Sutherlin offered a solution. Prohibit bird hunting in the territory, he said. He suggested legislators ban the shooting of any birds for ten years. Then the feathered friends could render "efficient service in the great warfare against the farmer's worst enemy." Sutherlin also became an early advocate of diversified agriculture. Again and again he warned farmers and ranchers not to put all their money and effort into a single crop. One bad year could prove disastrous.

For rural sections, far removed from telegraph and stage routes, the *Rocky Mountain Husbandman* served other purposes. It carried major national and international news. Governor Benjamin F. Potts' Thanksgiving Proclamation appeared requesting Montanans to celebrate in an appropriate manner. The produce market was also important. Flour was in good demand. XXX Willow Creek flour went for $6.65 a hundredweight. Madison and Gallatin XXX sold for only $6.00. Eggs were 80¢ a dozen. Potatoes brought $20 per ton. Cabbage paid $1.75 per hundredweight. Hay sold from $13 to $16 per ton.

With very few libraries scattered throughout Montana, reading matter was hard to obtain. As a result, page five of the *Husbandman* always had "The Home Circle" column that contained a short story, some poetry, little quips about daily life and tidbits of philosophy. "Days are bubbles on the stream of time which, in passing, burst forever." "The vices of the rich and great are mistaken for errors, and those of the poor and lowly for crimes."

Finally, Robert Sutherlin used a page of his newspaper to expound on the news and beliefs of Good Templars— people who preached against alcohol. "The Templar should have a clear head, an honest and sympathetic heart, and a ready helping hand." "There is nothing easier than to cultivate an appetite for liquor." "Drink cold water. Nothing will quench the thirst so well."

For today's student of Montana history, the *Rocky Mountain Husbandman* is a very important source. Beyond the local and territorial news, the correspondence from William Sutherlin is invaluable. As he travelled about Montana he wrote letters with descriptions of mining in Butte, agriculture in the Gallatin Valley, stock raising in the Beaverhead and accounts of new little towns as they sprang up here and there.

As Montana grew and subscribers to the *Husbandman* passed 1,300, Diamond City declined. Her peak days had been the 1860s, and by 1879, the town was little more than a shell. To the east, along the Smith River, White Sulphur Springs grew to become the seat of Meagher County. In 1879 the Sutherlins left Diamond City and set up operations in the new town.

Robert and William threw their full support behind White Sulphur Springs. They bragged about the beneficial qualities of the natural springs there. They encouraged expansion of the hot bath resorts and suggested that all Montanans visit the area to relax. The brick *Husbandman* building became a prominent feature of the White Sulphur Springs business district and testified to the Sutherlins' faith in the town.

In time, the *Meagher County News* and other newspapers appeared on White Sulphur Springs streets, but throughout the 1880s, the *Husbandman* was the only paper in town. Robert Sutherlin never forgot his promise to the Grangers. The paper continued as the leading voice for agricultural and farming interests in Montana.

William Sutherlin died in 1900. He had retained his interest in the newspaper from the beginning, but editorial policy and format had been under the guidance of Robert. In 1904, the *Husbandman* moved for a third and final time. North and west of White Sulphur Springs, Great Falls had become the nucleus of agricultural development in central Montana. Robert set up his printing press in this city and continued to issue his paper until he died in 1926. The journal survived its founder and continued publication until 1942. It retained the policies and editorial tone Robert Sutherlin had set for it almost sixty years before.

"We will labor with diligence to reach the highest standard of excellence," Sutherlin promised in 1875. "It shall be our endeavor to advance in every way possible the material interests and industrial pursuits of a people whose patronage and favor we hope to win and retain through merit alone. We shall ever be found boldly and fearlessly championing the cause of the sons of toil—commending the good, denouncing the wrong—unawed by fear and unswerved by favors."

Robert N. Sutherlin believed in agriculture. He believed in Montana. He kept his promises.

Wanted: A Chinook—The Winter of 1886-1887

Spring gently warmed the plains of eastern Montana. Stream banks filled with the run-off of melting snow. The rains came to refresh the land. Bright red and yellow blossoms of the prickly pear joined the more delicate shades of spring flowers. The new shoots of bunchgrass promised renewed feed on the open range. It looked like 1885 would be a good year.

Summer turned dry. Ranchers and cowboys looked westward for the boiling clouds of periodic thunderstorms, but found none. The green promise of the grasslands turned brown early, and dark clouds on the horizon meant range-fire, not rain. With the speed of the wind fires moved across the plains like a low, rolling wave. Thirty, forty, fifty miles an hour they came. They fanned out as they went. A fire might start with a lightning strike, a campfire, or a rustler's spark. Before long the flames would fan out perhaps five or ten miles wide. They raced on almost unchecked for up to one hundred miles, blackening the earth, destroying the dry grass, and leaving charred remains of wildlife, cattle and perhaps cowboys in their path.

Ranchers had no choice but to move their cattle from each burned-over range. Not until the following spring would the grass renew. Even then the feed would be less nutritious. True, it would green-up early, but with the mulch gone there was little to hold precious moisture around the roots. The next season's grass would not be as hardy.

Fall roundups in 1885 held the warning of impending disaster. Herd sizes had increased. Overcrowding and overgrazing became more obvious. There was a reason for the overstocked range. Declining prices for cattle on the eastern market persuaded Montana ranchers to hold their cattle through the winter rather than sell them at a loss. At Chicago, the price per hundredweight had slipped from $4.75 in 1882 to $3.90 and below by the fall of 1885.

Winter settled across the western plains of the United States late in 1885. In the South, already overcrowded ranges in Texas and Oklahoma felt the brunt of the blizzards. When the thaw came in 1886 and the drifted fences and coulees melted out, ranchers in that part of the country counted eighty-six percent of the herds dead. Quickly they moved to sell survivors. The market was already glutted. The price of cattle continued to drop when more were offered for sale.

If 1885 was dry, 1886 was parched. Again the rains failed to come and black, choking clouds of smoke filled the skies for weeks at a time. Cowboys tied bandannas across their faces to filter the air. Ashes and smoke stung their eyes. They tried to move herds out of the paths of fires onto unburned ranges and toward water.

New cattle came into Montana from the south. In the fall, ranchers expected to sell probably 200,000 head, but the Chicago market dropped even further—$3.70 per hundredweight and going down. It was better, some thought, to hold their cattle through the winter and hope for a change in 1887. Already overcrowded ranges became all the more choked with cattle—upwards of a million head.

"Beef is low, very low, and prices are tending downward," warned the *Rocky Mountain Husbandman* in September. "But for all that, it would be better to sell at a low figure, than to endanger the whole herd by having the range overstocked."

Cattlemen knew what was happening. They could see their overgrazed ranges. They knew even a moderate winter would prove hard. In an attempt to forestall disaster, they looked outside traditional ranges. Some 250,000 Montana cattle, primarily from Dawson and Custer counties, were moved northward to less crowded ranges in Alberta. Other ranchers cut out weaker cattle, cows and calves, bunched them into herds of 100 to 500 and drove them west. In the sheltered valleys of the Madison, Missouri and Deer Lodge they boarded these small herds with farmers who had feed to spare. Still other owners simply drove their stock onto the forbidden ranges of Indian reservations. All these were attempts to avoid disaster, but disaster was on its way. Sweeping out of the north, the winter of 1886-1887 began.

Wild game on the plains moved early to the sheltered Missouri River badlands that fall. Many animals drifted much farther south and west than usual. Birds that usually wintered in Montana disappeared south. Granville Stuart noticed that DHS horses and cattle seemed to have thicker,

Charles M. Russell sketched out the condition of Louis Kaufman's herd on a post card during the hard winter of 1886-1887.—*Montana Stockgrowers Association*

heavier coats of hair.

Cold and snow seldom visit Montana to stay before December, but on November 16 the temperatures dropped. Skies turned steel gray. Winds picked up. Old-timers remembered the storm not for its snow, but for the sharp, cutting, blowing ice. Like glass it cut through clothing. Where it lay in drifts it crusted, ready to shear the flesh from horses and cattle who broke through.

Kissineyooway'o the Cree and Metis called it—"it blows cold." First the gentle push of wind, then the whine through the bushes and branches. Then came the roar of an icy demon, screaming and overpowering all before it. White owls of the Arctic appeared. Cattlemen had never seen them before.

In a week the storm was over. Montanans looked for the relief of chinook winds—snow eaters—but it was too early. Temperatures moderated. Some snow disappeared, but not all. Across the white range an icy crust spread, covering dwindling forage. Two more blizzards came in December. In January there was even more intense cold, and more snow.

On the ninth of January it started snowing again. For sixteen hours it continued at the rate of an inch an hour. Temperatures fell to -20°F and held. As the storm started, the *Yellowstone Journal and Live Stock Reporter* expressed the concern of stockmen across the range. "WANTED" the small ad read: "WANTED—A rip-roaring, snow-eating, polar-paralyzing chinook. . . . Must have it!"

When the storm passed everyone looked west for warm winds. They did not come. Snow continued off and on. Temperatures dropped to -40°F and stayed, day in and day out. Then the big storm struck.

It began on January 28. For three days and three nights it blew, and snowed, and blew like no one could remember. The storm paused for a day, then continued until February 3. It raged from Canada to Wisconsin and Iowa. Thermometers dropped to -63°F. Ranchers could not see from the bunkhouse to the barn. Remaining cattle wandered into coulees, against hedgerows or fences, and died. Trapped in drifts up to their bellies some froze standing up; then drifted over.

No one asked cowboys to do anything special. Their job was to look after the cattle for a dollar a day. Weather made little difference. They dressed as well as they could. Bundled up in an extra pair of long underwear, two pairs of wool socks, two wool shirts, a couple pair of pants, overalls, and leather chaps, they readied themselves. Then they added a pair of wool gloves inside fleece mittens; a blanket-lined coat and a fur cap. Finally, before putting on their socks, cowboys rubbed their feet with snow, then dried them. If they wore boots, they stood in water then went outside so an airtight sheath of ice would form on the boots and insulate them. Some wore overshoes or sheepskin "packs."

Around their eyes cowboys rubbed lampblack or burnt matches to keep them from going snowblind. They cut eyeholes in black neckerchiefs and wrapped them across their faces. They headed out to try to drive whatever animals were left into sheltered areas; to pull cattle from the drifts. The wind, the ice, and the cold cut through their clothing. Many of them died like the cattle they tried to save. Their buddies tied the stiff bodies to their horses and took them back to the ranch, where they placed the bodies in snowdrifts to await the thaw when the ground could be broken for graves.

Storms and cold continued through February. From the first through the twelfth of the month the temperature in Glendive *averaged* –27°F. Driven before the winds, cattle roamed starving, staggering into towns, looking for food. Some died on the city streets. Five thousand invaded the infant town of Great Falls, eating garbage and young saplings the city had planted the previous year.

When the foreman for the Kaufman and Stadler cattle company had to tell his Helena bosses how the herd was doing in the Judith Basin, he turned to a young cowhand named Charlie Russell for a reply. The Missouri-born cowboy sketched a picture of a starving steer, ribs showing, coyotes in the background waiting for it to drop. "Last of Five Thousand" Russell captioned the post card. It told the story for Kaufman and Stadler and all Montana's cattlemen.

The chinook did not come until March. Joseph Scott, president of the Montana Livestock Association observed that if the warm weather had come twenty days later, there would be nothing left of the cattle industry in the territory. As it was, not much survived. Conrad Kohrs lost fifty percent of his herds. Granville Stuart counted seventy-two percent of the DHS cattle dead. Nelson Story tallied up seventy-five percent losses. Perhaps the hardest hit were the "E6" and "Turkey Track" ranches. Owners counted 27,000 head on their range at the fall round-up. By spring, only 250 were left. More than ninety-nine percent of their cattle had perished. Theodore Roosevelt, running cattle near the Montana-Dakota border, took one look at his starving herd and left the cattle business altogether. Total losses hit about $20,000,000—maybe more.

Speculators who had flooded the range with cattle hoping for easy profits found their herds and investments wiped out. English, Scottish and French companies went bankrupt. Texas, Iowa and New England firms did the same. In 1886 there were 220 separate cattle operations in Montana. The next year, only 120 survived. When absentee owners ordered the sale of their remaining cattle, the market dropped even below the dismal prices of 1886. During the summer of 1887 prices fell to $3.20 per hundredweight; by October they reached a record low of $2.50. Twenty-five dollars for a thousand-pound steer—if you had one. It was not much.

The Montana Stockgrowers Association held their annual meeting in Miles City during 1887. Recording secretary Russell B. Harrison documented the trials the industry had endured the previous year:

1st, The unprecedented drought that prevailed last Spring and Summer, causing a great shortness of food, making the cattle poor in flesh. . . .

2nd, The low price of beef that ruled in Chicago during the fall, shrinking our receipts materially. . . .

3rd, The very severe winter which has just passed, which brought general loss, more or less severe, depending upon circumstances, to every member. . . .

Warm winds that brought an end to the winter of 1886-1887 brought new grass to the range, mild optimism to those who had survived and change to the cattle industry. In smaller herds, with more winter feed and better shelter, cattlemen started again. They restocked and renewed the industry. "We are not here to bury our industry," Joseph Scott said before the stock growers in Miles City, "but to revive it." Optimistic? Yes! But the optimism proved justified.

At the Grant-Kohrs Ranch

Johnny Grant built a cabin in the Deer Lodge Valley. Conrad Kohrs ran cattle in four states and two Canadian provinces. What is today the Grant-Kohrs Ranch was once the largest and best-known operation in Montana. Begun in the 1850s, the home ranch is now a National Historic Site near Deer Lodge.

The ranch's story began in the middle 1850s. A Canadian trapper, hunter and mountaineer named Johnny Grant decided to settle in the Deer Lodge Valley. With his Bannock wife, Quarra, he set up a small ranch and built a cabin. Over the years his family became large and so did his operation. From a few head of cattle and oxen, Johnny Grant soon developed a herd of more than three thousand.

Each spring and summer he drove some of the animals to Fort Hall. There he traded these well-fed animals for travel-weary stock from Oregon Trail emigrants. He offered them one good animal for two weak ones. With the end of the travelling seasons, Grant drove the new animals back to the Deer Lodge Valley and began to fatten them on nutritious grasses. Johnny Grant was the first Montana cattleman of any note and the first truly open-range rancher in the area.

Prosperity made possible a new home for Johnny and Quarra Grant and their large family. In 1862 he hired Alexander Pambrun and "McLeod the hewer" to cut, haul and hew timber for his house. Built of logs and covered with clapboard, the house was the largest in Montana in 1865 when Thomas Dimsdale described it in Virginia City's *Montana Post:* "The dwelling house, which is large and two storied, is by long odds the finest in Montana. It appears as if it had been lifted by the chimneys from the bank of the St. Lawrence, and dropped down in Deer Lodge Valley."

Johnny Grant decided to leave Montana in 1866. Quarra died and he thought it best to take the children back to his native Canada. For $19,200 Grant sold the "farmhouses with household furniture, stables, corrals, ricks of hay, all my farming implements, wagons, yokes and chains, also my cattle, sheep, goats, and grain" to a tall, blond, thirty-one-year-old Danish butcher named Conrad Kohrs. This formed the nucleus of what became Kohrs 30,000-acre home ranch.

Kohrs was partners with his half brother, John N. Bielenberg, under the name Kohrs and Bielenberg Land and Livestock Company. Bielenberg handled the day-to-day operation of the ranch. He never married and soon earned a reputation not only as a bachelor, but also for his honesty and his sense of humor. "Anything you can't do on a horse isn't worth doing," he once observed. Kohrs mastered the financial end of the operation: marketing, banking and obtaining credit.

Conrad Kohrs also brought a woman to the ranch—much to John Bielenberg's disgust, at first. In 1868, Kohrs went east. He courted and married a girl he had known in Europe. That spring he brought his nineteen-year-old bride, Augusta, to Montana on a Missouri River steamboat. At first she was lonely so far from home, but she quickly adapted to life in Montana. She began fixing up the Grant house Kohrs had purchased. She added St. Louis, Chicago and European furniture. Inside and out, it became a showplace, "having seven finely furnished rooms on the first floor, besides a magnificently furnished parlor and a spacious dining room."

Less than a year after Augusta Kohrs first saw the Deer Lodge Valley, Kohrs' cattle herds began to overcrowd the area. As a result, Conrad Kohrs became one of the first Montana cattlemen to move east of the mountains, establishing a separate herd along the Sun River. Soon, cattle with a "C" brand on the left shoulder and a "K" on the left thigh could be seen east and west of the divide.

To market their cattle, Kohrs and Bielenberg established a network of butcher shops in Montana's mining camps. When mining went into a depression between 1869 and 1879, it became necessary to find other outlets.

Kohrs began driving his cattle to market as early as 1870. The route headed south through Idaho, then east along the old Oregon Trail toward Cheyenne where the Union Pacific carried his cattle to eastern markets. By 1881, the Utah and Northern Railroad had entered Montana. Kohrs could now use the U. & N. to market cattle.

Kohrs drove only three- to four-year-old steers to market. Herd size ranged from 1,000 to 3,000 head. An outfit consisted of a herd boss—Tom Hooban and Michel Oxarart were trusted favorites—seven to nine cowboys, a cook, and a horse wrangler. A mess wagon, a bed wagon, and a cavvy of 90 to 100 saddle horses accompanied them. In all, the 1,500-mile drive took about five months.

To expand and strengthen their herds, Kohrs and Bielenberg brought some of the first Shorthorn and Hereford cattle into Montana. They bred them with local stock to improve quality and size. John Bielenberg was also interested in improving the quality of saddle horses. As early as 1873, he imported thoroughbred stallions, breeding them to native mares. These stronger horses became known throughout Montana and carried the "Dutch K" brand on the thigh.

As livestock operations grew, so did the size of the Kohrs' home ranch in the Deer Lodge Valley. The old cabin where Johnny Grant and his family first lived became a bunkhouse. Here cowboys gathered after the day's work to relax. The place smelled of sweaty men, tracked-in manure, tobacco from roll-your-own cigarettes or plugs for chewing. About the hot, crackling stove they would sit, whittle, swap stories and lies and just "take the slack out" after a hard day.

Near the main ranch house, Kohrs built a buggy shed and horse stable. In the shed might be found several vehicles, among them a Dougherty wagon (or ambulance) of Johnny Grant's that had come to Montana by riverboat. Kohrs bought it with the ranch and used it to transport Augusta to Deer Lodge for the first time. In 1877, this same wagon was rushed to the Big Hole Battlefield to help transport wounded soldiers to a Deer Lodge doctor.

A series of barns and stables soon appeared on the ranch. Stallion barns housed John Bielenberg's blooded thoroughbreds. These included the Leeds Lion Barn, named for a famous English Shire stallion brought in for stud. Cattle, oxen and draft horse barns also added to the number of buildings.

In the 1880s, Conrad Kohrs built two important buildings on the ranch. First came a barn for race horses. He took great pride in raising these as well as his draft and work horses. Racetrack Creek, south of Deer Lodge, was a place where he exhibited some of these fine animals.

For the pleasure of refreshing drinks and a relief from summer heat, the Kohrs ranch added an ice house. Here blocks of ice cut in winter could be saved, using sawdust for insulation. On the south side of the ice house, various Chinese cooks had their summer bedroom. In addition to cooking sourdough bread, beef and beans for family and hands, the Chinese added garden vegetables, bacon and eggs, pies or cakes and sweet fried biscuits called "bannocks."

In 1883 three important things happened to Kohrs and his family. Initially, the Montana Union Railroad was constructed from Butte to Garrison, right past the Kohrs' ranch. Conrad Kohrs encouraged its construction as a positive addition to the Deer Lodge Valley economy and a market for his cattle. That same year, Kohrs bought into the DHS Ranch for $400,000. It was a record price at the time. A.J. Davis (D), Samuel Hauser (H), and Granville Stuart (S) originally founded the company near Fort Maginnis and present-day Lewistown. Stuart stayed on with Kohrs, managing the operation. In time this became the Pioneer Cattle Company, Montana's largest. It was but one of Kohrs' many companies.

On August 20, 1883, Conrad, Augusta and their three children—Anne, Katherine and William—left Deer Lodge with friends for a tour of Yellowstone National Park. The group took several wagons and spent seven weeks in the region. In his autobiography, Conrad Kohrs described seeing the steam rising from various geysers and springs. "It looked more like a big factory town than a bit of nature's wonderland far from civilization's interests," he observed.

As the decade of the 1880s passed, Kohrs became increasingly involved in cattle operations throughout Montana. He took part in the formation of the Montana Stockgrowers Association in 1884. He also ran successfully for the legislature and worked during the 1885 session for laws that assisted cattlemen.

From changes at the Kohrs' ranch it became obvious that the nature of the industry was changing. Fixtures soon included grainaries, hay meadows and haystacks, as well as feeding areas where a portion of the herd could be wintered. Such action helped Bielenberg and Kohrs avoid some losses during the disastrous winter of 1886-1887. Travelling the range that season, Kohrs described streams frozen solid and cowboys chopping them up to melt for water.

When the snows melted and temperatures rose after that

Conrad Kohrs as he looked in 1874 at Virginia City. An immigrant and pioneer cattleman, Kohrs was one of the first to take herds into Central Montana.

winter, Kohrs' losses proved less severe than many other ranches. His DHS/Pioneer herd in the Judith Basin lost about sixty-five percent. Overall, he averaged fifty percent losses. Because of his reputation as an honest man, Kohrs was able to borrow $100,000 to rebuild his herds. Hearing that Kohrs intended to stay in the cattle business after that winter, one Montana banker remarked, "Con, you have more nerve than any man in Montana." Kohrs' judgment was good. During the rest of the 1880s and 1890s, he continued to ship large numbers of cattle. Usually the totals varied between eight and ten thousand per year. One fall he sent out 365 railroad cars full of steers.

Many Montanans believed in Conrad Kohrs and trusted his judgment. Partly because of that trust, he was elected a delegate to the 1889 Constitutional Convention. He arrived at the convention a few days late because he was on a cattle buying trip. He left the day it ended for yet another such trip. Despite his many other interests—including placer and hydraulic mining at Pioneer—he kept a finger on all ranch operations.

To modernize the main ranch house, Conrad and Augusta decided on a brick addition in 1890. Contractors used bricks made by prisoners at the State Penitentiary in Deer Lodge. After completion of the work, a furnace replaced individual stoves for heating. A coal shed behind the house eventually replaced large stacks of firewood. Running water inside made it possible to do away with the traditional outhouse in back. "The new addition," Kohrs said, "gave us all the conveniences of the city and lightened the burdens of the housekeeper perceptibly—no carrying of wood for six or seven stoves. . . ."

Increasingly, Conrad Kohrs left management of the ranch to John Bielenberg and his son-in-law, John M. Boardman. The years from 1900 to 1918 were probably the best of Kohrs' life. In terms of cattle sales, 1909 topped them all with gross receipts above $500,000. Thereafter, Conrad Kohrs described operations as "gradually winding up." By 1915 the Kohrs ranch was but a small remnant of its former size.

During the winter of 1899-1900, Conrad and Augusta decided to live in Helena. Augusta so enjoyed the stay that Conrad surprised her on their wedding anniversary by purchasing a home in the capital city. He returned to the ranch regularly during summers until his death in 1920. Augusta continued to live in Helena, but because of her love for the old home, she kept it furnished and spent part of July and August each year in the Deer Lodge Valley. In the 1930s, Conrad Kohrs' grandson, Conrad Kohrs Warren, took over management of what had once been the largest ranch in Montana—the home of the state's "Cattle King."

When Augusta Kohrs died in 1945, Conrad Warren and his wife Nell carefully preserved the ranch house, its furnishing and all the outbuildings. Today the National Park Service has assumed control of the property and 219 acres. It is a small portion of an operation that once controlled over one million acres. It is an important monument all the same. It is a monument to Johnny Grant, Conrad and Augusta Kohrs, John Bielenberg and the many men and women like them who made the Montana livestock industry what it is today.

Timeline

1805-06: Lewis and Clark explore Montana.

1810: Gardening and livestock raising begins near fur posts.

1841: Father deSmet starts farming in Bitterroot and Flathead Valleys; U.S. Preemption Act, 160 acres for homesteaders or "squatters."

1850: John Owen establishes a fort in Bitterroot Valley; settlers follow.

1850s: Johnny Grant settles in Deer Lodge Valley; raises cattle.

1858: Granville Stuart arrives in Montana.

1862: U.S. Homestead Act provides 160 acres of free land per head of family; Conrad Kohrs and James Fergus arrive in Montana.

1863-64: Gold rush starts in Montana; new markets develop for agriculture and livestock.

1864: Montana becomes a territory; William Orr drives cattle over Mullan Road to Beaverhead Valley in partnership with Philip Poindexter.

1865: Montana Legislature passes a law regulating marks and brands on livestock.

1866: Kohrs and John Bielenberg buy out Johnny Grant in Deer Lodge Valley; Nelson Story brings first Texas cattle into Montana for mining camps.

1867: Patrons of Husbandry (Grangers) founded in East; Fort Shaw established on Sun River; Jesuits bring in first commercial flock of sheep.

1869: Union Pacific-Central Pacific Railroad completed in Utah; Kohrs moves first cattle into the Sun River area.

1870: Sheep well-established in Beaverhead Valley.

1872: Henry Sieben expands sheep raising to central Montana.

1873: U.S. Timber Culture Act provides 160 acres if timber is grown on part; Grangers organized in Montana by Robert N. Sutherlin.

1874: Joseph Glidden patents barbed wire.

1875: Sutherlin starts the *Rocky Mountain Husbandman* in Diamond City.

1876: Sioux and Cheyenne Indians are removed from eastern Montana plains.

1877: U.S. Desert Land Act grants 320 acres of land if part is irrigated.

1878: U.S. Timber and Stone Act permits acquiring more land for rock and wood.

1879: Fort Assiniboine established along Milk River in northcentral Montana; *Yellowstone Journal and Live Stock Reporter* starts in Miles City.

1880: Fort Maginnis is built to encourage settlement in central Montana; DHS Ranch is established in Judith Basin with Granville Stuart as manager; James Fergus moves farming and ranching operations from Helena to Armells; Utah Northern and Northern Pacific railroads enter Montana.

1881: James S. Brisbin publishes *Beef Bonanza*.

1883: Northern Pacific Railroad completed across Montana; "Teddy Blue" Abbott comes to Montana with a Texas trail herd; Pierre Wibaux arrives in Montana with French backing for the cattle business.

1884: Montana Stockgrowers Association formed to help unify industry; central Montana Vigilantes operating.

1885: "Bottom" falls out of the cattle market; livestock left on range.

1886: First Brand Book published by the Montana Stockgrowers Association.

1886-87: Hard winter, overstocking and overgrazing ruin open range ranching.

1887: James J. Hill completes St. Paul, Minneapolis & Manitoba Railroad across Montana to Great Falls; over 50% of Montana livestock companies go out of business.

1893: Cattle on Montana ranges total 100,000 more than 1886-1887.

1894: Chicago, Burlington & Quincy Railroad completed to Billings.

1895: Large, open range round-ups continue in northeast Montana.

1902: Owen Wister publishes *The Virginian*, romanticizing the cowboy.

1906-07: Hard winter brings 12%-13% livestock losses.

Suggested Readings

E. C. Abbott and Helena H. Smith. *We Pointed Them North.* New York: Farrar and Rinehart, 1939.

Nannie Alderson and Helena H. Smith. *A Bride Goes West.* New York: Farrar and Rinehart, 1942.

Everett Dick. *Sod House Frontier.* New York: Appleton-Century, 1937.

Robert H. Fletcher. *Free Grass to Fences.* Helena: Montana Historical Society, 1960.

Ernest S. Osgood. *Day of the Cattleman.* Minneapolis: University of Minnesota Press, 1929.

Marie Sandoz. *Cattlemen from the Rio Grande to the Far Marias.* New York: Hastings House, 1958.

David A. Walter. "Horns, Hoofs, Horses: The Cattle Industry and Its Cowboys." *Visual History of Montana,* Unit 3. Helena: Montana Superintendent of Public Instruction, 1975-76.

David A. Walter. "Montana Homestead: Farming the Dreams and Droughts." *Visual History of Montana,* Unit 5. Helena: Montana Superintendent of Public Instruction, 1977-78.

Recess time at the Columbia Falls school. The school house was a sign of a growing, stable community.

Chapter VII
Social and Urban Development

Alki, Big Horn, Montreal, Silver Bow, Virginia City—the list went on to number twenty. It was 1865 and these were Montana's first incorporated cities. Many more existed. Every little valley, every placer diggings, every collection of prospect holes fancied itself a town. From the beginning of settlement, Montanans scattered across the face of the land, but they gathered together frequently in communities of varying sizes. People who did not live in a town or city looked to them for supplies, information and entertainment. "A night on the town" has been a tradition to Montana from the days of miners and cowboys to the present.

Town building took place primarily during two periods—the mining rush of 1863-1890, and the homestead era from about 1909 to 1919. A few places grew up before the mining boom. Fort Benton along the Missouri and John Owen's fort up the Bitterroot Valley began in 1850. Soon these adobe posts became the center for separate communities. All communities—Montana's included—started as supply points. Towns were established to supply mining activity. Gold, silver and copper mining gave birth to places like Bannack, Helena, Granite, Zortman, Libby, Butte and countless others. Coal mining centers included Red Lodge, Roundup, Timberline, Stockett and Colstrip, to name a few. When petroleum exploration came to the state in the early 1900s, a new series of supply towns boomed, like Cat Creek, Oilmont and Shelby.

Mining was not the only inspiration for forming a town. Miles City provides a good example of a town begun to service the needs of a fort—nearby Fort Keogh. Later it served ranching and agricultural interests. Central and eastern Montana are dotted with communities small and large that sprang up to supply livestock and farming needs: Rapelje, Mizpah and Opheim; Sidney, Scobey and Broadus, among them.

Lumbering in western Montana served the same function as agriculture. Hamilton, Clinton, Whitefish and Missoula owe at least part of their beginnings to the forest products industry that grew in the mountains surrounding them. Those same mountains also provided recreation. This, too, justified a town. Hunter's Hot Springs and White Sulphur Springs by their very names describe their origin. With more recent forms of relaxation, tourism and skiing became important. Out of these activities came West and East Glacier, West Yellowstone and one of Montana's newest communities—Big Sky.

It is inaccurate to say that each town had only one reason for being. Many depended on several sources of income. Libby residents worked as miners and lumbermen. Whitefish residents found jobs in lumbering, then tourism. Helena started as a mining camp, then became a financial and governmental center. Many towns that started for one specific reason, really became permanent communities because they served as supply points for larger and larger areas. Fifty-six of these places also became centers of government as county seats. Such a designation was more than an honor—it meant permanence and added jobs. As a result, many bitter rivalries developed between communities contesting the location of a county seat.

Railroad towns also deserve mention. Nationally, it was common for a railroad to come into a territory or region and establish towns of its own. Often companies did this so they could sell their own town lots, but many of these communities became important centers of supply. Everywhere there are railroads in Montana, there are towns that owe them their origin. Billings and Dillon are excellent examples because they received their names from former railroad presidents. Havre, Great Falls and Townsend also illustrate typical railroad-born communities.

Establishing a town was one thing. Maintaining it proved another problem. Communities built around exhaustible, non-renewable resources stood a good chance of dying, or shrinking in size when those resources vanished. Gold camps like Diamond City, Maiden or Kendall, Garnet and Bannack are ghost towns because the gold is gone. Places like Marysville, Virginia City and Zortman are mere skeletons of once vigorous boom towns. Similar compari-

Billings, Montana, in 1882 when it was a very young town platted next to the Northern Pacific mainline.

sons can be made for vanished coal towns like Timberline, Cokedale and Washoe. Coal is no longer as important in Roundup and Red Lodge as it once was.

Agricultural towns that flirted with prosperity during the homestead days faded when rains and markets vanished. Gilman, Menard, Mondak, Ismay and others demonstrate the fickle nature of agriculture.

For all the towns that did not make it, many others survived and flourished. Places that began as local supply points became distribution centers for larger areas. Fort Benton first demonstrated the potential prosperity of a supply town while riverboats operated from 1860 through 1890. When railroads came, other cities rose in importance. Billings and Great Falls—Montana's two biggest cities—serve large regions. To a lesser extent, the same can be said for Glasgow, Lewistown, Bozeman and Kalispell. Providing goods and services is like a renewable resource. People continue to want more and more; a town keeps on growing. Warehouses, offices, courthouses and businesses indicate a city's reason for being.

Lumber, agriculture and visitors—tourists or students—should also be included among renewable resources that keep a town alive. A lumbermill, a plywood plant, an agricultural implement dealer, a ski lift and a campus provide this or that town a continuing source of income to keep it alive.

True, mining camps and towns often sprang up like weeds, but getting organized was essential if the place was to last. What did a city need to operate? Virginia City's charter—granted in 1865—provides some indication. The place started out about a mile and a half square. Inside those bounds, government was by a city council with aldermen and a mayor. Anticipating the needs and problems of Virginia City residents, founders also provided for a judge, a marshal and an attorney. A clerk, an assessor and a treasurer were needed for paperwork, taxes and monies to operate. A street commissioner proved essential if people wanted to get from one place to another. Voters—U.S. citizens, white males, twenty-one years old and residents for at least ninety days—had the responsibility of choosing all these officials. Nonwhite males received the right to vote by the end of the 1860s. In many communities, women could not vote until 1914.

Once elected, city officials had thirty-eight separate responsibilities, according to the charter. These fell into three general categories. First came taxation and finances—raising the money necessary to operate. Next came the duty to look after public health. Finally, Virginia City's officers had to supervise the general well-being of the community. This included providing streets, water, lights and a fire department. Later, cities added electricity, telephones, natural gas and street cars to those services. Also included in the well-being category came regulation of merchants, saloons, dance halls and places of prostitution. The Virginia City charter gave the council superficial authority over the sale of many items from bread and butter to bricks. The message read clearly: citizens must not be cheated.

Many communities received charters from the legislature or became incorporated. Where city organization did not exist, county commissioners had the responsibility to provide almost identical services. Helena residents, for example, did not want to incorporate. Voters turned down such action several times before finally approving it in 1881. They preferred to let county commissioners oversee the town.

Preserving a town's finances, health and well-being might have sounded easy. In practice, it proved anything but. Towns were full of life and temptations. "Hell-roaring, wild," one miner called them. Who had time to worry about paved streets and sanitation? When rains and spring run-off came, dirt streets turned into muddy rivers. If the camp happened to be confined within a narrow creek valley, the results might be comical. During a particular spring, residents in Helena set up ferry service to get from one side of Main Street to another. They even got plans for a giant wood and steel bridge and threatened to erect it. Finally local officials agreed to improve drainage.

Alice Gans' bedroom showed the popular style of decorating in the 1880s and 1890s.

Sewer systems consisted of a pile in back of each house, or a stream channel through town. Garbage, dead animals and sewage built up. During warm days it became too much to bear. More than one editor remarked that the smell was so bad you could see and taste the air. Growth brought other problems, particularly in the mining city of Butte. As the number of smelters and open ore-roasters increased, so did air pollution. Even the slightest inversion kept smoke in the city. Chemical fumes joined those of open sewers. The situation became severe. Smoke was so thick residents could not see. Street cars had to clang their bells constantly to warn pedestrians of their presence. Lung disease skyrocketed, and Butte doctors estimated seventy-one percent of the city's deaths were related to breathing the air. In 1885, anti-pollution campaigns began. Finally the city government forcefully closed down all open copper roasting in 1891. Only when smelters moved elsewhere did the situation really improve.

Because of its size, Butte's problems seemed extreme. Every town with a smelter, each camp with its coal and wood smoke, each community with open sewers or a marginal water supply had problems, however. Helena, which prided itself in the 1880s as one of Montana's model cities, had bad drinking water. Purification was primitive. When worms began coming out of faucets in Helena homes, the city council reacted by declaring the water system a public nuisance. Eventually, the water company cleaned up the system and fresh water returned.

Towns also had the potential for swift and sudden disaster. Communities from Miles City to Missoula sprang up with buildings of log and wood. Brick or stone structures—called "fireproofs" for obvious reasons—came slowly. It is not surprising, then, that "the fire fiend" visited several Montana communities. Before Montana became a state, Billings, Miles City and Livingston experienced major fires. Blackfoot City had a blaze in 1869 that destroyed most of the camp and it was never rebuilt. Helena survived three disastrous blazes in the space of the five years between 1869 and 1874. After each, residents rebuilt, erecting a few more "fireproofs." Following the last blaze, January 9, 1874, the city built a fire tower and hired a watchman. Residents even convinced the Territorial Legislature to pass Montana's first fire law, taxing all Helena residents and property owners one dollar to help support a fire department.

No town was immune from fire, even as brick replaced wood in buildings. During the evening of January 15, 1895, Butte experienced the worst blaze in its history. Flame erupted in the warehouse district. Firemen and spectators rushed to the scene. Suddenly a series of explosions rocked the area. Blasting powder stored in the buildings had ignited. More than fifty people lost their lives.

Other demons and diseases crept about city streets. Gambling dens, saloons, dance halls and red light houses sprang up in a town usually before the first church or school. Most cities had laws regulating or forbidding them, but they did bring people to town. Those sinning miners, farmers and cowboys spent money in more legitimate businesses, so city officials often ignored the "tiger dens" and "hurdy gurdies" unless violence broke out.

Sheriffs, marshals, judges and courts existed from the day Montana became a territory. Punishment for serious crimes was hanging, but before jails become common, whipping or banishment was also used. Outside existing court systems, various vigilante groups operated. Thomas Dimsdale's *Vigilantes of Montana* recounted the major activities of 1863-1864, but there were others. Few communities of any size or duration lacked at least one vigilante hanging. Helena's famous Hanging Tree claimed thirteen victims before a minister cut it down. One of those to die was James Daniels, hanged with a pardon from the governor in his pocket. Such action outside the law continued into the present century.

Montanans realized very early that hanging, whipping and banishment could not be the only forms of punishment. Most towns built some type of jail. These served to hold local offenders, but there was nothing for territorial or federal criminals. To remedy this, Congress appropriated money for a Territorial Prison in 1867. Construction began in Deer Lodge in 1870, and by 1871, the fourteen-cell facility was complete. Here the U.S. Government housed federal prisoners, and the territory paid one dollar per day for any criminals the district courts sentenced. For a while, an Eastern State Prison operated in Billings, but it proved short-lived. Deer Lodge became the only prison in Montana.

With all their problems, cities and towns still had something to offer. Call it "society," or "culture," or "civilization," if you will. Life in a city took the edge off Montana's frontier. It helped tame the land and the pioneers themselves. Topping the list of "high class" places in a community were private clubs. For men only, they offered a place to play cards, have a drink and talk business. Establishments like the Miles City Club, the Silver Bow Club and Helena's Montana Club provided these outlets. Newspapers, churches and schools helped "civilize" towns, too.

Newspapers represented a contact with the outside world—with "the states" and what had been home. The first newspaper began not long after Montana itself. *The Montana Post* started publication August 27, 1864, in Virginia City. Before long the *Montana Radiator* in Helena joined the field. Then came others. Each town had to have a newspaper. They became signs of status and prosperity. From the Absarokee *Enterprise* to the Zortman *Little Rockies Miner*, they appeared. Weeklies, semi-weeklies, tri-weeklies, dailies—as the town grew the frequency of the paper usually increased. Their titles reflected more than the towns in which they were published. They reflected the interests and composition of Montana. For German speaking residents the *Die Montana Freie Presse* (Free Press) and the *Staats Zeitung* (City's News) existed. Butte's *Tribune-Review* carried regular news from Cornwall for that city's Cornish residents. Three black newspapers circulated between 1894 and 1911. Other titles told the story and the audience at the same time: *Mining Journal, Live Stock Reporter, Montana Catholic, Silver Advocate, Populist, Union-Freeman, Fruit Grower and Farmer*.

Early Montana editors became as well-known as their papers. Thomas Dimsdale from Virginia City, Robert E. Fisk of Helena, James H. Mills at Deer Lodge and Joseph Wright in Bozeman ran early papers. W. D. Wright, Miles City, and John H. Durston, who began the *Anaconda Standard*, joined the group. They all had views on each and every public issue. No frontier editor worth his salt would back away from a good fight—editorial or otherwise. For his editorial views Robert Fisk got a black eye on one occasion and was shot at on another. Like all his counterparts from across Montana, he did not hide his convictions.

The columns of these papers were spiced with candid

Thomas J. Dimsdale was the editor of Montana's first newspaper, *The Montana Post*, and author of the first book published in Montana, *The Vigilantes of Montana*.

comments about politics and fellow editors. One editor observed a particular legislative session in Virginia City where "liquid refreshment flowed across hotel bars as freely as the water over Alder Gulch." They might characterize greedy businessmen as "selfish croakers," and if a territorial official did not work out he might be called an "ignominious fizzle." An editor might dismiss an opponent as a "whiskey pickled gerkin," or a "jackanape" and expect the same to be said of him in return.

Undoubtedly, two of Montana's most interesting early editors were J. Allen Hosmer and Lee Travis. Hosmer began publication of a newspaper called the *Beaverhead News* in Bannack during August of 1866. He was only sixteen years old at the time. Using a hand press, he issued the journal regularly until October. At the same time he wrote, printed and bound one of Montana's first books—*A Trip to the States in 1865*. In 1869, Hosmer started another paper, the *Virginia City Republican*. Two years later he tried again with the *Virginia City Telegram*. Both had short lives. In 1872, Allen Hosmer moved with his family to California where he became a lawyer.

Even more remarkable was Lee Travis. He decided to enter the newspaper field despite his generally poor health. On July 12, 1875, the first issue of his *Weekly News Letter* appeared on Helena's streets. By September the title had changed to the *Montana Daily News* and Travis claimed the largest circulation of any daily paper in the territory. At the same time, he wrote regular articles for Bozeman's *Avant Courier*. He was only fourteen years old. In January of 1876, he sold the *News* but by March of 1880 he was back in business with the *Morning Capital*. Again, his health forced him to sell out in October of that year. On February 6, 1882, he died. Editors from across Montana remembered his sparkling, bright and newsy papers. They described Travis as active, ambitious and of excellent character. Both Hosmer and Travis lived up to the finest traditions of Montana journalism. They were young and daring. Their newspapers brought the rest of the nation and the world to Montana.

For honors as Montana's first book, J. Allen Hosmer's *A Trip to the States in 1865* contested with Thomas Dimsdale's *The Vigilantes of Montana, or Popular Justice in the Rocky Mountains*. Both appeared in 1866. Hosmer printed his own. Dimsdale's volume came from *Montana Post* presses under the direction of D. W. Tilton. Tilton also received the contract to print the first volumes of the legislative journals in 1866. The next year, the Democratic newspaper in Virginia City did legislative publishing. For the remainder of the territorial years and into statehood, public printing contracts depended on political influence.

By 1868, Robert Fisk and the *Helena Herald* had entered the book publishing field with a Helena city directory, entitled *Historical Sketch and Essay on the Resources of Montana; including a Business Directory of the Metropolis*. Fisk had his wife, Lizzie, do the binding.

Although Fisk's volume and the ones that followed had short histories of Montana, it was not until 1885 that the first true history of the territory appeared. Michael A. Leeson wrote and compiled a 1,367-page book entitled *History of Montana, 1739-1885*. This large book attempted to cover all white exploration and settlement in Montana. It also included biographies of many prominent residents.

Men of God figured early in Montana's history. They had a profound influence in settling the region. Adventuresome priests like Fathers Pierre-Jean deSmet, Anthony Ravalli, Gregory Mengarini, and Joseph Giorda established Catholic Missions before the major influx of white settlement. With the gold rush, other Catholic priests came. Soon their parishes could be found in even the smallest communities.

Protestant ministers arrived early, too, serving miners and their families. Methodists A. M. Hough and Hugh Duncan came in 1864 and 1865. They preached in cabins and in crude churches that had dirt floors, logs for benches and roofs that leaked rain and snow. In 1876, Reverend William W. Van Orsdel joined the Methodist effort. More commonly known as "Brother Van," he travelled the state, taking time to preach and lead hymns wherever a congregation assembled. Daniel S. Tuttle travelled to Montana in 1867 as a twenty-nine-year-old Episcopal bishop for the entire territory. Headquartered in Virginia City with his cat "Dick," Tuttle soon became accustomed to the rough-and-tumble mining camp life.

Other missionaries and ministers arrived: Presbyterians, Congregationists, Baptists and more. In Chinese communities at Helena, Butte and Blackfoot City, religious services also took place. Montana boasted a fine Jewish synagogue in Helena and there were others in Butte and Billings.

When pioneers talked about civilizing they usually meant churches and schools. Having a newspaper, a church and a school indicated permanence. Early education in Montana was private. Lucia Darling's school in her log cabin at Bannack in 1863 was the region's first. Thomas Dimsdale of

Virginia City also gave private lessons. When the first Montana legislature met in 1864-1865, among the laws passed was one providing for public schools.

According to this statute, everyone between ages four and twenty-one had to attend school. In truth, few over sixteen years of age did so. The legislature did not set the length of the school year. Some schools ran for as little as thirty days a year. Most averaged about eighty-two. Many parents did not want school to interfere with work their children did in town or on the farm. As a result, the school year was short, usually during the fall and spring months.

Sarah Raymond of Virginia City became one of Montana's first public school teachers. She came to the territory by covered wagon in 1865 and started teaching in March of the next year. Her first class included about fifty students. She described them as the "worst set of children I ever saw or heard tell of." After the first few days of teaching, she felt so tired she thought she had been working in the mines. When the school term ended in June, she quit teaching for good.

Also among pioneers in Montana education was a Helena lawyer named Cornelius Hedges. He became territorial superintendent of schools in 1872. He eventually served four terms in the office and is regarded as the father of Montana's school system. When he started, his annual salary was only $1,200 per year, plus $600 in expenses. His duties included travelling to all the school districts to inspect them. He found teachers made only $68 per month. Many had little or no training. Hedges worked to get better training for teachers, to improve log cabin schools and to end racial segregation wherever he found it.

Women took an early interest in territorial education. Through their efforts, the 1883 legislature gave women the right to vote and hold office as local trustees and county superintendents. The first woman elected to county office was Helen Piotopowaka Clarke of Helena. She worked for many years to improve education in Lewis and Clark County. After that she devoted much of her life working to better Indian education on reservations.

Copies of early school rules and regulations show how thorough the education was. In the eighth grade, for example, all students had to pass courses in reading, spelling, arithmetic, English, writing and United States history. In

Cornelius Hedges came from New England as a young man, settled in Helena, involved himself in civic activities and became Montana's first Superintendent of Education.

reading, each student had to be able to identify the works of more than a half-dozen American and English authors. For a passing grade, everyone needed to read 112 different books before the end of the year. These included several by Mark Twain, Charles Dickens and James Fenimore Cooper. There were other titles, too, like *Gow's Good Morals and Gentle Manners*.

Rules for students of all ages were strict. No one could return to school after missing a day or leave school during the lunch hour unless he or she had written permission from home. Anyone falling behind in schoolwork was set back a grade. Other rules followed.

1. Every pupil is expected to attend school punctually and regularly; to obey promptly and cheerfully all

the directions of the teacher.
2. Any scholar who shall be absent one week without giving notice to the teacher, shall lose all claim to his or her particular desk.
3. Each scholar shall have a particular desk, and shall keep the same and the floor beneath in a neat and orderly condition.

As public education expanded in Montana, so did private schools. Various churches established high schools and colleges to help further education. The Catholic Church founded St. Vincent's and St. Aloysius academies for girls and boys in Helena during the 1860s and 1870s. Later they established two colleges, Mount St. Charles (now Carroll College) in Helena, and the College of Great Falls. All the while Jesuits and Ursuline Sisters worked to further education on several Indian reservations. St. Labre School in the Northern Cheyenne Reservation and St. Francis Xavier (Crow) were among these efforts.

Presbyterian schools included the Bozeman Female Academy in 1873 and the College of Montana at Deer Lodge in 1883. Today Trask Hall in Deer Lodge is a monument to the College of Montana and a long-standing commitment for higher education.

Methodists founded the Montana University at Helena in 1889. It operated at various locations in the area until 1923, when Methodists combined with the Presbyterians to form Intermountain Union College. Eventually this school united with Billings Polytechnic Institute to become Rocky Mountain College.

Other private schools came and went in Montana. Classical schools were common; so were commercial or business colleges. Much of the effort for higher education focused on state-supported schools. These came into being in 1893. That year the legislature established an agricultural college and experiment station at Bozeman, a school of mines "at or near Butte," a normal (teacher training) school at Dillon, and a university in Missoula.

The year 1893 proved busy for the legislature when it came to founding other state institutions as well. That same session the legislature established the Orphans' Home at Twin Bridges, the State Deaf and Dumb School at Boulder, and the State Reform School in Miles City. With the growth

Helen P. Clarke, daughter of pioneer Malcolm Clarke, was elected Lewis and Clark County Superintendent of Schools in 1882.

of Montana, other schools were needed. Northern Montana College at Havre, founded in 1913, was finally funded and began operation in 1929. In 1927, a second teacher training school began in Billings—Eastern Montana College. Succeeding legislatures changed the function of the Boulder River School and moved the facility for the deaf and dumb to Great Falls. The names of each institution changed from time to time as well. To these 1893 beginnings, Montana's major public facilities owe their origins.

What was a city? What was "culture" in nineteenth century Montana? Newspapers, churches, schools and private clubs played a part, to be sure. Yet life in a Montana city held more. The best way to see what a city had to offer is to look at one in particular.

Butte was Montana's largest community in the 1890s. Over 42,500 people crowded the hills and gulches around Butte in the decade after Montana became a state. To brag about all the city had to offer, the local Board of Trade (an early Chamber of Commerce) pointed to many things. Six bands, four opera houses, five artists and twenty restaurants existed to serve residents and visitors. The Public Library and Free Reading Room, with its 1,000 volumes, operated from the second floor of the Court House. To know what was going on residents read the Republican *Inter Mountain*, the *Tribune*, the *Times*, or the Democratic *Butte Miner*. A weekly labor paper existed entitled the *Butte Bystander*. Germans read their own paper, the *Montana Journal*. For other interests there were the "sensational" *Sunday Mercury*, the *Home Industry*, the *Advocate*, the *Mining World*, and the *Mining and Railway Review*.

If the need arose while in Butte, twenty-six doctors were available, including Charlie Can and Gee Young for Chinese patients. Four hospitals provided more intensive care. If all doctoring failed, there were six undertakers. Out of town a short distance were Catholic, Protestant, Chinese and Jewish cemeteries.

During the week, Butte's children received instruction in nine public elementary schools, one public high school, and one Catholic school. On Sundays families chose from twelve places of worship, including a Jewish synagogue, a German Lutheran church and an African Methodist Episcopal church. A workingman might belong to any of seven labor unions in Butte. These included the 3,000-member Miners Union, several railway brotherhoods and the Knights of Labor. For entertainment, thirty fraternal organizations and twenty social clubs operated. Masons, Hibernians, Good Templars and Foresters held regular meetings; so did the Crickett Club, the German, Italian and Scandinavian societies. Four National Guard units also headquartered in Butte.

Harry N. Hanson got a new suit and a new bicycle in 1896.—*A. J. Dusseau photograph, M.H.S.*

And, of course, there were saloons in the Mining City—156 of them.

To get about town the Butte Street Railway Company provided trolley service. A cable car line ran to Walkerville. To get out of town people took either of two stage coaches, or any of four railroads. Messages went via the post office, Rocky Mountain Bell Telephone or any one of three telegraph lines. Hoping the entire community would not go up in smoke were four fire departments and sixty-one separate fire insurance companies.

That was Butte. That was business, society, politics and culture in Montana magnified or miniaturized in every city, town or camp.

Inter-Collegiate Debate!
STATE University
vs.
Montana WESLEYAN

Auditorium, Thursday, Dec. 28
7:30 P. M.

COME AND HEAR THE

BOER
QUESTION DISCUSSED

The State Team Will Defend the Boers
The Wesleyans will Support the British
The Supreme Bench will Act as Judges.

Reserved Seats 50c.   General Admission 25c.
TICKETS ON SALE AT O'CONNOR'S DRUG STORE.

Poster advertising a public debate in 1898.

Montana's People Came from Someplace Else

Montanans came from someplace else. They came along the Old North Trail or across the high plains. They followed routes blazed by Bozeman and Mullan; they pushed north from Corinne. Assiniboine, Blackfeet, Cheyenne and Crow arrived centuries ago. Missouri and Canadian trappers probed the land only a few decades after United States independence. French and Italian priests followed. After them came a hodgepodge of midwestern miners, New England lawyers, ex-slaves, Orientals, Scandinavian farmers, Texas cowboys and others.

White settlement came in waves. First was the trickle of trappers and missionaries before 1864. Then gold opened a floodgate of miners and hangers-on. This group came primarily from the Mississippi River Valley, the South and Colorado. They looked to Montana not for permanence, but for quick wealth from its gulches and hillsides.

By 1880 and 1890 the third wave of settlement swept the region. Railroads brought pioneers intent on staying: merchants, lumbermen, farmers, smeltermen, workers with families. Between 1900 and 1920 yet another group advanced on Montana. Dry-land farmers came determined to make a go of homesteading on the plains.

After 1920 the last influx took place. Oil men, gas men, roustabouts and boomers came. Some found the quick wealth they sought; others left dreams and fortunes in dry holes across the land. To the fertile valleys during the same decade came Mexican emigrants. The sugar beet industry began to grow in Montana, and farmers saw in the Chicano a source of labor for the fields.

Who were Montanans? They were new faces, new languages and new settlers on the land. Nicknames slurred their origins—Cousin Jack, Frenchy, Black Mary, Portuguese Joe, Cajun Charley, Yankee Bob, Chinese Mary. That was a Montanan—someone from someplace else.

In 1865, Virginia City residents authorized Francis Thompson to serve as immigration agent for Montana. He travelled to New York and worked diligently to convince easterners that their fortune and future lay in Montana. Governor James Ashley heard of Germans and Scandinavians settling in Minnesota in 1869. He thought Montana should have a share. He employed an agent in New York to write and publish promotional material for distribution overseas. Soon the settlers began to arrive.

Bertha Anderson remembered the trip across the Atlantic from Denmark. It was a voyage all too typical for foreign emigrants. The five members of her family travelled steerage because they could afford nothing else. Their quarters constituted a solitary bunk in the hold of a ship. One hundred and fifty people crowded the single compartment. During the entire trip they did not undress. It was impossible to be alone. If the person in the bunk above became seasick, he vomited past the lower bunk onto the floor. Twice a day a sailor came down to try to clean the area. Water and food were stale at best. Lice and bugs infested clothes. After processing at New York and a long trip by "Emigrant Car" to Sidney, the Andersons made a home in Montana.

Fred and Lambert Naegele left Germany to settle in Helena. Their stationery store and print shop at 16-18 Warren Street became a focal point for other German settlers in the area. Soon the shop became the offices of the *Montana Staats Zeitung*, printed in German and published three times a week. For entertainment, Helena's German community formed the Harmonia Society. They built their own meeting hall at 110 Broadway. There, plays, recitals and entertainment became regular features. Brewer Nick Kessler, banker Theodore Kleinschmidt, jeweler John Steinmetz, grocer Fred Kuphal, clothiers Bernhard and Jacob Loeb and many others joined the Naegeles in Helena. They read the *Staats Zeitung*, served as officers in the Harmonia Society and became leaders in the Montana business community.

Europeans of various nationalities soon congregated in Montana's growing communities. West of Missoula, Frenchtown took its name from natives of that country. Long after original settlers passed from the scene, such traditional celebrations as St. John's Day (December 27) continued to exist. East of the Garden City, lumbermen from Finland congregated in the early 1890s. What is today Milltown was once known locally as Finntown for its ethnic concentration.

In the Gallatin Valley, the town of Amsterdam testified to the Dutch emigrants who first settled the area in 1893.

After years of struggling, their community flourished and they built a church. Old country traditions remain to the present. Hi-Line stations on the old Great Northern reflect the European bent of early railroad officials. Railroad agents sought homesteaders from these areas: Havre, Zurich, Lothair, Kremlin and Inverness.

Lewistown reflected a unique influx of two groups. In the 1880s, *metis* (French-Indian mixed bloods) drifted south out of Canada to escape retaliation. A rebellion against the Canadian government led by Louis Riel had failed. His followers now sought a new place to settle. To the valleys and hills of central Montana they came and here their descendants stayed.

Around the turn of the century Croatian craftsmen also began to settle the area. First one or two came, then friends, neighbors and acquaintances. By 1902 these skilled stonemasons were quarrying rock from the nearby hills, preparing lime in their own kilns and erecting impressive buildings. These structures reflected personal pride and urban permanence.

Croatians, Serbs, Ukrainians, Yugoslavs, Italians, plus other southern or eastern Europeans settled in many mining camps. Among them, Butte and Red Lodge enjoyed the greatest numbers and diversity. Ethnic celebrations livened the community year with festivals like the pre-Lenten "mesopost" or "leave out meat." A combination of private and public celebration laid to rest the sins of the past year. A dummy, "Slarko Veljacic," representing the bad luck, misfortunes and evils of the past year was tried. First there were mock efforts from a prosecuting attorney and a defense counsel. Then came a verdict from the audience jury— "Guilty." The dummy was condemned to death. First dancers stabbed the effigy. Next, participants dragged it through the streets and finally they burned it. Dancing, drinking and songs continued until the early morning hours.

Unique as a celebration of Montana's varied ethnic heritage is the annual Festival of Nations in Red Lodge. The week-long event features all the color and flavor of the many European settlers in the region. Dancing, songs and delicious foods are available. Here resident and visitor may taste Italian Risotto ala milanesa, Yugoslavian sarma and povitica, Finnish Teekakkuja, schnitzels and sauerbraten from Germany, English dumplings and Irish stew. Various native costumes and crafts also occupy a part of the festival, adding their splash of color and history.

Montana's heritage also includes the Oriental tradition. After the many placer diggings had been worked by white miners, Chinese came to glean the last grains of gold from the sand. (Missoula's Cedar Creek diggings had an Oriental population as early as 1865.) When A. K. McClure visited Montana in 1869, he reported 300 Chinese in Virginia City, and "twice as many in Helena." Blackfoot City residents also reported a sizable population of Chinese miners.

Never permitted to settle in white parts of town, Orientals soon erected Chinatowns on the outskirts. Butte and Helena had the largest Chinese populations, totaling over 3,000 by 1890. They usually congregated in urban areas, seldom settling in rural Montana.

Butte's Chinese population began to grow in 1876, when the first Oriental cabin went up on Main Street, just below Galena. As placer riches in Bannack and Virginia City faded Chinese miners moved to Butte. In addition to becoming miners, many became woodchoppers. Traditionally, this trade had fallen to the French-Canadians in the area, and during the early 1880s several flare-ups occurred between the two groups. Gradually Chinese abandoned woodchopping and took up truck gardens. Others went into the laundry and restaurant business. Some opened gambling houses.

The first Chinese temple in Butte went up in 1886, and by 1910 residents had erected a larger, two-story structure. Gradually shacks and shanties disappeared. Substantial, multi-storied brick and stone stores, restaurants and laundries took their place. As growing Butte crowded the Oriental section, Chinatown shrank to Galena and Mercury streets, between Main and Colorado.

Life in Chinatown was colorful to behold. Inhabitants of the section moved to and fro, their hair braided in queues. They wore loose-cut trousers, tight blouses of silk or cotton, and either broadbrimmed hats or the more traditional silk skull caps. On the shelves and in the store counters were an endless variety of exotic spices, herbs and teas. From the restaurants and gambling dens came the sounds of Oriental music.

Funerals attracted particular attention. Most Chinese

came to the United States intending to stay only until they made their fortune. True, many stayed the remainder of their lives and raised families, but it was common to retain Chinese citizenship and plan an eventual return. When death occurred outside China, festivities were as elaborate as friends and funds could make them. Decorated carriages and a bedecked casket made up the procession. Fireworks popped and exploded to ward off evil spirits. At the grave-side, a final meal was prepared and left; so the departed soul would have something to eat on the long journey ahead. After original burial, relatives often had bodies disinterred, packed in wooden kegs or metal boxes, and shipped to a final resting place in China.

Chinese populations gradually dwindled in Montana. Many white residents felt hostility toward Oriental workers in their communities. Particularly during times of high unemployment, a feeling existed that Chinese kept wages down and took jobs from white workers. At several times during the 1880s and 1890s, boycotts of Chinese businesses and workmen spread through Butte and Helena. Nationally anti-Chinese feelings intensified between 1900 and 1910. Many young Chinese realized business and social opportunities did not exist in Montana. They moved elsewhere. By the middle of the twentieth century, fewer than one hundred Chinese remained in Montana, most of them native-born.

Blacks made up another group that clustered in Montana's urban centers during the late nineteenth and early twentieth centuries, only to disappear in later years. From the first years of territorial government, a question existed on whether "colored" residents should vote. Some Republican editors, like Robert Fisk, spoke for equal rights. Less radical Republicans and many Democrats disagreed. Often public sentiment prevented qualified black voters from going to the polls.

Still their numbers increased. They came primarily from the Midwest and the South, and began to concentrate in Butte and Helena. Often the jobs they secured were menial: shoe shine parlors, servants, cooks, waiters, musicians. Few opportunities for other employment existed. Business directories list printers, druggists and physicians who were black. William Irvin served on the Helena police force for a number of years in the 1890s.

Unlike the Chinese, blacks generally integrated into community housing. In any particular middle-class neighborhood it was not uncommon to find the residence of a black and a white family side by side. Only in areas of education did segregation exist. Territorial school law required separate schooling for "children of African descent." Deer Lodge public schools enforced the law in 1873, removing a single black child from their schools. Then Superintendent of Schools Cornelius Hedges opposed both the Deer Lodge action and the law. Hedges, Robert Fisk of the *Helena Herald* and Territorial Governor Benjamin Franklin Potts worked to have the law changed. By 1882 school districts throughout the territory generally ignored the law. In 1883 the legislature changed it. "No child shall be refused admission to public schools because of race or color," the new statute read.

Like the Montana German community, Blacks in the state had a series of three newspapers between 1894 and 1911. J. P. Ball, Jr., began the *Colored Citizen* in 1894, "devoted to the social, moral and industrial interests" of Montana blacks. The paper lasted only a few short months and spoke primarily about Helena's campaign to become permanent state capital.

A second short-lived newspaper began publication in Butte on May 30, 1902. The *New Age* billed itself as the "leading race journal" of the Northwest. It wanted to be a medium to "bring the colored people of the state closer together." Like the *Colored Citizen*, however, it did not last a year.

When J. B. Bass began *The Montana Plaindealer* in 1906, he set out to found a more permanent publication. True to his word, he made this Helena paper last five years. Bass spoke out continually against laws and policies that hurt the black community. Chief among the issues Bass attacked was a 1909 miscegenation law, prohibiting intermarriage between whites and blacks or Orientals. Despite the *Plaindealer*'s protests, the measure became law. "God help us!" Bass exclaimed in an editorial the next week. The law remained on the books in Montana until 1953.

The Montana Plaindealer experienced financial difficulties in 1910 and ceased publication in 1911. Although the numbers of blacks in Montana remained about the same from decade to decade, they became an increasingly smaller percentage of the population. By the 1930s, many young blacks had left Montana for better opportunities in bigger cities.

The varied ethnic backgrounds in the makeup of Montana's population reveals the fact that residents "came from someplace else." There is a colorful foreign heritage of English, Irish, Scandinavians, Germans, Italians, Yugoslavs and Chinese. These people mixed with other emigrants from New England, Missouri, Mississippi, Colorado, Minnesota and California. Together, Montanans can take their cue from the Red Lodge celebration and truly enjoy a "Festival of Nations."

Lizzie

"My Dear Mother," began the letters. Elizabeth Chester Fisk wrote home to Connecticut almost every week. She came to Helena as a bride in 1867. Her husband, Robert, edited the *Helena Herald* that he had begun in 1866. He had returned to New England and married his Yankee school teacher sweetheart. Lizzie and Robert then came to Montana by riverboat up the Missouri. They settled in Helena and for the next twenty-five years called it home, raising six children. Regularly Lizzie wrote to tell her mother what life was like on the frontier.

"My Dear Mother" she would begin each time, and then continue with personal reflections on the nature and growth of Helena. "My first impressions of Helena have been generally confirmed," she observed soon after her arrival. "I like the place much; it is not like home, but there is a wide field for usefullness [sic] here, and entering upon the work earnestly and prayerfully one need never be lonely or disheartened."

Friends gave them a warm welcome and before long Lizzie said Helena felt homelike—almost. Helena was a town with no grass, no trees, no flowers, only dust and stone in the streets and yards. "Nothing grows here without irrigation" she said that first summer. Yet she planted a garden. Ditches along the major streets provided water for home use and gardening. When her mother sent flower and vegetable seeds, Lizzie worked to make her plans come true. As time and money permitted, Robert and Lizzie planted trees and shrubs. Faithfully she lugged buckets of water from the ditches to each plant, insuring its survival.

In 1869 Lizzie returned to Connecticut during the spring and summer to have her first child—"baby Grace." After a six-month absence she returned to Helena and noted a more urban atmosphere. In outward appearance Helena was wonderfully improved. The new stone and brick fireproofs were much more imposing structures than the hastily erected wooden shanties. Ladies appeared more stylish and dressy than when Lizzie left. They wore velvet cloaks and hats, handsome furs and elegant dresses. They tried to imitate eastern fashions.

Wife of Robert E. Fisk, Elizabeth Fisk, was anything but a passive observer of life in Helena in the 1860s and 1870s.

"Yes, Helena has wonderfully improved. I realized it when first I caught a view of the city ablaze with light on the evening of our return, and each day suggests some new comfort and pleasure from its altered appearance. Yet it seems to be all show. I have an undefined impression that we are resting on the brink of a precipice. It seems that some terrible calamity is impending."

She guessed right. In 1872 and again in 1874, fire destroyed much of Helena's business district. A letter on January 11, 1874, described the horror of the last blaze. "The fire alarm wakened us at about six o'clock on that morning. The wind had been blowing fearfully all night, and many times I had wakened and listened and thought what a terrible time for a fire! And when at last the bells began ringing the sound became interwoven with my dreams and I did not at once realize that what I dreaded had come to pass."

Hastily she dressed and ran outside to watch cinders falling all about the house. She filled all the tubs and containers in the house with water. Should a spark land on the roof it would be necessary to climb a ladder and douse it before the entire place caught fire. This done, Lizzie hurried downtown to check the progress of the blaze. Chinatown—where the fire started—had been destroyed. Guests at the International Hotel had just managed to escape with their lives before that building went up in smoke.

On her return, Lizzie passed the volunteer firemen at the hand-pump engine. The men seemed almost exhausted. They'd had no breakfast and could get nothing to drink. She quickly organized neighborhood women who boiled coffee and made sandwiches. "How gratefully the poor fellows received it."

Fire spared the Fisk home, but destroyed over $1,000,000 in property throughout the city. She wondered if the town would rebuild. Before she finished her letter, however, Helena residents had begun the process of clearing away debris and erecting new homes or businesses. Montanans were the same earnest people, not easily disheartened, whom Lizzie had observed a few years before.

The dynamic editor of the *Helena Herald*, Robert E. Fisk, came west with his brothers as pioneers of the northern overland route from Minnesota in the 1860s.

Montanans had another side. When Joseph Wilson and Arthur L. Compton shot and robbed a local rancher in 1870, vigilantes assembled. This mob removed the men from jail and hanged them from the old "hanging" tree in Dry Gulch. Again Lizzie recorded her impressions.

"We watched the crowd about the courthouse and jail," she said, "rushing and surging to and fro. Although they were as near as only three blocks up the street, yet not a sound could we hear. The silence was terrible, the hush of so vast a throng, moved as with one heart and speaking as with one voice that the men were guilty, and should be hanged at four o'clock on the old pine tree.

"To add to the gloom and horror it was a dark, drizzly day with frequent peals of thunder, a day such as we seldom experience here. For two hours before the executions took place the hills around and opposite the tree were thronged with people. Women and children were there and nearly every man in town. It was a relief to know the worst was over, when the misery of the poor wretches was at an end."

Life had its lighter moments. Grace's fifth birthday party provided an opportunity for twelve of her little friends to help celebrate. Refreshments included biscuits and butter, cold roast beef, preserved pears, a mold of jelly, candy and two large decorated cakes, one frosted in gold, the other in silver. Her gifts included a new white dress, a jump rope and a ball.

Raising children was anything but easy. "If one could only keep Grace away from the many disagreeable, ugly children who infest this part of town, she should be a very nice little girl," her mother remarked. They had no public schools in Helena from March through November, and nearly all the children in town were turned loose to "run wild."

Many years later, Lizzie was to reflect on the difficulties of raising all six children. "I wish," she said, "any woman who imagines it easier to bring up a family in the west than in the east might have her lot cast in Helena for a time. I suppose this is no worse than other western cities. We have today in Helena licensed gambling houses to say nothing of the saloons open all the time. The Coliseum is a low theater, I hardly know how to describe it where girls serve the drinks in booths and lure men in, and tonight to crown all we have at the Ming Opera House a wrestling match. There was also one last Sunday."

Time brought new sources of entertainment. When the Broadwater Hotel and bath opened in 1889, Lizzie, Robert and their children were among the first visitors. She described the hotel as a truly elegant place, and said both structures were on a grand scale, particularly the bath with its "immense expanse of water." On occasion they took the streetcar out to the facility. Everyone dined in the restaurant there while the children enjoyed the park and pool.

Lizzie busied herself with many civic as well as family duties. She became an active member of the Presbyterian Church and helped its founding in Helena. She worked to establish a public library before the 1874 fire, and to rebuild it after. Like other Helena women she took an interest in school affairs. She voted in school elections and even ran for the school board, although unsuccessfully. As part of the "Poor Committee" she helped raise money to assist families where the father was out of work. She visited the local "Poor Farm" to minister to its residents. When the legislature considered giving women the right to vote, or debated women's rights, Lizzie was among those testifying for the cause.

The Fisk household did not want for its own culture. Grace took art lessons and learned to paint well enough to win several prizes at the territorial fair. Other Fisk children took music lessons and played in the Helena Juvenile Orchestra. School and public drama provided other sources of entertainment. Family bookshelves also held all the latest novels, and current magazines like *Ladies Home Journal*, *Cosmopolitan*, *Century*, *Harper's* and *Atlantic*.

Helena grew and Lizzie noted its changes. Their Rodney Street home had once been the outskirts of town. By 1890, streetcars rattled past every fifteen minutes; electric streetlights burned on the corners; and subdivisions spread out east and west. Lizzie visited friends in one of the new housing tracts and discovered beautiful homes in barren surroundings. "No grass, no trees, no walks, but dust or mud." She resolved not to move from the shaded, settled part of town.

In July of 1891, the Fisks had their home wired for electricity—one single bulb in each room. "No more slopping of coal oil, cleaning of lamps, or breaking of chimneys," she rejoiced. "No heat or smoke, but a clear, steady light." Christmas provided a special treat. She lit the tree with lights instead of candles. No wax dripped on the floor and gifts. That pleased Lizzie.

Christmas was one of the most pleasant times of year. Family and friends gathered at the Fisk home, sometimes twenty-five or more. The meal was worth the wait: turkey, cranberry sauce, grape jelly, pickles, sweet and Irish potatoes, soup, Bavarian cream cake, coconut cake, coffee and nuts. Everyone exchanged gifts and reflected on the past year.

Lizzie Fisk confirmed her first impressions of life in Montana. There was a wide field for usefulness; a place to build a good home.

Fire! Fire! Fire!

It was 9:55 P.M. Butte began to settle down for the evening. For January 15 it was not too cold. Most of the snow had vanished. A nice evening, police officer Fred Krambeck thought as he walked back toward his beat. The year 1895 is off to a good start. He'd taken his "lunch" hour and gone home for a bite to eat. The warehouse district along the Great Northern tracks had been quiet. He hoped it would stay that way for the remainder of the night.

On Oregon Avenue, just where the tracks crossed, John Steinborn rushed to meet him. John's beat was farther west, but during Fred's break, John always patrolled the area to help out. "Fire!" Steinborn said. He'd noticed an orange flicker in one of the warehouses and turned in the alarm at box 72. Before they finished speaking, the clang and commotion of the fire engines interrupted.

Fire Chief A. D. Cameron and his assistant, John Sloan, hurried from their chairs when the alarm sounded. Before they had their white, gum rubber hats and coats on, the other men from the shift were responding: Sloan's brother, Ed, George Fifer, Sam Ash, Peter Norlund, Dave Moses, John Flannery, Dave and Bill Magee. Quickly the two teams of horses stepped into the hanging harnesses. The hose truck and the hook and ladder were out of the station in minutes. Down Arizona, across the Northern Pacific tracks, on toward box 72 and the warehouse district.

By the time the firemen arrived, a crowd of some two hundred had gathered. The Kenyon-Connell warehouse was ablaze, the flames spreading fast. John Flannery jumped off the hose truck as they passed a hydrant near the Great Northern tracks. He grabbed the coupling, looped it around the hydrant and began to make the connection. The hook and ladder swung past, as hose truck driver Dave Magee carefully reeled out the hose, laying a line from the hydrant to the fire.

Immediately Chief Cameron realized the corrugated metal on the side of the building would hinder efforts to extinguish the blaze. As he worked to get the kinks out of the hose, he instructed Ed Sloan to grab an ax and start tearing off the siding. Assistant Chief John Sloan pitched in to make quick work of it.

Dave Moses and Sam Ash grabbed the nozzle and waited for water. Pete Norlund started down the hose, taking out kinks. George Fifer went to check the other side of the burning building. Volunteer firemen began to arrive. Chet Burns asked what he could do and someone hollered for him to run to the hydrant and tell Flannery the crew was ready for water.

Suddenly from the structure came a small explosion. A puff of smoke rose ominously. Firemen dropped hoses and axes and ran for the hook and ladder. It was just burning oil going up. No danger, they decided. Soon they were back. The Sloans had a couple of sheets of metal stripped off. Flannery gave the hydrant valve a few turns. He saw the water surge through, and he gave it another twist.

Dave Magee jumped down from the seat of the hose truck, gum coat and hat on, horse blankets in hand. His first duty was to blanket the horses to prevent a chill. On the hook and ladder his brother Bill prepared to do the same. "Maybe we'd better drive away," he yelled from the driver's seat. "There's likely to be another explosion." Spectators mused on whether the warehouse contained any dynamite or blasting powder. Some said it did. Others thought for sure it didn't. It was 10:08.

Inside the 80-by-90-foot warehouse lay tools and equipment of a bustling mining camp: hoists, drills, compressors, pumps, nails, pipe fittings, picks, shovels and iron cornices to beautify the fine brick buildings. Tucked into the building's northwest corner was a bomb, waiting to go off. Here the firm of Kenyon and Connell had a powder room. Hercules powder and caps, fuse and dynamite, perhaps as much as forty or fifty boxes, each weighing fifty pounds. It was all packed into an area nine by fourteen feet. Butte City law prohibited such a quantity of explosives, but the camp was booming and soon the powder and dynamite was to be dispersed underground—at work in the mines. An unintentional jolt might set off the dynamite, so as a precaution, the owners lined the inside of the powder room with half-inch iron plates. The pieces were not large, only four by six inches—"rabble heads" they were called. These little plates of iron had been used to skim vats of molten metal in the smelters. Now larger "rabble heads" were used, and Kenyon-Connell had several thousand on hand. They stacked them around the powder room to prevent a stray bullet from piercing the building and setting off its contents. On two sides, there were thousands and thousands of "rabble heads"; on the other two sides were pipe fittings, nails and wire.

It was 10:08. Chief Cameron had returned to direct the Sloan brothers as they worked taking off siding. Dave Moses and Sam Ash were playing a stream of water on the growing flames. Pete Norlund was back, having kicked out the last of the kinks. George Fifer grabbed another ax. Dave Magee raised the first horse blanket above the backs of his team. Brother Bill made ready to get down off the hook and ladder and follow suit.

Every building within a radius of five miles shook. From Walkerville, and South Butte, from Meaderville and Rocker, frightened people rushed from their homes, from stores and saloons, from hotels. In the sky they saw a ball of fire rising several hundred feet. Windows all over Butte shattered at the force of the blast. Along Broadway and Main large store windows showered broken glass. The force of the blast blew many Butte residents off their feet.

Mary Leatham had just lain down with her sick daughter. Her little boy, Alex, had gone to see the fire engines. Her husband relaxed in the living room of their home on Utah Avenue. The roar of the explosion woke the sleeping girl, then pieces of iron —"rabble heads"—came flying through the window and struck the wall.

Dave Magee remembered a flash in front of him. In a blinding instant the fire crew disappeared. The hook and ladder went fifty feet into the air and crashed in fragments. When he came out of his daze, Dave Magee had both horses on top of him. His leg was broken. There was a horrible quiet. Smoke and dust clouded the air. Then came the cries and groans of the injured and dying. John Flannery, blown from the hydrant, realized he could do little by himself. He took off on a run for a telephone.

Once the shock had worn off, people began gathering from all over town. The explosion destroyed the Kenyon-Connell warehouse. The fire spread to the Butte Hardware Company facility nearby. Nevermind. There were bodies, parts of bodies, wounded. Someone helped Dave Magee out from under his dead horses, then helped him up town toward medical help at the Murray and Freund Hospital. Within five minutes people closed in, trying to help as well as they could.

Disaster struck a second time. An explosion equal to the first erupted from the Butte Hardware Company warehouse. Again, in violation of city ordinances, a large quantity of powder and explosives had been stored there. Again, the shrapnel of pipe, iron, nails and glass rained across Butte. Casualties grew in number. Now spectators held back. Should they rush to help victims or would there be another blast? As if in answer, a third explosion split the warehouse district. It was smaller and there was little left to damage. Few people were close enough to be killed.

It had ended. The flames burned for another four hours. Butte's fire equipment lay in ruins so there was no way to stem them. Of the firemen, only Dave Magee and John Flannery survived. The smell of burning flesh mixed with that of wood and metal. Rescuers began the gruesome process of gathering the dead, the mangled bodies and the survivors. Many had severe burns; others, concussions from the blasts; still others had ugly wounds from flying pipe, metal, iron and "rabble heads." The worst fire in Butte history had ended.

At least forty bodies were recovered when daylight made searching possible. Hundreds of others crowded Butte's hospitals. For the lucky, wounds were dressed and recovery was possible. For others, their names would soon be added to the list of dead. Parents and relatives crowded the city's undertaking parlors trying to locate family members missing since the horrible evening. For several weeks the process of identifying the dead continued. In all, fifty-seven died during fifteen minutes of horror in Butte's warehouse district. Alex Leatham never watched fire engines again.

From all over the world came assistance for the stricken city. William A. Clark cabled $1,000 from Europe for relief work. John Maguire held a benefit performance at the Opera House to aid victims and families. Each saloon passed the hat. Each union donated. Each church took a special offering. A relief committee formed the next day and began paying for medical attention. When someone needed a specialist in Spokane to save a torn arm, the money was there. In all, more than $45,000 was gathered and dispersed.

January 17, 1895, Silver Bow County Coroner, Joseph Richards, selected a jury and began an inquest. For two weeks witnesses came and went. Did you see the origin of the first large explosion? The second? What did you do? Where did you go? How were you hurt? Did anyone know exactly how much dynamite and powder the warehouses contained? Only a few boxes, some said. One remembered maybe forty. Another estimated at least ten tons.

It took the jury only three hours to make up its mind once testimony ended on January 31. The Kenyon-Connell Commercial Company and the Butte Hardware Company stood guilty of violating Butte ordinances. They had stored excessive amounts of explosives within the city limits. Next time the law should be more strictly enforced.

John Flannery returned to work at the central fire station on January 16. Dave Magee lay in the hospital. The remainder of the crew never answered another fire alarm. John Steinborn returned to his beat that next evening. Fred Krambeck did not. He had rushed to help the dying firemen after the first deadly explosion. He did not survive the second.

Timeline

1850: Ft. Benton and Ft. Owen founded.

1863: Bannack established; mining rush and urban development starts.

1864: Montana becomes a territory; Virginia City and Bozeman established; *Montana Post* first published.

1865: Virginia City incorporated; first school law passed; Francis Thompson promotes emigration.

1866: *Helena Herald* and *Beaverhead News* first published; first books printed in Montana appear; Sarah Raymond starts teaching public school.

1867: Rev. D. S. Tuttle and Lizzie Fisk come to Montana.

1868: Helena city directory published.

1869: Fires destroy Blackfoot City and damage Helena; St. Vincent's Academy founded, Helena.

1871: Prison in Deer Lodge opens.

1872: Cornelius Hedges becomes Supt. of Public Instruction; Helena again damaged by fire.

1873: Bozeman Female Seminary opened by Presbyterians.

1874: Helena again damaged by fire; Virginia City loses election for territorial capital.

1875: Lee Travis issues the *Weekly News Letter;* hangman's tree in Helena cut down.

1876: Custer defeated at Little Big Horn, and Ft. Keogh established; "Brother Van" arrives in Montana; first Chinese cabin built in Butte.

1877: Nez Perce Indians flee across Montana.

1878: Montana Collegiate Institute founded in Deer Lodge.

1880: Utah Northern and Northern Pacific railroads enter Montana.

1881: Helena incorporated.

1882: Billings founded.

1883: Northern Pacific railroad completed; Roundup founded; Miles City damaged by fire; racial segregation prohibited in Montana public schools; Great Falls founded.

1884: Helen Clarke becomes Lewis and Clark County Supt. of Schools; Miles City, Silver Bow and Montana Clubs formed.

1885: M. A. Leeson publishes first history of Montana.

1886: *Montana Staats Zeitung* begins publication; Chinese temple built in Butte; first street cars begin operation in Helena and Butte.

1887: James J. Hill builds his railroad into Montana; Glasgow founded.

1889: Montana becomes a state; *Anaconda Standard* first published; Montana University established and Broadwater Hotel opened in Helena.

1891: Havre founded.

1892: First election for capital: Helena, Anaconda, Butte, Bozeman, Great Falls, Deer Lodge, and Boulder receive votes.

1893: State establishes major colleges, universities and institutions; Hamilton founded; Dutch settle in Gallatin Valley.

1894: Helena defeats Anaconda for permanent state capital.

1895: Warehouse fire in Butte kills 57.

1900: Croatian stonemasons begin to settle in Lewistown.

1906: J. B. Bass begins *Montana Plaindealer.*

1907: Washoe founded.

1909: Homestead era begins and creates new towns; Mount St. Charles College founded in Helena; Billings Polytechnic Institute begins.

1916: Homestead boom reaches its peak.

1917: U.S. enters World War I.

1920: Oil discovered at Cat Creek.

1924: Colstrip established and mining starts.

Suggested Readings

Paul W. Adams. *When Wagon Trails Were Dim.* np: Montana Conference. Methodist Church, 1957.

Larry Barsness. *Gold Camp: Alder Gulch and Virginia City, Montana.* New York: Hastings House, 1962.

George Lubick. "Cornelius Hedges, Frontier Educator." *Montana, the Magazine of Western History*, Vol. 28, No. 2 (Spring, 1978).

Montana Writers' Project. *Copper Camp.* New York: Hastings House, 1943.

Daniel S. Tuttle. *Reminiscence of a Missionary Bishop.* np: Whitaker, 1906. (Also available in paperback, 1976.)

A Northern Pacific train at Cinnabar, Montana, in 1896.—*F. J. Haynes photo, M.H.S.*

Chapter VIII
Travel Across the Land

Jerklines, bullwhackers, double-tripping, gandydancers, hoghead, motorman, flivver, eighteen-wheeler, Jenny—one hundred years of slang tells the history of Montana transportation. From ox trail to jet trail the story of moving people and merchandise is an exciting one. Likewise, the story of transportation and communication is also important.

Montana and distance go together. It is a long way from one corner of the state to another. Montana is a long way from eastern and Pacific Coast markets, too. The problem of getting what Montana produced to market—fur, gold, copper, cattle, wheat—demanded more and better transportation. The same can be said for getting people and finished goods into Montana. Methods of transportation have undergone major changes during the years from first settlement to interstate highways.

Early travellers and explorers took routes of least effort. Lewis and Clark and later fur trappers usually came to Montana following the Missouri River. Some followed this waterway to Three Forks and beyond. Others came via the Yellowstone. Still others, generally Canadian trappers like David Thompson, used western rivers like the Clark's Fork and Kootenai as highways. From the rivers trappers headed overland. Sometimes they followed existing Indian trails. Sometimes they struck out and blazed their own way.

The U.S. government realized the need for transportation in the West. In the early 1850s Congress authorized several people to explore and map routes across the West. Isaac Stevens, governor of Washington Territory, received orders to investigate the northern region. In 1853 and 1854, he and his men, including John Mullan, surveyed the area from Minnesota to the Pacific Coast. They were looking for the best possible route for a transcontinental railroad. Eventually transcontinentals crossed Montana, including the Northern Pacific, Great Northern, and Milwaukee railroads.

Before this took place, there was a need for better trails and roads. Fort Benton was the head of river navigation on the Missouri. Walla Walla, Washington, held a similar position on the Columbia River. To join these two ports, Captain John Mullan received instructions to build a road in 1858. Mullan and his men worked on the route for four years. They built bridges, cut flat roadways into steep hillsides, and laid logs together in muddy spots. When the Mullan Road was finished in 1862, it was one of the most modern in the nation. Freighters could travel the 624 miles in about a month.

When word of Montana gold strikes reached Minnesota in the early 1860s, anxious residents looked for a route westward to riches. Under the leadership of such men as James L. Fisk, several wagon trains followed the northern route. They used about the same path Mullan and Stevens had laid out a decade before.

Other prospectors pushed into Bannack, Virginia City, and other placer diggings using different routes. Some followed the old Oregon Trail as far as Fort Hall, Idaho, or Salt Lake City, Utah. From there they headed due north. When the Union Pacific Railroad completed tracks to Utah in 1869, the jumping-off point for Montana became Corinne, Utah. This route to Montana was known as the Corinne/Virginia City Road. It saw a lot of use by people eager to get to the goldfields. Many freighters also entered Montana this way. They brought goods from the nearest railroad to the mines and growing towns.

Colorado had enjoyed a gold and silver rush in 1859, but by 1863 many prospectors looked for someplace else to strike it rich. Montana offered that opportunity. To encourage settlers from Colorado, and provide a "short cut" from the Oregon Trail, Montanans pushed development of the Bozeman and Bridger trails.

John Bozeman and Jim Bridger charted these roads from a point near Cheyenne, Wyoming, along the Big Horn Mountains into Montana. From there the trail went up the Yellowstone, over Bozeman Pass, and on to Virginia City. These routes enjoyed much popularity, but they passed through lands the government had promised to the Indians. Warfare was nearly certain. Despite repeated efforts to keep the route open, hostile Sioux and Cheyenne often closed it

Stages stopped every day at George Slack's Fishtrap saloon and post office along the Big Hole River.

during the summer. Snow did the same in winter. Despite dangers and hardships, miners and settlers pushed on to Montana.

As transportation *to* Montana was important, so transportation *in* Montana proved equally essential. When the First Territorial Legislature met in Bannack during 1864-1865, they passed thirty-nine laws dealing with mining. They also passed thirty-five dealing with transportation. To Montanans of that period, transportation took second place only to mining.

Gradually transportation companies developed to handle Montana's needs. Famous stage lines like Wells, Fargo and Company, and Ben Holladay's Overland Mail and Express Company, Murphy, Neel and Company, or the Diamond R replaced these. Even more specialized operations built and operated toll roads, bridges, and ferries. The route over McDonald Pass, west of Helena, was a toll road. Ferries on the Big Horn, Yellowstone, Clark Fork, and later Missouri River operated for many years.

Stagecoach and wagon travel appears romantic today. In truth, the rides were long, dirty, and hard. As many as twenty or thirty people crowded into and on a stagecoach. Leather curtains at the windows could be rolled down for some weather protection. Without heat, however, a good buffalo robe was the only source of warmth. For the driver and those riding outside, heavy buffalo and fur coats or rain slickers offered protection from the weather. Stages ran night and day. Drivers changed. Passengers could "lay over" at a stop, but if time was a factor, they usually pushed on. Travel from Corinne to Virginia City or Helena normally took four or more days. When there was light traffic, a company might use a smaller wagon, or jerky. The name said it all.

Freight did not have to move as fast as passengers. Ox and mule teams, rather than horses, provided the motive power for these wagons. Oxen could manage about two miles per hour, mules two and one-half. Oxen were cheaper to purchase and more reliable if the weather or roads were poor. Freighters used either type.

Freighters used six or seven pairs of animals to pull heavy wagons. Over rough spots, double or triple teaming might be necessary. In a team, the animals closest to the wagon were known as wheelers, front mules or oxen were leaders, and those in between were called swingers. In an ox train, a bullwhacker walked on the left, beside the team. He kept them moving by yelling, cracking his long whip above their heads, and using a variety of language guaranteed to move anything. On a mule team, a "skinner" played the same role as the bullwhacker. He controlled the mules using a jerkline, a rope or rein connected to the lead animals.

By the mid-1880s, railroads began to replace mules and horses. In isolated sections of Montana, stagecoaches and freight wagons continued to operate into the early 1900s. Only the advent of the railroad and then the automobile replaced them.

Steamboats, like wagons and stagecoaches, occupied an important place in early Montana transportation history. Before them, other craft had plied the rivers. Fur trappers used various boats: hide-covered bull boats, logs dug out for canoes, mackinaws, rafts, and keelboats to transport furs and merchandise.

Large-scale river transportation in what is now Montana began in 1859. On July 17, the paddlewheeler *Chippewa* arrived at Fort Brule, also known as Fort McKenzie or Kipp's, near the mouth of the Marias. Pierre Chouteau's American Fur Company owned the boat and made enough money on the trip to justify doing it again. The next year the *Chippewa* pushed farther upriver, and docked at Fort Benton. The *Key West* did likewise in 1860.

For the third time, the *Chippewa* headed toward Fort Benton in 1861. Packed in her hold was a variety of goods. Food and trade items that made up the government's annual payment to the Blackfeet took up part of the space. Twenty-five kegs of powder lay in the bottom of the boat. Also hidden inside was whiskey. The American Fur Company planned to use whiskey in the Indian trade, even though it had been illegal since 1834.

Just short of Fort Benton, a deckhand on the *Chippewa* decided he needed a drink. With candle and cup he crept into the ship's hold to tap a liquor keg. The whiskey caught fire. Soon the entire boat was ablaze. Moments later—after passengers had escaped—the fire reached the powder kegs. After the smoke cleared, survivors discovered packages of beads and *Chippewa* pieces up to three miles away from the disaster. No other boats tried to reach Fort Benton in 1861.

Snags, burst boilers, ice, fire, and many other hazards made steamboat travel dangerous. During the heyday of riverboat travel, more than two hundred and fifty shipwrecks occurred in the Missouri. The *Chippewa* was only one of many. After the *Chippewa* came an ever-increasing number of "mountain boats." These vessels had a shallow draft, requiring as little as eighteen inches of water to float when empty and about four or five feet when loaded. They varied in size and capacity. Their length ranged from one hundred and fifty to two hundred feet. Most carried over four hundred tons of cargo. Indian, military, mercantile, and mining items filled their holds and crowded their decks. Growing passenger lists indicated the large number of miners and settlers who took this route to or from Montana's goldfields.

Usually, the first boats began to arrive in mid-May. They continued plying the muddy waters until July or August. Rarely did they start earlier or continue longer, but a wet year and heavy run-off changed that. The year 1878 had both, and the *Big Horn* reached Fort Benton on April 29. As late as September 23, the *Colonel McLeod* arrived in the city. Both dates stand as records.

Dry years restricted river traffic. In 1874, the Missouri ran so low that boats had trouble making Fort Benton at all. They dropped much of their cargo at Carroll, above the mouth of the Musselshell. Freighters and military units opened the Carroll Trail between this point and Helena. The road enjoyed some later use, depending on how far the boats could get. Like Carroll, Cow Island became a civilian and military freight depot. Goods from this point usually went through Fort Benton by wagon, then south to Helena and elsewhere.

How long did it take to ship something 2,000 miles from St. Louis to Fort Benton? Times varied with weather conditions and the speed of the boat. Travellers allowed at least one month. Sometimes it took two. Not everyone travelled all the way from St. Louis. People boarded at Sioux City, Omaha, and elsewhere. Some boats did not make complete round trips. Upon arriving at Fort Benton and the "upper river," they worked all summer moving freight and passengers between Fort Benton and Cow Island, or Fort Union. "Double tripping" the rivermen called it.

Boat owners made good profits—as much as $70,000 a trip. Such companies included firms like the Montana and Idaho Transportation Line, I. G. Baker and Company, and the Benton Transportation Company. Steamboat operations were not confined to the Missouri alone. As early as 1864, the *Chippewa Falls* and *Alone* went up the Yellowstone, carrying the Sully Military Expedition. The ships reached a point near the mouth of the Big Horn River before turning back.

Successful steamboat pilots became legends in Montana. Among the most noteworthy were Joseph LaBarge and Grant Marsh. LaBarge started as a fur trader for the American Fur Company in 1831. He was only sixteen years old. When he was thirty-one, he bought his own boat. He first reached Fort Benton in 1862, piloting the *Shreveport.* Until his retirement in the 1880s, he made trips and maintained an excellent record for safety.

Grant Marsh was also young when he began his life on the Missouri. At twelve, he became a steamboat cabin boy. He first reached Fort Benton in 1866 with the *Luella.* Only thirty-four at the time, Marsh earned the respect and gratitude of miners when he decided to keep his boat on the upper river through the summer. Finally, in September, he started down with a load of miners and gold. His cargo, estimated at $1,250,000 in gold dust, was reportedly the richest single load ever to leave Montana.

This daring captain became even more famous for his exploration and operation on the Yellowstone River. As part of a U.S. Army survey effort, Marsh pushed the *Key West* up the Yellowstone in May of 1873. He managed to reach the mouth of the Powder River before low water turned him back. Two years later he took the *Josephine* and a load of soldiers even farther. After passing Pompey's Pillar, he reached a point about sixty miles from Yellowstone National Park. When he turned around, someplace between present-day Billings and Laurel, he set a record for navigation on the Yellowstone.

Of all Marsh's activities, undoubtedly the most famous was the rescue of wounded soldiers from the Battle of the Little Big Horn in 1876. He managed to get the *Far West* to the junction of the Big Horn and Little Big Horn. From there he transported survivors seven hundred miles to Bismarck in less than fifty-four hours.

Riverboat traffic on the Missouri and Yellowstone declined when railroads arrived. No more graphic illustration is needed than to note that twenty-one boats docked at Fort Benton in 1887. There were three in 1888. The railroad had reached Benton late in 1887. Boats had become outmoded. River transportation did continue, however, well into the 1900s. Paddlewheelers served as grain carriers for much of the period. U.S. Army Corps of Engineers snag boats worked the river into the 1940s. One of these, the *Mandan,* docked at Fort Benton on June 20, 1921—the last steamboat to reach this historic port. Construction of Fort Peck Dam in the 1930s sealed off riverboat traffic from the upper Missouri.

Paddlewheelers plied other Montana waters. When the Great Northern reached the Kootenai River area in 1892, new goldfields were booming to the north in Canada. Before long more than one-half dozen boats travelled the upper Kootenai, led by the *Annerly.* They carried supplies and people from the railroad to the mines near Fort Steele. On the return they handled ore. Then the mining boom faded. The Great Northern built a branch in Fernie, and by 1915 there was no need for steamers on the upper Kootenai. Boating lasted longer on the lower river. Not until 1957 did the last ship—the *Moyle*—leave Kootenai Lake.

For pure pleasure, Montanans and tourists enjoyed other steamboats on various western lakes. St. Mary's Lake near Glacier and Flathead Lake enjoyed the largest number of ships. The Flathead Lake boats carried some freight and also herded logs to various sawmills. By 1932, the last freight boat had been dismantled. Passenger traffic, which boomed between 1908 and 1915, dwindled because highways and railroads came into the area. The last passenger boat left Flathead Lake in 1954. Lakes in Glacier National Park still have passenger boats during the summer.

No form of transportation or communication had the impact on Montana and the West that railroads had. They moved goods and people with ease. In the public eye, a

FROM
CHICAGO OR ST. LOUIS

We give you a first-class ride

BY WATER or RAIL to ST. PAUL.

From there to BISMARCK via the great

NORTHERN PACIFIC RAILROAD.

From Bismarck on the excellent new Passenger Steamers
of the

FORT BENTON TRANSPORTATION COMPANY

To all points in the Northwest.

We ride you through the

GRANARY OF THE WORLD,

The largest Farms in America, and immense Stock Ranches,
to the Republic's Mint,

MONTANA.

DISTANCES ON YELLOWSTONE RIVER
From Fort Buford to

Glendive	148	Rosebud	274
Powder River	200	Big Horn	348
Fort Keogh	237	Little Big Horn	398

OVERLAND DISTANCES
From Fort Benton to

Sun River and Ft. Shaw	60	Phillipsburg	320
Helena	140	Maria's Cros'g, Simmon's Ferry	75
Blackfoot	170	Fort Belknap	90
Diamond City	175	Blackfoot Agency	140
Deer Lodge	195	Fort Walsh / Cypress Mountain. B.A.	160
Butte City	240		
Missoula	260	Fort McLeod "	225
Bozeman	240	Fort Edmonton "	475
Virginia City	265		

Stages leave BENTON for HELENA Daily.

Northern Pacific Express
Connects at Bismarck with the

THE BENTON LINE EXPRESS

Through to all important points on the Missouri River between

BISMARCK, FORT BENTON, HELENA, M. T.,

And intermediate points.

T. C. POWER COLLECTION

Advertisement for the mixed transportation system dominant in Montana during the Territorial period, railways and overland stages.

railroad also represented prosperity. During the 1860s and 1870s, Montanans considered almost anything to encourage railroad construction. Free land, no taxes, financial bonuses, and outright bribery were considered. Finally, the race to Montana focused on the narrow-gauge (rails three feet apart) Utah and Northern and the standard-gauge Northern Pacific (four feet, eight and one-half inches between the rails).

Utah and Northern (U.&N.) tracklayers, or gandy-dancers, first entered the territory on March 9, 1880. In a ceremony on Monida Pass, officials drove a specially-engraved silver spike to mark the event. By December of the next year, U.&N. rails had reached the Butte area. Meanwhile, the Northern Pacific (N.P.) crews approached Montana from the east and west. Near Glendive, the first N.P. rails came into Montana during late December 1880. Montana officials took the same silver spike used at Monida Pass, reengraved it, and drove it once more in celebration.

For the next two years, Northern Pacific crews pushed track through the territory. Finally, in August of 1883, workmen joined the two sections near Gold Creek. Henry Villard was serving as president of the Northern Pacific. He wanted a grand celebration for his transcontinental line. Villard brought dignitaries from all over the world in several special trains. On September 8, he had a rail taken up, and at Gold Creek all the world watched as the "last rail" was laid again.

Among all Montana's railroads, the Northern Pacific stood out as unique. Congress chartered the line as a land grant railroad. This meant that for every mile of track laid, the company received free land. Railroad officials could then sell the land and use the money to pay for construction costs. Congress tied some strings to the deal, however. Land the railroad received lay in alternate one mile square blocks (sections) on both sides of the track. The government kept the remainder. Furthermore, the railroad could not have mineral land, or patented homestead, or mining property. In return for this land, the railroad had to carry all U.S. government freight free or at a reduced rate.

The history of the Northern Pacific land grant became a complicated and confusing story. The railroad never did get all the land promised to it. Some mining and lumber interests felt the company wanted to take all the "good" land. The N.P. provided more free freight service to the government

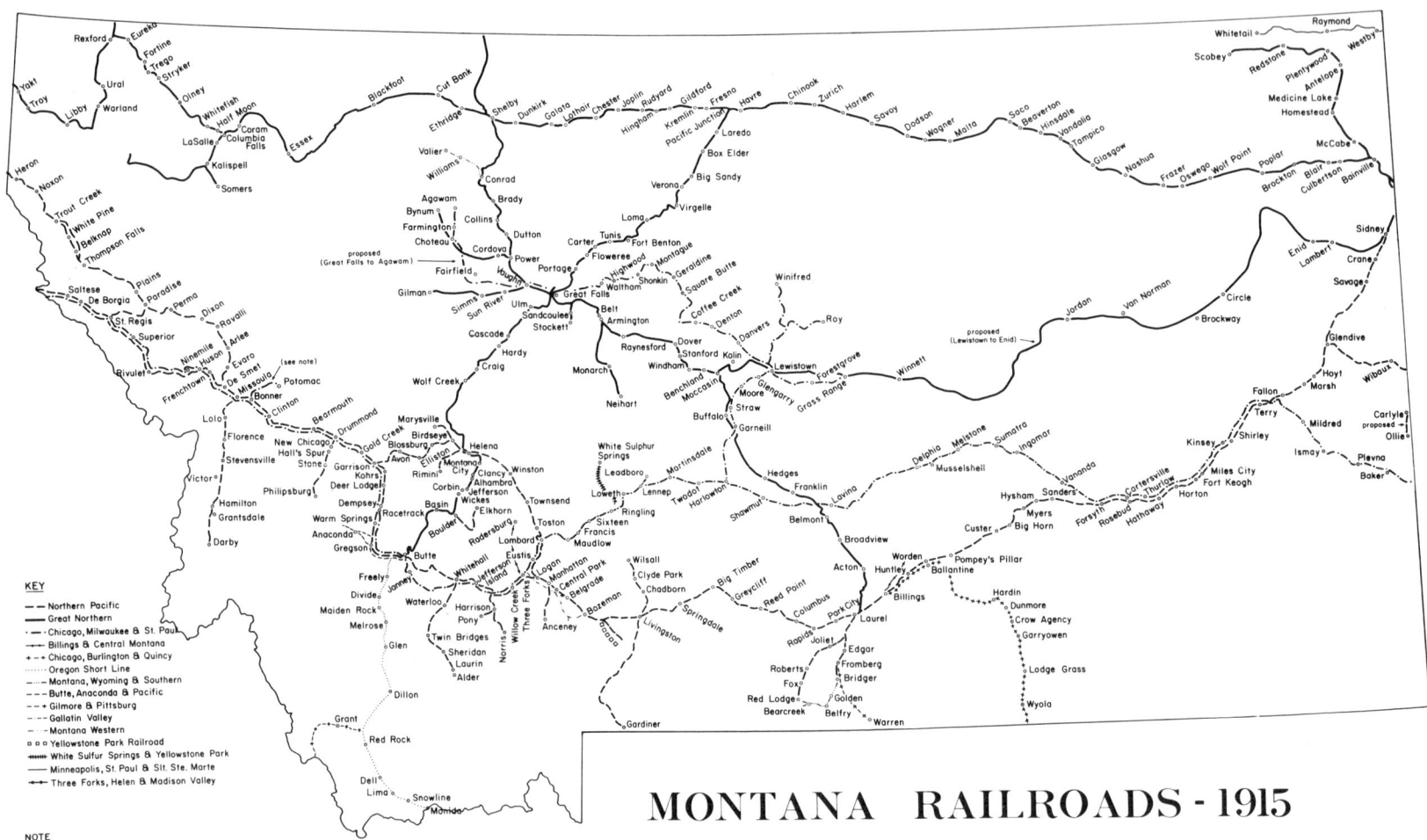

MONTANA RAILROADS - 1915

than it received in land sales.

The Utah and Northern and the Northern Pacific divided Montana's railroad traffic between themselves in 1883, but not for long. Minneapolis businessman James J. Hill decided to push his St. Paul, Minneapolis and Manitoba Railroad into Montana and on to the mines at Butte. While one set of gandydancers drove spikes across the Hi-Line toward Great Falls, another set worked on the Montana Central Railroad between that point and Helena. By November of 1887, Hill had through trains running between Helena and St. Paul. Two years later, the "Manitoba" served Butte.

Jim Hill came to dominate railroad affairs in Montana like no other man. In the early 1890s, Hill renamed his line the Great Northern and decided to make it transcontinental. Construction pushed west from Havre, over Marias Pass, into the Kalispell and Kootenai River areas. Then crews worked on to the Pacific Coast. He did all this work, as he had his earlier construction, without land grants or government aid. So strong was Hill's financial position that during the 1890s he managed to get control of the Northern Pacific. He also held the Chicago, Burlington and Quincy Railroad, which had a branch to Billings in 1894. Hill combined these and some smaller companies into the Northern Securities Company. In 1904, the U.S. Supreme Court ruled that Hill had a monopoly on rail transportation in the Pacific Northwest. The Court ordered the Northern Securities Company dissolved.

One other transcontinental railroad joined Hill's Great

Northern and the N.P. in Montana. The Chicago, Milwaukee and St. Paul had built through the area by 1909. The Milwaukee joined the other two lines in promoting Montana. All three companies encouraged homesteading in eastern and central Montana to develop the land and markets. Still a fourth line entered the northeast corner of the state to get into the act. The Minneapolis, St. Paul, and Sault St. Marie reached Whitetail in 1913. It worked to develop agriculture in that region as the other railroads had done farther south.

From the main lines, countless branch lines and independent railroads poked into the many valleys and communities of Montana. Montana Western, Bitterroot Valley Railway, Yellowstone Park and White Sulphur Springs, Montana Southern, Gilmore and Pittsburgh, and the Montana, Wyoming and Southern were but a few. Among the most substantial was the Butte, Anaconda and Pacific (B.A.P.). Copper mine owner Marcus Daly built the line in 1894 to transport ore from Butte to his smelter in Anaconda. Although it never did reach the Pacific, the B.A.P. did hold one national record. In 1913, it became the first major U.S. railroad to use electricity instead of steam for all its power.

Many larger companies toyed with the idea of electrifying. The Milwaukee decided to try. In 1914, it began using this type of power between Harlowton, Montana, and Avery, Idaho. Farther west the Great Northern did likewise, getting its trains over the Cascade Mountains in Washington. By the late 1960s, the B.A.P. switched from electricity to diesel. The Milwaukee did the same in 1975, marking the end of an era for long-distance, electric railroading in the western United States.

When the Milwaukee completed construction through Montana in 1909, the state had almost 5,000 miles of railroads. Nearly everything travelled by rail. Passenger service using "name" trains became the ultimate in comfortable travel. People remember the "Empire Builder," the "North Coast Limited," and the "Hiawatha" for luxury. Other trains like the "Copper City Special," the "Gallagater," and the "Skiddoo" covered shorter runs. Passenger revenues dropped as cars, buses, and then airplanes took over. Passenger trains grew smaller and ceased altogether. During the 1930s some companies tried using single, self-powered "Budd Cars." Like large baggage cars with a few seats, these saved passenger runs, but not for long.

By the 1960s, the Milwaukee was out of the passenger business altogether. N.P. and G.N. operations dwindled to two trains each. The Union Pacific ran one into Butte. Smaller lines had no passenger service at all. In May of 1971, the U.S. government took over all passenger service in Montana and most of the nation with the creation of AMTRAK.

Where railroads once monopolized freight transportation, trucks began to take increasingly larger parts of the traffic. To improve efficiency, the G.N., N.P., and Burlington again tried to consolidate. In 1970 they succeeded with the formation of the Burlington Northern Railroad. The Milwaukee Railroad struggled along as the other transcontinental in Montana, but in 1978, it declared bankruptcy. Today Montana still has 4,800 miles of railroad track. Gradually the figure grows smaller as less profitable lines are cut. Railroads are still very important and efficient freight movers. But they are no longer so all-important as they once were in the 1880s and 1890s.

For almost seventy years another form of rail transportation existed in Montana. Street railways operated in Montana's seven major cities from 1883 to 1951. These lines joined the business district with the railroad depot, the smelt-

The Lower Broadwater streetcar in Helena in front of the Broadwater Hotel and Natatorium about 1900.

131

er, or residential area. Begun as horse car lines, street railways had switched to steam, cable, and then electric power by the 1890s. Trolley cars became part of everyday life for many Montanans. The motorman took everybody to work, to school, or to play. Longer lines connected cities to places like Milltown near Missoula, the Broadwater Hotel outside Helena, and Gallatin Gateway south of Bozeman. Despite their service and comfort, streetcars could not compete with the automobile. By the 1920s trolley companies began to fold. Companies in Billings, Bozeman, Helena, Great Falls, and Missoula went down in that order. Butte's ceased running in 1937. Anaconda held on until 1951, thanks to the copper company's subsidy providing transportation for smelter workers. In most cities buses continued service when streetcars quit.

If the train impacted the last century, the automobile did the same for this century. Serious citizens felt certain that autos would be only a passing fad when they first appeared. Only the rich could afford them. They lacked comfort and durability, but they were versatile. In a car you could go anywhere you could find a road, and some places you could not. People in Montana's rural areas took a particular fancy to the new-fangled device.

A good roads movement developed across the nation. These organizations worked to improve roads and promote laws helping motorists. Newspapers began carrying more advertisements for cars and more frequent stories about people who used them. State and federal governments became involved in bettering highways and driving conditions. The Montana Highway Department began in 1913 to meet such needs. Until 1916 states and counties handled road construction and maintenance. That year the federal government started financing a proportion of that work.

Promotion played an important part in developing Montana highways. Ford Motor Company and Glidden Auto Tours encouraged tourists to see Montana by car. For the truly venturesome, there was the Yellowstone Trail to follow from Minneapolis to the National Park. First a motorist bought a guide booklet. Then he cranked up his auto and followed a series of yellow posts and arrows across the plains and through the canyons all the way to Yellowstone's geysers. During the 1920s and 1930s, petroleum companies and the Montana Highway Department issued free road maps. Soon gas stations and motor courts could be found in most Montana towns. Tourism increased.

Truck and bus transportation developed with the automobile. As both grew larger, rail service decreased. Demands rose for even better roads. Where gravel and dirt would not do, oil and pavement took over. U.S. highways became main thoroughfares. State and county roads served as feeders. Finally, to provide the best in road transportation, the U.S. government decided in 1956 to construct a

Construction of the Interstate Highway system improved transportation and changed the face of the land. I-90 near Huson.—*Montana Highway Department photograph*

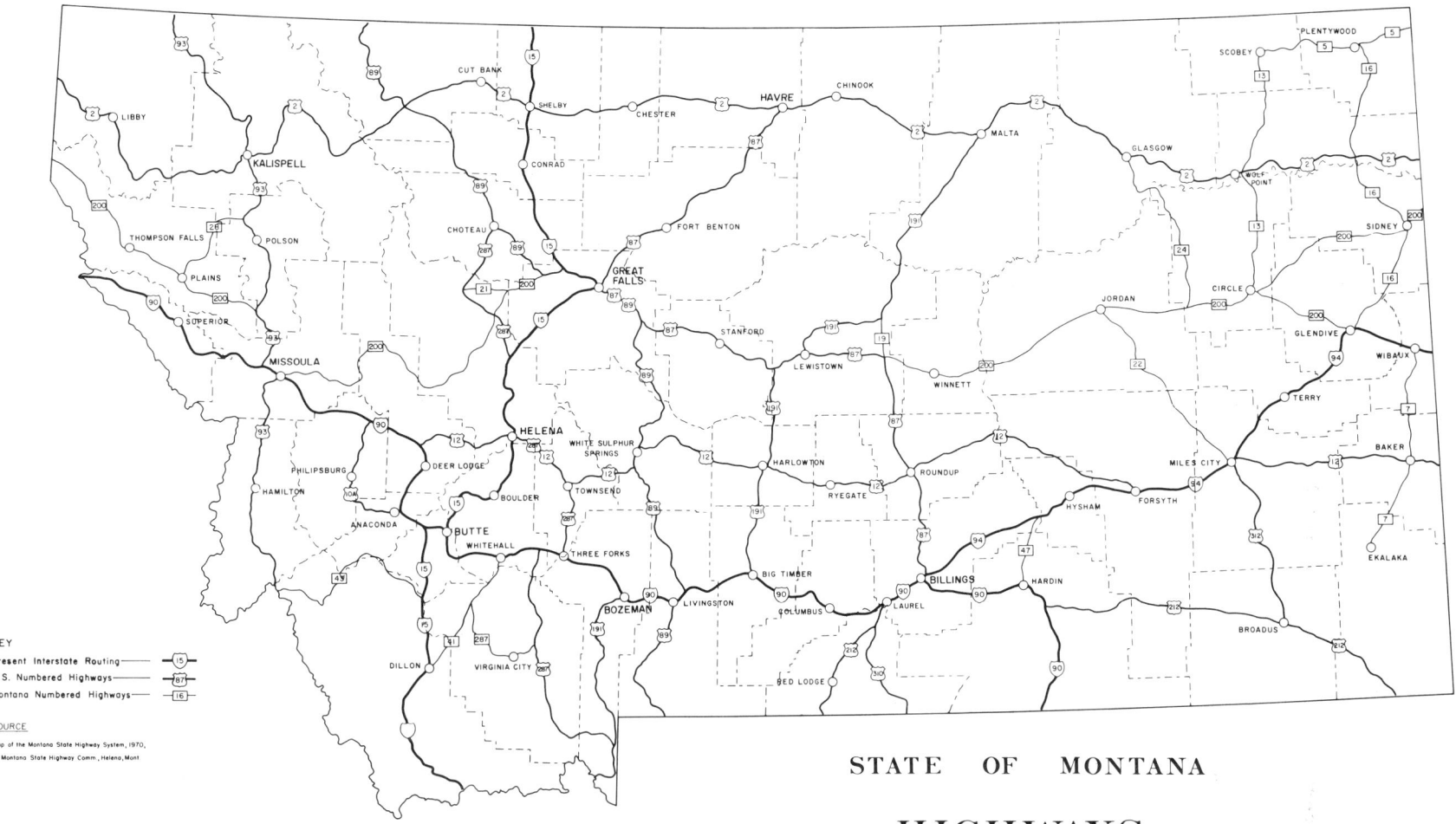

STATE OF MONTANA

HIGHWAYS

network of interstate highways. In Montana I-90 and I-94 promised faster east-west travel. I-15 did the same for north-south traffic. By the late 1970s, highway statistics told the story. Cars, motorcycles, semi-trailer trucks, and buses crisscrossed over 10,000 miles of U.S. highways and more than 1,200 miles of interstate. Additional thousands of miles in state and county roads joined even the remotest parts of Montana.

Air transportation shared the automobile's route to success. When J. C. Mars flew the first airplane in Montana at the state fair in 1910, spectators gaped in amazement. Helena businessmen decided to promote their community and offered $10,000 to the first person flying across the Continental Divide—provided it was done west of Helena. Mars' partner, Cromwell Dixon, accepted the offer and cashed the check after his successful flight on September 30, 1911. Unfortunately, Dixon died the next week in a plane crash at a Spokane fair.

Undaunted, other flyers in their flimsy wood and cloth planes buzzed from one county fair to another. T. T. Moroney impressed legislators in 1913 with a flight around the capitol dome in Helena. In gratitude, they named him Montana's official aviator. The same year Katherine Stimson carried Montana's first airmail letter. She flew from the fair grounds in Helena to the downtown post office.

Commercial air service came to Montana on March 3,

1933. On that date what is now Northwest Orient Airlines first joined Montana with Minneapolis. Air service expanded the next year when National Park Airways connected Great Falls, Helena, and Butte with Salt Lake City. Eventually, National Park Airways became Western Airlines. In 1951, Frontier Airlines entered the state from Denver and the southeast. Service on all the air carriers improved from propellers to jets in the middle and late 1960s.

Private pilots also began to crowd the Big Sky. Like the car, planes originally belonged only to daredevils. With Montana's vast distances, farmers and ranchers quickly discovered the advantage of the airplane's speed. To provide some control of private and commercial flight, legislators established the Montana Aeronautics Commission after World War II.

Montana's militia took to the air along with everyone else. The Air National Guard was created in 1947, and in February of 1955, the first helicopter arrived to support Army National Guard units. Today jet fighters and jet helicopters serve as modern replacements for the horse-mounted militia of a century ago.

Airplanes demonstrated a potential for more than passengers and mail. Farmers discovered they could "dust" crops with ease. The U.S. Forest Service began dropping smokejumpers into remote forest fires and dropping fire retardant on larger blazes. Air freight handled everything from big packages to small cattle herds. Ford Tri-Motors, DC3s, Convair 580s, and 747s represent new jargon and a new era in Montana transportation.

Progress and change affected communication as well as transportation. In the early 1860s, it took a long time to get a letter from Bannack to Helena or some other mining camp. By stage or steamboat it might be several months before a loved one in "the states" received mail. Months more passed before the reply came. When Virginia City businessmen suggested a telegraph line to Salt Lake City in 1866, promises of

Cromwell Dixon prepares to leave the State Fairgrounds in Helena in 1911 on his historic flight across the Continental Divide.—*N. A. Forsyth photograph, M.H.S.*

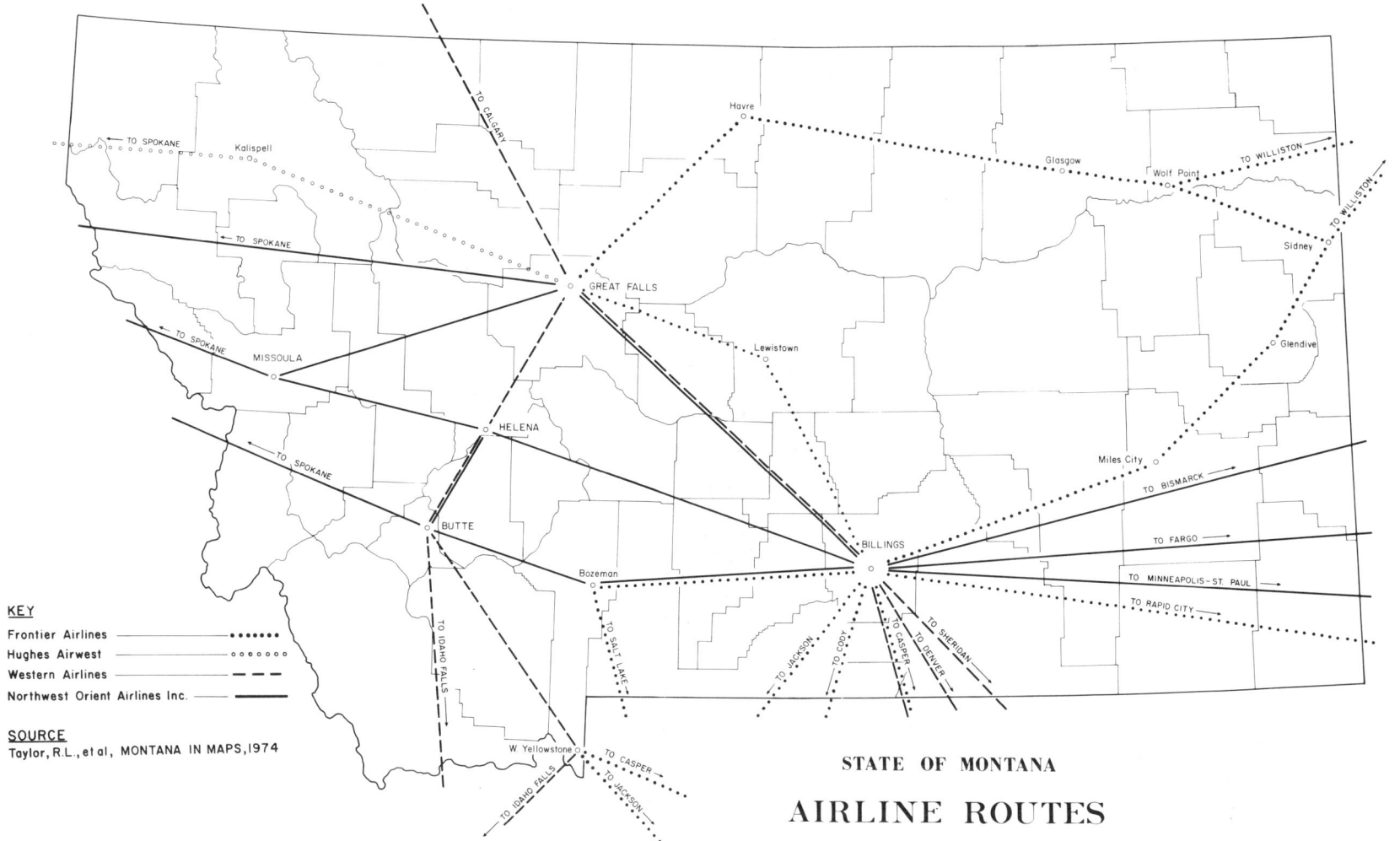

STATE OF MONTANA

AIRLINE ROUTES

aid came pouring in. By November 2, all the poles were in place and the wires ready. "The telegraph between Great Salt Lake and Virginia City is finished! Montana forms a part of the civilized world! Citizens! Hang your banners on the outer walls! Montana is no longer an unknown territory!!"

By 1867, telegraph lines reached Helena. They began to branch out and by the end of the 1870s, extended to Missoula, Fort Assiniboine, and Fort Keogh. Frequently buffalo rubbed against the poles, knocking them down. Sometimes weather and wind snapped the wires. When a courier had to get word of the Custer Battle to Washington, the closest telegraph was in Bozeman. Wires were down. Finally the rider reached Helena and the message went out. During the next decade, the network of civilian and military lines kept growing.

Alexander Graham Bell experimented with telephone communication in 1875 and 1876. Within two years, Montana residents recreated his experiments and played with small telephones. For a state of such vast distances, the application was obvious. On February 21, 1882, Montana's first telephone exchange began operating in Butte with sixteen subscribers. By August, telephone lines joined Butte and Helena. During the next year, the Rocky Mountain Bell Company expanded service to Missoula, Anaconda, Deer Lodge, and points in between. Other companies established lines in the Sun River Valley and Bozeman areas.

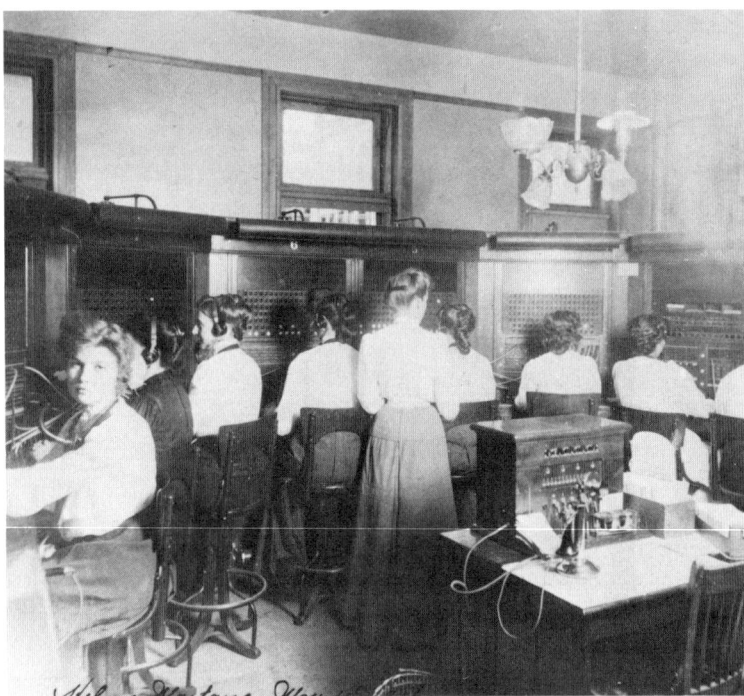
"Hello, Central"—the main switchboard in Helena, 1906.

Radio and television served further to break down Montana's sense of isolation. KDYS began broadcasting as Montana's first radio station in 1922 under the sponsorship of the *Great Falls Tribune*. Today more than fifty radio stations cover the dial. Television began with four-hours-a-day broadcasts from Billings' KOOK-TV in 1953. From a single station and tiny screens in heavy wooden cabinets, to twelve broadcasters and plastic portables, TV brought the world to Montana.

Distance and Montana go together. Across that distance and across Montana's history spread a wide variety of transportation types. They range from plodding oxen to streaking jets; from steamboat mail to TV's instant replay. Transportation and communication have helped Montana grow. They have brought people and machines to work the land and to mine the earth. Wagons, boats, trains, trucks, and planes have also carried Montana's produce to market. Telegraphs, telephones, radios, and television have brought the rest of the world and nation to Montana. They have brought change to the face of Montana.

Welcome Aboard a Steamboat

Welcome aboard! Is this your first time on a Missouri River steamboat? Well, I'm the captain and I'd be pleased to show you about and give you a bit of history along with the tour. Watch your step there. That rope is fastened to the starboard capstan and is tied to the tree over yonder. It keeps us at shore. Those two capstans are like steam-powered winches. You wrap a rope around it, apply a little steam and it starts turning slowly. Either one will pull the entire boat. But I'm ahead of myself. I'll tell you about that when we're talking sailing techniques.

This ship is what they call a "mountain boat." Let me explain. The Missouri between St. Louis and Fort Benton is divided into two parts. Most of it—say the first 2,000 miles to Cow Island—is what we call the "Sandy River." The river runs pretty smooth; drops maybe only eight and one-half inches each mile. Almost any boat can make it with a good skipper. But there are problems. It's still shallow in spots. And those shifting sandbars will ground you in a minute. Those snags, the trees and branches washed down, will tear a hole in the bottom so fast the boat'll go down before you can snap your fingers. There are plenty of dangers on the sandy river.

The last stretch between Cow Island and Fort Benton is the "Rocky River." Here the old Missouri cuts through really rugged land and drops more rapidly. Two feet per mile, I'd say. You still find snags, but the main dangers are rapids, loose boulders, and rocky reefs. It takes a lighter boat to travel the river above Cow Island most years. Those are the mountain boats, like this one. Sure there are wet years, like '78 when almost any boat could get up to the fort. Most of the time, however, if you and your freight are going straight through, you want a mountain boat.

How do you tell them apart? It's pretty easy. Take a look at the bow—up front. This design is what we call a "spoonbill," kind of flat and rounded. It sits high in the water, slips over the sand bars more easily, handles well in tricky currents. Mountain boats also have a pretty shallow draft. They don't take much water to sail, even when loaded. This little beauty takes only twenty inches of water when it's

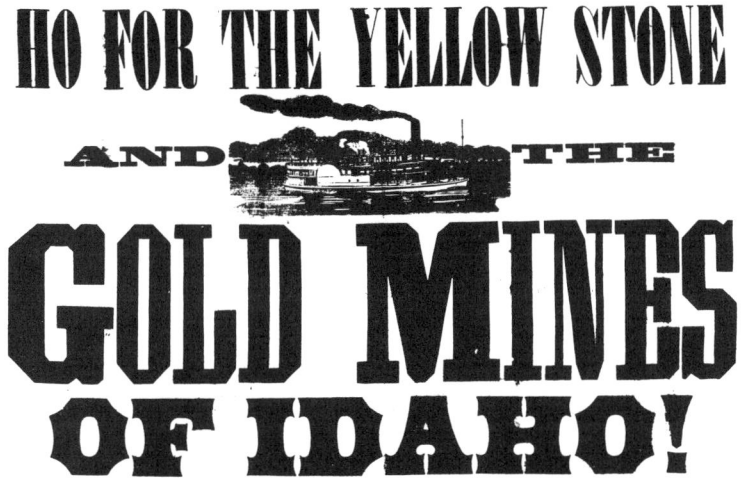

Advertisement for steamboat passage in 1863 up the Missouri to mines at Virginia City and Bannack.

light, four and one-half feet draft when it's fully loaded.

While I'm talking statistics, let me give you all the particulars. We're 189 feet long; 33½ feet wide; and the hold is 5 feet deep. Empty, this ship weighs in at 400 tons; but it'll carry easily 500 tons of cargo. It cost nearly $25,000 new when it was built in 1870. Mind you, it's not the biggest boat the Missouri ever saw. If you wanted to go for pure size, you'd have to see the *Montana*, *Dakotah*, or *Wyoming*.

Those were big boats—all built about the same time. Think of it, 252 feet long, almost 49 feet wide, a hold 6 feet deep and costing more than $36,500 new. They weighed nearly 960 tons each and drew almost two feet of water light. And could they carry cargo! The truth is, the *Dakotah* holds the Missouri River record for most freight: 900 head of hogs, 5,200 railroad ties, and another 450 tons of cargo. Imagine that. That was some boat. But the three of them were too big for mountain boats. They made it to Fort Benton on wet years, but generally they ran the lower river, or even the Mississippi.

Hey, I'm just talking away. Let's get on with the tour. You're leaning against the jackstaff. We've got that tall flag-type pole at the very front of the boat to help me when I'm in the pilothouse, up top. With a flag flying from the jackstaff, I can get an idea of how much the wind's blowing, and which way. Sighting down it, I know about how far away something is, like a snag, for instance. I can plan my turns to miss it.

The other spars and derricks up here are all important. We use the derricks to lift heavy cargo on board. They're also useful for "grasshoppering." See those two poles sticking up along each side? That's what we call a grasshopper's leg. Say we hit a sandbar. Every boat does several times a day with that river constantly shifting course. Anyway, when we hit a sandbar, and the bow's hung up, the crew lowers those poles into the sandbar as deep as they'll go. Then they take that rope strung through the block and tackle on top, run it through the pulley on the bottom, and give it a twist around the capstan. With starboard and port "legs" in place, you apply steam to the capstans and it begins to lift the front of the boat, using those poles like stilts. That's grasshoppering. With the paddlewheel turning hard, you can push forward—kind of inching across the sandbar. Usually it takes more than one "hop" to get across. If we're really stuck, sometimes I reverse the paddlewheel and it churns water under the boat. This washes away built-up sand. We back off the sandbar and look for a way around it.

There are a couple of other ways of getting over a sandy stretch. Remember I said I'd tell you how those capstans come in handy? Well, sometimes we send out a crew with a rope in the skiff—one of those two small "lifeboats" in back. They reach shore and head upstream to find a sturdy tree, then tie it off. If there are no trees available we can use a "dead man." We just take a large log, head away from the shore upstream a bit, and bury it firmly in the ground with a rope attached. This is where the capstans come in. We wrap the other end of the rope around the capstans and begin to winch ourselves upriver. It sure beats cordelling. The early keelboat people did that with men on shore pulling the boat along.

One more last resort for getting yourself free. Remember this if you ever need it. Take several men and put them on either side of the boat with a good strong chain. Have them drag the chain under the boat—kind of sawing back and forth as they go. That Missouri lays down a lot of sand, but the current will also wash it away when the chain loosens it. Sometimes this'll free the boat and you can back it off the sandbar.

Come on down the main deck. Those stairs lead to the cabins, and we'll head up there in a minute. Behind, you notice the two stacks. We try to keep them painted black and looking sharp. Between them you see the company emblem. Most riverboat firms have some kind of letter or symbol up there. The "Block P" from the Benton Transportation Company was probably as famous as any. It's kind of like advertising, I guess.

Right below those stacks are the boilers—three of them. They're 38 inches by 22 feet if you're interested. We try to keep an operating pressure of about 130 pounds of steam. There are the steam lines running overhead toward the back of the boat. They provide power for the two steam engines. The engines provide the power for the paddlewheel, which is 18 feet in diameter and 24 feet long. Of course, the rudder is back there, too.

In between the back of these boilers and the end of the engine compartment is the boat's main cargo area. It's maybe seventy to seventy-five feet long. Here, and up front by the derricks, we haul all kinds of freight: mine machinery, equipment, bags of wheat and ore, animals, you name it. Lots of people assume all the animals in Montana came overland and that's not true. Some of that fine breeding stock came by riverboat. Why, we will carry just about anything for twelve cents a pound. The main deck serves as a passenger area, too. For those who cannot afford a cabin, you can buy space on the deck with the freight and animals—and the wood. I forgot to mention the wood.

All that cordwood stacked along the side will be used up in no time once we start upriver. Boats stop about every other day to replenish their wood supply. Some boats tried to use the coal you find along the Missouri, but it just didn't work. Generally we pay "wood hawks" or Indians to cut wood and stack it by the shore. If there's none available, we have to stop and send the crew and even passengers out to cut it. No wood, no fire under the boiler, and no steam to make the paddlewheel go. It's that simple.

Usually we keep the deck as full as we can. The more freight, the larger the profits. The owners of this boat expect me to bring in from $16,000 to $60,000 a season. Sure they'd like to have the $250,000 Durfee and Peck reported clearing in 1872, but I think that's a little high, myself. Anyway, I keep the deck full and even put stuff in the hold. There's some freight that won't get damaged too much down there. And—promise you won't tell, this is off the record—if we're carrying whiskey for the Indian trade, we keep it below. We can generally sneak it by the government inspectors. I'm not saying I like to do it, but there's money in it, and a lot of booze goes upriver illegally.

Okay. Come up the stairs to the passenger deck. It has eight cabins on each side, and will hold about thirty passengers. Some boats hold more, some less. My wife and I—and our little girl—have the forward cabin on the starboard or right side. Opposite, to port, the clerk has his cabin and office. He keeps track of the freight and passengers, collects the money, and all that. It's $300 a trip from St. Louis. Can you believe people will pay that for a cabin? If I were going to the goldfields, I think I'd go with one of the $100 deck tickets. Wouldn't you?

Anyway, back of our two cabins, there's one for the crew, and another for the cook. The male passengers then get the next two on each side. Toward the back are the really nice cabins for ladies or families. You'll notice those are well back from the boilers. That's why they're first class. It's a little cooler back there, and if those boilers ever blow, there's less chance of the ladies being blown to pieces. Enough of that. Very few boats ever explode and go down. Snags, ice, and bridges sink more boats.

Here, take a look in one of these nice cabins: two bunks,

Missouri River steamboat at an upriver landing stacked with passengers and cordwood.

a large lower and a smaller upper. In that space under the lower bunk you tuck your travelling bags, boxes, boots, shoes, washbowl, and pitcher. Some people drive a nail or two into the wall for hanging coats or other bags. Beyond the bunk the cabin is only 3-by-6 feet. It's not much, but the best we've got. The carpeting on the floor helps spruce up the place, too. One door opens outside to the promenade or walkway around the cabin deck. The other door opens into the main cabin. Cabin passengers eat here with my family and me. We set a nice table—silver, china, canned vegetables, and generally fresh meat. Sometimes we carry a steer or two on board to butcher part way upriver. Generally we hunt buffalo or game as we go.

Behind the cabins is a nice open deck where you can walk during the trip. Lots of passengers do their sightseeing from up here—away from the animals and freight below. Those two doors way in the back? Those are the rest rooms. They're just outhouse types with open holes leading down through the deck over the paddlewheel.

Let me take you up to the pilothouse. Some ships have what we call a Texas deck. That's a deck above the passenger cabin where the captain and crew live. Those are generally bigger boats. There are few Texas decks on mountain steamers. Come on in the pilot house. The glass all around makes it easy for me to see. You'll notice we've got the ship's name printed brightly on the front and sides. The wheel, whistle, and some of the gauges are here. These windows open for July and August trips. You need some type of circulation in those badlands come summer.

Did you notice all the freight the crew is loading? The levee here is crowded with everything Montanans will need for the coming season. It's hard to think of supplies for the year coming only once. Imagine what it would be like if you could buy clothes, food, toys, and equipment only once each year. That's what those miners and merchants have to do. Usually one boat carries most of the materials a store will stock for the year. That's why the levee's crowded, and Fort Benton will look just the same.

You should see Fort Benton! There's maybe a half mile of riverbank with boats tied up during the spring and early summer. You'll see kegs, barrels, boxes, crates, and packages in a thousand different sizes. You can count over five hundred different items in my cargo alone. Got a minute? Read down the list of household items we're carrying this trip. Mind you, this doesn't count all the mining supplies, howitzer ammunition, food, newsprint, tobacco, clothes, and other things we're packing in. Read the list:

> Almanacs, book clasps, brooms, brushes, candles, candle molds, candlesticks, ironstone china, butter churns, clocks and parts, ivory and hard rubber combs, cooking kits, cooking utensils, cups, cutlery, indigo dye, glass goblets, griddles, hearth tools, ink, lamps and parts, matches, mirrors, pen holders, pen points, pencils, pie plates, pots and pans, soap, spice grinders, starch, stoves and parts, tallow, tea kettles, teaspoons, waffle irons, washboards, washtubs and buckets, water tumblers, and whiskey glasses.

That's quite a bit of stuff, isn't it?

We're going to be leaving port in a couple of days, I hope. The water is rising, and it looks like a good year. This is not one of the faster boats, but she's a good one. It'll take us about six weeks to make Fort Benton, so we should be there in mid-June. If you want to talk about fast ships, you should have seen the *Far West*. She set the record for the 1,700-mile run from Sioux City, Iowa, to Fort Benton in 1872. Martin Coulson piloted her that trip. He challenged Grant Marsh and the *Nellie Peck* to a race. They had to make regular stops for freight and passengers—and wood, naturally. But the *Far West* tied up at Fort Benton in seventeen days and twenty hours out of Sioux City. That's fast. The *Nellie Peck* was only three hours behind and that's not bad either. Remember now, they weren't travelling twenty-four hours a day. About 3:00 A.M. to 9:00 P.M. is all you can turn. By night you might hit a snag, so it's best to tie up and wait for light.

Listen, you've probably got other things to do, and I've kept you on board long enough. You remember us if you ever want to go upriver. It's a lot of fun on a river steamboat, wind blowing and paddlewheel splashing behind. Step carefully, now. Drop by next time we're in port.

Jim Hill Built a Railroad

Hill County sits on the Canadian border, along the northern edge of Montana. It straddles a set of railroad tracks now owned by the Burlington Northern. Built by the St. Paul, Minneapolis and Manitoba Railroad, and then owned by the Great Northern, that railroad was the creation of a unique man, James Jerome Hill. Hill County serves as a monument to a great man's influence in Montana.

The story of Jim Hill began in Ontario, Canada, in 1838. On a small fifty-acre farm, Hill was born September 16. With his older sister, Mary, and his younger brother, Alec, Jim spent the first ten years of his life growing up on the farm. They worked hard with their father and mother to provide a living for the family. In the evening, by lamp or fire light, their parents often read to them. The Hill family library was small, but it provided a good start: a one-volume collection of Shakespeare's works, another book of Robert Burns' poetry, a Bible, and a dictionary.

Sunday was a day for church and relaxation. After reading passages from the Bible, the family went to nearby Rockwood for church. The afternoon belonged to the children for play. Favorite among the boys' sports was hunting. Jim became an excellent shot with a rifle. The boys also built bows and arrows from the trees and brush nearby.

At age nine, an accident happened that blinded Jim in one eye. A newly built bow snapped in his hands and the arrow flew backward, tearing the eyeball from its socket. A local doctor managed to return the eye to its place and to restore muscular control. He could not restore sight. From that time on, Jim Hill could see only shades of light and dark in that eye. In later life no one knew or suspected. Both eyes twinkled with delight when Hill was happy. They flashed with anger when he became upset. During his lifetime he read long and hard. Jim Hill did not let his handicap stand in his way.

For his first thirteen years, James Hill was simply James Hill. That year he discovered and read of Napoleon's exploits. The history so impressed the young man that he took the name of Napoleon's brother—Jerome—as his own middle name. Thereafter, he used James J., or J.J., or Jim Hill.

In 1872 when this picture was taken, James J. Hill was just beginning to expand his railroad lines to the West. By 1893 he completed his own transcontinental railroad, the Great Northern.

At best, Jim Hill's early years had been filled with hard work. Then, at fourteen, he assumed responsibility for the family. His father died on Christmas Day, and as the oldest son, Jim worked to provide for his mother, sister, and brother. For the next two years he clerked in a general store. He earned a dollar a week at his first job, but learned valuable lessons in business. He developed good handwriting and perfected bookkeeping skills.

By the spring of 1856, Jim Hill was seventeen. Ontario lacked the adventure he sought in life, so he decided to leave Canada and try his luck in the bustling cities of the United States. By July 21, 1856, he had established himself in St. Paul, Minnesota. He secured a job as an agent for a steamboat company. The city held all the adventure young Hill wanted. He worked long and hard. On one occasion he heard yells from the busy waterfront and rushed out to discover someone drowning. Quickly shedding his jacket, he dived in and pulled the boy to safety.

During evenings he strolled the city with a girl friend. He hunted bear in nearby forests. He won and lost a few fights in the rough-and-tumble city. In a sense of public service, he joined the local militia and the volunteer fire department—Minnehaha Engine Company Number 2. Here he manned the pump-bars that supplied the hoses. He ran with the hook and ladder. He proudly wore the company's red and blue shirt and the helmet.

When the Civil War broke out, Jim Hill joined other Union-minded young men in St. Paul and volunteered. Even with only one eye, Hill was the best shot in his militia unit; so it was with some disappointment that he faced his rejection. No one-eyed men in the army, the inspecting doctor had told him. During the conflict, Hill supported the local company as well as he could. On their departure and return, he arranged fitting celebrations.

By the time the Civil War ended in 1865, Jim Hill had gained valuable experience in the trade, freighting, and transportation business along the upper Mississippi River. He saw Minnesota's first steam locomotive arrive in the fall of 1861. Hill soon handled the affairs of both railroad and riverboat companies in St. Paul. During the late 1860s he became more and more involved in railroad promotion. He also became increasingly interested in a young lady named Mary Theresa Mehegan. On August 19, 1867, the two married. "I am the head of the house now and live at home," Hill wrote to a friend. "All's well."

Hill decided to go into business on his own the same year he married. He became involved in promoting trade north of St. Paul along the Red River in Canada. He also saw opportunities in coal. "My idea is to get as many people using coal as possible," he said. For the next ten years he worked hard, making St. Paul a distribution point for the region and gaining a percentage of the profits for himself. His success was well-assured by the end of 1876. He sat down and wrote, "I have much to be thankful for this year. I have had a fairly prosperous business and my wife and five children are all in good health and happy."

In 1877 Hill joined with several associates in Canada, England, and the United States to get control of the small St. Paul and Pacific Railroad. Arrangements were completed the following year. Hill then began the task of making the line a profitable carrier. By 1880 the company had become the St. Paul, Minneapolis, and Manitoba Railway. Its lines extended to Winnepeg, Canada, and into what is now North Dakota. James J. Hill was its manager. He would spend the rest of his life operating that line and its successors.

During the early 1880s, two transcontinental railroads pushed across the northern plains and mountains to the Pacific. South of the Canadian border, the Northern Pacific completed construction at Gold Creek, Montana, in 1883. A few years later, the Canadian Pacific tied Montreal with Vancouver. In between the two lines lay millions of undeveloped acres in North Dakota and Montana. Three Montanans encouraged Jim Hill to take a long hard look at their part of the country. Paris Gibson, Charles A. Broadwater, and Martin Maginnis recognized Hill's ability and thought his railroad could help them develop Montana.

Martin Maginnis served as Montana's territorial delegate to Congress from 1872 to 1883. From this vantage point he kept his finger on the political pulse of the region. Gibson and Broadwater had more economic visions. About the time the Northern Pacific was laying its first rails in Montana, during 1881, Paris Gibson talked with his old friend. Near the Great Falls of the Missouri, Gibson reported excellent coalfields. The falls themselves provided an endless source of energy. Certainly this area had the potential of a great city.

Broadwater encouraged Hill to look not only at the region about the Great Falls, but also at the gold, silver, and copper potential in Butte. Among Hill, Gibson, and Broadwater, a plan began to develop. Gibson would secure land near the falls and found a city. Hill would extend the Manitoba along the Missouri River from its present terminus at Devil's Lake, North Dakota. From Great Falls, Broadwater would build the Montana Central railroad south to Helena and Butte.

During the spring of 1884, Hill yielded to pressure from the two vocal Montanans. He travelled to Helena on the Northern Pacific, then rode with Gibson and Broadwater to the Great Falls. The men visited, hunted prairie chickens, and spent their nights around a camp fire, talking about old times and Montana's future. Hill returned to St. Paul and thought. He sent a geologist to study Sand Coulee coal. He sent other observers as well. By 1885 his mind was made up—he would extend to Montana. "With a railway to the Falls and cheap coal, I see no reason why it is not the cheapest and best place in Montana to reduce the ores of that whole country," Hill told Broadwater.

The "grand progress" or the "long march forward," as Hill called it, began in 1886. In that year Manitoba crews graded 774 miles and laid 400 miles of new track. "I do not feel at all tired," Hill noted at the end of the year. But ahead lay an even more awesome task. During the summer of 1887, Hill's crews laid 783 miles of track. It was more than had ever been completed in a single year by any railroad company. By November, Helena residents could board the Montana Central, change to the Manitoba at Great Falls, and head east to St. Paul.

By 1889, Hill had decided to cross the Rockies and mountains to the west and extend his line all the way to the Pacific Ocean. He wanted a transcontinental railroad. He planned to build the best possible line, in the shortest distance, and on the lowest grades with the least curvature. His reason was simple. "Our policy is to cut down our grades and put the whole road in condition to give such low rates that opposition enterprises must be bankrupt." A better-built railroad meant a more profitable railroad. Hill built the best.

December 11, 1889, explorer John F. Stevens found a pass between the Marias and Flathead rivers. The wind whipped about his heavy clothing. The temperature stood at nearly forty below. Undaunted, Stevens checked his calculation. He had found a low, level pass across the Continental Divide. The next year Hill pushed his newly-created Great Northern Railroad westward over that pass.

The construction task of 1890 was even more impressive than that of 1887. Prairies provided small challenges for track builders compared to the deep cut valleys and rugged mountains west of Havre. At Cut Bank Creek the Great Northern constructed one of the largest trestles in the world. Track gangs struggled up canyons, bridged a hundred rivers and streams, and blasted cuts and tunnels. At any time a special train with Jim Hill on board might show up to see how work was going. He directed even the smallest details, including the location of water tanks and the length of sidings. After two years of work the dream came true on January 6, 1893. The Great Northern stretched from St. Paul to the Pacific.

The same year he completed the Great Northern, a financial panic swept the United States. Many railroads built on speculation or without Hill's care went bankrupt. The Northern Pacific was one. Hill joined other financial leaders, like Edward H. Harriman of the Union Pacific, in a contest for control of these lines. When the dense political and financial smoke of these battles had cleared, Jim Hill controlled the Great Northern and the Northern Pacific. Together, these companies owned the Chicago, Burlington and Quincy Railroad. To provide a form of unified management, Hill created the Northern Securities Company, Limited, in November of 1901.

To many businessmen, this combination of railroads represented the best arrangement for the future of the Northwest. To others it represented a monopoly. To still others, like President Theodore Roosevelt, it was a trust that needed busting. In 1902 Roosevelt had the U.S. government bring suit against the Northern Securities Company. Two years later the Supreme Court ordered it dissolved. Despite the court's ruling, the three railroads continued to play important roles in the development and growth of the region. In a sparsely settled land, there was little room for intensive competition. Hill's vision finally became reality in 1970 with the creation of the Burlington Northern. The new company combined the lines Hill had united under the Northern Securities Company almost seventy years before.

Jim Hill recognized that Montana's land had great potential for development. Paris Gibson predicted, "These lands, which may be classified as semi-arid, are better fitted for growing wheat than any lands I have ever seen." Hill agreed. He worked to encourage settlement along his railroad. Farmers would provide markets for goods carried on his railroad, while they grew grain, vegetables, and cattle that Hill could carry to the Midwest. He put it simply: "If the farmer was not prosperous, we were poor."

During the early decades of the 1900s, Hill had the Great

Northern promote farming and settlement on the plains of Montana and North Dakota. The Great Northern helped Montana's Agricultural Experiment Station establish demonstration farms. The company provided free transportation for extension agents and operated special railroad cars that carried information on crop rotation, irrigation, and dry-land farming techniques.

Hill took an immediate interest in communities and people all along his railroad. When someone wrote asking about his "philosophy of life," Jim Hill replied that there were no new recipes for success. "Get knowledge and understanding. Determine to make the most possible of yourself by doing such useful work as comes your way." Opportunities come to everyone at some time, Hill went on. "Then it depends upon him, what he makes of it, and what it will make of him."

How should you prepare for life? Hill had other suggestions. He recommended that every boy and girl learn to be "obedient and affectionate and considerate of others." They should take advantage of all the education they can get, he said. Anyone who did this, Jim Hill believed, "has all the preparation for life that it is possible to give."

James Jerome Hill lived a full life. On May 29, 1916, he died at his home in St. Paul. The "Empire Builder" was gone. Paris Gibson believed no other man better realized the potential of Montana and the northwest than Hill. Businesses in Havre, Great Falls, and elsewhere along Hill's railroad, closed in mourning. At 2:00 P.M., St. Paul time, May 31, 1916, every train on the Great Northern stopped. Every telegraph and telephone ceased operation. For five minutes employees, passengers, young and old, paused to honor the man and his greatness.

The *Great Falls Tribune* remembered Hill not for his death, but for what he left Montanans. "He dreamed a dream of the future . . . ," the newspaper said. He worked to achieve his vision and make his dream come true. The Burlington Northern and the lines that came before it mark Hill's dream in Montana. Counties like Hill, and towns from Culbertson, to Havre, to Kalispell, to Troy are monuments. Perhaps James J. Hill provided his own epitaph in 1880 when he said: "When we are all dead and gone, the sun will still shine, the rain will fall, and this railroad will run as usual."

Timeline

1853-54: Isaac Stevens looks for possible railroad route in Montana.

1859: *Chippewa* reaches Marias River; construction begun on Mullan Road.

1860: *Chippewa* and *Far West* reach Fort Benton.

1862: Mullan Road completed.

1864: *Chippewa Falls* and *Alone* travel up Yellowstone River; Bozeman Trail opened by John Bozeman.

1866: Telegraph completed from Salt Lake City to Virginia City; Wells Fargo & Company begin operations in Montana.

1867: Indians attack forts on Bozeman Trail; John Bozeman killed by Indians.

1868: Bozeman Trail closed and forts abandoned.

1869: Union Pacific completes first transcontinental railroad in Utah.

1876: *Far West* picks up wounded after Battle of Little Big Horn.

1880: Utah and Northern Railroad enters Montana from south and Northern Pacific enters Montana from east; Dillon founded.

1881: Utah and Northern reaches Butte.

1882: Billings founded; first Montana telephone exchange in Butte; street railways in Billings.

1883: Northern Pacific completed in Montana.

1886: Street railways in Butte and Helena.

1887: Railroad reaches Fort Benton; Manitoba Railroad reaches Helena.

1893: Jim Hill completes Great Northern Railway.

1901: Northern Securities Company formed by Jim Hill.

1907: Montana Railroad Commission established by legislature.

1910: J. C. Mars flies first plane in Montana.

1911: Cromwell Dixon first to fly over Continental Divide in Montana.

1913: Katherine Stimson carries first airmail letter in Montana; Butte, Anaconda and Pacific Railroad first U.S. railroad to use electric power; Montana Highway Department established.

1916: Jim Hill dies in St. Paul, Minnesota.

1921: *Mandan* is the last steamboat to dock at Fort Benton.

1922: KDYS in Great Falls is first Montana radio station.

1933: Commercial air service begins in Montana.

1937: Last trolleys operate in Butte.

1947: Montana Air National Guard created.

1951: Last trolleys operate in Anaconda.

1953: KOOK-TV in Billings is first Montana TV station.

1954: Last passenger boat operates on Flathead Lake.

1955: First Montana National Guard helicopter arrives.

1956: Interstate highway system begun.

1957: *Moyle* is last steamboat to operate on Kootenai Lake.

1970: Burlington Northern Railroad created.

1971: Amtrak created for passenger traffic.

1978: Milwaukee Railroad declares bankruptcy.

Suggested Readings

Robert G. Athearn. "Railroad to a Far-Off Country—The Utah and Northern," *Montana the Magazine of Western History* Vol. 18 #3 (Autumn, 1968).

Merrill G. Burlingame and K. Ross Toole. *A History of Montana,* Vol. II, Chap. XIX, "Transportation and Communication," pp. 53-84 (3 Vols. New York: Lewis Historical Publishing Co., 1957).

William E. Lass. *A History of Steamboating on the Upper Missouri River* Lincoln, Neb.: University of Nebraska Press, 1962.

Rex C. Myers. "Trolleys of the Treasure State," *Montana the Magazine of Western History* Vol. 22 #2 (Spring, 1972).

Robert L. Peterson. "The Completion of the Northern Pacific Railroad System in Montana: 1883-1893," in *The Montana Past: An Anthology,* edited by Michael P. Malone and Richard B. Roeder. (Missoula: University of Montana Press, 1969).

An oil rig in the first field to be developed in Montana, Cat Creek, just east of Lewistown about 1929.

Chapter IX
Industry Expands

Montana's State Seal has a pick, a shovel, a plow, and the Spanish terms for gold and silver across its face. Certainly Montana came into existence as a territory because of the mining boom in gold and silver. Equally certain, agriculture continues to play a vital part in Montana. Yet the history of the territory and state is more than the story of mining and agriculture. Spread across the land are many other businesses. The people who changed Montana from a wilderness into a modern state have been merchants, bankers, dam builders, lumbermen, craftsmen and laborers in countless trades.

Businessmen actually predated mining in Montana. Traders who followed Lewis and Clark brought goods to exchange for furs. Every fur post from David Thompson's in the west to Manuel Lisa's along the Yellowstone was, in truth, a store. No money changed hands, but trading with tobacco, guns, beads, metal hatchet heads, and flour, these early businessmen bought furs. At season's end the plews (skins) went downriver to St. Louis or Fort Vancouver where the trader sold them for money. Each spring the process began anew. The fur trader was a merchant, buying and selling.

Many pioneers brought the necessary equipment for placer mining with them. It was not much. A pick, shovel, and gold pan could get a man started. Before long, however, the miner needed additional supplies. Maybe he needed some lumber to build a sluice box or a rocker. What if he lost or broke his shovel? Then, too, a man might develop a yearning for some canned peaches or milk, some flour, a slab of bacon, a shot of whiskey or some feminine companionship. A few months of hard work wore out a pair of boots, or Levi's, or a red-checked flannel shirt. In every mining district, a town sprang up to supply those wants.

There is no way to know how many grocery stores, meat markets, general stores or saloons actually operated in Montana. In 1867, the Mercantile Agency of R. G. Dun and Company attempted to name businesses in the new territory. It counted 83 pioneer traders. Two years later the Montana Publishing Company issued a *Statistical Almanac* and proudly listed "2 tanneries, 1 foundry, 7 flouring mills, 17 sawmills, 15 distilleries and breweries, 4 furniture factories, and several wagon and harness factories" in Montana. By 1875, R. G. Dun and Company's tally had grown to 292 merchants in over 50 towns and villages. Virginia City alone had 41.

Clearly, the number of businesses grew as the population grew. Many people went into business after they failed to strike it rich mining. Others originally came to Montana with the idea of establishing some type of store. A major problem all merchants faced was one of supply. Goods could be obtained by overland freight from Utah and the Union Pacific, or on an annual basis by riverboat. At best, orders came not by the day or week, but by the month or year. Imagine trying to order enough of a product to last an entire year.

Miscalculation or a long, hard winter meant scarcity. Prices rose. No better example exists than the flour famine at Virginia City during the spring of 1865. Heavy winter snows closed supply routes. Flour stocks dwindled. Prices hit $150 per hundred pounds, and more. Townspeople took matters into their own hands. They gathered together all the supplies in Virginia City and doled them out in small quantities at lower prices.

Most prices in far-off Montana ran high. Coffee sold for $1.10 per pound; rice for 60¢; tobacco from $8 to $12 per pound; eggs, $1.50 per dozen, cracked or not; and a can of corn or peaches brought $2.00. One housewife reportedly spent $1,050 on food alone during her first three months in Montana. Only meat remained relatively cheap because of wild game and a generally adequate beef supply.

Pennies, nickels and dimes were in short supply on the frontier during the first few decades. "Two bits" became the basic price for many items, like a spool of thread. Miners expected to pay 50¢ for a bottle of writing ink, and $1 to mail the finished letter to "the states." Candles ran 60¢ per pound, ax handles, $1.25 each. Drinking glasses or mugs cost $12 per dozen, and beer to fill them, $12 a keg. One dance at the

Flour mills, such as the Judith Basin Roller Mill in Lewistown, were one of Montana's early industries.

local hurdy gurdy cost $1. All this came out of a miner's earnings when gold brought between $17.50 and $18 per ounce.

Despite high prices, Montana's population continued to grow. So did the number of businesses. This increase is easily reflected in the R. G. Dun tabulations. From 292 merchants in 1875, the totals jumped to 1,954 in 1885, and 4,859 a decade later. The figures increased steadily as years passed, reaching 10,000 in 1915, and topping 30,000 today. Prices for goods and services varied with local and national conditions. Improved transportation lowered prices. Increased supplies also dropped prices as did depressions in the early 1870s, the 1890s, the early 1900s, and the Great Depression of the 1930s. Inflation had the opposite effect. During the 1880s, from 1914 to 1919, and after World War II, prices rose as inflation made the dollar worth less.

Getting enough money to start a business was a challenge. No sooner had the first mines and stores begun in Bannack and Virginia City, than people began to lend and borrow money. In some cases it was nothing more than using credit. Individuals often had an account at the grocery or hardware store. They settled up every month. Larger companies might pay their bills every three months. Sometimes cattle companies paid annually, after the fall roundup.

Checks or bank drafts appeared in Montana before banks. Someone would come with a check on a Salt Lake City or St. Louis bank. Local merchants knew the bank was good, and knew the customer, so they cashed it. Other places took no checks and extended no credit. Several early "no credit" signs included: "Honor thy Father and Mother, but Not Stranger's Checks," and "To Trust is to Bust, to Bust is Hell; No Trust, No Bust, No Hell."

Money became a business itself, and banking was born in Montana. The first bank was the Ben Holladay/W. L. Halsey operation out of the Virginia City Stage Office that opened in August of 1864. They offered to buy gold dust and cash government checks or bank drafts from major cities. But this operation lasted only six months. Credit for opening the first permanent bank went to someone else.

B. F. Allen and J. H. Millard started their banking firm along Alder Gulch in September of 1864. Allen lived in Iowa and provided the money. Millard went to Virginia City and opened the bank. Right away he had a problem—the vault doors did not arrive. He wanted to give miners and merchants a sense of security, so he had wooden doors installed and painted to look like a heavy metal safe. Anyone visiting the bank for the first few months was not permitted to get too close to the vault doors in case they discovered the secret. Finally the real doors arrived and Mr. Millard rested easily at night. When Allen and Millard sold out in 1866, Millard took 100 pounds of gold dust back to Iowa as profit.

Interest rates from that period show why banking proved profitable. Interest of 2 percent a month was considered reasonable. Many early businessmen, like lumberman Anton Holter, paid 10 percent per month on money they borrowed. The highest recorded interest was charged at Trout Creek diggings—1 percent a day or over 365 percent a year. No wonder banking was profitable, and no wonder more than thirteen banks operated in Virginia City during its first years.

S. T. Hauser realized the need for a national bank in Montana. He began borrowing money in 1864 to establish one. He received a charter for the First National Bank of Helena on April 5, 1866. Other private banks appeared in Helena and Virginia City. For the first few years, only these two towns had banks, and Helena became Montana's financial center. Other communities soon attracted banks of their own. By 1870 Deer Lodge had one. Bozeman's First National Bank began in 1872, and Missoula's in 1873. The latter bank is the longest continually-operated financial institution in Montana.

Into the 1880s banks continued to appear in most communities. These were either private or national banks. When a major financial depression hit in 1893, banks folded. By 1900, only twenty-one continued operations. After statehood, Montana's legislature permitted state banks. By 1900, twenty-two had received charters. Hamilton's Ravalli County Bank—founded in 1895—is the oldest still operating.

Banking prospered during the first decade of Montana's history—1864-74. It boomed beyond belief between 1900 and 1920. Homesteaders flooded eastern Montana to secure their patch of land. They needed loans for housing, food and farm equipment. Eager bankers were there to provide the money. Before long both settlers and bankers had overextended themselves. When the price of grain jumped between 1914 and 1917, people thought that surely they had it made. Then weather, grasshoppers and markets turned against them. Depression swept across the agricultural sections of Montana like wind-blown dust.

In 1920, Montana had 426 banks. In 1925 only 227 remained. One hundred and ninety-nine banks had folded—103 in 1923 alone. There had been too much competition and too much optimism. Too much money had been loaned with too little security. Failures continued to mount as the 1920s turned into the national depression of the 1930s. By the end of that decade, Montana had just over 100 banks. The figure stayed about the same for nearly twenty years. Population growth in the 1960s and 1970s brought the figure up, but more cautiously and soundly than during the early 1900s. Today more than 160 banks and financial institutions provide money for businesses, homes and individuals. These firms carry on a tradition as old as Montana itself.

Montanans invested more than money in developing the territory and state. Many, many hours of work went into each business. As miners, ranchers, farmers and lumbermen took their living from the land, they sought someone to process their produce. Industry came to Montana.

Simply put, industry took raw materials—ore, grain, produce, fruit, livestock and trees—then ground, melted, cooked, canned or sawed it into something consumers could use. Although not a major manufacturing state, Montana developed business as an important link between the land and its people.

Manufacturing got its start in the region during the fall of 1845 or the spring of 1846. Father Anthony Ravalli brought two grinding stones with him from Europe when he came to St. Mary's mission. Before long, Jesuits in the Bitterroot, and later at St. Ignatius, produced more flour than they or the Flathead Indians could consume. Extra sacks were sold to American Fur Company posts along the Missouri. Montana had a manufacturing business.

During the early territorial period John Owen (Stevensville), Moise Reeve (Frenchtown), F. L. Worden and C. P. Higgins (Missoula), P. W. McAdow and Tom Cover (Bozeman), and George Thomas (Three Forks) erected flour mills. Others did, too, until more than a dozen mills ground and sacked flour by 1868. Flour mills could be found near most major population centers. Soon flour, which sold regularly for $30 to $40 per hundred pounds in 1863 and 1864, dropped to less than $10 per hundredweight. Bozeman and Missoula were early centers for the industry. In time Lewistown, Billings, Kalispell and Great Falls had large, prosperous mills. Beginning with the Cataract Milling Company, which Paris Gibson founded in 1885, Great Falls became a center for flour production. Flour brand names like "White Satin," "Rex," "Sapphire," "Occident" and "Ceretana" spread across Montana.

Other food processing followed the flouring mills. Every early mining camp had a meat market. Conrad Kohrs discovered the advantages of raising and selling the beef as early as 1864. By 1885, other businessmen began concentrating entirely on meat packing, purchasing beef from nearby ranchers. In Miles City and Great Falls, meat packing

Thomas C. Power dominated Upper Missouri River trade and transportation for many years at Fort Benton. His investments included cattle, freighting, supplies, banking and other businesses.—*Lawson photograph, Helena, M.H.S.*

companies formed that year. The number grew slowly but steadily and eventually included such firms as the Great Falls Meat Company, Hansen Packing Company in Butte, J. R. Daly in Missoula, and Billings' Pierce Packing and Midland Empire Packing companies. During the 1920s and 1930s an unusual product developed, in the processing of wild horse meat. Cowboys rounded up most of the remaining wild horses in central and eastern Montana. Plants in Miles City and Butte processed as much as 450 animals a day. They sent the products for use across the country as dog food and even as roasts or steaks for human consumption.

Cattle in Montana also provided a source for the dairy industry. The Gallatin, Boulder, Beaverhead, and Deer Lodge Valleys prided themselves in butter and cheeses. No territorial or state fair was complete without an exhibition of these products. J. N. Kelly began one of the first commercial dairy operations at Big Timber in 1895. Marcus Daly started one near Hamilton in 1896. For many years, however, cheese and butter shipped in from the Midwest sold for less than Montana-produced items. Through the work of the Agricultural Extension section of Montana State University, farmers began improving livestock and dairy production techniques.

Likewise, fruit and vegetable canning grew from a local industry to a major business in the 1940s and 1950s. Over time, the smaller Montana firms were unable to compete with larger national corporations, and they ceased operation. In July of 1915, the first commercial cannery in Montana opened near Stevensville. It processed cherries, peas and beans. Bozeman, Billings and Red Lodge canneries soon followed. Frozen food production flourished briefly at Glendive from the mid-1940s to the mid-1950s. Joseph Crisafuli and sons froze corn on the cob for national distribution. Like their food-processing counterparts across the state, the Crisafuli operation was not able to sustain itself because of limited markets and high transportation costs. Today only large, national companies purchase and process Montana produce.

Sugar beet production provides another example of a Montana food industry that struggled against national marketing problems. I. D. O'Donnell and a group of Billings businessmen raised enough money to construct Montana's first sugar beet factory during 1904 and 1905. Under the name Billings Sugar Company, the plant handled 55,000 tons of beets, producing 161,000 bags of sugar in 1906. Great Western Sugar Company took over the Billings operation in 1917 and built another short-lived plant in Missoula. Amalgamated Sugar Company (later American Crystal Company) built plants in Whitehall and Missoula following World War I. It never operated the Whitehall facility. Utah-Idaho Sugar Company built a plant in Chinook during 1925. The Holly Sugar Corporation entered the Montana sugar beet business the same year at Sidney. Holly built a second plant at Hardin in 1937. Cane sugar imports made beet sugar profits marginal for many years. Today only the Sidney and Billings plants survive.

For one year, Montana had a unique industry headquartered in Big Timber. The Sweet Grass Woolen Mills processed 6,000 pounds of wool between 1901 and 1902. It turned out the "finest blankets" in the state. It was a brief industrial attempt that failed because of larger, outside competition. The building stands today in Big Timber as a reminder of Montana's industrial hopes and dreams.

Smelting and industry go together in Montana. Miners started with placer gold. What settled in the bottom of a pan or sluice box was relatively pure. When they turned to lode or underground mining for gold and silver, processing became important. In simple terms, metal mining followed four steps. Miners dug the ore from the ground. Stamp mills crushed the rock and concentrators removed useless quartz or other undesirable minerals. Finally, these concentrates went through the smelter where a combination of heat and chemicals changed the mineral—gold, silver, copper, zinc, or other metal—into a bar or ingot.

Initially, a single miner could do some of this in small quantity. With an arastra—similar to a grinding stone—he could crush the rock, and using water or perhaps mercury, separate out a concentrate. From there, some type of smelting was needed. Early on, ores and concentrates left Montana by wagon and riverboat for Colorado, Baltimore or even Europe for smelting. As each metal industry expanded, a series of mills, concentrators and smelters grew up to handle the processing. These operations made up Montana's first heavy industry—one that continues today.

Precious-metal mills and smelters existed in various sizes in mining camps across Montana. Glendale, Wickes/Corbin, Cooke City, Butte, Basin, Maiden, and other camps sported their stacks and tailings ponds. Early pictures or sketches of Montana cities and towns emphasized smoke billowing from these industries. It was a sign of prosperity and of a future.

Copper processing began almost a decade after the first major ore strikes in Montana. It was not until the late 1870s that the first successful copper smelters added their smoke to city skylines. Butte miners knew copper, gold and silver existed in the region's ore deposits. The presence of each metal in a smelter or mine designed for a different one created endless problems. Copper, particularly, was difficult

Blasting crew at work at the 1900-foot level in one of the Butte copper mines.— N. A. Forsyth photograph, M.H.S.

and expensive to process. W. A. Clark was among the first to experiment with freighting the ore out of Montana for processing in Colorado, Baltimore, Swansea, Wales and Freiberg, Germany.

Clark was also the first to establish a smelter capable of handling copper in Montana. His Colorado and Montana Smelting Company began processing copper in 1879. Within two years Charles A. Meader was managing the Montana Copper Company smelter in Butte. A. M. Holter and S. T. Hauser opened the Parrot Silver and Copper Company, producing the first blister copper in the region.

All this paled in comparison to the rich output of the Anaconda Mine and the efforts of Marcus Daly. He realized the need for a large smelter and discovered an ideal location twenty miles west of Butte, on Warm Springs Creek. By 1884 the town and smelter at Anaconda were a reality. To start, the plant handled 500 tons of ore each day. By 1887 additional facilities increased capacity to more than 3,000 tons. In 1902 the "New Works," or Washoe Smelter, began handling Anaconda ore at the rate of 5,000 tons per day.

Washoe was the largest smelter in the world at the time. Its smokestack eventually reached a height of 585 feet, towering over the Deer Lodge Valley.

Butte's Boston and Montana Copper Company realized that they, too, needed a better place for a smelter. Rejecting sites along the Big Hole and Jefferson rivers, they settled on a location near the Great Falls of the Missouri. In 1890 this smelter began production. Eventually, the Anaconda Copper Mining Company assumed operation of the Great Falls facility. Anaconda later closed the smelting operation and used the plant for electrolytic processing of copper and zinc.

Copper production continues at Butte and Anaconda today. The state has three other smelting operations, however. The American Smelting and Refining Company (ASARCO) in East Helena handles lead and zinc. The Stauffer Chemical Company near Silver Bow processes phosphorus. The Anaconda Company's aluminum plant at Columbia Falls has been handling that metal since 1955.

Montana industry converts other raw materials into finished products. Today refiners in Billings, Laurel, Wolf Point, Great Falls, and Cut Bank produce petroleum products for the state and region. Montana's oil boom began in 1919. When the crude oil started pouring from wells at Cat Creek, Cut Bank, Williston Basin, Kevin-Sunburst, Dry Creek, Elk Basin, Soap Creek and elsewhere, refineries quickly followed to convert the "black gold" into usable products. Miles City and Lewistown had refineries in 1921. By the end of the 1920s, more than a dozen refineries and cracking plants operated across the state. Gradually these plants have been consolidated to six facilities. Some of the crude oil processed in the state comes from fields outside Montana. Naturally the oils, gasoline and asphalt produced are marketed regionally from Wyoming and the Dakotas to Washington. Like smelting, Montana's petroleum refining industry transforms raw materials taken from the land into a product the state and nation can use.

Another of Montana's major industries predates the formation of the territory and state. From the moment the first Montana resident cut lodge poles, or fashioned a travois, or built a campfire using wood, Montana had a new industry. When early trappers and traders came, they—like the Indians—turned to the forests as a source of building material. Cabins, forts, and camp fires marked expanded use of forest products.

First attempts at sawing lumber employed whip or pit saws. Pioneers literally dug a pit and laid a log over it. One man stood on top, another at the bottom. They pulled a saw up and down through the log. When missionaries arrived, the need for lumber increased. Father Ravalli receives credit for operating the first sawmill in Montana at St. Mary's. Ravalli's mill first turned out sawed boards in 1845.

As with most other industries, the mining rush to Bannack and Virginia City spurred the expansion of lumbering. Riverboats needed cord wood for fuel. Miners needed homes, sluice boxes and stores. Bannack had a sawmill by late 1862 to meet its needs. Between 1863 and 1865, literally dozens of steam-and-water powered lumber mills began operating across western Montana. Among the more notable were Thomas Cover and P. W. McAdow's mill near Bozeman, A. M. Holter's Virginia City operation, Nick Redding in Helena, and the Frank Worden/C. P. Higgins mill at Missoula. Demand and prices were high during the middle 1860s. Miners paid between $125 and $140 per thousand board feet, buying lumber as fast as it could be cut.

When placer mining declined in the late 1860s and 1870s, lumber production slumped with it. Prices dropped to $50 to $60 per thousand board feet. By the end of the decade production had picked up only moderately. Forty-two mills operated and about six million board feet was sawed annually. Prosperity waited just over the horizon in the form of the steam locomotive.

The Utah and Northern, Northern Pacific, Manitoba, and Montana Central Railroads all built in Montana during the 1880s. Trains needed wooden ties beneath the rails. They needed wooden trestles to bridge coulees and canyons, timber to line tunnels, and cord wood in the tender to keep the fire going under the boiler. Demand for wood was large and big companies formed to meet it. Eddy, Hammond and Company, of Missoula, grew to become the Montana Improvement Company, which operated throughout western Montana. The Montana Improvement Company cut timbers and wood for the railroads. They also provided mine timbers and cord wood for smelters like Marcus Daly's growing operations in Butte and Anaconda. Daly owned part of the

Lumber mills like this one at Hamilton, have been an important part of Montana's economic development.

company, and so did the Northern Pacific Railroad on whose land much of the timber was cut. Through its government land grant, the NP became Montana's largest private land owner in the 1880s. Many of the alternate sections it received were forested.

How important was lumbering in early Montana? An old picture will tell the story. Photographs of Helena, Missoula, Virginia City and elsewhere show surrounding hillsides completely barren of trees. They had been cut for building and for fuel.

The federal government attempted to curb excessive use in the 1870s and 1880s. Companies like the Anaconda Company, Montana Improvement Company and the Northern Pacific violated the letter and spirit of the law. They acquired title to vast tracts of forest lands, sometimes fraudulently, and cut indiscriminately on government land as well as their own. When the government tried again in 1891 with the Forest Reserve Act, companies moved to buy up anything left. During the 1890s, over 100 mills cut lumber in Montana. There were 21 in the Bitterroot Valley alone. The largest mill in the state was the Blackfoot Milling and Manufacturing Company at Bonner. It turned out 240,000 board feet a day in 1890. By 1900 Montana's lumber mills processed over 255 million board feet annually.

President Theodore Roosevelt tried yet another time to limit lumbering abuses. The federal government began legal action against the Big Blackfoot operation and W. A. Clark's Western Lumber Company in 1905. This had little effect, for other companies expanded timber operations in the state. Michigan and Minnesota forests had been heavily cut during the 1800s. Now companies from that region looked west to Montana for new territory. By 1907, firms like the J. Neils Lumber Company started purchasing land in what became Lincoln, Sanders, Lake and Flathead counties. In 1923 the

153

company abandoned Minnesota and set up headquarters in Montana. Others joined the move.

Montana lumber companies owned most of the non-government timber land in the state by 1910. The Northern Pacific and Anaconda Company held more than 70 percent of the unreserved forest land. These firms, and others, began cooperative efforts like the Northern Montana Forestry Association. Among their main goals was the prevention of forest fires. 1910 proved a real challenge.

Early on, the summer of 1910 turned hot and dry. Before long 90 major blazes and more than 3,000 small fires burned in western Montana and northern Idaho. In August the forest literally blew up. Fires combined. The heat created hurricane force winds, spreading flames in a path 130 miles long and 20 to 35 miles wide. An area about the size of Connecticut went up in smoke, as did nearly eight billion board feet of timber. Eighty-five people lost their lives, most of them fire fighters. Another 125 were missing and never found. Out of the disaster came improved efforts at fire fighting and detection. The first fire lookouts went up. Airplanes, fire crews and eventually smokejumpers brought sophisticated fire fighting to Montana timber lands.

Conditions in Montana's forests proved hard for lumbermen year around, not just during fire season. Accidents with saws, axes, teams, logging railroads and machinery claimed a toll. Working hours were long—at least ten per day. The six-day week was common and wages remained low. Small wonder that radical labor organizations like the Industrial Workers of the World (IWW or "Wobblies") began organizing timber workers between 1905 and 1917. IWW organizers were aggressive and persuasive. Workers listened and resolved to fight their employers, if necessary. The IWW and Montana lumber mill owners had a major confrontation in 1917. The union wanted better conditions. Owners faced poor markets and declining profits. During the summer of that year, the IWW declared a strike. There was violence on both sides. September 1, Montana Lumber Manufacturers Association members met in Missoula. Under the direction of Kenneth Ross, they worked to correct some of the poor conditions in the woods. The government suggested logger/owner cooperation and the Loyal Legion of Loggers and Lumbermen came into being. The eight-hour day began in the forests. Loggers went back to work.

Lumber production after World War I fluctuated with the market. During 1923 it peaked at 436 million board feet cut. Depressions hit in the 1930s and 1960s, with prosperity sandwiched in between. Today modern technology makes it possible to use trees more completely. Particle board, plywood, woodchips for paper, and bark for lawn decoration are a few examples. Timber management on private and forest service land also seeks to insure continued production. But it is an industry still plagued with controversy. Clear cutting, wilderness and insect control issues often create arguments between environmental groups and lumber producers. Historically, lumbering has had a vital part in Montana's past. With proper management, it will continue to play an important role in the state's future.

Wood once served as Montana's only source of energy. Gradually, however, electric power came to dominate the field here, as it did nationally. Montana's electrical output has come from two other resources—coal and water. Early generating plants used coal or coke. In eastern portions of Montana today, this still makes up the primary source of generating power. Most Montana-Dakota Utilities customers receive electricity from coal-fired generating plants, for example. Colstrip plants 1 and 2 burn coal practically at the mine, providing electrical power for customers both in Montana and the Pacific Northwest.

Helena and Butte residents first enjoyed the marvel of electricity in August and November of 1882. Curiously, Helena had electrical service even before New York City. Other cities developed electricity quickly: Bozeman (1885), Billings (1887), Livingston (1889), Kalispell (1892) and Havre (1898).

Billings holds the honor as the first Montana city with hydroelectric power. When the Billings Water Power Company began operating their small plant in 1887, they proudly boasted the best lighted city in the West. One streetlight glimmered in each block of the business district and on every other block in residential sections.

Bigger things were yet to come. In 1890, the Black Eagle Dam at Great Falls diverted water through generators. The electricity powered the Boston and Montana smelter, the city and its streetcars. The next year, dams on Flint Creek and

Rocky Creek provided hydroelectric power for Philipsburg and Bozeman, respectively.

A major change took place in both the electrical and mining industry when hydroelectric power came to Butte. Samuel T. Hauser of Helena constructed Canyon Ferry Dam east of that city in 1898. Most of the power generated followed transmission lines to Butte. In 1899 and 1901 dams on the Big Hole and Madison Rivers added their power to Butte's industry. More and more dams rose in Montana canyons: Bonner, Big Fork, Hauser, Rainbow Falls.

The most important man in the history of Montana's power industry was John D. Ryan. Ryan ran the Anaconda Company in Butte by 1910. In this position he controlled the industry which used most of Montana's hydroelectric power. He then set out to control the production of that power. Through a series of legal and financial maneuverings, he forced early developers like S. T. Hauser to sell out. In 1912 he was ready to form the Montana Power Company—overnight one of Montana's largest industries. Consolidated under one corporate roof were the Butte Electric and Power Company, the Madison River Power Company, the Billings and Eastern Montana Power Company, the Missouri River Power Company, the Great Falls Water Power and Townsite Company, and the Thompson Falls Power Company. By 1913 Montana Power acquired or absorbed forty-four different companies. John D. Ryan controlled more than 85 percent of Montana hydroelectric output.

Montana Power continues to provide most electrical service in central and western Montana. In the extreme north and west, Pacific Power and Light serves some communities. In the east, Montana-Dakota Utilities is the major distributor. In more sparsely settled rural areas, a series of twenty-five Rural Electrification Administration cooperatives (REAs) provide service to farmers and ranchers. The REAs began in 1936. With the three major companies, they are responsible for the fact that almost every home in Montana has electrical service. The labor-saving changes electricity made possible on the farm was one of the major developments in Montana after 1940.

Electricity ushered in the modern age for Montana. Electrified copper mining and smelting, streetcar and railroad transportation, home or street lights, and cream separators;

John D. Ryan, powerful executive head of Amalgamated Copper, Anaconda Copper and Montana Power Company. From 1909 until his death in 1933, Ryan was one of the most influential figures in Montana's economy.

the change has been profound. Something else came to Montana that changed the state's way of thinking—the tourist.

Actually, tourism in Montana is old. One of the first tourists visited the area before it became a territory. In 1855 wealthy Irish sportsman Sir George Gore came to hunt big game in the Powder River country. He had Jim Bridger as a guide, and brought along 20 servants, 112 horses, 12 yoke of oxen, 6 wagons, and 21 carts containing arms, ammunition and all the luxuries of home. He slaughtered game throughout the region until the Indians had to protest his excesses.

Over the years Montana residents have never hesitated to write friends and relatives back east boasting the region's beauty. Tourism increased. Yellowstone National Park became the nation's first in 1872, testimony to the country's interest in unique scenery. Hot springs resorts like Hunter's Hot Springs, White Sulphur Springs, Boulder, Elkhorn and

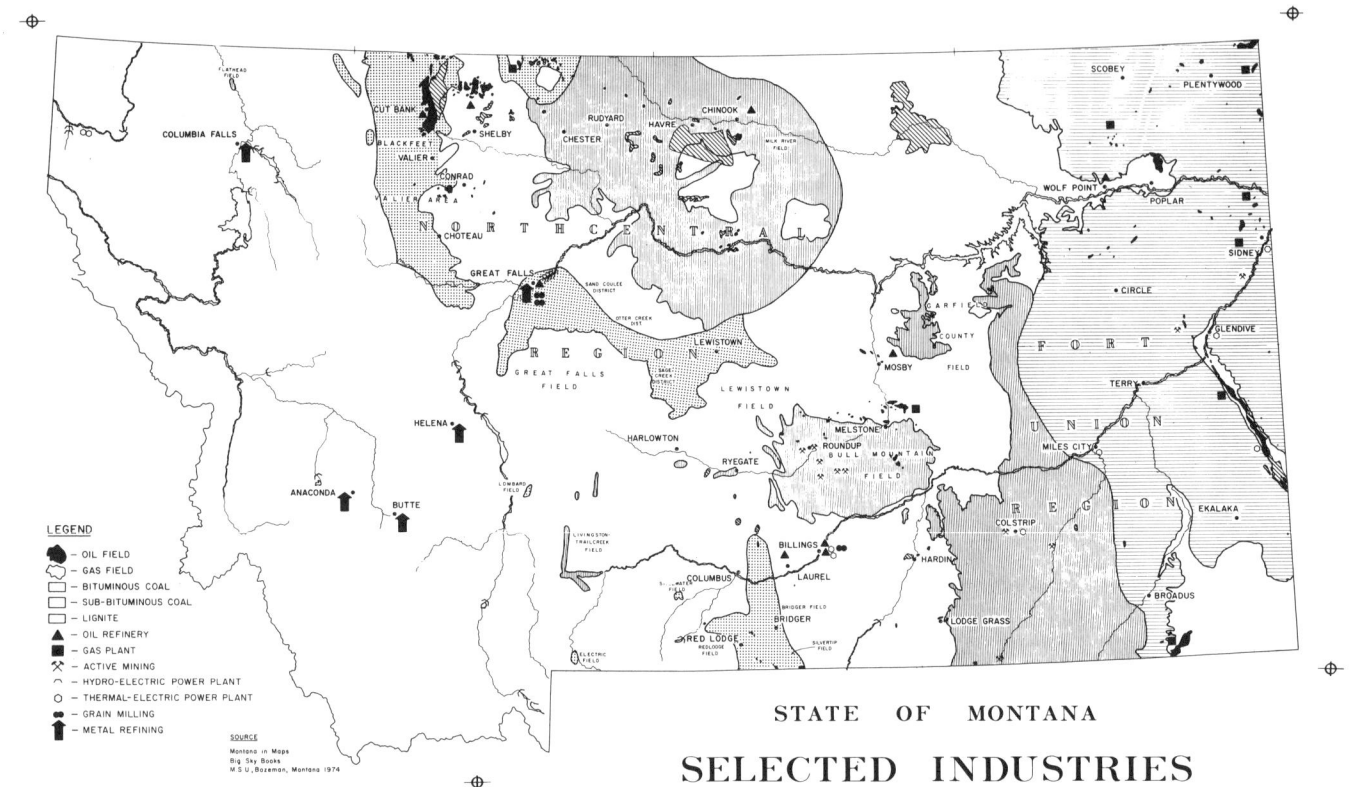

STATE OF MONTANA

SELECTED INDUSTRIES

the Broadwater Hotel provided another source of tourist business. When the railroads arrived in the early 1880s, Pullman passenger cars carried even more tourists to see Montana. For the first ten years after the railroads' arrival, visitors spent an estimated $50,000 a year in Montana. By early 1900 this had jumped to almost half a million dollars. Then came the automobile.

A car made it possible for the tourist to go where he wanted when he wanted. Overnight the tourist industry topped the $1,000,000 mark. The local Board of Trade became the Chamber of Commerce. "The Chamber" encouraged tourists to come visit and stay. Dude ranches developed to give out-of-state residents a taste of western life. Glacier National Park, 1910, preserved another section of the state for the sight-seeing public. The state began setting aside parks, monuments and recreation areas in 1936. Today these state sites number seventy-seven.

In 1930 the state decided to encourage tourist travel officially. The Highway Commission, through the efforts of Robert Fletcher, began a series of promotional campaigns. They sent out brochures. They placed historic markers along highways. Each year during the Depression, more than a million tourists came to Montana and left $25,000,000 annually. It was quite a boost for the state's economy. During the next two decades the number of visitors who came and the dollars they left increased. In 1954 over three million visitors spent almost $100,000,000. Today estimates reach above four million tourists and $350,000,000. Tourism is Montana's third largest industry, behind agriculture and mining.

Montana's State Seal is not large enough to include symbols for all the businesses and industries that make up our economy. Merchants, bankers, smelters, lumbermen, factory workers and tourists join miners, farmers and ranchers in developing the land and contributing to Montana's economic growth.

Hard Work Built Montana

Hard work built Montana. The land gave nothing freely. Trapping, mining, cutting timber, shoveling coal, running machines, doing laundry, baking, pouring molten metal—hard work built Montana. The workingmen and women who came to the territory and state soon saw benefits in cooperation. Newspaper printers were the first to organize, not long after Montana became a territory.

Printing required skill and experience. The few typesetters and printers who joined the rush to Virginia City in 1864 prided themselves in their trade. Some sources say the first group to form included employees at the *Montana Post*. They asked for and got some of the best wages in the territory—$75 to $100 per week. Three years later, Helena printers chartered the first real Montana union—Local 95 of the International Typographical Union. For more than a century, this union represented its members in Montana's capital city.

The history of unionism in Montana can be dated from the formation of the Butte Workingmen's Union in 1878. This story began on June 10 of that year. Owners of the Alice and Lexington Mines decided to reduce wages from $3.50 to $3.00 per day. Work stopped. Miners began to march down the hill from Walkerville into Butte, led by a brass band. The miner's wage was a standard for all Butte workers, leaders explained. If employees yielded to the mine owners' demands, all Butte would suffer.

Over 300 Butte workmen joined the new organization, paying $2.50 for the initiation fee, and $1.00 per month in dues. The union also offered free medical care and insurance against wage cuts. On June 19, 150 miners—again with a brass band in the lead—marched up the hill to talk to the Alice Mine manager. Marcus Daly had been in Butte only a couple years, handling affairs for the Walker Brothers of Salt Lake City. He listened to the men. He heard their arguments and understood that none of Butte's other mines were cutting wages. By late July, miners were back to work at the Alice and Lexington at $3.50 per day. They had won.

Miners dominated the Butte Workingmen's Union from the start. Gradually they began to encourage non-miners to

Miners' Union Day parade at Granite, Montana, in the 1880s. In mining towns this was always a festive occasion.

join the trade-oriented Knights of Labor. By 1885, Butte had switched from silver to copper mining, and the union decided to change its name to reflect its make-up. Some 1,800 strong, the group began the Butte Miners' Union, largest of its kind in the West. Members built an impressive $13,000 hall for a headquarters.

Unionism in Butte grew with the expansion of mining and the town itself. The Silver Bow Trades and Labor Assembly came into being in 1886. Within five years most of Butte's 6,000 workers belonged to one affiliate or another. The Miners' Union continued to dominate and achieved enough strength in 1887 to get a closed shop in most Butte mines. This meant a miner had to join the union to get a job. The growth continued, made possible, in part, by the political and economic struggle historians call "The War of the Copper Kings."

William Andrews Clark, Marcus Daly, and later F. Augustus Heinze battled to control copper, Butte and Montana politics. Miners' unions became important allies. When the Western Federation of Miners formed in 1893, Butte became the site of Local No. 1. Through the 1890s, Butte was the "Gibraltar of unionism." Its membership supported Western Federation's efforts to improve working conditions throughout the West.

Between 1893 and 1906, important changes took place. The Western Federation of Miners turned increasingly toward socialism and radical action. In 1905 Federation leaders Charles Moyer and Bill Haywood met with socialists Eugene Debs and Daniel De Leon in Chicago to form the Industrial Workers of the World. A year later F. Augustus Heinze sold his interests in Butte to the Amalgamated Copper Company giving them complete control of Butte's mines and smelters. Gradually the mining company came to dominate the leadership of Butte's mining unions. The stage was set for a confrontation.

Rustling cards made matters worse. December 1, 1912, the mining company began a system whereby each miner had to have a rustling card—company approval—before he could seek work in the mines. The company or a foreman could take the card at any time, thus killing a man's hope for work. Miners hated the system and voted not to work under such conditions. The management-dominated union refused to call a strike.

By June 13, 1914—Miners Union Day—tensions were high. The annual parade soon erupted into a fist fight. Miners, fed up with changes in recent years, sacked the Union Hall and destroyed many records. When Western Federation officials came to try to quell the unrest, miners almost lynched the spokesman and finally blew up the Miner's Hall.

The violence not only destroyed a building, it killed the union. Anaconda Company officials moved quickly to take advantage of the situation. In September they declared the open shop in all Butte mines. On October 6, the Anaconda Company had the courts depose Socialist and pro-labor mayor Lewis Duncan. Likewise, Socialist newspapers were smashed. The Company had won.

During World War I, federal and state action supported businesses against union organization. National Guardsmen and federal troops kept Butte quiet, or served as warnings of what would happen if miners struck. In 1917, IWW organizer Frank Little was hanged. In 1920 Company gunmen fired machine guns on union pickets, killing two and wounding sixteen. Only with New Deal legislation in the 1930s did Butte miners reorganize under the Mine, Mill and Smelter Workers.

Again, the history of unionism was not smooth. Mine, Mill and Smelter Workers affiliated with the Congress of Industrial Organizations (CIO). Mine-Mill became more and more liberal. Some leaders and members became identified with Communism. In 1950, the CIO expelled Mine-Mill. Butte miners developed a bitter hatred for the CIO and stayed with their own organization.

At the same time changes were taking place in Butte mining operations. The Anaconda Company began to move away from underground mining and toward an open-pit technique. The Berkeley Pit was soon Butte's major mining facility. The Steelworkers Union also began active campaigns to recruit members in Butte, cutting into Mine-Mill strength. Probably the peak of Mine-Mill power came in the 1959 strike. It lasted 181 days and was the longest in Butte's history. After that, the Company's move to open-pit mining became more pronounced. So did Steelworkers' success in recruiting new members. In 1967 Mine-Mill combined with its larger competitor. When underground mining ceased in 1975 only a few hundred members of the miners' union remained.

Butte labor history is a colorful one. But the history of Montana's union organizations extends beyond mines and smelters. Certainly the 6,500-member Butte Miners' Union represented the largest block of workingmen in the city around the turn of the century. There were other unions. In these organizations is found the breadth of Montana's labor experience. A Butte business directory of the period listed thirty-three separate groups:

Building Trades Council
Amalgamated Society of Engineers
Barbers' Union
Bakers Union
Blacksmith and Helpers Union
Bricklayers Union
Brotherhood of Stationary Engineers
International Building Laborers Union
Butte Butchers Union
Carpenters' Union
Cigarmakers' International Union
Clerks' Protective Union
Cooperative Lathers' Union
Horseshoers' Union
Hotel and Restaurant Employees Union
International Association of Machinists
International Brotherhood of Boiler Makers and Iron Ship Builders
International Journeymen Plasterers Union
International Typographical Union
Iron Moulders' Union
Job and Express Union
Laundry Workers' Union
Mill and Smeltermen's Union
Musicians' Union
National Brotherhood of Electric Workers
Painters, Paper Hangers and Decorators' Union
Plumbers and Gas Fitters' Union
Shoemakers' Union
Street Railway Employees Union
Teamsters Union
Tailors' Union
Tin, Sheet, Iron & Cornice Workers' Union
Workingmen's Union

Other Montana cities were not far behind in organizations. Missoula had 23 labor unions during the first decade of this century. Billings had 19 and Great Falls, 12. Today more than 425 separate labor organizations exist throughout the state. Historically, they have played a vital role in representing many of Montana's workingmen and women. At the same time they indicate the many different skills required to keep the state's economy healthy and active.

From Wheat to Flour

A special type of gold brings millions of dollars into Montana. These nuggets are not of heavy metal found in gulches and veins. They are small kernels of wheat harvested annually from one end of Montana to another. Gathered together in grain elevators, Montana wheat eventually travels to flour mills across the nation and around the world. From these mills comes the flour that feeds countless men and animals.

To understand the making of flour, it is necessary to understand the make-up of a wheat kernel. On the outside it looks like a single unit. Actually, there are three separate parts. The outer shell, about 14 to 15 percent of the wheat, is the bran. This is rich in niacin, riboflavin and thiamine (plus other B-complex vitamins). Humans do not digest bran fibers very thoroughly, however. Bran is included in whole wheat flour, but generally it is removed and made into animals' feeds.

Wrapped inside the bran is the endosperm. This is about 83 percent of the kernel and is the source of white flour. "Enriched" flour has more B-complex vitamins and iron added to it than are lost when the bran is removed. Also tucked into the kernel is the wheat germ—the embryo or sprouting section of the seed. This is less than 3 percent of the kernel, but contains quite a bit of fat and oil. If it is included in flour, like whole wheat, it increases the chance of spoilage. Usually it is removed in the milling process. Some wheat germ is sold separately for human consumption. Much joins bran as mill feed for animals.

Simply put, flour production removes the wheat bran and germ, then grinds the endosperm into a fine powder. The story actually begins with the growing cycle of wheat itself. After each harvest the land is fallowed, then plowed and planted. Soon winter and spring wheat brightens the land with green shoots. During summer, they mature to gold and the harvest begins. Combines and grain trucks bustle with activity. Names like Hard Red Winter, Durum and Hard Red Spring wheat mark the produce. For Montana it means between 130 and 150 million bushels of wheat. At 60 pounds per bushel, that is approximately 8½ billion pounds of wheat a year.

After combining, wheat is moved by grain truck to a local elevator. Over 240 such elevators dot Montana. From there by truck again, by railroad hopper car, or perhaps by barge from Lewiston, Idaho, the grain heads for a flour mill. Much wheat leaves Montana. Some is bound for more populated states. Other shipments make their way to the Orient and Europe. Some wheat remains in Montana and is ground into feeds or flour in any of three mills. They have familiar names like General Mills and ConAgra in Great Falls or Peavey in Billings.

Grinding wheat into flour is not a new industry for Montana. The process began in the Bitterroot Valley in 1845. Father Ravalli brought two round millstones from Europe. Soon he had a water-powered mill processing local grain. In a simple, one-step technique, the grain was fed between a moving stone and a stationary base (a second stone). Take a clump of dirt between your hands. Rub them together and watch the fine particles fall, much as the ground flour did in Father Ravalli's mill. Montana's early flour mills followed this simple process. By using a series of stones and regrinding the wheat, it was possible to make excellent flour. By the 1870s, Montana had mills in a dozen locations, all water-powered.

During the late 1800s and early 1900s, three important changes took place in the milling industry. First, other sources of power began to replace flowing water. Steam and eventually electricity came to power increasingly larger mills. Mill stones also gave way to a roller mill process. Looking very much like a series of overgrown wringers from old-style washing machines, these rollers made it possible to grind flour more gradually. This produced more and better flour per bushel.

Edmund La Croix invented a machine in 1865 that made the third improvement. Called a middlings purifier, this device took the ground wheat (middlings), sifting them on a screen, while blowing air through. This separated bran and wheat germ from the ground endosperm. Middlings could then be reground, finer and finer, producing smoother flour. These three technical improvements made possible the construction of larger mills. Over the years these plants replaced small community operations.

Grain elevators along the Great Northern at Dutton. Wheat for flour is Montana's agricultural "gold." —*Great Northern Railway photograph, M.H.S.*

A modern flour mill is a study in mechanical engineering and cleanliness. Montana's three mills operate on what is called a closed system. Once the grain enters the mill, it is processed entirely by machine until it is bagged for shipment to the consumer. Several floors of machinery, along with miles and miles of tubes and conveyors, handle the wheat en route. A flour mill is clean for reasons of safety as well as sanitation. Excessive amounts of dust would be harmful for workers to breathe, and dust might lead to fire or explosion.

Impressive is the fact that nearly half the milling process involves getting the wheat clean and ready for grinding. Chemists inspect the wheat when it arrives at the mill. Diseased grain has already been rejected. Now inspection and classification takes place. This includes grinding, sifting and baking small quantities to determine quality. Protein and water content varies. Most Montana wheat ranges from 10 to 18 percent protein and averages 11 percent moisture. Both figures change according to the wetness of the growing season. Less moisture generally means higher protein content.

Once testing and grading is done, cleaning begins. First a separator screens out sticks, stones and other foreign objects. Next, an aspirator blows air through the grain to get rid of chaff, leaves and light debris. Barley, oats, cockle and other seeds still may be mixed in with the wheat, so a series of disc separators eliminates those elements.

Wheat kernels have now passed through the first series of cleaners and purifiers. There is yet another round. A machine known as a scourer roughs up the kernel, rubs off impurities, and gets the product ready for more machinery. In the next series of steps, magnets, washer-stoners and high-speed impactors take over. They remove even the smallest metal parts and rocks that remain. Impactors kill any insects or larva that have managed to survive to this point.

Once cleaning is completed, the wheat is tempered. Grain may start with only 11 percent moisture. For ideal processing, it needs to have 15 to 16 percent. Tempering adds that moisture, making it easier to separate bran from the endosperm and then grind the endosperm into fine flour. Once tempered, the wheat goes through an Entoleter—an impact machine that breaks and removes any unsound wheat. Only the best kernels are now left for grinding.

"First break" in milling terms means the first time wheat is sent through a set of rollers. This splits the kernel open and starts the grinding process. From this point on, the wheat flows through a series of rollers, sifters and middlings purifiers. It goes through five times, if necessary. The germ and bran are removed. A seemingly endless series of giant sifters—resembling large shaking boxes with different sized screens—sort the various products. Even though the endosperm makes up 83 percent of the wheat kernel, modern technology can get only 72 percent of that endosperm ground into flour. The remainder joins the bran and germ in a variety of products.

How fine is fine flour? To measure it, you need to think in terms of microns. A micron is .001 of a millimeter. After grinding, flour may range from 1 to 150 microns in size. Different bakers want different types of flour, but a standard home flour is 132 microns. That is approximately 1/10 of a millimeter. A metric ruler will demonstrate just how tiny that is.

All-purpose flour we buy in stores is only one type produced. This is a bleached and enriched flour for home use. Nationally, it makes up less than 15 percent of the flour sold. Montana's mills make other types for more specialized demands. Bakers require a particular flour for each variety of bread found on supermarket shelves. Cakes, crackers, pies and pastries also need different flours, as do pretzels and macaroni products. General Mills, ConAgra, and Peavey, as well as other mills across the nation, grind flour to suit the needs of those using it.

The remaining 28 percent of the wheat kernel, which does not become fine or "patent" flour, finds other uses. Nothing is wasted—every bit of the wheat that enters a mill is made into a usable product. Some of the bran and germ is used by humans in such things as breakfast cereals and baking. They are rich in B-complex vitamins, and together have over 25 percent of the protein found in wheat. The protein also makes them useful in animals' feeds. These range from livestock and poultry feeds to pet foods. Some finely ground flour that does not become patent flour is used in glues, like wood and paper glues found around homes and schools.

Flour is probably the most widely used product in the world. Every nation and culture has some form of bread product made from flour. The grinding process is one that has undergone major changes in the last century. No longer do small, water-powered mills in individual communities provide for America's baking needs. Hand-in-hand with Montana's wheat industry, milling forms an important part of the lifestyle we enjoy today. The history of each slice of bread, each hamburger bun, and each cookie includes the story of flour milling in Montana.

Timeline

1806: Fur traders start Montana's first "business"

1845-46: Father Ravalli establishes first flour and saw mills in Montana

1855: Sir George Gore visits Montana

1863: Gold rush starts; lumber and retail sales industries start in Montana

1864: Montana created; first bank established in Virginia City

1865: Virginia City flour shortage; smelters begin operation in Montana

1866: First National Bank of Helena established

1867: R. G. Dun lists 83 businesses in Montana; first labor union established

1870: First Deer Lodge bank established

1872: Bozeman gets a National Bank; Yellowstone National Park created

1873: First National Bank of Missoula established; U.S. Timber Culture Act passed

1875: R. G. Dun lists 292 Montana merchants

1878: Timber Cutting Act and Timber & Stone Act passed Congress; Butte Workingmen's Union established

1879: First Montana copper smelter established by W. A. Clark in Butte

1880: 42 lumber mills operate in Montana

1881: Utah & Northern Railroad completed to Butte

1882: Montana Improvement Company formed; first electric lights in Butte and Helena

1883: Northern Pacific Railroad completed across Montana

1884: Anaconda town and smelter established

1885: R. G. Dun lists 1,954 Montana merchants; flour mill established in Great Falls; meat packing industry begins in Miles City

1887: Manitoba (Great Northern) Railway completed to Great Falls and Helena; Billings gets hydroelectric power; closed shop declared in most Butte mines

1889: Montana becomes a state

1890: Copper smelting begins in Great Falls; first hydroelectric dam built at Great Falls

1891: U.S. Forest Reserve Act passed

1893: Silver panic and depression hit U.S. and Montana mines and banks; Western Federation of Miners formed

1895: R. G. Dun lists 4,859 merchants in Montana; Hamilton State Bank established; dairy industry starts in Big Timber

1898: Canyon Ferry Dam built

1901-02: Woolen Mill operates in Big Timber

1905: U.S. Government begins legal action against timber cutting abuses in Montana; IWW formed

1906: Sugar beet factory opens in Billings

1907:	J. Neils Lumber Company first enters Montana
1910:	Forest fires destroy 8 billion board feet of timber, kill 85; Glacier National Park created
1912:	Montana Power Company formed; Rustling Card system begins in Butte
1914:	World War I begins in Europe; Butte Miners' Union Hall destroyed; open shop declared in Butte mines
1915:	First Montana fruit canning plant opens at Stevensville
1917:	U.S. enters World War I; major lumber strike
1919:	Montana oil boom begins
1920:	426 banks in Montana
1921:	First petroleum refineries established in Miles City and Lewistown
1923:	103 Montana banks fail; lumber production peaks
1925:	227 banks left in Montana; sugar beet plants open in Chinook and Sidney
1929:	New York Stock Market crashes
1930:	Nationwide depression begins; tourist industry develops in Montana
1933:	New Deal legislation leads to rebirth of miners' union in Butte
1936:	REAs begin operation in Montana
1937:	Sugar beet plant opens in Hardin
1939:	World War II begins in Europe
1940:	100 banks remain in Montana
1941:	U.S. enters World War II
1945:	Crisafuli's open frozen food processing plant in Glendive
1950:	Mine, Mill & Smelter workers expelled from CIO
1955:	Aluminum plant begins operation in Columbia Falls; Berkeley Pit starts in Butte
1959:	Longest strike in Butte history
1967:	Mine, Mill & Smelter workers combine with Steelworkers' Union
1975:	Underground mining ceases in Butte
1978:	160 banks operate in Montana

Suggested Readings

Rita McDonald. "Commerce and Industry" in *A History of Montana*, ed. M. G. Burlingame and K. Ross Toole. 3 Vols. New York: The Lewis Publishing Co., 1957.

Michael P. Malone and Richard B. Roeder. "The Modern Montana Economy: 1920–1975," in *Montana: A History of Two Centuries*. Seattle: University of Washington Press, 1976.

K. Ross Toole. *Twentieth-Century Montana: A State of Extremes*. Norman: University of Oklahoma Press, 1972.

Theodore Wiprud. "Butte: A Troubled Labor Paradise." *Montana, The Magazine of Western History*, Vol. 21, No. 4 (Autumn, 1971).

Cover of a promotional brochure distributed by the Chicago, Milwaukee & St. Paul Railroad to encourage homesteading in Montana.

Chapter X
Land for Homesteads

"Montana is the last of the good states to be developed, and will be settled with a rush." The Milwaukee Railroad wanted to encourage homesteaders in Montana. So did the Great Northern, the Northern Pacific, the Burlington Railroad, and the State of Montana itself. Settlers came with a rush. In the space of twenty years—from 1900 to 1920—central and eastern Montana went from a sparsely settled province to a region peppered with homesteads, new towns and new counties. Historians call this period the Homestead Era. It was the last great agricultural land rush in the history of the American West.

Homesteading in Montana began officially on August 1, 1868. On that date David Carpenter filed his claim for 160 acres of land in the Helena Valley. He became the first person in Montana to take advantage of the 1862 federal Homestead Act, designed to promote western settlement. For a small filing fee, a man could claim 160 acres of government land as his own. If he lived on it and improved it, the land was his, practically free, after five years.

Easterners believed 160 acres was enough land for any man to farm and support his family. Westerners knew that scarce rainfall and near-desert conditions made it almost impossible to survive on 160 acres. As a result, Congress tried again in 1877 with the Desert Land Act. The new law offered a settler 640 acres at $1.25 an acre. The farmer had to irrigate a portion of that land and live there for three years. Some farmers took advantage of this legislation. Many cattle outfits abused it through dummy entries, tying up vast ranges for their livestock.

Once more Congress tried to encourage irrigation, because water proved all-important for successful agriculture in the western United States. In 1894, the Carey Land Act made it possible for states to contract with private companies to develop irrigation projects in the West. Less successful than anticipated, the Carey Act was supplemented by the Newlands Reclamation Act (1902). For the first time the federal government itself contributed money to promote irrigation. In Montana this legislation led to several successful projects. Dams captured the water, ditches took it to the fields. Notable were the Huntley Project east of Billings, the Lower Yellowstone Project near the North Dakota line, as well as the Milk and Sun River Projects in north-central Montana.

Still a lot of Montana and the West remained unsettled. Through the efforts of Montana Senator Joseph M. Dixon, and others, Congress passed the Enlarged Homestead Act of 1909. This doubled the amount of federal land a person could settle and claim. It sparked Montana's homestead boom. Senator Dixon also played a major part in opening much of the Flathead Indian Reservation to homestead settlement the same year. This action brought large numbers of settlers into the southern Flathead Valley. The ease of homesteading improved when the Three Year Homestead Act (1912) reduced "proving up" time from five years to three. It also allowed a homesteader to be absent from his land for up to five months a year.

Montana had a lot of land to settle. Between 1868 when David Carpenter began the process and 1920 when the homestead boom ended, Montanans used these federal laws to claim over thirty-two million acres. In addition, the Northern Pacific Railroad (NP) sold substantial portions of its land grant to settlers. Between 1900 and 1917 alone, the NP peddled almost eleven million acres of land. Their prices ranged from $1.25 to $8.50 per acre.

In short, there was plenty of land and plenty of people to settle on it. Why did such a large homestead rush take place in the eighteen years after 1900? Availability of land was only one of four important reasons.

Agricultural technology had come a long way by 1900. Steam and eventually gasoline tractors, steel moldboard plows, grain drills, discs, harrows, mechanical binders, and threshers made farming possible on a much larger scale than ever before. Improving agricultural techniques provided another explanation for the boom. In the 1890s a South Dakota farmer named Hardy Webster Campbell discovered, as had other plains farmers, that proper soil cultivation con-

Hardy Webster Campbell promoted dry land farming throughout the West. Many homesteaders used his methods.—*Nebraska State Historical Society*

served available water. What Campbell did that his western neighbors did not was to publicize his findings. Soon everyone heard about the "Campbell System" and read publications like *Campbell's Farming For Profit*, *The Western Soil Culture*, *Campbell's Progressive Agriculture*, and *Campbell's Scientific Farmer*.

Hardy Campbell stressed deep fall plowing, sub-surface packing, light seeding with thorough cultivation before and after, and alternating periods of summer fallow and summer tillage. Others, like F. B. Linfield of the Montana Agricultural Experiment Station at Bozeman, disagreed that a single "system" existed for dry-land farming. They did feel dry-land farming was possible, however. Through the years the Experiment Station issued many circulars, bulletins and reports on farming in Montana. They also conducted Farmers' Institutes throughout the state to educate those involved in agriculture. These publications and presentations stressed the need for water and soil conservation. They also suggested planting shelter belts and growing diversified crops. In branch stations and demonstration farms throughout Montana, the Agricultural Experiment Station exhibited these techniques and assisted local residents.

There were other dry farming experts. Hardy Campbell eventually went to work for the Burlington and the Southern Pacific railroads as they tried to promote homesteading along their lines. Jim Hill of the Great Northern also had his

Thomas Shaw served as the Great Northern Railroad's agricultural expert. He wrote booklets explaining how to farm the Montana plains.—*University of Minnesota*

expert Thomas Shaw, a professor from the Minnesota Agricultural College. By 1910, Shaw was touring the Great Northern Route in North Dakota, Montana and Washington, to encourage and promote dry farming.

Of all the factors that led to the homestead boom in Montana, promotion was probably the most important. Who promoted it? Primarily, it was the railroads. Perhaps the Milwaukee Railroad started it when they drew settlers to the Musselshell Valley and Judith Basin where they had just laid tracks. Montana's other railroads were not far behind. Together the Milwaukee, Northern Pacific, and Great Northern spent thousands of dollars on publications and brochures designed to encourage homesteaders. They distributed this literature in the East and Midwest, and even in Europe—primarily Germany and Scandinavia.

F. B. Linfield of the Montana Agricultural Experiment Station in Bozeman worked to help and encourage dry land farmers in Montana.—*Montana State University Archives, Bozeman, Montana*

Homesteaders came by the thousands. To encourage them the railroads offered reduced fares as well as special rates and cars for their belongings on the overland trip. For as little as $22.50 homesteaders could bring family, equipment and livestock from St. Paul to Montana in a boxcar. For more comfortable accommodations, "Zulu" sleeping cars were available. The railroads did even more. They contributed thousands of dollars to the Montana Agricultural Experiment Station to aid in teaching farming techniques. They subsidized demonstration farms at places like Adams, Terry, Lake Basin, Chester, Havre, Baker and Roundup. "Better Farming Special" trains, and members of the Experiment Station staff travelled the state free to help provide information and promote farming. It worked. Available land, technological improvements, "scientific farming" and a splash of promotion brought homesteaders to Montana. More than one thousand entry claims a month went through the Great Falls Land Office. Nearly two hundred and fifty settlers got off the train at Havre in one evening alone. What awaited them? For one thing, there was uncertainty; for another, there was hard work.

At the depot a railroad agent, or perhaps a private "locator," offered to show them the land and get them settled. Some of these men were honest and some were not. Many settlers found good land, but others were less fortunate. With filing fees paid, and claim in hand, the homesteader and his family now had a hunk of the Montana prairie to call their own.

The first order of business was constructing a home. "Kits" of wood and tar paper were available from lumber stores in the area at about $100. Perhaps they brought the material with them. They built two-, three-, or four-room green lumber and tar paper shacks. To keep out the wind and cold, homesteaders covered the walls with newspapers or blankets. Around the shack's base they banked dirt or sod. Less affluent settlers built lean-tos, dug caves in hillsides or erected sod homes.

A stove in the center of the cabin provided heat for the winter they knew lay ahead. Fuel was another matter. Some wood existed along river and stream beds, but it was not enough. More than likely, the family took the wagon, or borrowed the neighbors', and visited a local "coal mine."

Often this consisted of little more than a lignite outcropping on a neighbor's place. Here they cut bricks of the dark material. They stacked it around their cabins for insulation from the winds, and for eventual stove fuel.

The first year often proved to be the hardest, because they had no income until they harvested the first crop. As a result, many homesteaders secured jobs in the nearby towns that had sprung up to support them. To ferry themselves to town, some bought cars. The Studebaker wagon or Model T parked behind their shack now became a symbol of Montana's first commuters.

With the new settlers came new terms of speech. Cowboys called the newcomers "Scissorbills"—a person who did not know what he was doing. "Honyocker" probably came from cowboy slang, too. The original term was "hunyak," a racial slur directed at early Slavic immigrants. Many Montanans thought of these "Honyockers" as ignorant people doomed to failure. Looking back—after the boom had passed in the 1920s—other Montanans questioned the wisdom of anyone foolish enough to think they could make a go of it on the plains with 320 acres, a few dollars, and no experience. True, many homesteaders between 1900 and 1918 lacked farming experience. Yet they brought to Montana that same diversity and optimism that characterized earlier rushes, like those for gold and cattle. And like those who had arrived years before, they came as young men and women. They were intent on making their fortune and future here, despite the odds. Homesteaders brought a wide range of experiences. They brought enthusiasm.

To support the new arrivals, a series of boom towns sprang up. Existing railroad sidings or cattle towns took on new airs. Along the Hi-Line, Wolf Point, Glasgow, Malta, Havre and others experienced the influx. Plentywood, Scobey, Jordan, Ryegate, Baker and many more filled in the map of eastern Montana. The state's population grew enormously. Montana began the 1900s with just over 240,000 residents. Ten years later it had increased to 376,000. By the peak year of 1917, upwards of 600,000 called Montana home.

The boom was an explosion not just in towns and population, but also in counties. Take a map and draw a line from Glacier National Park to Yellowstone National Park. East of that line, Montana had thirteen counties in 1910: Carbon, Cascade, Chouteau, Custer, Dawson, Fergus, Meagher, Park, Rosebud, Sweet Grass, Teton, Valley and Yellowstone. By 1920, thirty-eight counties occupied the same area.

"County-busting" became the political game of the decade. Men like Dan McKay played it well. McKay was a fast talker, rode the "biggest horse in the Milk River Valley," and in a few minutes of conversation could convince anyone that their town should be the seat of a new county. Why did they want new counties? They wanted to be close to the people. What better way to do that than have your own county? Montana's Legislature accommodated them in 1911 and 1913. The Leighton Act of 1911 left the creation of counties generally to local desires. By the time those desires had cooled, Montana had increased the number of counties from twenty-eight to fifty-six. Unquestionably, county seats today are closer to home than they might have been in 1910; but where property assessments and populations have fallen since those boom days, financing county government becomes an increasing burden for residents.

Optimism ran high after 1909. The land was there. Promoters and hustlers were peddling it. Providence and politics seemed to cooperate. In the decades before railroads and chambers of commerce erased "Great American Desert" from the maps of the West, people had a visual reminder that rain was sparse west of the One Hundredth Meridian. The period from 1909 through 1916 seemed to belie that reality. At the same time the homestead boom was warming up, nature cooperated with rainfalls in excess of sixteen inches a year across eastern Montana. Even more helpful, the moisture came in the late spring and early summer, when it was most needed for good crop production.

Hardy Campbell, Thomas Shaw and others pointed to wheat yields of twenty-five bushels an acre in 1910. By 1915-1916, these had jumped to thirty-five to fifty bushels. And wheat prices were high. World War I engulfed Europe in 1914. England and France needed wheat. Montana grew it. Prices rose to $2.00 per bushel. Then in 1917, the United States entered the war. "Food Will Win the War!" the government said, stabilizing the price of wheat at $2.20 per bushel. Good yields and good prices made farming a profitable venture. Bankers rushed in to take advantage of the eco-

Display of the Northwestern Development League at an agricultural fair during the "wet years" before the droughts.

nomic upswing. The newly created Federal Reserve System proved willing to make money available for agricultural loans. Before long Montana had not only new counties and towns, but a bank and a grain elevator in each—symbols of prosperity.

The bubble burst in 1917. Prices did not come down but neither did the rain. In Glasgow, 20.5 inches of rain had fallen during 1916; in Ekalaka, 13 inches fell. During 1917 each received only 7.8 inches. In 1918 they had even less. Rainfall at Valier dropped similarly: 19 inches in 1916, 11 inches in 1917, 5.6 inches in 1918. The same happened at Sidney, Poplar, Valentine, and dozens of other points across northern and eastern Montana. Grimly the Montana Agricultural Experiment Station reported the most unfavorable

It's time for a parade—Richland County has been formed and Sidney is the county seat.

growing seasons for dry-land farming "of which we have any record."

To make matters worse, the Rocky Mountain migratory locust visited the state—grasshoppers. The state made available 10,000 pounds of white arsenic. Communities gathered together in "mixing bees," combining the poison with bran mash to spread in fields and kill the pests. Farmers pulled grasshopper-catching machines across their lands. One farmer reported collecting 56 bushels of the insects on 231 acres. Another claimed he caught and sacked over 800 pounds of the pests in two hours' time. Experiment station staff suggested a bright side to the picture. Grasshoppers made good chicken feed. But the damage was done. In many areas, what the drought did not wither, the grasshoppers ate.

Then the World War ended. The "boys" returned home, and prices went back to less than $2.00 a bushel for wheat. By 1919-1920, the lack of rain, the grasshoppers, and a depressed market had swept through eastern Montana like a prairie fire. Some moved to town for good. Others gave up altogether and returned "home."

Conditions amounted to a "disaster" for the state. The Legislature met in special session during 1919 and passed bills to relieve the situation as much as possible. House Bill 12 tried to "Provide for any Inhabitants, Who by Reason of Misfortune Resulting from Drought, Hail or Unfavorable Climatic Conditions, Have been Rendered Destitute or in

MONTANA COUNTIES - 1915

Need of Aid." The politicians could not bring rain or improve the market for grain.

Many banks, once so eager to be part of the seemingly endless prosperity, found they had to foreclose on farm loans. Even with the land, they could not sell the property and recover their losses. It meant financial disaster for them as well as their customers. Between 1920 and 1925, nearly two hundred banks failed. It reflected the agricultural depression that had already covered the region.

The Milwaukee Railroad people had been right. Montana was one of the last good states to be developed. Certainly the homesteaders settled it with a rush between 1900 and 1917. They brought with them the same excitement and spirit Montana had witnessed in earlier "rushes." Homesteaders, Honyockers, Scissorbills, pioneers—call them what you will, they made Montana. Abandoned shacks and bank buildings mark the sites of those who came and left. Modern Montana agriculture is a tribute to those who came and stayed.

You Need a Homestead in Teton Country!

Ladies and gentlemen, boys and girls: It gives me great pleasure to be here today on behalf of the Great Northern Railway. Yes sir, the Great Northern Railway—your ticket to a new and better life in Montana. You heard me, folks—Montana. Today I'm here to inform, to educate, to elucidate each and every one of you on homesteading in Montana—The Treasure State.

Treasure there is in Montana, folks. Land. That's what Montana has, land. And a piece of that prosperity is yours for the taking. This is 1912, gentlemen and ladies. It's 1912, and before you know it another year will slip right through your hands. Don't delay. Listen, if you will, to the knock of opportunity at your door this very day.

"What do I need to do?" you're asking yourself. Let me tell you. First, you need to visit Montana. We're talking today about Teton County, Montana. You need to get yourself on a train and see Teton County. There are 3,000,000 acres in this fine land, in this county alone, and only a small part is now under cultivation. Some is mountainous, some is grazing and timber land, but thousands of acres are free government land. And there's nearly a million acres in the Blackfeet Indian Reservation. I have no doubt that in the near future this, too, will be opened for white settlement. But you can't take advantage of this opportunity standing here. You need to visit Montana. See Teton County yourself.

When you arrive, one of our agents will be pleased to show you a parcel of available land. The Homestead Act of 1909 says you—and you, too—are entitled to 320 acres of that land. Pick out the piece you want. Visit the local land office. Make your claim for 80, 160 or 320 acres of Teton County. There are papers to sign, of course. You need to certify that you've not already claimed land nor used homestead rights earlier.

"What if I'm not a U.S. citizen?" Good question, sir. There's no problem. If the United States of America is your permanent residence and you've filed first citizenship papers, you can take advantage of this opportunity. When you become a full citizen, the land is yours. And you soldiers or sailors can also get land. Make your claim and receive credit for military service when it comes to proving up on your land.

Now you're asking yourself, "What does it cost?" I'll tell you. If you file on 80 acres, the commission and fee is $8.00. On 160 acres it's $16.00 and for a full 320 acres you pay only $22.00. There may be some other fees in the county clerk's office, or elsewhere, but these are small. The Great Northern itself is prepared to take you and your family from St. Paul to Teton County for less than $50. You heard me right—less than $50 for you, sir, your wife and kids. We'll also take what we call emigrant moveables to get you started—up to 20,000 pounds.

You can begin now setting aside what you'll need. Get two, maybe four, horses or mules to break the land. Take along a cow or two for milk and butter, and some chickens, hogs, or sheep if you've got 'em. Take along feed, of course, and plenty of grain for seed. Experienced homesteaders tell us you'll also want about 2,500 feet of lumber for corrals and out buildings. A small portable house, say 500 fence posts, and some trees and shrubbery are also nice. Lumber's about $40 per thousand feet in Montana, so you may want to take it with you. For $100 to $150 a small home can be bought here. The price is a bit higher in Montana.

Now I can see you counting up those costs and wondering if you can do it. Let me read a letter we've received from a Mr. W. T. Cavett in Dunkirk, Teton County, Montana. He says he arrived on his land two years ago with "money enough to file on a homestead, build a cabin and a grub stake for a month." Mr. Cavett netted himself $25 per acre for his wheat and $37.50 an acre for his flax last year. Here's another letter from Mr. James Ryan at Conrad, also in Teton County, Montana. Mr. Ryan bought—mind you bought—prime land at $22 an acre. He paid for it in two years. He says here some of his neighbors paid for theirs with one crop. Can you afford it? Sir, let me tell you, you can't afford not to take advantage of this opportunity!

When you've claimed your land, the government gives you six months to bring out your family and belongings. Get yourself situated. Build a house. Put your land under cultivation. By the second year you need to have 20 acres on a 320-acre homestead seeded. For a 160-acre parcel the requirement is only 10 acres. When you apply for final proof at the end of three years, you must have one-eighth of the total acreage under cultivation.

You heard me, sir. I said three years and the homestead's yours. The new government law makes this possible instead of waiting five. This same law also says you can leave your land for up to five months each year. Spend the winter in town—get a second job. You can still take advantage of this opportunity for free land. Can't wait three years? If you've filed on 160 acres you can commute or buy the land after only 14 months. Pay the government $1.25 and it's yours. Commutation's not possible on 320-acre homesteads or if the land's got coal or minerals.

Now I just heard a man over there turn to his wife and say, "I'm not a farmer." To you, sir, I want to say neither were Mr. Cavett and Mr. Ryan before they went to Montana. The Great Northern Railway has in its employ an agricultural expert to answer your every question. Professor Thomas Shaw of the Minnesota Agricultural College has thoroughly studied farming in this region. He's available to help and advise you.

Now Professor Shaw tells me Teton County gets over sixteen inches of rain a year. The key, he says, to successful cultivation is retaining that moisture. Plow five or six inches deep when you're breaking the land. Disc and harrow immediately to conserve moisture. After each rain renew the cultivation. Now he goes on to suggest getting to Montana early in the spring and breaking as much land as possible that first year—before it gets too dry. By mid-May you want to have some Durum wheat and flax in. These will be your money crops. Then put in feed and home crops. You'll want to plant white hulless barley, oats, corn for fodder, potatoes, beans, rutabagas and garden vegetables.

Come August and September take some of the land you broke early and put it into winter wheat. Here's another money crop. The next spring break more land, and plant more oats, barley and flax, along with some rye and alfalfa. Other crops should include the corn, potatoes, beans, rutabagas, and garden vegetables you planted the first year. Of course, several of these may be omitted, but there is always safety in variety. The process continues the third year, and so on.

Yes sir. Yes ma'am. Professor Shaw has it worked out so you can learn to farm. Montana's Agricultural Experiment Station and the Great Northern's own experts are also there to help. In Teton County you'll find new friends and neighbors with a season's farming under their belts. They'll give you a hand. And that's another thing. Farming is hard work, I'm here to tell you. But folks, you'll get to know fine people in Montana—friendly ones. They're starting their futures, just like you. They'll help when they can.

Now you kind folks have listened to me long enough. The Great Northern Railway has packed the cars of this "Farming Special" with all kinds of exhibits and machinery. We want to show you what's waiting in Montana. Over here, on my right, you'll see corn, melons and rutabagas like you've never seen before. Take a look at the shocks of wheat from Teton County we've brought along. Read the figures. Look at the maps and see where land is still available. We've got a little pamphlet here by Professor Shaw. You'll want to read it. It's chocked full of helpful farming suggestions. And here's a list of emigrant moveables you'll need. I'll be around, folks, to answer your questions. Before I go, I'd like to have you remember two things. Remember E. C. Leedy, Great Northern Railway, St. Paul, Minnesota. You write to us, and we'll answer your questions. And you remember Teton County, Montana—it's waiting for you.

Richland County is Born

Richland became Montana's newest county on May 16, 1914. Split from Dawson County—one of Montana's oldest—the fledgling county represented the rapid growth of homesteaders in the region. It also illustrated a desire for more localized self-government. Richland County was created by "county splitting" or "county busting." This political process doubled the number of counties in the state in the space of fifteen years from 1910 to 1925.

Homesteaders began flooding Montana after the Enlarged Homestead Act passed Congress in 1909. The same vast expanse of land that brought homesteaders frustrated them when it came to government. County seats frequently lay many miles away. Jealousies and frustrations also arose as new outlying residents often accused established citizens and towns of ignoring their needs. Complaints of high taxes, poor roads and bridges, or inadequate service brought suggested changes in government. The most common change included creation of a new county centered in a growing area of homestead development.

Prior to 1911, establishing a new county depended on winning approval from the Montana Legislature. That year, however, the legislature responded to demands for new counties by passing the Leighton Act. Dr. I. A. Leighton of Jefferson County authored a bill that made it possible for fifty percent of the voters in a particular area to sign a petition requesting creation of a new county. If the proposed county met certain requirements, then residents of that area could vote on whether or not they wanted their own government. Homesteaders near Sidney thought it was about time for such a change.

Sidney sprang up in Dawson County on Montana's eastern border in 1888 as a cattle town. It stayed generally small and served as a center for the vast ranches scattered in the area. Homesteading in the early 1900s changed that. Old towns took on new life, and new communities were established: Fairview, Enid, Savage, Crane, Fox Lake/Lambert, Girard, and Sioux Pass among them. Suddenly Glendive, the Dawson County seat, seemed miles away in distance and interest.

When Representative Walter D. Kemmis of Sidney and Senator J. M. Boardman of Poplar were elected in 1912, they made known their feelings. This rich homestead land on the eastern edge of Dawson County should have its own government. The idea of Richland County began to take root like the growing wheat. Both Kemmis and Boardman cooperated to get a bill creating Richland County through the 1913 legislature.

In mid-February the issue began to heat up. Jim Metcalf, editor of Glendive's *Dawson County Review,* opposed Richland County and said what he thought of its chance in the legislature. Harry G. Ketcham of the *Sidney Herald* wasted no time in saying what he thought of Jim Metcalf. The *Herald's* front page on February 21, 1913, was filled with Ketcham's views. Lies from the "slimy pen of Slippery Jim Metcalf," Glendive's "pin-head pencil pusher," Ketcham called the *Review's* comments. He went on with a string of adjectives designed to wilt any criticism. Metcalf was a beastly, nondescript brute; damnable, dirty, disgusting, full of cunning cussedness, and a disgrace to Montana journalism, Ketcham wrote.

When the legislative smoke cleared, the Richland County bill had passed and lay on Governor Sam V. Stewart's desk awaiting his signature. Stewart vetoed the measure. He suggested that promoters use the Leighton Act. Harry Ketcham blamed the governor's decision on the "wire-pullers of Glendive."

After less than a month's breather, Richland proponents began organizing for a new campaign. Sidney residents formed a committee to circulate petitions and obtain signatures. They kicked off their drive on April 30, adding other members to their group from around the region. Veteran county promoter Dan McKay joined the effort, giving his advice and counsel. So did M. A. Frissell, publisher and editor of the *Fox Lake Promoter,* which first appeared late that June.

Richland County supporters zeroed in on a few selected points to push their arguments. Of most interest was lower taxes. A strong feeling existed that Sidney residents paid high taxes to support Dawson County and Glendive. In return they received little. That was point number two. We are "Grass Orphans" one resident complained. Better roads, bridges and services would all come with Richland County. Finally, supporters stressed the need for a more localized government; a government that was closer to the people.

Throughout summer and fall the petition campaign continued. Opponents appeared. Sometimes it was an editorial in the *Glendive Monitor,* the *Paxton Pilot,* or the *Fairview Times* criticizing Sidney for wanting to hog politics in the new county. Sometimes it was a man on horseback or in a Model T circulating petitions against Richland County. Sometimes the man asked residents to sign a petition invalidating their signature on a pro-Richland petition. By mid-December 1913, Richland's backers had enough signatures to feel assured of success. They presented them to the Dawson County Commissioners—as prescribed in the Leighton Act—and asked for a special election.

Through December of 1913 and January of 1914, Dawson County officials counted signatures on the various petitions and counter-petitions. The *Sidney Herald* admitted it would be close, but pledged itself to "standing by our colors until victory perches on our banners or we are defeated." January 28, 1914, word came from Glendive that the required signatures were there. Leighton Act provisions had been met. On May 16 residents of the proposed new county would vote on its creation.

Now new contests began. In addition to the county-splitting issue, voters had to select a site for the county seat and officials to staff newly created offices. Sidney, Enid, and Fox Lake (Lambert) filed immediate petitions for the "beautifully colored plum." Fairview joined shortly. Republicans, Democrats and Progressives also wasted little time in nominating candidates for each county office.

Glendive threw in the towel once the petition to create Richland County had been approved. Representatives of the Glendive Commercial Club expressed their best wishes for the cause during late January. In a friendly editorial dated February 10, 1914, J. R. Widmyer, editor of the *Glendive Independent,* extended his and Glendive's support: "If the new county is formed, the people in its territory have our well wishes for a happy and prosperous future."

The race for county seat soon narrowed to lively campaigns on behalf of Lambert and Sidney. M. A. Frissell kept up the honor of Lambert in the pages of the *Fox Lake Promoter,* but the Sidney Commercial Club overwhelmed all opposition. First in February, then in March, they sponsored huge banquets to boost Sidney's campaign. One hundred and forty voters were royally fed and entertained. Then the Commercial Club branched out and put on similar feeds in Crane, Lambert, Girard, and Sioux Pass. Sidney supporters made the circuit again in May before the election. This time they brought around the "Right Honorable" Dan McKay who convinced all but the staunchest critics that Richland County was a must.

County splitting sentiment was not universal, despite McKay's golden words. Weekly articles in the *Sidney Herald* and constant talks by the Richland County Committee tried to convince residents that the new county would mean lower taxes and better services. Sidney businessmen promised to make a building available for a courthouse should that community get the designation—no need to build something expensive, they said. Some opponents feared a consolidated county high school would have to be built in Sidney. No, Sidney supporters said. Each community should have their own schools. Sidney would pay for the cost of any schools in that community without county taxes, thank you.

"RICHLAND COUNTY IS CREATED" the inch-high headlines proclaimed across the *Sidney Herald.* Saturday, May 16, 1914, voters approved the new county 1,094 to 448. Sidney became the new county seat, receiving 848 votes; more than all its competitors combined. Lambert finished second with 425. Enid and Fairview trailed with 168 and 119. Sidney was proud—"the Gem City, the prosperous, pushing, progressive new permanent county seat." Monday, May 19, Sidney residents celebrated the double victory. Flags, banners and bunting floated from every building. All businesses closed. Led by the Sidney Concert Band, a parade wound through the city streets. After the band came 46 "gaily bedecked and handsomely decorated" automobiles, followed by all the school children from high school to first grade. The parade ended at the baseball field where the city team beat the high school boys 9-2. A tennis match and gun club shoot concluded the celebration.

Not long after the election, county commissioners gathered in Sidney to find a home for county government. They leased the Valley Mercantile and Lumber Company building. After some remodeling, it was fit as "temporary" office space. New officials had to provide their own desks, chairs, and equipment, however. From nearby saloons and businesses they borrowed tables and chairs until money came in for more permanent fixtures.

In April of 1916, County Commissioners decided it was time for a better arrangement. They asked voters to approve construction of a new building. But Richland County residents were serious about maintaining lower taxes. They turned down the issue, 1,339 to 380. In 1919 Richland County became a victim of county splitting itself when sixteen townships on the western edge separated to become part of McCone County. Now would be a good time to build a permanent courthouse, commissioners reasoned. Again, voters overwhelmingly rejected the plan.

By 1926, county officials and residents had had enough. The Valley Mercantile and Lumber Company sign still showed on the front of the building. The wooden floors were worn through with heavy traffic. Walls creaked in the wind and leaked cold in the winter. Voters decided now was the time for a new building. On May 4, 1928, the county dedicated an impressive, domed structure. "Temporary" tables and chairs borrowed fourteen years before were returned.

Richland County today is testimony to the faith its early settlers and promoters placed in it. Its formation represents an era in Montana history and politics when homesteaders flooded the plains and new counties crowded the map. Perhaps the words of congratulations from the *Dawson County Review* provide a fitting tribute: "The new county is one rich in resources which are now being developed by a splendid class of settlers. It has a number of good towns which are populated by wide-awake, progressive citizens.... Richland is carved from one of the best portions of eastern Montana and is destined to become one of the best counties in the state from every standpoint."

Timeline

1862: U.S. Homestead Act passed.

1864: Montana becomes a territory.

1877: Desert Land Act passed by Congress.

1883: Northern Pacific Railroad completed across Montana; railroad gets land grant.

1887: Manitoba (Great Northern) Railway completed to Great Falls and Helena.

1889: Montana becomes a state.

1893: Montana Agricultural College established at Bozeman; Montana Agricultural Experiment Station begins operation.

1894: Carey Land Act passes Congress; Hardy W. Campbell begins to promote dry farming.

1901: Rosebud and Powell Counties created.

1902: Newlands Reclamation Act passes Congress; first Montana Farmers' Institute held.

1904: Mondak established.

1905: Sanders County created.

1908: Baker and Ryegate founded.

1909: Enlarged Homestead Act passes Congress; Flathead Reservation opened for Homesteading; homestead rush to Montana begins; Milwaukee Railroad completed across Montana; Dutton and Lincoln Counties established.

1910: Professor Thomas Shaw begins to promote dry farming for the Great Northern Railway; Antelope founded.

1911: Leighton Act passes Montana Legislature; Musselshell County created.

1912: U.S. 3-Year Homestead Act passed; Gilman founded; Hill and Blaine Counties established.

1913: Sheridan, Fallon, Big Horn, and Stillwater Counties created.

1914: Toole, Richland, Wibaux, Mineral Counties created; Lambert and Flaxville established; World War I begins in Europe.

1915: Phillips and Prairie Counties created.

1917: Wheatland and Carter Counties created; U.S. enters World War I; wheat reaches $2.20 per bushel; homestead boom peaks; drought begins across Montana.

1918: Drought worsens across Montana.

1919: Glacier, Pondera, Roosevelt, McCone, Garfield, Powder River, and Treasure Counties created; World War I ends; wheat market deteriorates.

1920: Liberty, Daniels, Judith Basin Golden Valley counties created; bank failures begin.

1923: Lake County created; 103 banks fail in Montana.

1925: Petroleum County is the last county created in Montana.

Suggested Readings

Belvian W. Bertino. *The Scissorbills.* New York: Vantage Press, 1976.

Orland E. Esval. "Member of the Crew." *Montana, The Magazine of Western History,* Vol. 27, No. 4 (Autumn, 1977).

Dale Eunson. *Up on the Rim.* New York: Farrar, Straus and Giroux, 1970.

Marie Peterson McDonald. *After Barbed Wire.* Glendive: Frontier Gateway Museum, 1963.

David A. Walter. "Montana Homestead: Farming the Dreams and Droughts." *Visual History of Montana,* Unit 5. Helena: Montana Superintendent of Public Instruction, 1977-78.

Dan Whetstone. *Frontier Editor.* New York: Hastings House, 1956.

Jeannette Rankin speaking to well-wishers in Washington, D.C., just before she was sworn in as America's first female member of Congress, April 2, 1917. Carrie Chapman Catt, women's rights leader, stands alongside. —*Library of Congress*

Chapter XI
Power Politics

On October 1, 1889, Montana voters went to the polls. They faced the most important question that had yet been put to them. Delegates to Montana's third Constitutional Convention produced a document that needed voter approval before Montana could become a state. There were some minor controversies over the constitution, but the election results indicated how eagerly citizens wanted statehood. Over 24,000 voted for the constitution. Only 2,274 opposed it. A new period in Montana's history began.

As a state, Montana got off to a shaky start. In the October elections voters also selected a full list of state and county officials. Democrat Joseph K. Toole defeated Republican Thomas C. Power for governor. Republican John E. Rickards was elected lieutenant governor, and another Republican, Thomas H. Carter, defeated Martin Maginnis for Congress. These elections were close, but nothing was irregular. Legislative elections, however, were a different story.

In the state senate Republicans and Democrats split evenly with eight members each. The same happened in the house of representatives where each party won twenty-five seats. But in the house elections, five seats from Silver Bow County were disputed. No one seemed capable of determining who had actually won. Control of the legislature carried with it the power to select Montana's two U.S. Senators. Who would claim it—Republicans or Democrats? The legislature was paralyzed. Rather than settle the issue, representatives from both parties met separately during the entire legislative session, from November 1889 to February 1890.

The First Legislature became a farce. The biggest problem was the selection of two U.S. Senators, which only a joint session of the senate and house could accomplish. To prevent taking a ballot, Democrats in the senate refused to attend. Without a majority present the senate could do nothing—not even organize. This went on for twenty-four

For many years Senator Thomas H. Carter was the leader of Montana's Republican party. Twice elected a U.S. Senator, Carter generally represented conservative and business interests.

days. Finally the senate organized, but it still remained hopelessly split. Senators did not pass any legislation sent to them from the house. Meanwhile, house Republicans and Democrats continued to meet separately. In January 1890, the parties made the situation even worse. They both selected two senators. Montana sent four senators to Washington in 1890!

Republicans chose Thomas C. Power and Wilbur Fisk Sanders. Democrats selected W. A. Clark and Martin Maginnis. All four had been very active in territorial politics. Clark wanted desperately to represent Montana in Washington, but with the Republicans in control of the U.S. Congress, the outcome was sealed. Power and Sanders became Montana's first senators. Clark would have to wait ten years for another opportunity.

In Montana the 1890s were trying years. The economic boom of the 1880s, which had powered expansion in the mining, timber and railroad industries, suddenly collapsed in 1893-94. It was a jolt to everyone and it affected politics immediately. The trouble began far away from Montana. In February 1893, the first of many eastern industrial corporations declared bankruptcy. This set off a panic and then a full-scale economic depression. By summer, thousands of workers were without jobs all across the nation. In Montana the first effects were felt in the mining industry as the demand for metals declined. Specifically, it was silver that really created the problem.

In August 1893, hoping to slow down the depression, Congress repealed the Sherman Silver Purchase Act, refusing to buy silver for minting coins. Silver mining was big business in Montana. Suddenly mines in Elkhorn, Butte, Philipsburg and Granite were threatened. "God help the miners," one Butte newspaper headline read. Politicians reacted. Republicans and Democrats scrambled to be the first to issue complaints about the government's action. They demanded that silver money be coined again. Along with the two major parties a third political party, the Populists, made even more noise.

Populists had organized in Montana in 1892. They had originated a few years earlier in the Midwest and South where farmers were angry at railroad companies. But in Montana they were mostly interested in political reform and silver. Some who became Populists, like *Boulder Age* editor Will Kennedy, had already engaged in political reform. Kennedy and others convinced Montana in 1889 to use the Australian or secret ballot for all state elections. This made Montana one of the first states to adopt the Australian ballot. In the 1892 election the Populists ran several candidates, including a woman for attorney general, Ella Knowles. She and the rest lost, but in 1894 they were more successful.

In 1894 people listened as Populists spoke forcefully in favor of political reforms. The depression, the Populists said, was due to actions of the few Americans who owned the big corporations. Populists advocated government ownership of the railroads, a federal income tax and direct election of U.S. Senators by the people. They won three state senate and thirteen state representative seats in Montana in 1894. Two years later the Populists joined up with the Democrats in electing a governor, Robert Burns Smith. Populists never truly challenged the two major parties. Their reforms failed, but their popularity indicated how the political scene changed in Montana during the depression.

The depression affected more than just mining. Banks closed in many cities—in Helena four of the six banks folded in 1894. All of the railroads in the state declared bankruptcy. By December 1893, 20,000 Montanans were out of work. That was nearly one-third of the entire work force. It was a frightening time. Montanans worried as they read of violent labor strikes in eastern states. Jobless men loitered. In Butte the situation was particularly bad. In April 1894, over four hundred of Butte's jobless joined William Hogan's "Industrial Army." Hogan, one of Butte's unemployed, planned to join a "March on Washington" organized by Ohio's Jacob S. Coxey. Coxey demanded unemployment relief from the government. What followed could have been written by a novelist.

Hogan's bedraggled "Army" stole a Northern Pacific

FOR PLACE OF LOCATION OF THE PERMANENT CAPITOL OF THE STATE OF MONTANA.

VOTE FOR ONE.

CITY OF ANACONDA...	
TOWN OF BOULDER...	
CITY OF BOZEMAN....	
CITY OF BUTTE......	
TOWN OF DEER LODGE.	
CITY OF GREAT FALLS.	
CITY OF HELENA.....	

1892 ballot for the selection of the permanent state capital. No winner was determined and a second election was held in 1894 when Helena became the capital.

train in Butte—Hogan claimed he "borrowed" it. From Butte they sped at full throttle toward Dakota. "We are running this train," Hogan told railroad officials. Finally federal troops halted them in Forsyth. Hogan and forty of his men were found guilty of stealing the train. Hogan himself was sentenced to six months in jail. It was a bizarre event, but it did indicate the desperation of the times.

Populists and William Hogan were not the only political attractions in 1894; another issue captured public interest. For nearly two decades Marcus Daly and William A. Clark, two Butte copper barons, had jousted with each other within the Democratic party. Clark blamed Daly for his defeat in the 1888 election for Territorial Delegate. In 1894 they fought again. This time the issue was which city would become the permanent state capital. Helena had been the capital since 1875, but the constitution provided that voters finally determine what city would be the capital. An election in 1892 brought no clear winner. A second election was held in 1894.

The contest was between Daly's planned city, Anaconda, and Helena. Clark, naturally, championed Helena. It was a serious question, but the campaign had its comic side. Anaconda supporters, for example, published a pamphlet titled *Helena's Social Supremacy*, which poked fun at Helena's pretensions to culture. The authors described the clothing, habits and activities of Helena's citizenry, including how many top hats, canes and spats were visible on the city's streets. Daly's forces asked workingmen if they really wanted the capital in such a place as Helena. In return, Clark warned Montanans not to vote for Anaconda unless they wished to be fitted with a "copper collar," referring to the power of the Anaconda Copper Company. Helena eventually won the honor as capital city.

The capital question did not end the Clark-Daly feud. Clark still wanted a seat in the U.S. Senate. His way was blocked when the Republicans swept the 1894 elections. Republicans Lee Mantle of Butte and Thomas H. Carter of Helena became senators. Mantle's term expired in 1899, and Clark decided to get that Senate seat no matter what the cost. He organized his support and then boldly tried to buy votes in the 1899 legislature. It was a case of blatant political corruption. In the midst of Clark's vote-purchasing, Fred White-

Marcus A. Daly photographed in New York City during the last years of his great feud with W. A. Clark.

side of Flathead decided to risk everything and expose Clark. Whiteside presented his evidence of corruption to the legislature, yet Clark won the senate election anyway.

Clark went to Washington, but Whiteside did not give up. Joined by Marcus Daly and Senator Carter, he urged the Senate to investigate. After enough evidence was produced to indicate election fraud, Clark resigned his seat and returned to Montana. It was an embarrassing affair. Paris

Gibson was selected to fill Clark's vacant chair in the Senate. Two years later Clark finally became Montana's junior senator and fulfilled his longtime desire.

Montana's politics were not as corrupt as this episode might suggest. It was Clark's burning desire to be senator and Daly's determination to block him that produced these unusual results. It is only fair to note that political corruption occurred in other states as well. As long as legislatures chose U.S. Senators it was possible for a few individuals to control the elections. That changed in 1913 when the Seventeenth Amendment to the U.S. Constitution was approved. It provided for the direct election of senators by the people.

Clark's success in 1901 was part of a larger story that affected Montana politics in yet a more negative way. This second battle in the so-called "War of the Copper Kings" began with Marcus Daly's sale of the Anaconda Copper Company to a huge corporation—the Amalgamated Copper Company. Amalgamated was owned by the Standard Oil Company. Clark took advantage of this new situation and claimed that Daly had sold out to a powerful corporation that would dominate and strangle Montana. Clark pledged to defend the state. As an ally, Clark enlisted the support of a young and aggressive mining engineer and smelter owner, Fritz Augustus Heinze. Heinze, son of German immigrants, arrived in Butte in 1889. By 1900 he had his own smelter and producing mines and was at odds with Amalgamated. Heinze, also a Democrat, adopted the same attitude as Clark. The Amalgamated would snuff out all of the small miners and operators in Butte; someone had to defend Montana's interests.

After his election in 1901, Clark did not support Heinze for long. Daly had died in 1900. Clark was in the Senate and had no more use for his alliance with the controversial Heinze. The third battle of the Butte copper wars commenced. This time it was the solitary Heinze against the copper giant—Amalgamated. The results of this struggle practically poisoned Montana politics.

The conflict began in the mines under Butte and ended up in the courts and the legislature. Amalgamated intended to control all of the copper production in Butte. They purchased the Anaconda, W. A. Clark's holdings and several other companies, including the Boston and Montana Copper Company. Fritz Heinze had purchased a mine, the Rarus, which adjoined Boston and Montana Company mines. Heinze soon became a significant obstacle to the Amalgamated's control of Butte mining.

Heinze was a brilliant mining engineer and in the course of working underground he had learned Butte's complex vein system. The interior of the Butte Hill was a maze of fractured copper veins extending for miles. Heinze used what was known as the Apex Clause of the federal mining law actually to steal copper from the Boston and Montana (now Amalgamated) mines. The Apex Clause stated that, from the surface where a vein "apexed," a miner could follow that vein wherever it went, even if the vein darted off underground into the area directly below another individual's claim. From his mines, the Rarus and the Minnie Healy, Heinze tunneled deep underground into the Amalgamated mines and brought out ton upon ton of rich copper ore.

Between 1900 and 1903 Amalgamated lawyers went to work above ground to halt Heinze's piracy. Below ground, Amalgamated miners engaged in a genuine battle with Heinze's men over the ore. Both fights threatened to blow the lid off Butte and the state. Amalgamated's lawyers found out that Silver Bow courts would not give them a just hearing. Heinze had managed to control the judges, particularly Edward Harney and William Clancy. As each case came before Harney and Clancy, they ruled in Heinze's favor, angering and frustrating the Amalgamated all the more. No one had ever stumped Standard Oil as Heinze did in Butte. Henry Rogers, chairman of Standard Oil's board and president of Amalgamated, was determined to get Heinze out of the way.

Using the *Montana Standard*, which Amalgamated had purchased from Daly, and other daily newspapers bought by the company, Rogers' men in Montana began a media campaign against Heinze. But Heinze was popular with miners. Through his own newspaper, the *Butte Reveille*, he portrayed himself as a modern David battling a corporate Goliath. Finally, Rogers used the only weapon he knew would be effective. In October 1903, after nearly three years of frustration, the Amalgamated held a gun to Butte—they announced a complete halt of the company's operations. Thousands of miners were out of work. Butte and the entire state suddenly realized how much power Amalgamated had when they chose to use it. The mines would reopen, Amalgamated's newspapers told Montanans, only when the legislature passed a special law allowing court cases to be transferred out of Silver Bow County. This change of venue law was the only way Amalgamated could find to get around Heinze's judges in Butte.

The tactic worked. Governor Joseph K. Toole called a special session of the legislature in December 1903. In short order they passed the "fair trials bill," which gave Amalgamated its right to change venue in civil cases. It was a sad affair, but the giant copper trust made its point—Butte's and Montana's economy needed the mining industry. Heinze, of course, organized his forces to block passage of the "fair trials bill." He called his forces the Anti-Trust Party, and, while their purpose was to defeat Amalgamated, Heinze's people did suggest some important political reforms: tax revision, creation of a public service commission to regulate railroad rates, and the initiative and referendum. Once the special session was over on December 10, everyone breathed a sigh of relief. The mines reopened. The crisis had passed.

It was the last act of the "War of the Copper Kings." Heinze sold his mining interests to Amalgamated in 1906 for $12 million. He took himself out of Butte and Montana politics. Amalgamated itself left Montana in 1915 when it sold its holdings to the Anaconda Company. Heinze went to New York and entered the banking business with his brothers. Yet, the copper market still attracted him. In 1907, through his new United Copper Company, Heinze tried to control the copper market on Wall Street. His plan failed, although his financial scheme helped set off the Panic of 1907. Heinze died in 1914 at the young age of forty-five. He had been a brilliant schemer, a man with boundless energy. His role in Butte and Montana politics was tarnished, but it is difficult to find a completely honest politician involved in the "War of the Copper Kings."

While Daly, Clark, Heinze, Henry Rogers and others struggled over Butte copper, other individuals and issues had impact on Montana. In the first two decades of the new century, Montanans faced many challenges, including a World War, labor strife, a huge increase in population, severe drought, and the political antics of a group called the "Wobblies." It was what historians call "the Progressive Era."

It was a period of reform. Reformers wanted to increase political power in the hands of citizens and decrease it in the hands of corporations and political "bosses." It was a time when new political faces appeared. These were the years when Joe Dixon, Jeannette Rankin, Thomas J. Walsh and Burton K. Wheeler first won major campaigns.

A reform mood in Montana began with the Populists. It was accelerated by reactions to political corruption during the "Wars of the Copper Kings." Robert Smith, the Democratic-Populist governor from 1897 to 1901, and his successor, Joseph K. Toole, encouraged reform politics. The most important changes expanded direct citizen participation in government. In 1906 voters overwhelmingly approved a constitutional amendment providing for the initiative and referendum. This allowed citizens to petition for ballot measures without legislative approval. One newspaper called it an "End of the Bosses." It was not the end of power politics in Montana, but it did stimulate additional reforms.

Even more stunning were three other political changes. Montanans were only too aware of the power held by political bosses. In both major parties key individuals chose candidates without much voter involvement. In Wisconsin and Oregon reformers had instituted direct primary laws that gave voters the power to select party candidates. In Montana efforts to enact a similar law failed at first. In 1911 Miles Romney of Hamilton, Thomas J. Walsh of Helena and others formed the People's Power League to enact direct legislation laws. Using the 1906 initiative, they were successful in passing a constitutional amendment in 1912 that provided for direct primaries. In the same year they enacted an amendment for the direct election of U.S. Senators. Never again would Montanans have to endure the embarrassment of a senatorial election farce like Clark's in 1899. Reform legislation enacted in 1912 made that election one of the most important in Montana's history. In 1912 voters also approved a presidential preference primary law and a corrupt practices act.

Even with these victories, one major electoral reform remained unaccomplished. Beginning even before statehood, Montana women had agitated to gain the vote. Time and again they failed. Ella Knowles Haskell, the energetic Populist candidate for attorney general in 1892, led the women's suffrage movement in the 1890s. After the turn of the century, it was fiery Jeannette Rankin of Missoula who campaigned tirelessly for women's suffrage. With great organizational ability, Jeannette finally led her forces to victory in 1914. Two years later she became the first woman in American history elected to Congress. This was truly a crowning achievement for progressives in Montana.

Montana's legislators took reform seriously, too. Across the nation "muckraking journalists," as they were called, wrote of barbaric working conditions in American industry, of child labor excesses, of political corruption, and of poisoned food. Montanans were as concerned as anyone. And the legislature acted between 1913 and 1917 to correct abuses. They enacted laws regulating child labor, punishment of juveniles by courts, and even school attendance. Men and women working in industry were protected by laws governing work hours and safety. In 1915 a Workmen's Compensation Law was enacted to aid workmen injured on the job. In 1907, the legislature created the Montana Railroad Commission to regulate railroad rates. In 1913 they established the Public Service Commission to regulate other public utilities in Montana.

The new century also introduced new politicians to Montana. Outsiders have always commented on the exciting people Montana has sent to represent them in Washington. Our senators particularly have been noteworthy. They have had that quality of combining talent with dynamic personalities. Three of these exceptional people entered Montana politics during the progressive period.

One of them was Joseph M. Dixon. In the course of his political career he served as Missoula County attorney from 1894 to 1897, as a state representative in 1900, as Congressman from 1903 to 1907, as U.S. Senator from 1907 to 1913 and finally as governor from 1921 to 1925. He came to Missoula from North Carolina in 1891. He studied law, joined a law firm and became active in local Republican politics. In 1896 he married Caroline Worden, daughter of Missoula founder Frank L. Worden.

Throughout his career he was known as a direct and honest man. He held to principle and was something of a crusader. A staunch defender of popular government, he supported progressive reforms and consistently battled against the political power of Anaconda and other corporations. More than once he fought with political bosses. In the U.S. Senate he sided with the Progressives. He was an admirer of Theodore Roosevelt. When Roosevelt tried for the presidency in 1912, it was Joe Dixon of Montana who ran his national campaign. In Montana Dixon and his allies tried to break the Amalgamated's grip on state politics, but it was an uphill fight. Once in the governor's chair, as we shall see later, he finally achieved a major reform affecting the mining companies.

The second man to emerge in the progressive years was

Ella Knowles ran for Montana Attorney General in 1892 and lost to Henry Haskell whom she later married. She was later active in the women's suffrage movement in Montana. —*Progressive Men of Montana (1913)*. M.H.S.

Thomas J. Walsh represented Montana in the U.S. Senate from 1923 to 1933. He gained national attention when he exposed the Teapot Dome scandal during President Harding's administration.—*John A. Glander, Manitowoc, Wisconsin, photograph*

a scrappy Wisconsin-born lawyer who came to Helena in 1890. Thomas J. Walsh also made his reputation as a liberal antagonist of the Anaconda Company. He was an expert on mining law and often found himself in court arguing on behalf of injured workmen. Walsh consistently sided with the laboring man against the corporations. In the Democratic Party Walsh was respected for his legal mind, his diplomacy and his liberal views. After losing campaigns for Congress in 1906 and the Senate in 1911, he finally went to Washington in 1913. He remained in the Senate until his death in 1933. In the 1920s he became something of a national hero in his relentless investigation of the famous Teapot Dome scandal.

The last of the trio is the most powerful and influential of the three. Burton Kendall Wheeler came to Butte in 1905 after graduating from the University of Michigan law school. Born in Hudson, Massachusetts, Wheeler was twenty-three when he arrived in Butte. Like Dixon, Wheeler was dedicated to preserving the democratic process of government. He was also a determined pacifist and, like Walsh, a champion of the laboring people. Throughout his political career, Burton K. Wheeler could never be accused of being ordinary or boring. He was Montana's most controversial politician in the twentieth century.

Wheeler practiced law in Butte and took part in local Democratic politics. He soon realized how much power the Amalgamated wielded. Amalgamated owned nearly every daily newspaper in the state, except the *Great Falls Tribune*, and with that power they effectively controlled information. For Wheeler, it was depressing. Montana politics seemed anything but democratic. Nonetheless, he entered politics himself. At first, he says in his autobiography, "I was naive" when elected to the legislature in 1911. In that session he supported Thomas J. Walsh for U.S. Senator. Amalgamated wanted Walsh defeated. The "company" won in 1911, but when Walsh was elected senator two years later he rewarded Wheeler's support by getting him appointed U.S. District Attorney in Butte.

It was as district attorney that Wheeler first became notorious. The "company," of course, already knew that they could not buy him. But once the United States went to war in 1917, Wheeler angered many more persons than Anaconda Company officials. Anti-war radicals, some of them members of the Industrial Workers of the World (the "Wobblies"), agitated against the war. Citizens demanded that Wheeler charge these people with violations of anti-sedition laws. Wheeler refused to harass them, even if most Montanans thought they were Bolsheviks, the party name of communists in Russia. Wheeler was a pacifist himself, and would not violate the radicals' civil rights. Because of his stand, Wheeler became known as "Bolshevik Burt." In 1918 he resigned his post. Two years later he ran against Joe Dixon for governor and lost. But that was not the end of

Burton K. Wheeler addresses voters from the back of a truck during his 1920 campaign for governor.

Burton Wheeler's political career. He went on to become a U.S. Senator in 1923.

The Wobblies did far more than create problems for District Attorney Wheeler. The IWW was the creation of socialist labor leaders in 1905. When they came to Montana to organize lumbermen, fruit pickers and miners, they came to the strongest union labor state in the West. The labor history of Montana is fascinating, violent and complicated. Beginning with the Butte Miners' Union in 1878, miners and smeltermen organized to protect their interests. In 1893 Butte became the first local of the Western Federation of Miners. The WFM was an aggressive union and engaged in violent confrontations with police and federal troops throughout the West. In Butte, however, the wars between the copper barons allowed the union to grow and avoid conflict.

By the time the Wobblies came, the climate had changed. In 1906 Amalgamated refused to increase miners' wages. Union members split over what to do. Should they strike? Amalgamated answered the question by shutting down the mines just as they had in 1903. The strike died before it was born. The split in the union widened. When the company tried to bar the more radical union members from working, tensions grew. Amalgamated instituted a so-called "rustling card" system for job placement in the mines. Only miners with cards could work, and only non-agitating workers got the cards. Wobblies pointed to this obvious discrimination as reason for more radical action against mine owners. By 1914 tensions within the union became explosive. On Miners' Union Day, June 3, 1914, a riot ruined the annual celebration. Conservative and radical union members continued to argue. Finally, on June 23, a brief street battle and then twenty-five dynamite blasts levelled the Miners' Union Hall.

The blasting of the Butte Miners' Union remains something of a mystery to this day. At the time, some blamed the Wobblies; others thought the company's men actually did it. Whatever the truth, unionism in Butte suffered wounds lasting several years. Not until 1917 did miners have another union. In the midst of this turmoil the IWW continued to evoke fearful reactions from Montanans. In 1917 they agitated against World War I, claiming it was a capitalist's fight, not a worker's war. The Wobblies were never very strong, but the patriotic hysteria during World War I made them more threatening to those who expected to find subversives at work everywhere.

The final and most shocking incident in the Butte labor troubles in these years came in 1917. Wobblies took advantage of a mining disaster and resultant strike to stir up more interest in their organization. On June 8 a horrible fire deep in the Speculator Mine left 164 miners dead. Poor safety conditions were partly to blame. Miners struck the mines in angry protest. Into Butte came a very aggressive IWW organizer, Frank Little. He spoke long and hard in July of 1917. Shouting against the war, against the Anaconda Company, and against the capitalist system, he angered nearly everyone. On July 28 the *Butte Daily Post* asked, "How long is it [Butte] going to stand for the seditious talk of the IWW agitator?" The answer came on August 1. Six men dragged Little from his sleep and lynched him from a railroad trestle west of town.

Panic swept the city. Was Butte in for another siege of

The wreckage of the Butte Miners Union Hall after twenty-five dynamite blasts on June 23, 1914, levelled the building.

labor violence? Governor Samuel V. Stewart called a special session of the legislature. Federal troops came to Butte. An anxious calm existed. Most people deplored Little's murder, although he had been regarded as a traitor—one of the many who would not support the war effort. Emotions ran high. German-Americans were watched closely. Even eating German foods was discouraged. The result was the passage of a Montana Sedition Law that made it a crime to speak against the government. The Montana Council of Defense was created to act as a citizens' watchdog agency to punish those who refused to support the war. It was a frightening time. Until World War I concluded in November 1918, Montanans endured a fearful period when many of their civil rights were curtailed.

The end of the decade brought relief from political tensions, but yet another disaster struck the state. Drought nearly destroyed Montana's agriculture. That calamity is part of Montana's agricultural and social history. Montana politics emerged from the war years severely tested. The 1920s and 1930s, however, would bring a new set of political problems. Fortunately, Montanans found the resolve and strength to meet them.

The Farmers' Conference in Wibaux provided an opportunity to share problems and plan united action. The Nonpartisan League was active among eastern farmers during the 1920s.

Senator Clark of Montana

He was one of the "Big Four" of the Democratic Party in Montana. Along with Samuel T. Hauser, Marcus Daly and Colonel Charles A. Broadwater, William Andrews Clark played a major role in shaping Montana as a territory and state. Yet, of the four men, Clark was clearly the dominant personality. He was the most ambitious, and the most successful. With dark, piercing eyes and wild, brushlike chin whiskers, he was a man few Montanans had not heard of by 1900. His biography is a capsule history of Montana's economic and political development from gold rush days to the new century.

He was born on January 8, 1839, in Connellsville, Pennsylvania. The Clarks were farmers. William worked with his father and attended the Laurel Hill Academy before the family moved to Iowa in 1856. Next he taught school for a time in Missouri and then studied law in Mount Pleasant, Iowa. Judging from his acute legal actions later in life, he must have applied himself to his legal studies. In 1862, however, he journeyed west to the Colorado gold fields. The next year found him in Bannack just as the great strike was made at nearby Alder Gulch.

In Virginia City Clark made some initial money by mining a small claim. His interest soon turned to trade. Supplying miners, he reasoned, was a much surer business than prospecting. He sold flour, tobacco and other provisions shipped from Salt Lake City. By 1865 Clark had located at Ophir Gulch west over the divide from Helena. There he opened the "California Store" with a partner named Fraser. Years later Clark remembered how quickly he sold out of lemons, olives and other tropical delights freighted in by camel train from California. Among his friends at Ophir was S. E. Larabie, later one of Clark's business partners.

From Ophir, Clark visited briefly at LaBarge City. Soon after, the town took its permanent name, Deer Lodge. In 1867 Clark went east and entered a partnership with R. W. Donnell of New York to merchandise goods to Montana gold camps. As busy as he was, he also secured a mail contract between Walla Walla and Missoula in 1868. The following year Clark sold goods at Helena and then moved his business to Deer Lodge. There he and Larabie established a mercantile store. By 1872 their business was thriving and they opened a bank.

To say that W. A. Clark was enterprising and ambitious is an understatement. Mining still attracted his interest. In 1872 he purchased several mines in Butte. These mines, the Original, Colusa, Mountain Chief and others were silver properties. To learn more about mining, Clark spent two years studying metallurgy and engineering at Columbia University in New York. Once back in Montana, Clark bought other mines in Butte. By 1879 he had enough capital to organize the Colorado and Montana Smelting Company and erect the first smelter in Butte. In the following year he built the Moulton Mill and Mine works at a cost of $500,000. Later, he invested in the huge United Verde Copper Company in Arizona, an investment that actually brought Clark more riches than his Montana properties.

In later years he continued to invest. Eventually, he owned interests in mines in Arizona, Nevada, Utah, Idaho, New Mexico and Maine. He also purchased newspapers, including the *Butte Miner.* He owned a sugar plantation and refinery in California, a furniture factory in Los Angeles, a wire factory in New Jersey, a coffee plantation in Mexico, street railways and utility companies in Butte and Missoula and a stone quarry in Maine. Long before the idea of industrial conglomerates became popular, Clark became a one-man conglomerate. By his early forties he was a man of great wealth. But it was Clark's political activities that made him so influential in Montana.

Clark became a prominent Montanan. He began to be more and more the man in the spotlight. In 1876 Territorial Governor Benjamin F. Potts selected Clark as Montana's official orator at the Philadelphia Centennial Exhibition. Taking the role seriously, Clark spoke as a one-man promotion for Montana's riches and opportunities for new residents.

When the Nez Perce fled through Montana in 1877, Clark again stepped to the front. This time he led a company of volunteers to the aid of Colonel John Gibbon at the Battle of the Big Hole. In the same year he was elected Grand Master of the Masonic Lodge of Montana. Clark simply expected to be at the center of affairs. His entire life reflected this expectation. Just about everything he set his mind to do, he achieved. And he lived in a style to match his expectations. In 1876 he built a lavish mansion in Butte at a reported cost of $76,000. Later he spent millions purchasing European art and furniture. He built another costly residence on Fifth Avenue in New York. W. A. Clark did things in grand style.

It was in the 1880s, however, that Clark actively entered Democratic politics. Here, as in other pursuits, Clark expected to be one of the important people. He was not disappointed. His wealth, his prominence in mining and his talents assured him a primary position in Montana politics. In 1884 he was an elected delegate to the Constitutional Convention and became president of the convention. In that role he served ably. When another Constitutional Convention met in 1889, Clark was a delegate once again, and again he served as the convention president. Before the 1889 convention, however, Clark took his first fall and engaged in his first political fight with Butte mining rival Marcus Daly.

Just how the famous Clark-Daly feud began is unclear. It may have begun in a dispute over mining properties in Butte, a tangle over water rights or a dozen other possible conflicts. In 1888 it boiled down to one election. In that year Clark ran as a Democrat for territorial delegate against Republican Thomas H. Carter. Montana was strongly Democratic, particularly in the mining districts. Clark expected to win. When the votes were tallied, Clark could not believe the results—he had lost. Where had he lost the election? Solid Democratic precincts had gone for the Republican Carter. Clark smelled political foul play. The only explanation was that Daly had instructed his miners to vote for Carter, denying Clark the office he wanted so desperately. Clark charged Daly with political sabotage. Daly denied it.

There was ample evidence that Daly had done what Clark claimed. But there was no conclusive proof. It made no difference to Clark; he knew what had happened. When the selection of the permanent state capital became an issue in 1894, Clark was determined that Daly's town, Anaconda, would not be selected. Clark supported Helena and both men spent huge sums of money. When the voters selected Helena, Clark felt at least partially vindicated. In Helena he was a hero. But this was not Clark's ultimate ambition. He still

William Andrews Clark looks the part of financier, copper baron and politician that he was in this classic photo of him in the prime of his life.

wanted to go to Washington, D.C.

Senator Lee Mantle's senate seat was up for election in 1899. The legislature met in Helena in January to conduct business and select a U.S. Senator. Clark's men were there, including his lawyer, John B. Wellcome. They came with money to buy W. A. Clark his senate seat. Daly's forces, of course, were just as determined to block Clark's try for the Senate. Everyone knew of Clark's bribery, but no one objected until Fred Whiteside, a state senator from Flathead, decided to trap Clark's men in their dirty work. Arranging with two other legislators to be decoys, Whiteside accepted $30,000 in bribe money and then exposed the whole business to the legislature. In an emotional speech before his fellow legislators, Whiteside presented the evidence and challenged the bribed legislators to "tell us the price and sit down." Even more remarkable was the fact that Whiteside had spurned an offer of $300,000 to keep quiet about the whole affair. It was a daring move on Whiteside's part, but Clark's men had done their job too well. Clark won the election.

Clark went to Washington, but his senate seat was soon to be snatched from his grasp. Daly, Senator Carter and Fred Whiteside convinced the Senate to investigate the Montana election. The investigation uncovered much of what had happened. It was clear that his senate seat was in jeopardy, but before the Senate could act, Clark resigned. Once again Montana was embarrassed, and once again Montana was without a senator. But the story was not over yet. Back in Montana, Clark's men took advantage of Governor Robert Smith's absence from the state to persuade Lieutenant Governor A. E. Spriggs to appoint W. A. Clark to fill the seat just vacated by Clark himself! It was an incredible action. Upon his prompt return to Montana, Smith appointed Paris Gibson of Great Falls to the Senate. The Senate refused to seat either Clark or Gibson. Again Montana was without full representation in Washington.

Clark had lost a second time. On his third try, however, he was not to be denied. When Carter's seat came up for election in 1901, the legislature finally sent Clark to Washington. Now in the Senate, Clark lost his enthusiasm as a Daly rival. Marcus Daly had died in 1900, and Anaconda itself had been purchased by the Amalgamated Copper Company. Although Clark had used Anaconda's sale to the copper trust as an issue in his 1901 campaign, he soon allied with Amalgamated and actually sold them some of his mining properties.

In the Senate, Clark represented Montana's industrial interests. He fought to defeat President Theodore Roosevelt's conservation programs, believing them to be a threat to Montana mining and timber interests. He also worked unsuccessfully for federal aid to irrigation programs in the

West. Nevertheless, the stigma of political corruption dogged his life in the Senate. No one could forget how he had tried to buy his way into office.

He left Washington in 1907, after only one term. He spent the remainder of his life managing his far-flung investments and travelling between his residences in Butte, Paris, New York, and Santa Barbara, California. On March 2, 1925, William Andrews Clark died in New York City. A remarkable life was over; a life dominated by ambition, wealth and power. Like many titans of industry, he was misunderstood by most of his contemporaries. Rivals painted him as an arch villain. Supporters claimed he was a man of high purpose and great deeds. Neither appraisal is accurate, but both reflect parts of his character. To Montanans he was a symbol of what a man could accomplish on the frontier and how easily the pursuit of power can corrupt.

We Are at War

Until the summer of 1914 few Montanans, other than Slavic immigrants, had ever heard of Sarajevo, Bosnia. In that remote town on June 28, 1914, an assassin took the life of Austrian Archduke Franz Ferdinand. This act set into motion the greatest war to that time in European history. World War I, which many expected to be short, became a nightmare. It developed into a war of attrition. Opposing armies fired relentlessly at each other from deep trenches. The United States tried to remain neutral. President Woodrow Wilson avoided conflict with the warring nations at every turn. But it was no use. Finally, as Wilson said in his war message in April of 1917, America, "God helping her, she can do no other." America was at war.

In Montana the war had surprising effects. Some were positive, but most were negative. As the war in Europe dragged on in 1915 and 1916, American farm products became more and more important to war-torn European nations. Wheat and other commodity prices rose sharply. Montana's farmers shared in this sudden prosperity, particularly those farmers in the new agricultural districts along the Hi-Line. Weather conditions were favorable in those years, and the homestead boom of earlier years meant prosperity for thousands of new Montana farmers. Once the United States had entered the war, the federal government set guaranteed prices for wheat and urged farmers to plant as much as they could. Food could win the war, farmers were told. The prices remained high throughout the war even in the face of the first signs of drought. World War I was a boon to Montana agriculture.

The war boosted agriculture, but it disrupted Montana politics. America's entry into World War I was controversial. Across the nation there were many protests. German-Americans did not want to fight against their homeland. Irish-Americans objected to an American alliance with Britain as long as the British government held Ireland in colonial chains. Socialists objected to the war, too. They called it a "rich man's fight," a war that no worker should support. Socialist labor unions, like the IWW, urged workers to ignore the draft. Montanans were not immune to these ideas. Germans, Irish, and socialists throughout the state questioned American participation in the war. Their harsh criticism of the war made other Montanans angry enough to demand that the critics be silenced.

The Wilson administration acted quickly to generate support for the war in 1917. They created a National Council of Defense. Congress and Wilson asked each governor to create a statewide Council of Defense as well. In the summer of 1917 Governor Samuel V. Stewart complied and appointed the Montana Council of Defense. The council was not a state agency, although Governor Stewart served as *ex officio* chairman. Prominent and interested citizens from across the state composed the council. They volunteered their time and energy to the war effort. Council members helped organize county councils, local loyalty leagues, and other patriotic groups. It was all done with the best intentions, but soon trouble arose. Patriotic Montanans became too zealous. They pushed citizens too hard to buy Liberty Bonds and contribute to the Red Cross. Their gentle encouragement quickly turned to harassment.

A pro-war hysteria developed in Montana in 1917 and 1918. Part of this feeling came from fear. There was a fear of radical politics associated with the Industrial Workers of the World (IWW). There was fear of the Non-Partisan League (NPL)—an organization of socialist farmers that originated in North Dakota. The IWW and NPL had criticized the war and urged Montanans to resist American entry. When citizens complained to U.S. District Attorney Burton K. Wheeler, he refused to be stampeded into hasty action. Wheeler would not prosecute war critics. He knew how easily emotions could rule in time of war. "Most of the cases looked ridiculous to me," Wheeler later explained, "and I refused to bring indictments." Federal District Judge George M. Bourquin was just as reluctant to find anti-war agitators guilty of violating vague sedition laws. Newspapers across the state, however, labelled the war critics as "Bolsheviks," "anarchists," "bomb-throwers," and worse.

The war issue entered Montana politics dramatically when the state's lone representative to Congress, Jeannette Rankin of Missoula, voted against war in 1917. She was one of many in Congress who voted against war, but most Montanans disagreed with her vote. Almost as an effort to prove

Montana's 2nd Infantry leaving Helena for France on October 24, 1917.

how loyal Montana truly was, the Council of Defense and the county councils worked hard to sell Liberty Bonds and generally promote the war effort. They were suspicious of any unusual political activity. When IWW organizer Frank Little came to Butte, newspaper editors across the state demanded to know why Little should be allowed to speak openly against the war. Thugs lynched Little in August, but that only increased tensions. Then, in January of 1918, Judge Bourquin found a Rosebud County rancher, Ves Hall, not guilty of seditious speech. It was too much for the superpatriots. They demanded that something be done to punish anti-war "traitors."

The Ves Hall case was a turning point. Hall supposedly had remarked at the time of the *Lusitania* disaster that Germany had rightfully sunk the ship because it was carrying munitions of war—the *Lusitania* was an unarmed passenger ship torpedoed by German submarines killing over 1,100 persons. Ves Hall had also criticized American participation in the war. Montanans angrily denounced Bourquin's verdict. The next month Governor Stewart called a special session of the legislature to deal with war-related problems. The chief problem was a developing drought and a severe shortage of crop seeds. But the aggressive war-supporters took advantage of the opportunity. Governor Stewart himself set the mood when he opened the special session in February of 1918. He warned the "slackers" and "idlers" to get behind the war effort. They were "traitors in our midst," Stewart declared. In quick succession the legislature passed a Sedition Act and formally made the Council of Defense a state agency. The Sedition Act, actually written by U.S. Senator Henry L. Myers of Hamilton, made it a crime to criticize the government or officials of the United States. Armed with the new legislation, the council and its county groups now went after everyone who did not sufficiently support the war.

The council lost no time in granting itself extraordinary powers of subpoena and investigation. Supposed "slackers" had to appear before the council and defend themselves. Some meekly contributed more to the Red Cross or purchased more war bonds; a few objected. One who objected was Simon Schneider, a Mineral County farmer. "If [President] Wilson makes England give back all the territories it has taken from Germany," Schneider blurted out in defiance, "I will buy one cow's worth [of Liberty Bonds], if not, you will have to be satisfied with five dollars for the Red Cross." The council charged him with violating the Sedition Act. He was finally cleared, but in the meantime Schneider experienced the worst kind of abuse from suspicious neighbors.

It was a frightening time. People reported secret stockpiles of weapons at supposed enemy bases in the mountains. Others reported sighting German airships cruising the Bitterroot Valley. One person even swore an enemy plane landed near Hamilton! When strikes erupted in lumber camps and mines, the fear increased. Who was to blame? Were the strikers operating as enemy agents? Burton Wheeler later said the hysteria simply "made many people completely lose their sense of justice."

The Council of Defense lost all perspective in 1918. They ordered libraries throughout the state to burn books written in German. They banned use of the German language. German songs could not be sung. German Lutherans and Mennonites could not pray in German. There seemed to be no limit to infringements of civil rights. Council members thought they were doing their patriotic duty, but they went too far. And there was violence. In May 1918, Mickey McGlynn, an NPL organizer, suffered a beating in Miles City. Local citizens saw McGlynn as dangerous and took the law into their own hands. Montana's Attorney General Sam C. Ford demanded that McGlynn's attackers be punished. They were never brought to trial. This incident was the beginning of the end to the pro-war hysteria, but only the end of World War I itself terminated the council's activities.

Ironically, Montana had given heroically to the war effort. Nearly ten percent of the population went off to fight. Due to a mistake in the state's draft allotment, 40,000 Montana men found themselves in the army. It was a larger burden than any other state had to carry. Montana's farmers produced bumper crops. And the majority of citizens bought more than their share of Liberty Bonds and contributed to the Red Cross. Still, the war years left more scars than Montana deserved.

Politically the repercussions of the war years were enormous. The socialists, of course, lost nearly all the meager population support they may have had before strikes, demonstrations and Frank Little's murder damaged their cause. Jeannette Rankin, who had received support from IWW and NPL leaders, lost her bid for the Senate in 1918. Burton Wheeler, the district attorney who had defended socialists, resigned his post under pressure. Wheeler could not shake the "radical" label. When he battled and lost to Joseph Dixon for governor in 1920, a few angry voters actually attacked him.

Politics aside, perhaps the most destructive wartime experience for Montanans was an agricultural calamity. The great wartime boom collapsed as suddenly as it had appeared. The decline began in 1917. First along the Hi-Line and later throughout eastern Montana, the plentiful rains stopped falling. The drought came and lasted three years. Rainfall was one-third of previous years. Wheat production dropped in some areas from 25 bushels per acre to only 2.4. High summer temperatures, hot winds, great clouds of grasshoppers and unyielding dryness devastated Montana farmlands. Thousands of farmers gave up. Many of them were homesteaders who just a few years before had come with such high hopes. The end of wartime demand dropped agricultural prices. In 1919 and 1920 many farmers who had braved the drought could not hold their land. Their crops brought less than one-half the price they had received only two years before. It was a calamity that left over 10,000 farms vacant by 1925.

As a new decade began in 1920, Montanans hoped that it would bring fewer problems than the last. That wish would be only partially fulfilled. But it is certain that Montanans were better prepared for the future than they had been in 1910 or 1914. They knew what could happen when law and civil rights were disregarded. They found out how quickly nature could turn a fertile field into bone-dry dust. They discovered how strong they could be when the times demanded it. And, most importantly, they understood how close the tie was between Montana people and their land.

Timeline

1888: W. A. Clark loses territorial delegate election to Thomas H. Carter; Will Kennedy founds *Boulder Age.*

1889: Montana achieves statehood.

1889-90: First legislature meets amidst great confusion.

1892: Populists organize in Montana; Ella Knowles runs for attorney general.

1893: Financial panic affects Montana mining and banking; many Montanans unemployed; Western Federation of Miners organized with Local #1 in Butte.

1894: Banks fail and railroads go into receivership; Butte Industrial Legion "borrows" NP train in Butte; Helena selected as permanent state capital.

1896: Populist Robert Smith elected governor.

1899: Amalgamated Copper Company purchases Anaconda Copper Company; Fritz Heinze comes to Butte; W. A. Clark elected but not seated as U.S. Senator.

1900: W. A. Clark elected U.S. Senator; Marcus Daly dies in New York.

1902: Joseph M. Dixon elected to Congress.

1903: Amalgamated closes Butte copper mines in fight with Heinze; Governor Toole calls special session of legislature to pass "fair trials bill."

1904: Dixon reelected to Congress.

1905: Industrial Workers of the World (IWW or "Wobblies") founded in Chicago; Burton Wheeler comes to Butte.

1906: Heinze sells out to Amalgamated; voters approve initiative, referendum, and recall procedure.

1907: Railroad Commission established to monitor freight rates in state; Joseph M. Dixon elected U.S. Senator.

1909: IWW "free speech" fights in Missoula.

1910: Fires burn western Montana forests.

1911: Miles Romney and others found People's Power League; Henry L. Myers elected U.S. Senator.

1912: Voters approve direct primaries law.

1913: Public Service Commission established; Thomas J. Walsh elected U.S. Senator; Burton Wheeler appointed U.S. District Attorney in Butte.

1914: World War begins; women get the vote in Montana; blasting of Butte Miners Union Hall; Fritz Heinze dies.

1915: Workmen's Compensation Law passed.

1916: Jeannette Rankin is first woman elected to Congress; Non-Partisan League organizes in Montana.

1917: U.S. enters World War; Jeannette Rankin votes against war; Frank Little lynched in Butte; loggers strike in western Montana; Montana Council of Defense organized; drought hits Hi-Line counties.

1918: Drought spreads throughout state; Ves Hall case; Governor Stewart calls special session of legislature.

Suggested Readings

Thomas A. Clinch, "Coxey's Army in Montana," *Montana the Magazine of Western History* Vol. 15 (Autumn 1965).

C. B. Glasscock, *The War of the Copper Kings*. New York: Bobbs-Merrill, 1935.

T. A. Larson, "Montana Women and the Battle for the Ballot," *Montana the Magazine of Western History* Vol. 23 (Winter 1973).

Sarah McNelis, *Copper King at War: The Biography of F. Augustus Heinze*. Missoula: University of Montana Press, 1968.

K. Ross Toole, "The Genesis of the Clark-Daly Feud," *Montana the Magazine of Western History* Vol. 1 (April 1951).

Theodore Wiprud, "Butte: A Troubled Labor Paradise," *Montana the Magazine of Western History* Vol. 21 (October 1971).

Machines like the tractor made farming much easier.

Chapter XII
Montana in the Twenties Was A Time of Trial

The end of World War I in 1918 brought great rejoicing across the nation. Montanans joined in the celebration. Too many Montana men had gone to war and too few had returned. Many of those who returned found their farms in desperate shape. Worse than the drought, however, were the generally poor economic conditions. A nationwide recession kept demand and crop prices low. Wheat, Montana's chief cash crop, had brought high prices in 1917-1920. Between August and December of 1920, however, wheat dropped from $2.22 to $1.26 per bushel. By December of 1921, the price was only 86¢ per bushel. With little or no income, farmers had difficulty paying bills and meeting land payments.

It was a poor beginning for a new decade. Hundreds of homesteading families had left their farms by 1920. They could not endure the conditions. Many of the homesteaders—far too many—had taken up farming for the first time when they came to Montana in the decade before World War I. In Liberty, Hill, Toole, and Pondera counties, for example, seventy percent of the homesteaders without a farming background left the land. Those who did not leave often lost their farms anyway. The hard years were accompanied by thousands of mortgage foreclosures. From 1921 to 1925 over 20,000 farmers lost their land. Foreclosures averaged over 300 per year in the 1920s. In Hill County alone, over ninety percent of the mortgaged farms faced foreclosure during the 1921-1925 years.

There was a bright side to Montana agriculture in the 1920s. Those who came through the hard years realized the importance of increased farm efficiency. They bought gasoline tractors by the hundreds. They invested in harvester-thresher combines. They increased the size of their farms. They diversified their crops. They began to manage their farms in a scientific and businesslike manner. In short, Montana farmers modernized faster and more completely than ever before.

The first gasoline-powered tractors used in Montana came in the 1890s. It was not until about 1915, however, that they became popular.

After 1917 implement dealers brought tractors into Montana by the trainload and sold them very quickly. The earlier tractors were heavy and less maneuverable than newer models, yet the later models still had sufficient power to pull two or three plows. The purchase of new tractors peaked in 1928. By the 1930s there were over 20,000 tractors in operation in Montana, more than a tenfold increase in one decade.

Farmers also purchased harvester-threshers in record numbers in the 1920s. Until 1924 harvester-threshers were comparatively rare in Montana, but it did not take long for farmers to recognize the immense benefits they received from the use of these machines. By 1929 there were nearly 6,000 in use in the state. In addition to tractors and harvester-threshers, farmers also purchased trucks at a furious pace. All of this meant greater efficiency on the farm.

The great advance in farming in Montana during the 1920s was in the general modernization of farming techniques. Dry-land farming, farming with no irrigation and little rainfall, was perfected on experimental farms operated by Montana State College in Bozeman. In the "Fairway Farms Project" M. L. Wilson and his colleagues at Montana State developed new methods to improve crop yields, protect soil fertility, conserve resources, and modernize farm economics.

Farmers put more land into production and had higher yields per acre in the 1920s than they had in the previous decade. The use of tractors and harvesters meant that farmers hired fewer day laborers. But the machinery did increase maintenance and fuel costs. Nevertheless, the result was a real increase in farmers' incomes.

The banking industry in Montana, which had grown dramatically before World War I, fell on evil days in the 1920s. In 1905 there were just over 50 banks operating in Montana. By 1920 there were 425 banks open for business. The tremendous increase in Montana's population—due mostly to the homestead boom after 1909—accounts for a

Oscar Melby and sons on their farm at East Coalridge working with a Fordson tractor. —*Syverud Collection, M.H.S.*

larger demand for banking services. But the banks expanded much too fast. Even the prosperity of the war years could not justify such an increase.

The crisis began in the last months of 1920. While crops were good in 1914, 1915 and 1916, banks lent money to farmers on very generous terms. The general economic inflation encouraged more lending. Land values had increased sharply during those years. The poor crop years of 1918 and 1919, however, brought trouble. Low yields per acre and declining crop prices in 1919 and 1920 made it difficult for farmers to make their loan payments. They simply did not have enough income. Banks foreclosed on these loans, but the banks were no better off with the land than were the farmers. It was not long before the banks themselves could not meet their own demands. "This period," one commentator wrote, "has been one long dripping tunnel—a veritable nightmare. Each day brought new disasters."

As one country bank after another experienced problems and closed their doors, individual depositors rushed to withdraw their money. People lost confidence in their local banks. As these worried bank customers withdrew their money, other banks weakened and collapsed. Between 1921 and 1926 more than one-half of Montana's commercial banks failed. Two hundred and fourteen closed their doors during these years.

Most of the bank failures were in communities located east of the Continental Divide. Just over fifty-six percent of the banks in these localities failed, while west of the Divide only thirty-eight percent of the banks ceased operations. More importantly, the failing banks were much more likely to be in small rather than medium or large communities. Over seventy-two percent of the busted banks were located in towns of less than 1,000 population; forty-two percent of them were in communities with less than 300 people. In those very small towns, practically everyone kept his or her cash in those banks; when the banks failed, so did the town. Whole communities suffered terribly.

Many of the banks that closed probably deserved their fate. During the homestead boom, small banks seemed to appear practically overnight. The bank "presidents" were often little more than fast-talking traders who took advantage of the population increase. Some of them conducted business in an "unusual" fashion. In a 1919 Broadus bank, wooden boxes served as counters. The only "vault" was a tin box that the manager slipped under his bed each night for safekeeping. Other banks accepted shares of promised cattle and sheep sales as loan payments. It is little wonder that banks that operated in this manner had little protection when the crisis struck.

The Twenties was a time of trial, but some industries prospered. Oil production in Montana came of age. The first strikes had been in southeastern Montana during the war years. In the mid-1920s, however, drilling crews struck "black gold" in the Kevin and Sunburst oil fields near Shelby. These finds did not rival those in Texas and Oklahoma, but they did bring major oil companies to Montana. Drilling rigs tested promising areas all over the state.

Coal production, which had been limited to deep mines in Roundup and Red Lodge, came from new areas. By the early 1920s, the Northern Pacific Railroad desired a cheaper source of coal for its locomotives. They began strip-mining at Colstrip in Rosebud County. Stripping the coal was easier than constructing deep mines. Huge electrically powered shovels simply stripped off the shallow earth above the coal and dug it out by the ton. It was the beginning of a new era in Montana coal mining. In 1929 alone the N.P. mined three million tons of coal at Colstrip.

Butté's fabulous copper mines continued to prosper, but the Anaconda expanded its operations outside of Butte. In 1922 it purchased a brass company in Connecticut. One year later the company bought one of the world's largest copper mines in Chile. Anaconda entered a new phase of its corporate existence. Butte became less important. In future years Anaconda relied less and less on Butte copper.

All of these economic pressures had a telling effect upon politics in the 1920s. The agricultural depression placed great pressure on the state. This was very evident in eastern Montana. Farmers listened more and more to radical voices. Angry farmers blamed railroads, grain purchasers and others for their problems. In Plentywood, a group of socialists began publishing a remarkable newspaper in 1918, *The Producers News*. During the next nineteen years, editor Charles E. Taylor (sometimes called "Red Flag Taylor") made *The Producers News* notorious in Montana and the northern plains.

Taylor was a confirmed Communist. He sincerely believed that the Soviet system could save the world. Particularly, he felt, it could save the depressed agriculturalists in Montana and the Dakotas. It is impossible to determine how many genuine Communists there were among the paper's readers, but copies could be found in many if not most Sheridan County homes in the 1920s. Taylor claimed that the farmers' economic problems could be traced to the evil capitalist system. A radical change, he claimed, was the only political action that could rescue farmers from their predicament. In 1922 and 1924 socialist candidates won nearly every Sheridan County office. The return of agricultural prosperity in the late 1920s made the socialist's message less powerful. Nevertheless, the success of *The Producers News* and Sheridan County's socialists indicates how agitated farmers were in those years.

State politics opened the 1920s with a bang in the governor's race. Pitted against one another were Burton K. Wheeler and Joseph M. Dixon. Wheeler, a Democrat with support from labor organizations and socialist farmers, was a controversial man. He had angered many citizens during the war years when he refused to prosecute alleged war resisters. He had attacked the political power of the Anaconda Company and practically existed on controversy. This election, however, proved to be one of his sternest trials.

Joseph M. Dixon, the Republican candidate from Missoula, was also disliked by the Anaconda Company. Dixon was a reformer, and he had been very critical of Anaconda's high-handed political methods. Anaconda disliked Dixon less than Wheeler so they threw their support to Dixon. The campaign was nasty. At every opportunity the opposition charged Wheeler with the wildest kinds of ideas. They claimed that he was a Communist and favored "free love." They warned voters that Wheeler's election would mean revolution. Dixon struck a middle position in the campaign, but even he called Wheeler dangerous and radical. Montana's voters decided on Dixon as governor in 1920.

In office Dixon tried to reform state government. He fought hard to enact a new tax system, one he thought was fairer to workers and farmers. It was an uphill fight. In the end he won only a few battles, and he lost his bid for re-elec-

A steam tractor plowing a field in the Bitterroot Valley.

tion in 1924. Even Dixon's mild reforms were too much in the 1920s. Montanans preferred conservative leadership in the governor's office. Democrat John E. Erickson, a conservative who enjoyed the support of the Anaconda Company, remained governor from 1925 to 1933.

Although Montanans voted for conservatives in state offices, they continued to send liberal politicians to Washington. Senator Thomas J. Walsh had been in the Senate since 1913 representing Montana and doing a good job. Few knew of him outside of the state. But suddenly in the mid-1920s he became a national figure. He gained this fame as a no-nonsense liberal. Walsh demanded fairness in government and was determined to blot out political corruption wherever he found it. Tom Walsh of Montana was the man who exposed and prosecuted the Teapot Dome Scandal, the worst political scandal in American history to that time.

Thomas J. Walsh was born in Two Rivers, Wisconsin, in 1869. He attended local schools and graduated from law school at the University of Wisconsin in 1883. After spending several years in Dakota Territory, he came to Helena in 1890. He soon became a familiar figure in the capital city, especially among Democratic politicians. He developed a reputation as a defender of the workingman and a political reformer. T. J. Walsh was known throughout the West as the leading authority on mining law.

Democrats in Montana realized how talented this intense lawyer from Wisconsin was. They urged him to run for office, first in the state legislature and then for Congress. He failed in his bid for Congress in 1906, and failed again in a bid for a Senate seat in 1911. Finally, in 1913, Tom Walsh went to Washington to join Henry L. Myers in the Senate. As a senator, Walsh consistently supported progressive legislation. He stood for tax reform, a lower tariff, and women's suffrage. He was such an energetic and capable senator that in 1922 he held more committee assignments than any other senator. One of those committee assignments put him in the middle of the famous Teapot Dome scandal.

In 1922 the Senate began investigating rumors about

fraud in the Navy Department. The suspects included two cabinet members and several other important politicians. The charge was that they had acquired government oil properties illegally. Walsh spent months mastering the legal tangle surrounding the case and then he exposed the entire scandal. Walsh became a national celebrity. With the help of Burton K. Wheeler, who had joined Walsh in the Senate in 1923, Walsh pursued the issue to its conclusion. The whole affair nearly destroyed the Republican administrations of Warren Harding and Calvin Coolidge. Walsh's reputation as a fair but scrupulously honest man led to his selection as Franklin D. Roosevelt's attorney general in 1933. Tragically, Walsh died on his way to take the oath of office in Washington.

Montanans struggled through the Twenties only to face even harsher conditions in the next decade. Another cycle of drought began in some areas in 1928. There had been a few years of relative prosperity, and dry-land farmers, particularly, had learned how to improve their farming techniques. In fact, dry-land farmers in the so-called "Triangle" region in north central Montana led the nation in experimentation.

M. L. Wilson of Montana State College in Bozeman developed several new methods for conserving resources and improving dry-land farming techniques in the famous Fairway Farms Project. On these experimental farms Wilson and his colleagues tested several types of farming systems and designed new methods of handling farm economics.

Montana farms had been transformed during the 1920s. There were hundreds more tractors and combines operating on the large wheat fields along the Hi-Line. Farms and ranches were bigger, and those who had made it through the hard years were stronger for their experience.

Montanans from east to west had been toughened by the difficult years. Some had lost all of their savings when local banks collapsed. Others lost their farms or went further into debt. But the 1920s, unknown to everyone, was only a testing ground for the even harder years during the Great Depression. Montanans faced the tough 1930s with a greater respect for their abilities. They understood more completely how their fates were tied so closely to the condition of the land.

A Governor Under Pressure

Most Montanans thought that Senator Joseph M. Dixon had retired from politics in April 1917 when he sold his newspaper, *The Missoulian,* and moved to a ranch near Flathead Lake. He had earned his retirement, they thought. For nearly twenty years, Joe Dixon had served his state honorably. He had fought enough political battles. Up on his ranch, Dixon seemed to enjoy his new life thoroughly. He worked with characteristic energy. Joe Dixon never had done anything halfway. He built a creamery and ran a fine herd of Holstein dairy cows. In 1918 he planted wheat and rye. He tended a medium-sized orchard, too.

Dixon was optimistic about the new venture. He invested heavily to make his ranch the best equipped in the area. But these were the worst years for agriculture in the Flathead. The drought came in 1917 and worsened the following year. Dixon watched his crops wilt and dry up. His Holsteins produced less and less milk and the creamery failed. Along with his neighbors, Dixon lost money. His retirement was going to be as much of a test as politics had been. In 1919 his crops improved, but Dixon was forced to comment that "farming is not a prosperous business."

It was too much to expect that Joe Dixon would retire permanently from politics. He was too influential. Other Republicans continued to seek his advice. Dixon watched from the sidelines as Republicans feuded, corporations continued to influence political decisions and progressive legislation failed to pass in the legislature. These concerns and more brought Joe Dixon back into the political arena. In 1920 his name was on the ballot. Dixon was running again; this time he sought the governorship.

Joseph Moore Dixon was born in Snow Camp, North Carolina, on July 31, 1867. Raised in a prosperous Quaker family, young Joe had a pleasant childhood. He attended Quaker schools, worked on the family farm, and went to church regularly. At the age of nineteen, Dixon left North Carolina to continue his education at a Quaker college in Earlham, Indiana. At Earlham College he was active in a debating society and took an interest in journalism. Politics captured his attention, too. From these early days on, he

Joseph Dixon who came to Montana from North Carolina became a newspaperman, served in Congress and the U.S. Senate, and ended his political career as a one-term governor in the 1920s.

remained a Republican. Dixon returned to North Carolina in 1889 to finish his studies at Guilford College, and then he decided to seek opportunity in the West. In Missoula, Montana, lawyer Frank H. Woody, a cousin of Dixon's father, agreed to apprentice Joe in the study of law.

Dixon arrived in Missoula in the spring of 1891. He was apprehensive as he took his first look at the rough frontier town. It was a busy place with the promise of opportunity, but it still presented quite a contrast to North Carolina or Indiana. He began practicing law in 1892. He was successful, and four years later he married Caroline Worden, daughter of one of Missoula's founders. His interest in Republican politics did not take long to surface. Missoula County Republicans elected him party secretary in 1896. Five years after his arrival, he was already involved in local politics and making a mark in Missoula.

Dixon was a political reformer by nature. Whenever the opportunity arose, he argued for the common man's interests. Above all, Joe Dixon believed that democracy worked best when more people participated at every level. This view led him to support women's suffrage, direct primary laws and other political reforms that expanded democracy. He nearly ran for the legislature in 1898. Two years later he acquired the major ownership in *The Missoulian* newspaper. In the outspoken style of country journalism of the day, Joe Dixon made his views known in the newspaper. In 1900 he sought and won election to the legislature as a Republican representative from Missoula County.

In the legislature Dixon found that Republican politics revolved around the personality and power of Senator Thomas H. Carter. Montana's first member of Congress and U.S. Senator from 1895 to 1901, Carter was a conservative, close to the Anaconda Company, and a man Dixon struggled against for years. Over Carter's objections, Dixon won the Republican nomination for Congress in 1902. In the fall election, he defeated Democrat John B. Evans. The reform-minded Joe Dixon went to Washington in 1903 and won re-election the following year.

Congressman Dixon became U.S. Senator Dixon in 1907. He achieved few victories in Congress, but voters knew Joe Dixon to be a principled and reliable man. He had sponsored legislation Montanans wanted, including bills to improve irrigation and to open Montana's Indian reservations for settlement. He was known as a man of accomplishment. Once in the Senate, Dixon increasingly allied himself with the more progressive wing of the Republican Party. Thomas H. Carter, who had returned to the Senate from Montana in 1905, stood with the conservative faction. In Montana and in the Senate the two men feuded publicly. They especially disagreed on the issue of the direct popular election of U.S. Senators. Dixon supported it; Carter denounced it.

Both men were out of the Senate by 1913. During his one term in the Senate, however, Joseph M. Dixon acquired a national reputation. He supported and sponsored several important progressive bills, including a stiff inheritance tax, reform of the railroads, and lower tariff rates. With each Senate vote, Dixon moved closer and closer to a break with the national Republican leadership. In 1912 he broke and supported Theodore Roosevelt for President on the Progressive or "Bull Moose" Party ticket. Dixon served as Roosevelt's national campaign manager. Dixon worked so hard in Roosevelt's behalf that he lost his own bid for re-election to the Senate. Helena's Thomas J. Walsh beat Dixon in 1912 as Democrats everywhere rode Woodrow Wilson's popularity into office. Roosevelt lost and so did Dixon.

Joe Dixon returned to Montana in 1913. He returned to his newspaper and the relative calm of Missoula. But it was a difficult adjustment to make. His political interests and opinions had not changed. In his editorials in *The Missoulian* Dixon made it plain that he believed that Montana's political problems were due mainly to the Anaconda Company's meddlings in politics. He lashed out at his old enemies, Thomas Carter and the conservatives. He warned Montanans that they stood to lose popular government if Anaconda and other conservative forces held sway. Dixon demanded that Anaconda stick to copper mining and leave politics to individual citizens. It was a familiar fight. By 1917 Dixon had to admit that he was tired and that *The Missoulian* was simply losing too much money. Reluctantly, he sold the paper and retreated to Flathead Lake.

Politics continued to pull on Joe Dixon. He watched with anger and dismay in 1919 as conservatives and Anaconda tried to destroy Montana's direct primary law. He could remain in political retirement no longer. He announced his candidacy for governor in March 1920. The campaign of 1920 and Dixon's tenure as governor would prove to be the mos trying episodes in his entire career.

Speaking of his possible election as governor, Dixon complained to a friend in 1920: "I dread it. I would hate to live in Helena for four years to begin with and it is a dog job anyway." Nonetheless, he campaigned energetically and won the Republican nomination. His opponent in the general election was Democrat Burton K. Wheeler, a progressive-minded politician like himself. The Anaconda Company liked neither candidate, but Wheeler as governor was too much for them to take. They saw Burton as a dangerous radical—a man who would attack industry and propertied interests in the state. Reluctantly, Anaconda threw its support behind Dixon—the man who had fought against them for years.

The campaign was one of the roughest in Montana history. Anaconda and its allies unleashed a smear campaign against Wheeler. His connections with the Industrial Workers of the World and the Non-Partisan League made him an easy target. Anti-Wheeler newspapers predicted revolution if he won the election. It was an emotional campaign. The anxieties, fears and anger generated by World War I and the horrible drought helped create a tense political atmosphere. Dixon used it to his advantage. He called Wheeler a radical. He accepted the Anaconda Company's support, and he won the election by a surprisingly large margin.

Governor Joseph M. Dixon turned out to be anything but grateful for Anaconda's campaign support. He had presented himself as a moderate during the campaign, but he had not turned his back on progressivism. Dixon was still determined to reform government. He was still determined to enact a higher tax on metal mining companies. As he told a colleague, "You haven't seen me sign anything away." Governor Dixon was determined to be an independent man in Helena.

It was not an easy time to be governor. Montana agriculture had not recovered from the drought. Crop prices remained low; per-acre yields continued well below average. State finances were in sad shape. Some small banks had failed and business was generally depressed. Strong action had to be taken. Dixon's legislative program aimed at tax reform. In Dixon's view, the mining companies, oil producers and the rich were not paying their fair share in state taxes. It was time, Dixon told the legislature, to end corporate dominance of the state.

He introduced a bold program of higher mining taxes, an income tax, inheritance taxes and the creation of a tax commission to collect taxes fairly across the state. Conservatives fought Dixon every step of the way. At the end of the regular legislative session in 1921, Dixon's plan was in shambles. Angered by this, Dixon called a special session of the legislature in March 1921. It was a daring move. He battled with the opposition and won. The special session enacted an inheritance tax and passed a constitutional amendment creating a tax commission.

It was Dixon's fate, however, to be a one-term governor. These were hard times and no governor could have remained popular long. Yet, events seemed to conspire against him. In 1922 he fell into a nasty controversy when he fired Deer Lodge prison warden Frank Conley. It was charged that Conley had used state property for personal benefit. Conley denied it and took the case to court. It was a low point for the governor, and his opponents took advantage of the whole controversy. Conley was exonerated by the court. Meanwhile, Dixon lost valuable support in his own attempts to streamline government and reform the state tax structure.

The Conley affair weakened the Dixon administration. In 1924 Dixon lost his bid for a second term. Democrat John Erickson, with backing from the Anaconda Company, easily defeated Dixon. The conservatives had finally removed the governor they so detested. But Dixon had the last word. While Anaconda and its political allies concentrated on defeating Dixon, the voters approved Initiative 28. This measure—one that Dixon had called the most important tax reform—placed a one percent tax on the gross proceeds of metal mining. No longer could Anaconda avoid paying a fair tax. In defeat Joe Dixon had won a major victory.

He left office in 1925 to begin his second retirement from politics. Just as before, he could not remain inactive for long. In 1928 he contested Burton Wheeler for a seat in the U.S. Senate. Wheeler won the election. Even that defeat did not leave Dixon in retirement. Newly elected President Herbert Hoover tapped him for assistant secretary of the interior in 1929. Nevertheless, Dixon's days as a candidate were over. He had served his adopted state well. Few others could boast of his achievements. When he died in May 1934, Montanans of both parties mourned his passing. Joseph M. Dixon left a legacy of political independence and the importance of defending one's beliefs when under fire.

Making Dry Farming Pay

The great homestead land rush in Montana after 1909 brought thousands of new farmers to Montana's central and eastern plains. This is an area of broad plains and sweeping vistas. There are few forests and even fewer mountains. There is little to block the wind, little to protect man and animal from a harsh climate. Much of the land is best suited to grazing, but there are large areas where the soil sustains dry farming. Dry farming is agriculture without irrigation and without significant amounts of rainfall. It is a type of farming that demands much different techniques from those used in wetter and milder climates.

When the homesteaders first came, nature was kind. There was enough rain to sustain good crops. Yields as high as fifty bushels per acre were harvested near Havre in 1915 and 1916. These were boom conditions. The favorable climate did not last. Dry years from 1917 to 1921 made nonirrigated farming most difficult. The result was a disaster.

There were many causes of the agricultural depression. Weather conditions, of course, played the largest role. But there were some farmers who were able to save their land and endure the bad times. What did they do that other farmers did not? First, these successful farmers did not go further into debt buying additional acres when crop prices and crop yields were high. They were cautious. Second, they did not spend available cash on nonessential items such as larger automobiles. They lived within their means. Third, they practiced conservation in agriculture. These farmers made the most of their land and the available water. They wisely built up reserves to carry them through the dry years.

In 1920-1921, M. L. Wilson of the Montana Extension Service at Montana State College in Bozeman studied the most successful dry farming methods. He wanted to determine how farmers could operate efficient dry-land farms. What Wilson found out helped to establish new dry farming techniques.

Successful dry farmers all practiced some form of diversified farming. They did not rely solely on the great cash crop of the region—wheat. Most had large gardens. They tried to raise enough vegetables to feed their families adequately. More than that, they usually grew far more than they could eat in one season. They stored the surplus to carry them in poor years. They also raised livestock and planted more than one variety of crop. Some kept several dairy cows and sold milk and cream at local markets. Others raised turkeys, geese, chickens and hogs.

"What we make over and above our living expenses we save," one dry farmer commented in 1923. "The big trouble," he continued, "is that we don't yet know how to farm this country, nor have we learned to control the grasshoppers and cutworms." During those trying years in the 1920s, the farmers learned which crops grew best. They also learned how to retain moisture in the soil and how to build earthen silos for grain or silage storage. Those who learned these and other techniques were better prepared to endure the next drought in the 1930s.

The dry-land farmer's two worst enemies were drought and wind. Pests such as grasshoppers, army worms, cutworms, and other insect crop eaters often made poor conditions even worse. But the basic problem for dry farmers was how to overcome the lack of moisture. To retain soil moisture, farmers developed several methods of fallow farming. Instead of planting all of their tillable acreage, they left one or more large sections free of crops for a season or an entire year. Sometimes they plowed these fallow fields, but if the land had been tilled for too many years this could lead to soil erosion when the wind blew. When that happened, tons of topsoil could blow away during a single season.

To solve both problems—low moisture and soil erosion—farmers planted shelter belts. Box elder, green ash and white elm trees were preferred in constructing shelter belts. A long row of box elder trees backed by another row of the same could protect a large field from wind. In the winter the shelter belt caught drifting snow and thereby added to the moisture storage in the soil. Alongside these shelter belts farmers often planted all kinds of fruit trees, vine crops and gardens.

Dry years, however, still meant lower wheat crop yields. Dry farmers had to plan for these poor years. They learned to build up reserves. They stored rye, hay, corn, barley and other secondary crops to feed horses, cattle, hogs and chickens. For storage they developed unique hillside and trench silos. Digging right into a hill or plowing out a trench, farmers packed hay and other silage fodder tightly into the earthen silo. If done properly, there was very little spoilage and silage could be preserved in this way almost indefinitely. During the dry years some farmers were even successful in putting up Russian thistle hay as silage.

In his studies M. L. Wilson found that some cultivation methods were better than others. The earlier suggestion—the so-called Campbell System—had encouraged deep plowing. When the drought and winds came, deep plowing proved a disaster. The loose soil simply blew away. Dry farmers learned that they should till the soil to a shallow depth—just enough to shear off the weed roots—and leave a clod mulch of dirt. This helped retain moisture in the soil and prevent erosion. Instead of the large discs used in earlier days, dry farmers in the 1920s began using wire-pronged cultivators that cut just below the surface.

In the constant effort to conserve water resources, some farmers constructed natural irrigation systems. Following methods pioneered by William Cowan of Box Elder, farmers trapped water from melting snow or heavy rains in dikes and ditches gouged out of the land. By carefully arranging these dikes along the land contours, they could flood an entire field. Cowan had irrigated over one-half of his farm in this method as early as 1898. He estimated that most farmers could easily irrigate one hundred acres or more using this system. Of course they could not expect to irrigate their large wheat crops, but garden and secondary crops were irrigated in this fashion.

The heart of dry farming in north central Montana was wheat production. In good years some of the world's hardiest and highest protein wheat came from this region. Wheat farming in the 1920s, however, was a much different operation than it is today. Tractors were in use but new harvester-threshers were just being introduced. Most of the work was done by men and horses. At harvest time huge, lumbering steam-powered threshers accomplished the final process of sorting the straw from the grain.

When wheat was ready for harvesting there was no time to waste. Threshing crews worked from earliest light to near darkness to complete the job before foul weather or time injured the crop. Threshing required much labor. It depended upon plenty of human and animal muscle power. It required great teamwork. Local farmers pooled their equipment and labor on large threshing crews that travelled from farm to farm.

The threshing machine was a steam tractor equipped with a long conveyor belt. The conveyor carried the grain into a set of toothed cylinders where the wheat kernels were separated from the chaff. Then the mixture dropped onto a moving screen where the heavy kernels fell to a tray below. A powerful fan, directed across the screen, blew the straw and chaff to a long slanted pneumatic tube that sprayed the residue onto a straw stack. It was a marvelous machine for its day. It was nothing compared to the combines of today, but that one machine did the work of many, many men.

The hard labor of threshing was in "feeding" the threshers. Pitching the mown grain into wagons, driving a two-horse team pulling the laden wagon right next to the conveyor and finally pitching the grain onto the conveyor was hard work. The machine itself had to be fed. It needed fuel and water to keep up a boiler full of steam to power the conveyor, sifters and fans. All of this kept a large crew of men and boys working for days before one farmer's wheat could be harvested.

The typical dry farm operation, then, relied on wheat as a cash crop, but it also incorporated several different operations if it were to be successful. The farmer raised livestock to feed his family and bring in additional cash. He planted fruit trees, gardens and specialty crops for food and sale. Poultry and dairy products also enhanced the farmer's standard of living.

One successful farmer near Havre in the mid-1920s owned 640 acres of land. He planted spring wheat on most of it, but he also grew oats, corn, rye and potatoes. A large garden supplemented his food supply. He owned several work horses, three milk cows, sixty sheep, two hogs and fifty chickens. With a ten to twenty bushel per acre yield on his wheat crop, a large hay and grain crop yield, sales of wool, milk and eggs, he realized a good profit each year. He had planted a series of shelter belts, constructed sturdy silos and built three irrigation dams to divert water to his crops.

Not all dry farmers could claim this man's success. He ran a model farm. His experience, and that of others like him, demonstrated that men could adapt to a difficult climate and bring from the land a bountiful harvest. The stories of the dry farmers in Montana are true tales of sacrifice and triumph equal to any told about life in mining or lumber camps. It is another chapter in the larger story of Montanans' relationships to their land.

Timeline

1917: America enters World War I; drought affects Hi-Line counties.

1918: World War I ends; drought spreads across Montana.

1920: Joseph M. Dixon defeats Burton K. Wheeler for governor.

1921: State banks begin closing in communities across the state; Dixon calls Special Session of the legislature.

1922: Conley controversy over Deer Lodge prison management.

1923: Senator Thomas J. Walsh begins investigation of Teapot Dome scandal.

1924: Wheeler runs for vice-president on the Progressive Party ticket; strip mining begins at Colstrip; John E. Erickson defeats Dixon for governor; Initiative 28 approved by voters.

1928: Drought returns to Montana.

1932: Franklin D. Roosevelt elected president; Red Cross aid given to depressed counties in Montana.

1933: Senator Thomas J. Walsh dies.

1934: Governor Joseph M. Dixon dies.

Suggested Readings:

J. Leonard Bates. "Thomas J. Walsh: His Genius For Controversy," *Montana The Magazine of Western History*, Vol. 19, No. 4 (Autumn, 1969).

Jules A. Karlin. *Joseph M. Dixon of Montana*, Part 2: *Governor versus the Anaconda, 1917-1934*. Missoula: University of Montana Publications in History, 1974.

K. Ross Toole. *Twentieth-Century Montana: A State of Extremes.* Norman: University of Oklahoma Press, 1972. Chapter 3.

Burton K. Wheeler and Paul Healy. *Yankee From the West.* NY: Doubleday, 1962.

Downtown Billings, Montana, in the 1930s. —*Petek Studios photo, Billings, M.H.S.*

Chapter XIII
The Challenge of the Twentieth Century

Montanans had good reason to be proud of their state in 1930. True, the first four decades of Montana's statehood had been peppered with political controversies, labor strife, agricultural booms and busts, dramatic growth in mining industries, and a steady increase in population. But with a relatively small population, they had tamed a huge wilderness. They had built an economy and society of impressive dimensions. The state's frontier period had long since passed by 1930. Montana had grown from infancy through adolescence and into adulthood. Now as a mature state it faced significant challenges. Montana's problems and opportunities, however, continued to follow an historic pattern—they were closely related to the land and natural resources.

The Great Depression affected every region and state in the nation. It was a devastating experience. Urban areas felt the awful weight of general unemployment. One family in four had someone out of work. On the western plains the Depression was almost incidental to a greater calamity. The drought Montanans experienced from 1917 to 1920 returned in 1929 and 1930. This time it was worse, much worse. Rainfall fell in such small amounts in 1929-1931 and again in 1934-1937 that crop failures were even more disastrous than before. As if this were not enough, prices for agricultural commodities declined steadily throughout the Depression. Thousands of farmers lost their land. Those who somehow held on had to settle for subsistence living—no profits and no luxuries.

The drought ravaged the Hi-Line counties. Farmers in those counties had improved their operations during the 1920s. They had invested heavily in machinery and used advanced dry-land farming techniques. But the large acreages and high expenses left them vulnerable. In 1930 Montana dry-land farmers had to spend a larger proportion of their incomes on necessities than ninety percent of American farmers. Over fifty-four percent of Montana's farms carried heavy debts just as the drought began. When the dry years dragged on in the 1930s, it soon became clear that Montana did not have the financial resources to protect its agricultural people.

Montanans, of course, were not alone. When voters across the nation went to the polls in 1932, they chose as president the dynamic governor of New York, Franklin D. Roosevelt. Roosevelt's administration wasted no time in 1933. In three short months FDR engineered a series of programs—the New Deal—to restore prosperity to American factories, cities, and farms. It meant spending millions of dollars in federal funds. Although Montanans were defenseless against the drought, Montana did contribute significantly to the formulation of New Deal farm policies. Professors M. L. Wilson and Elmer Starch at Montana State College had experimented during the 1920s with new dryland farming techniques. In the Fairways Farm Program they tried crop rotation, farm production controls, and family farm management. Their work led to the New Deal's Domestic Allotment Program. Under this policy, farmers received payments from the federal government for holding specified amounts of land out of production. This helped stabilize prices and improve crop lands.

Montana suffered more than just agricultural losses during the Depression. Montanans from all occupations and in every corner of the state faced hard times. In the rural areas, where sixty-nine percent of Montana's families lived, one in five households needed some type of relief aid by 1935. The situation was worse in the cities. Three in ten households needed public support there. Montana's tax base simply could not provide funds for this level of relief. Besides, the legislature and Governor John Erickson took a conservative course. Instead of spending more, they cut the budget. Governor Erickson knew that only the federal government had the financial resources to provide genuine relief.

The Red Cross, particularly in drought-stricken counties, delivered thousands of dollars worth of supplies to needy families in 1932. Even more money was spent on seed loans for farmers, but it was still not enough. It was Roosevelt's New Deal that finally brought genuine relief to Montana. Montanans were uncertain about taking aid from the federal government, but they had little alternative. Before the Depression lifted, Montana received millions of dollars in agricultural and industrial loans, federal relief payments, and construction projects. In fact, Montana was second in the nation in per capita dollars spent by the federal government. Montanans needed them. By 1935 just under twenty percent of all Montana families depended on public assistance.

The largest single federal expenditure in Montana during these years was the gigantic Fort Peck Dam project on the Missouri River. Begun in 1933, it took more than six years and over 10,000 workers to build the dam—the largest of its kind in the world. In Glasgow the Depression lifted as soon as the Fort Peck project began. The city turned into a center of furious activity almost overnight as laborers, engineers, and construction specialists came to the huge Public Works Administration project. There were so many workers that fifteen boom towns suddenly appeared at or near the dam site along the Missouri. The completed dam was gigantic—a 250-foot high earthen barrier that backed up the Missouri for 135 miles.

The federal government spent money in Montana in many other ways during the 1930s. Roosevelt's New Deal provided employment to thousands more Montanans. The Works Progress Administration (W.P.A.) built courthouses and school buildings throughout the state. It repaired roads and bridges, and even provided work for writers and artists. Another government agency, the Civilian Conservation Corps (C.C.C.), hired young men to work in national forests and on government range lands. They cut new forest trails, built outbuildings, fought fires, built pack bridges, and worked on hundreds of other projects.

The W.P.A. and C.C.C. could not provide work for everyone. Many remained unemployed. The worst pockets of unemployment were in the cities and larger towns. Many rural people came to the cities hoping for work, but finding none they soon had to take relief in order to live. The Federal Emergency Relief Administration (F.E.R.A.) joined state and local governments to provide millions of dollars in direct relief payments. Half of those on relief in Montana were under the age of twenty. Over one-third of the heads of households receiving public assistance were between the ages of twenty-five and forty. A large proportion of the most productive Montanans had to rely on federal and state relief to endure the Depression.

The Depression also had a profound effect upon Montana politics. When Senator Thomas J. Walsh died, Governor John Erickson had to appoint a replacement. Erickson resigned as governor and the new governor, Frank H. Cooney, appointed Erickson to the Senate. Some questioned Erickson's political ethics in going to Washington. Meanwhile, Governor Cooney soon had problems of his own. He realized how important it was that Montana raise enough money to match federal relief and loan funds. Without matching state monies, Montana stood to lose potential federal dollars. Conservatives in the legislature fought Cooney and refused to vote for more taxes. They even tried to impeach him. Tragically, Cooney died of a heart attack in 1935.

Roosevelt's New Deal was not popular with all Montanans. There were continual arguments among politicians about the best means to handle the Depression. After Governor Cooney's death, Elmer Holt of Miles City filled out the term. In 1936 voters elected former Congressman Roy E. Ayers of Fergus County as the new governor. Ayers served until 1941.

The hottest political disputes in Montana centered around Burton K. Wheeler, Montana's dynamic liberal senator. Wheeler had been one of Roosevelt's earliest supporters. By 1937 Wheeler began to disagree with some of FDR's policies. Wheeler objected to FDR's controversial plan to alter Supreme Court membership in 1937. Wheeler withdrew his support of the New Deal. Suddenly there was an open split among Montana Democrats—some followed Wheeler, others remained loyal to FDR.

Senator James E. Murray of Butte, the man elected in 1934 to fill the seat held by Walsh and then Erickson, led Montana's loyal Roosevelt Democrats. Wheeler allied with conservatives he had previously fought. In 1938 there was warfare between the two Democratic factions. In that year conservative Democrats actually joined with Republicans to

Senator James E. Murray of Montana, one of the steadfast liberals in the 1930s, served longer than any other Montanan in the Senate—twenty-seven years, from 1933 to 1961.

defeat the ultra-liberal congressman from Butte, Jerry O'Connell. Ironically, O'Connell suffered under charges of being a radical—similar to those hurled at Wheeler so many years before. O'Connell fell victim to Wheeler's political power. By the end of the decade, Burton Wheeler stood as the conservative, while Senator Murray led the liberals.

As politicians feuded and the Depression continued, signs of change and improvement appeared in the Montana economy. In the face of paralyzing droughts, Montana agriculture limped through the early 1930s. New Deal agricultural programs under the Agricultural Adjustment Administration (A.A.A.), however, provided millions of dollars in loans and technical assistance. Thousands of Montana farmers received federal payments to compensate for lower crop production. The federal government also helped improve water resources in the state. In cooperation with the State Water Conservation Board, federal dollars helped build new irrigation dams and reservoirs across Montana.

In 1936 one of the most profound changes in Montana's rural life began. Rural electric cooperatives, with financial aid from the Rural Electrification Administration (R.E.A.), organized throughout Montana. These rural electric cooperatives were non-profit corporations using low-interest loans to build and maintain power lines. For the first time electricity came to farms and ranches. Before R.E.A. only six percent of Montana's farms and ranches had electricity. It meant a new age for Montana agriculture. A new world of power equipment and domestic appliances came to farm families.

Economic prosperity returned to Montana and the rest of the nation as a result of World War II. Agriculture, coal, oil, and lumber production, and general business activity increased in the 1940s and early 1950s. Agriculture, particularly, was blessed with good conditions. The rains returned to the plains. The demand for agricultural products increased during and after the war. Farmers invested in more machinery and became more specialized. Larger farms and ranches became the norm as the number of family farms continued on the decline. Montana specialized in two products: wheat and cattle. Since World War II, Montana's beef production had steadily increased, making it the eighth largest in the nation. In wheat production Montana now ranks fourth, with 4.7 million acres under cultivation. Montana agriculture continues to be diversified, but the trend toward larger capital investments and specialization has become dominant since the 1950s.

Copper mining in Butte had fallen on bad days during the Depression. Demand for copper was so low that Anaconda operated at only ten percent of capacity. The war, of course, brought a renewed demand for copper, but Butte would never again be so important to the Anaconda Company. The company purchased huge copper reserves in Chile and Mexico. In the 1950s, however, Anaconda decided to tap the enormous supply of low-grade copper in the Butte Hill through open-pit mining. The Berkeley Pit operation on the east end of Butte kept copper mining alive in Montana's milehigh city and changed the city's face forever.

In wood products and oil industries the war brought more activity. Montana's production of lumber and oil has never been a dominant force in the state's economy, but increased nationwide demand after the war helped increase production. This was particularly true in the forest products industry. More timber was harvested to supply the home-building industry. A large pulp and paper mill opened near Missoula in 1957. In recent years home building has even regenerated the log house and spawned companies in the Bitterroot and Thompson Falls areas who specialize in log homes. When demand for oil products began spiraling in the late 1940s, oil exploration in Montana increased overnight. In 1951 the vast reserves of the Williston Basin were discovered in eastern Montana. This new oil boom helped make Billings one of the fastest growing cities on the plains.

Perhaps the Montana industry that benefited most from the economic boom during the post-war years was tourism. Americans took to the highways in the 1950s, and Montana attracted its share of travellers. Glacier and Yellowstone National Parks, Montana's famed fishing and hunting opportunities, and the new sport of snow skiing drew thousands of out-of-state visitors each year. Better highways and improved air travel service continue to increase the state's tourist business.

Montana politics took another new turn during and after World War II. Jeannette Rankin again won election to Congress in 1940. When Roosevelt asked Congress for a declaration of war against Japan, Jeannette stood alone against war—it was the second time she had voted no on war. Burton K. Wheeler, after withstanding several challenges to his political power, finally lost popular support in 1946. The final chapter for Wheeler began with his stiff resistance to any war preparedness in 1939-1941. Wheeler, a committed pacifist, feared that Roosevelt's actions would drag the United States into the raging European war. He misjudged Montanans on this issue. Always the independent man in politics, Wheeler fought against the reintroduction of the draft. He tried to block FDR's military commitments to Great Britain. Consistently, Wheeler argued against any kind of war preparation right up to the bombing of Pearl Harbor in December 1941. As World War II wound down in 1945, Wheeler again criticized Roosevelt's foreign policy. This time he questioned American relations with the Soviet Union. The Russians, Wheeler warned, were a serious threat to world peace. Evidently Montana voters thought it was time for a change, for in 1946 they voted against Burton K. Wheeler in the primaries. He left the U.S. Senate and the public arena in 1947. An important chapter in Montana political history had ended.

The post-World War II years brought new faces into Montana politics. Montana continued to prefer conservative governors and liberal representatives to Washington, particularly in the Senate. Senator James Murray remained a liberal stalwart throughout the 1950s. Until his retirement in 1961, Murray worked aggressively for progressive legislation, including unsuccessful efforts to establish public water power generation in Montana through the Missouri Valley Authority (M.V.A.). Murray hoped that the M.V.A. could build more dams on the Missouri and bring even cheaper electrical power to Montanans. His dream never became a reality.

The most remarkable Montana politician to emerge in these years was Mike Mansfield of Missoula. A novice in politics and a professor at the University of Montana, Mansfield ran for Congress in 1942 and won. After five sessions in the House of Representatives, he narrowly won election to the Senate in 1952. Mansfield's political style and his advocacy of liberal programs, however, made him one of Montana's most popular politicians. More importantly, he rose quickly to national leadership. His expertise in foreign affairs, and even more, his ability to work successfully with politicians, regardless of their philosophies, led to his selection as Senate majority leader in 1961. Mike Mansfield of Montana held that position longer than any man in American history. Mansfield retired from the Senate in 1976, but his knowledge of Asian affairs led to his appointment in 1977 as American ambassador to Japan.

Montanans sent a second liberal Democrat to the Senate in 1961. Lee Metcalf of Helena had much more political experience before his election as a senator than had Mansfield. He had moved up through the political ranks, including time spent in the state legislature, on the Montana Supreme Court, and four terms as western district congressman. Once in the Senate, Metcalf became one of the strongest liberals in the West. He supported labor legislation, backed progressive social issues, and raised some serious questions about the utility industry. Most important to Montanans, Lee Metcalf was an aggressive conservationist. Perhaps his greatest achievement was sponsorship and success in passing the Wilderness Act of 1964. For the first time Americans stopped using natural resources without concern for future generations and set aside large forested regions as wilderness preserves. Metcalf also sponsored legislation to protect wild and scenic rivers. On the eve of his retirement in 1978, Lee Metcalf died unexpectedly of a heart attack.

Montana's congressional delegation was split during the three decades after World War II. Liberal-minded Democrats held the western district seat tightly in their grasp. The lone exception was Republican Dick Shoup who won two terms, 1971-1975. Mike Mansfield, Lee Metcalf, Arnold Olsen, and Max Baucus went to Congress from the western district, and each one reflected the more liberal viewpoint of their constituents including organized labor. In the eastern district, voters consistently sent conservative Republicans to Congress. Even when Democrats Leroy H. Anderson, 1957-1961, and John Melcher, 1971-1977, won election, they reflected the conservative agricultural constituency they represented.

The most important changes in Montana politics, however, took place at the state level. Post-war conditions forced most states to modernize their operations. Montana was no different. The Depression had demonstrated how important an efficient state government could be. It would take several years, but in the 1950s, 1960s, and 1970s Montana lawmakers moved forcefully to improve state government.

The first important change came in 1949. Legislators passed a sweeping reform of school funding in the state. They constituted a School Foundation Program that dispersed state monies to school districts across the state. This was a giant step toward upgrading and equalizing educational opportunities for all Montana children. A second improvement in state government was the establishment of the Legislative Council in 1957. For years legislators had complained of the increasing complexity of issues that faced them each legislative session. The Legislative Council became a professional research and bill-writing arm of the legislature. The council did the complex technical work necessary to produce the best possible legislation.

Even with these improvements, state government still drew criticism for being too slow and unresponsive. Critics spotted two problems. The enormous number of overlapping state agencies was one. The antiquated nature of the 1889 Constitution was another. At the polls in 1970 voters acted on both problems. A constitutional amendment gave the legislature power to begin a sweeping executive reorganization of government. Through legislation passed in 1971, over one hundred state agencies were combined or transformed into just nineteen. Executive reorganization simplified state government, made it more accountable to citizens, and gave the governor more direct control over the bureaucracy.

Another constitutional amendment approved in 1970 called for a special election to choose delegates to a consti-

The man who held the position of Senate Majority Leader longer than anyone in American history, Senator Mike Mansfield, served Montana and the nation with statesmanlike ability.

tutional convention—the fourth in state history. At the special election in November 1971, voters chose one hundred delegates to meet the following year in convention. Meeting at the state capitol in Helena, the delegates did a superb job of writing a much shorter and more flexible document to replace the old constitution. Experts across the nation called it one of the best that had ever been written.

There were many Montanans, however, who were not so certain. Mostly conservatives from rural areas, they questioned changing from bienniel—every two years—legislative sessions to annual sessions. They charged that it was simply a waste of taxpayers' money. Voters approved the new constitution by a narrow margin, but in 1974 critics managed to get a constitutional amendment passed that returned the legislature to biennial sessions. Critics also challenged the constitutional provision for statewide property tax assessment. Previously tax assessment had been handled by the counties. On the whole, however, the 1972 Constitution proved itself to be a considerable improvement over its predecessor.

Montana has had a series of remarkable governors since World War II. On the whole they have been conservative, but that has been traditional throughout Montana history. What is unusual is that four of the seven post-war governors were Republicans. Montana has been predominantly Democratic since statehood. The first of these Republican governors was Sam C. Ford. Ford was the courageous state attorney general during World War I who finally challenged the actions of the Council of Defense. In office from 1941 to 1949, Governor Ford took a moderate course of action. He supported many efforts to streamline and modernize government, but he achieved no great breakthroughs. His Democratic successor, John Bonner, was a liberal. The legislature was in a conservative mood during Bonner's one term, 1949 to 1953. It was under Bonner, however, that the School Foundation Program became a reality.

In 1952 Montana voters elected one of the most colorful governors in the state's history. Republican J. Hugo Aronson, nicknamed "The Galloping Swede," won election to two terms, holding office from 1953 to 1961. A robust man with a ruddy complexion and hands that showed a life of hard work, Aronson was a conservative. Although few thought of

Governor J. Hugo Aronson (1953-1961) who was nicknamed the "Galloping Swede."

him as a politician, he was a skillful administrator and stood forthrightly behind his convictions. Another Republican, Donald G. Nutter, followed Aronson into office in 1961. Nutter was far more conservative than Aronson, but his death in a plane crash in January 1962 ended any opportunity to pursue his governmental plans. Republican Lieutenant Governor Tim Babcock took over and then won election in his own right in 1964.

In 1968 the Republican string of governors was broken when Forrest Anderson defeated the incumbent Babcock. Anderson had served in the legislature, on the Montana Supreme Court, and as attorney general. He was known as an exceptional politician. It was during Anderson's single term, 1969 to 1973, that executive reorganization took place. While he was governor Montanans elected one of the most liberal legislatures in state history. Made up of environmentalists, reformers, and young politicians, the legislature passed many laws designed to clear corruption from state government and protect the environment. Anderson's successor, former Democratic Lieutenant Governor Thomas L. Judge, continued Anderson's liberal politics. Judge won a second term in 1976.

On two points all Montanans, regardless of political party or occupation, can agree. Contemporary issues are more complicated than ever before, and today's decisions affect Montana's future more than any in the past. Montana's natural resources have been its source of wealth. It is no surprise, then, that environmental issues are among the most challenging to surface in recent years.

Even before the passage of the national Wilderness Act in 1964, wilderness advocates had worked tirelessly to include more and more of Montana in the wilderness system. The Montana Wilderness Society, founded in 1958, has succeeded in promoting several wilderness areas in the state, including the sprawling Bob Marshall Wilderness Area near Lincoln and the huge Selway-Bitterroot Wilderness Area on the Idaho-Montana state line—the largest wilderness in the nation. Recreational vehicle owners, miners, lumbermen, and other developers have been vocal in their opposition to "locking up" any more land in such areas. Many battles have been fought over the question, and it is unlikely that easy solutions will be found.

The most heated environmental controversy since World War II, however, has involved coal mining. Earlier in the century coal miners descended into deep mines at Roundup and Red Lodge in eastern Montana. In 1924 the Northern Pacific Railroad began strip-mining at Colstrip in Rosebud County. Montana has the largest coal reserves of any state—well over one hundred billion tons. It is easy to mine. In some areas in eastern Montana only a few feet of soil cover rich coal veins. In the 1960s and 1970s a controversy raged. How much coal should be mined? Could the land be reclaimed and put to agricultural use again after mining? Environmentalists in the legislature passed tough laws requiring mining companies to reclaim mined land. They also passed the highest coal severance tax in the nation in 1973.

An even larger controversy developed when Montana Power Company's subsidiary, Western Energy, decided to build large coal-fired electrical power generation plants right on the coalfields in eastern Montana. Environmentalists and eastern Montana ranchers fought it. They formed the Northern Plains Resource Council in 1971 to block future coal development, particularly in the Rosebud County area. In several public hearings and in state and federal court, both sides argued the fine points of coal development over and over again. Nevertheless, two large power plants were built at Colstrip, and coal production continued to soar. In 1972 over ten million tons was stripped from the land, and in 1974 the tonnage increased to over fourteen million. Montana Power and four Pacific Coast utilities planned two more power plants—Colstrip 3 and 4. Environmentalists quickly opposed them. The battle moved into the courts and construction waited.

Ranchers and environmentalists maintain that rushing to mine coal in eastern Montana is a mistake. The land, air, and water, they argue, will never be the same. Montana cannot afford to damage its environment. Coal companies, on the other hand, point to America's energy needs. Energy supplies are scarce, and Montana's coal can save the nation from a devastating energy crisis. The dispute is far from over.

Coal mining and other environmental issues are not the only difficult questions Montanans have faced since World War II. There are many others. But most issues revolve around the question of resource development—using the land. Just how much development should take place in Montana? What kind of life do Montanans desire? What do the people want? How best can Montana achieve a better life for its citizens? The challenge of the twentieth century is to answer these questions in the democratic manner Montanans have always cherished.

To Tame the Missouri

Hot winds blew across Hi-Line counties again in 1929. They had blown before in 1917 and 1918. Farmers who remembered the first drought braced themselves. Within two years Montana's northern tier of counties looked like a dust bowl. Crop yields dropped sickeningly. Supplies of seeds became scarce. Then, just as drought conditions worsened, Montana farmers felt the first weight of the Great Depression that put millions of people out of work across the nation. Economic growth in Montana and neighboring states slowed to a crawl. Montanans added their names to unemployment rolls. Crop prices dropped, making conditions even worse for drought-plagued farmers.

Valley County was one of the most depressed Hi-Line counties in 1931-1932. The future looked bleak. Nearly eighty percent of the county's farmers expected to lose their land. Many left the area before their families were destitute. In the early months of 1932 the Red Cross came to Valley County to help. In a short time they distributed over $100,000 in supplies. The federal government took action, too. In 1932 the Department of Agriculture distributed $432,623 in federal seed loans to over 1,400 area farmers. Everyone knew this aid would not be enough; they needed something much greater than seed loans and Red Cross supplies to rescue Valley County.

Across the nation in 1932 voters went to the polls hoping for a political solution to the lengthening Depression. For the first time since Woodrow Wilson, they sent a Democrat to the White House—New York Governor Franklin Delano Roosevelt. Roosevelt's vague campaign promises suddenly became reality in March and April of 1933. He called the program a "New Deal" for the American people. To relieve unemployment, Roosevelt's New Deal employed men all over the nation in public works jobs. The Public Works Administration (P.W.A.) hired thousands to build bridges, repair roads, construct courthouses and more. P.W.A.'s largest single construction project materialized in remote Valley County, Montana, far away from Washington, D.C., and major urban centers. Across the Missouri River the P.W.A. built the world's largest hydraulically filled earthen dam—Fort Peck. The Fort Peck project was that "something" that Valley County so desperately needed, more than Red Cross and seed loans.

The idea for a dam across the Missouri, near the historic site of old Fort Peck, had been suggested long before the Depression. Businessmen, shippers, agriculturalists, and politicians in downstream states had wanted a dam for years. They hoped a large dam would control devastating floods, and they expected river navigation to be improved as well. In the mid-1920s the Army Corps of Engineers studied the Fort Peck site. A dam could be built there, they believed, but it would be an enormously expensive project. Presidents Calvin Coolidge and Herbert Hoover rejected the plan. Too costly, they said. But Franklin D. Roosevelt saw the Fort Peck project as a great opportunity. It would provide jobs for thousands of unemployed people and build a great river-taming dam at the same time.

The Fort Peck project was popular with nearly everyone. The Corps of Engineers saw it as a great challenge—so much of a challenge they were not sure how to accomplish the feat. Politicians and businessmen in Iowa, Nebraska, and Missouri were pleased. Fort Peck meant jobs for unemployed Montanans. It meant political rewards for Democrats like Senator Burton K. Wheeler who worked hard to get the project approved. Everyone was in such a hurry in 1933 that the P.W.A. actually approved the dam before they had decided how to build it. But there were some people in Valley County who objected. They lived in the fertile Missouri bottomlands soon to be flooded by the dam. Ironically, these were the only prosperous farmers in the whole area. They annually harvested some of the best alfalfa seed in the nation. There were only one hundred landowners affected, and after some protest they finally sacrificed their land for the Fort Peck Dam.

No one was sure just what the dam might cost. The best initial estimate was $65 million, making it one of the largest public works investments to that time in American history. They planned to build a giant earthen barrier across an eight-thousand-foot gap between two river bluffs. The building materials were there at hand—millions of tons of clay soil. The dam's projected size was enormous. When completed Fort Peck Dam would be over 250 feet high, 21,000 feet long,

The famous "Million Dollar" bridge at Fort Peck Dam site. The project provided many jobs for Montanans during the Great Depression. —*U.S. Army Corps of Engineers photo*

and 50 feet thick. It would create a lake 16 miles wide, over 135 miles long, covering 249,000 acres, with more than 1,500 miles of shoreline. At its deepest, Fort Peck Lake would be 220 feet deep.

Even more remarkable than its size was the construction method used. Rather than simply dig soil and deposit it across the river channel, engineers scooped clay from the river bed and piped it with water to the dam site. There the earth-water mixture was rolled and compacted. Using huge dredges—floating barges equipped with powerful bladed scoops—workers gouged out 125 million cubic yards of earth to form the dam. That was enough material to fill a train of boxcars that would nearly encircle the globe at the equator. In addition they built a massive bridge across the Missouri—the famous "million dollar bridge"—to supply necessary construction materials.

Three miles to the east of the earthen barrier, the finished dam featured a massive concrete and steel spillway. Extending for nearly a mile, the spillway discharge channel is the most visible structure at Fort Peck Dam. The spillway releases overflow lake water to the Missouri River, some nine miles below the dam, through sixteen huge gates. Finally, construction crews strung a 154,000-volt powerline over 250 miles from Rainbow Falls on the Missouri to the dam site. It was another construction record at Fort Peck—it was the longest single electrical feeder line ever built.

Actual work began in October of 1933. Glasgow, Montana, became a scene of furious activity almost overnight.

Floating dredges and slurry pipeline at Fort Peck Dam site in 1935. "Million Dollar" bridge is at left. —*U.S. Army Corps of Engineers photo*

Engineers, laborers, equipment, and supplies transformed Glasgow into an army-like depot and command center. With several dozen dry-land farmers ready to cut timber along the Missouri, Army Engineers organized the first work crews on October 23, 1933. For some of those farmers it was the first pay they had received in over two years. They worked for fifty cents an hour. That may not sound like a sizeable wage today, but many jobs in Glasgow paid only twenty-five cents an hour at the time. Everyone worked an average of thirty-four hours each week. For the first time in over three years, Valley County men had the prospect of bringing cash home to their families.

Engineers did not change the Missouri's flow until they had completed four huge diversion tunnels. They dug these tunnels through rock-hard shale near the dam site. They had to finish the tunnels and divert the river's channel before the actual dam could be completed. It was another supreme challenge. No one had ever tried to tunnel through this type of shale before. It took nearly three years and the labor of over four thousand men to build the thirty-two-foot diameter steel-lined tunnels. Years after the dam had been completed, the Corps of Engineers installed two hydroelectric power generators at the mouths of the diversion tunnels. They built the first powerhouse in 1943 and completed the second in 1961. Together the powerhouses can generate over 165,000 kilowatts of electricity.

The Fort Peck project required the most sophisticated construction skills available. Building the "million dollar bridge" demanded the best welders, carpenters, and heavy construction specialists that could be hired. Constructing the four electrically powered dredges meant hiring shipbuilders. Experienced "sandhogs"—tunnel workers—came to punch through the diversion tunnels. Cement workers, surveyors, heavy equipment operators, electricians, railroad men, and many other craft workers found employment. While Valley County men filled many of the jobs, thousands of workers had to be imported.

People from every section of the nation came to work at Fort Peck. Into an area empty of towns came over ten thousand workers and their families. To house bachelors, the government built barracks. A small town—Fort Peck—grew up practically at the construction site. But this was not sufficient to house everyone. A series of hastily built "boom towns" soon appeared along the Missouri's banks. Families hammered together small homes in settlements given colorful names such as Wheeler, Delano Heights, New Deal, Square Deal, and Cactus Flat. Little business districts boomed. Grocery stores, drugstores, cafes, hardware stores, honky-tonk saloons, and even a red light district called "Happy Hollow" lived briefly off the workers' payroll earnings. For six years—1934 to 1939—the Fort Peck area was home to these people. A community developed. Its people organized social clubs, theater groups, Boy Scout and Girl Scout organizations, a library and many other community institutions. With the completion of the dam, many families remained in Montana, moving to other areas in the state. Four decades after, in the summer of 1977, several hundred returned to Fort Peck to celebrate their achievement and reminisce about those strenuous days at work on Montana's greatest construction project.

Building Fort Peck Dam was not without hazards. Working with the clay slurry, constructing the railway, digging the diversion tunnels, and fabricating the spillway entailed dozens of very dangerous operations. With so many complicated construction projects proceeding at the same time at record speed, mishaps were unavoidable. But the disaster that struck on September 22, 1938, shocked everyone. Nearly eighty percent of the dam had been completed. Seemingly, the great river had been tamed. Then in the early afternoon, earth near the diversion tunnels broke loose and slid into the lake. Nearly two hundred men raced for their lives. Equipment, railroad track, pipe, tons of gravel, and huge boulders moved, fractured, and tumbled. In a few moments over five million yards of earth shifted. Eight men died and five percent of the dam had been destroyed. Engineers redesigned that portion of the dam. Within a few months they had completed the entire project.

Fort Peck was one of the New Deal's largest construction projects. It was the single largest expenditure of federal monies in Montana during the Great Depression. Man has seldom changed the land as dramatically as he did at Fort Peck. Where a powerful river once coursed without restriction, a giant barrier and lake appeared. Today Fort Peck Dam controls the Missouri, provides electrical power, aids river navigation, and offers recreation to thousands of visitors each year. Government investment totalled over $160 million. But to those hard-pressed people in Valley County, and to the thousands who came to work, Fort Peck Dam was far more than just a government investment. Fort Peck Dam stands today as a testament to their labor and the significance of government action in the face of hard times.

An Independent Man in Politics

When Americans thought of Montana in the 1930s and 1940s they pictured scenes from Glacier National Park or the mines at Butte. If they thought of politics one name came to mind—Burton Kendall Wheeler. True to what has become a Montana political tradition, Burton Wheeler forcefully represented his state in the U.S. Senate. First elected to the Senate in 1922, he held the seat until 1947. Political independence and controversy dominated Wheeler's career. He was one of the state's most colorful and most important politicians. His career provides an inside glimpse at Montana politics during the first half of the Twentieth Century.

Burton K. Wheeler was born in Hudson, Massachusetts, on February 27, 1882. The Wheeler family had lived in New England for generations. His father was a cobbler. They were not poor, but there were few luxuries in the Wheeler house. By religion they were Quakers, although Burton's mother was a Methodist. The Wheeler household reflected strong religious beliefs. Although Burton was never particularly religious, he retained a sincere respect for other people's beliefs and defended their right to hold them. From his father he learned to hate war and fight intolerance. Growing up in a Catholic factory town as a Protestant introduced Burton to the realities of religious intolerance. An asthmatic child, he avoided fights and learned to use his quick wits.

In high school Burton showed his teachers the logical turn of mind that was to become one of his hallmarks throughout his career. He was not particularly studious in school, but by graduation day he had resolved to attend college and study law. It was 1900 and the nation had just climbed out of a lengthy economic depression. Wheeler went to work immediately to earn his college education. First as a stenographer, next as a clerk, and then through numerous other jobs he finally earned enough and headed west to the University of Michigan in 1901. In almost storybook fashion, Burton worked his way through college doing odd jobs, including selling books door-to-door. While selling books in Illinois he met Lulu White, the woman he married in 1907. He applied himself to his studies, won election as class president, and graduated in 1905.

Burton Kendall Wheeler on the campaign trail in the 1920s.—*N. B. Cresswell photo, M.H.S.*

Rather than return east or remain in Michigan, Wheeler continued his own westward movement. After looking for a favorable position in several western states, Wheeler landed in Butte during October of 1905. Butte did not strike Wheeler as very promising, but after a shifty gambler left him financially unable to continue his travels, he decided to give the rough mining community a try. It was not long before Burton Wheeler had established a reputation in town as a very capable and honest lawyer. In 1909 he began his Montana political career as a delegate to the Butte Democratic Convention. To his surprise he was elected party chairman and urged to run for the legislature in 1910. He won that contest and took his seat in Helena in January of 1911.

Wheeler represented Silver Bow County, and many legislators assumed that he would vote with the "Company" (Anaconda Copper Mining Company) on most issues. They soon found how wrong they were. Wheeler was an independent politician. When balloting began for U.S. senator, Wheeler supported Thomas J. Walsh of Helena. The Company was determined to defeat Walsh. Wheeler steadfastly supported Walsh even after one man offered him $9,000 to vote against Walsh and another threatened him. Wheeler further angered the Company when he introduced legislation supporting organized labor, mine safety, and other measures. One fellow legislator predicted that Wheeler would not be reelected in Butte. He turned out to be right, but Montana and the Company would hear much more from Burton Wheeler.

In 1913 Thomas J. Walsh was finally elected to the Senate. Wheeler had been one of his most consistent supporters. In recognition of his support and his exceptional abilities, Walsh saw to it that Wheeler was appointed U.S. District Attorney—the youngest in the nation at the time. This new position proved no safer politically; Wheeler found himself involved in more controversies. He prosecuted cases against the Northern Pacific Railroad, prominent businessmen guilty of land fraud, and other powerful interest groups. He had even more enemies among conservatives. Regardless of warnings, District Attorney Wheeler did his job as he believed it should be done. Consistently he tried to protect the weak from the powerful. His most controversial actions, however, came after the United States entered World War I.

The war became an emotional issue in Montana. Many people opposed the war altogether. They spoke against the war and urged men to avoid the military draft. Other Montanans were frightened by the large number of foreign-born people living in the state. There were numerous complaints lodged against German-Americans. Foreigners, or aliens, were feared as enemy agents or worse. Wheeler refused to prosecute aliens or those who spoke against the war. He maintained that they had violated no laws. Soon there were complaints against Wheeler.

The Montana Council of Defense charged that he was aiding the anti-war groups in the state. Pressure mounted to remove him. His opponents said he was a radical. They called him a "Bolshevik," referring to the new rulers of communist Russia. "Bolshevik Burt," as some nicknamed him, remained true to his principles and refused to be swept along by the pro-war hysteria. Even when he was subpoenaed by the Montana Council of Defense, he refused to engage in what he called a "witch hunt."

In 1918 Wheeler bowed to the opposition. Because his friend, Senator Thomas Walsh, faced a tough reelection campaign, Wheeler resigned as district attorney rather than hurt Walsh's chances. Two years later Burton Wheeler stood as a candidate himself. This time he ran for governor against another liberal politician, former Senator Joseph M. Dixon of Missoula. That campaign in 1920 was one of the hardest fought in Montana history.

Those opposed to Wheeler charged him with every sin imaginable. Of course, they called him a radical and suggested that if he were elected, radical miners and farmers would control the statehouse. One newspaper editor even claimed that he advocated "free love." In vain Wheeler protested these charges. The Company supported neither Dixon nor Wheeler in the primaries, but they certainly preferred Dixon to the former district attorney. The campaign was so rough that Wheeler was physically attacked several times. In Dillon angry voters charged the speaker's platform yelling that he should be lynched. Wheeler made a quick exit, raced to a nearby railroad siding, and hid in a boxcar as angry voters milled around outside. Some now called him "Boxcar Burt." He lost the election. Evidently voters believed the stories about Wheeler's socialist leanings. In 1922 Wheeler was running for public office again, this time for U.S. Senator. After his sound beating in 1920, most gave him little chance to be elected. He fooled them all. In a year that saw Republicans victorious across the nation, Wheeler easily won. In 1923 Burton K. Wheeler went to Washington to begin one of the most remarkable senatorial careers in American history.

Wheeler did not change his politics when he entered the Senate. He continued to act on behalf of laborers and farmers. For several sessions he tried to enact legislation to aid farmers during depressions when crop prices dropped. He also fought hard to revise railroad legislation and thereby provide lower freight rates for farm commodities. And he continued to be an independent politician. When Attorney General Harry Daugherty in the Coolidge administration used his power to halt a railroad strike, Wheeler questioned his tactics and motives. Daugherty criticized Wheeler. The dispute electrified the Senate. Here was a first-term senator from Montana challenging the chief legal officer of the nation. Wheeler's questions eventually led to a full investigation of Daugherty and to the attorney general's resignation.

In 1924 the Democrats nominated a conservative representative of business interests as their presidential candidate—John W. Davis. Wheeler and other liberal Democrats complained, charging that there was no real choice between Davis and the Republican Coolidge. To give voters that choice, Wheeler bolted the Democratic party in 1924 and ran for vice-president with presidential nominee Robert M. LaFollette of Wisconsin on the Progressive party ticket. They had no real chance, but in Wisconsin and Montana they had a lot of support. Once again Wheeler showed everyone that he thought and acted independently of political parties and political bosses.

Coolidge was reelected in 1924. Four years later Burton Wheeler was up for reelection to the Senate. He won that contest easily. Evidently Montana voters approved of his independent style. They also approved of Wheeler's aggressive prosecution of corruption in Washington. Wheeler and his fellow Montana senator, Thomas J. Walsh, unceasingly exposed many scandals, including the famous Teapot Dome oil scandal. The 1930s, however, brought far heavier challenges than political corruption. By early 1930 a nationwide economic depression begged for solution. There was a demand for change. Burton Wheeler recognized this and became the first major politician to endorse New York Governor Franklin D. Roosevelt for president.

After Roosevelt won the election of 1932, he brought new men and new ideas into government. Burton Wheeler remained a steady supporter of Roosevelt's "New Deal."

New Deal legislation used bold measures to restore prosperity. Wheeler believed in using federal money. He fought hard to get the huge Fort Peck project in eastern Montana approved. He supported farm legislation designed to increase farm incomes. But he did not follow Roosevelt blindly. In 1934, for example, he reversed his own support for the Indian Reorganization Act—a bill that ironically carried his name as a co-sponsor, the Wheeler-Howard Act. The legislation specifically rejected the goal of Indian assimilation into white society. Wheeler believed in bringing Indians into the mainstream of American life. Rather than continue his support, he worked to amend the bill. Wheeler was not afraid to change his mind and to do it publicly.

In 1937 Wheeler endured a test of will that would have destroyed most other politicians. After supporting Franklin D. Roosevelt for four years, Wheeler broke with FDR over a controversial presidential plan to add members to the Supreme Court. Wheeler led the fight against the president's "Court Packing Plan." Across the country he spoke on the issue. He called it an abuse of executive power and warned citizens that the president wanted too much power. It was a direct challenge to Roosevelt. In Montana the issue split the Democratic party—Roosevelt supporters versus Wheeler supporters. When asked if he trusted Roosevelt, Wheeler replied, "I put my trust in laws rather than in men." Wheeler helped turn the tide against the president's plan. Of course, this angered FDR, but Wheeler survived the conflict and was elected to his fourth Senate term in 1940.

Montanans respected Burton Wheeler's stand on the Supreme Court issue. Even conservatives admired his strength under fire. Even Anaconda Company newspapers applauded him. He had barely recovered from the Supreme Court battle when he again locked horns with FDR. This time the issue was war. In late 1939 war rocked Europe, and the United States tried to stay clear of the conflict. Wheeler's upbringing and his experience during World War I made him an opponent of war. In the Senate he fought every piece of legislation that he thought might drag the nation closer to war.

Wheeler's opposition to the war began his decline. As sincere as he was in his anti-war stance, more and more Montanans agreed with other Americans that the Germans and the Japanese had to be stopped. The attack on Pearl

Harbor, of course, settled the issue. The United States went to war. The next five years were Burton Wheeler's last in the Senate.

In 1946 he was beaten in the primaries by Leif Erickson. In 1947 he said goodbye to the intense atmosphere of Congress. He spent the next eighteen years practicing law in Washington, D.C., and returning home to Glacier National Park for vacations. He continued to support labor and farm interests. He warned of a serious international threat posed by the Soviet Union's foreign policies. But more than this, Burton K. Wheeler left a giant legacy to Montana. When he died on January 6, 1975, just short of his ninety-seventh birthday, he left behind a seventy-year record of public service and involvement that inspires Montanans of all political beliefs. His personality, actions, and sincerity made him, as one commentator put it, "almost a party unto himself." That is as Burton Wheeler wished it. To the end he remained an independent man in politics.

Timeline

1929: Drought hits the Hi-Line counties.

1932: Franklin D. Roosevelt is elected president.

1933: T. J. Walsh dies, John E. Erickson appointed U.S. senator; Frank Cooney becomes governor; Fort Peck Dam project begins; Civilian Conservation Corps comes to Montana.

1934: James E. Murray elected U.S. senator; Wheeler-Howard Act giving Indians soverignty passed; four-month copper strike paralyzes Butte, and Mine, Mill and Smelter Workers Union gains recognition.

1935: Governor Cooney dies, Elmer Holt becomes governor; Works Progress Administration (W.P.A.) begins work in Montana.

1936: Roy E. Ayers elected governor; Jerry O'Connell elected western district congressman; Rural Electrification Administration (R.E.A.) begins work in Montana.

1937: Senator Wheeler leads national fight against FDR's "court-packing" plan.

1938: Jacob Thorkelson defeats Jerry O'Connell for Congress; Fort Peck Dam construction accident kills eight men.

1939: Completion of Fort Peck Dam.

1940: Jeannette Rankin elected western district congresswoman, her second time in Congress; Sam C. Ford elected governor.

1941: Jeannette Rankin votes against war a second time, this time as the lone opponent to American entrance into World War II.

1942: Mike Mansfield elected western district congressman.

1943: Bearcreek Coalmine disaster near Red Lodge kills 70 men; first powerhouse at Fort Peck built.

1946: Wheeler defeated in primary by Leif Erickson; Zales Ecton elected U.S. senator; Wesley D'Ewart elected eastern district congressman.

1948: John W. Bonner elected governor.

1949: School Foundation Program established by legislature to aid in funding public schools.

1950: CIO ejects Mine, Mill and Smelter Workers for radical activities.

1952: J. Hugo Aronson elected governor; Mike Mansfield elected U.S. senator; Lee Metcalf elected western district congressman.

1954: Orvin Fjare elected eastern district congressman.

1955: Anaconda opens aluminum plant at Columbia Falls.

1956: LeRoy Anderson elected eastern district congressman.

1957: Legislative Council established by legislature; Hoerner-Waldorf builds pulp and paper plant near Missoula.

1958: Montana Wilderness Society founded.

1959: Lee Newspapers buy Anaconda newspapers in Montana.

1960: Donald G. Nutter elected governor; Lee Metcalf elected U.S. senator; James C. Battin elected eastern district representative; Arnold Olsen elected western district congressman.

1961: Second powerhouse built at Fort Peck.

1962: Governor Nutter killed in plane crash; Tim Babcock becomes governor.

1964: Tim Babcock elected governor; Wilderness Act passed.

1965: Reapportionment of Montana's legislature ordered by federal court.

1967: Longest copper strike in Montana's history.

1968: Forrest Anderson elected governor; John Melcher elected eastern district congressman; Libby Dam begun on Kootenai.

1969: Large-scale strip mining begins at Colstrip; Constitutional Revision Committee established to review 1889 Constitution.

1970: Executive reorganization approved by voters as constitutional amendment.

1971: Northern Plains Resource Council formed; Richard Shoup elected western district congressman; copper strike; Executive Reorganization Act passed.

1972: Thomas L. Judge elected governor; Constitution written and later approved by voters.

1973: Coal tax passed, highest in the nation; Jeannette Rankin dies.

1974: Max Baucus elected western district congressman.

1975: Burton K. Wheeler dies.

1976: Mike Mansfield retires from U.S. Senate; Ron Marlene elected eastern district congressman; John Melcher elected U.S. Senator.

1978: Lee Metcalf dies; Montana Supreme Court Chief Justice Paul Hatfield appointed U.S. Senator; Max Baucus elected U.S. senator; Pat Williams elected western district congressman.

Suggested Readings

Michael P. Malone, "Montana Politics and the New Deal," *Montana the Magazine of Western History* Vol. 21 (January 1971).

Michael P. Malone & Richard B. Roeder, "The Recent Political Scene: 1945-1975," in *Montana: A History of Two Centuries* (Seattle: University of Washington Press, 1976), pp. 288-302.

Bob Saindon & Bunky Sullivan, "Taming the Missouri and Treating the Depression: Fort Peck Dam," *Montana the Magazine of Western History* Vol. 27, No. 3 (Summer 1977).

Burton K. Wheeler, *Yankee From The West* (New York: Doubleday, 1962).

Education is an important part of Montana life and history. Children leave the Deer Park school in Flathead County at the end of the day.—*Mel Ruder photograph, M.H.S.*

Chapter XIV: Montana: Our Land and People

Montana's history is a story of land and people. Any account of the past or present, and any hope for the future can be expressed in terms of people on the land. Obviously Montanans have changed the area since the first men dug fire pits. More subtly, the land has changed Montanans. Montana. It is our land; we are its people. Over the years authors, poets, historians and painters have tried to capture the experiences that make us Montanans.

Montana is something to experience, certainly. Yet no one can personally do everything. Likewise, Montana and Montanans cannot exist as an island in the nation or world. Through education, we have learned about ourselves. We have learned valuable skills.

Fur trappers packed books with their traps. Thomas Dimsdale and Lucia Darling rang school bells shortly after gold was found. So education has always been an important part of Montana. From isolated one-room cabins, to large Class AA high schools, the business of education goes on. Today Montana has more than eight hundred public elementary and secondary schools. There are also another eighty private schools in the state. Increasing education costs have moved many districts toward consolidation. Each year fewer and fewer one- and two-room schools survive. All the same, the personal touch of individual instruction and attention is something we work to save.

Elementary and secondary schools are controlled by local school boards. Assistance and direction come from a county superintendent and from the state Superintendent of Public Instruction. Through the state superintendent's office, federal educational programs are administered. Training or materials are also provided to insure the best possible standard of education in the state. Teachers organizations like the Montana Education Association and the Montana Federation of Teachers also provide training at annual conventions. The State Board of Education sets statewide policy. Among its other duties are minimum curriculum requirements and school accreditation. The board's decisions to include the teaching of United States and Montana history and to specify teacher preparation in Native American studies indicate the important place Montana's past has in preparing for the future.

Post-high school education also has an important place in Montana's history. People realized very early that education was vital to the growth of the region. Rocky Mountain College in Billings has the longest heritage in the state's educational tradition. It is a combination of several earlier schools. These include Montana College at Deer Lodge, the private Montana University and Intermountain colleges in Helena and others. Rocky, the College of Great Falls and Helena's Carroll College are the present church-supported colleges in Montana.

The state itself has not been short in fulfilling its duty to provide higher education. Beginning with the series of 1893 laws establishing major university units, the system has grown (as have the schools themselves). Largest among these schools is Montana State University in Bozeman. It is followed by the University of Montana in Missoula. Eastern, Montana Tech, Northern and Western Montana colleges speak for the geographic breadth in other state schools. Today these units are administered by a Commissioner of Higher Education and a Board of Regents. They set policy and spending levels. Daily administration falls to the presidents at each college or university.

The state also oversees vocational and technical centers. These schools in Billings, Butte, Helena, Great Falls and Missoula have assumed an important role in training young women and men for essential careers in Montana. The separate communities in which these centers are located also exercise some control over the schools. Thorough training for careers in vehicle mechanics, radio broadcasting, office management and construction are now possible for Montanans through Vo-Tech education.

Community colleges offer another educational option to Montanans. Dawson, Miles and Flathead community colleges prove that education is a lifelong process. Some of their graduates receive an Associate of Arts degree before proceeding with additional work at another state college or university. Many more stay in their respective communities better prepared for their role in them. Across the land Montanans continue to pick up new skills and polish old ones.

Being a Montanan is also sharing; sharing what we know and are with others. Western Heritage Center, Museum of the Northern Plains, Montana Historical Society and Museum of the Rockies are institutions devoted to telling us something about the land on which we live. They tell us about the people who were here before us and the history they left. More and more counties and communities have come to realize the importance of preserving the past. Museums and historical societies operate in more than eighty towns and cities. There is no better way to study and appreciate Montana than to start in a local museum or attend the meeting of a local historical society. These buildings and groups are filled with stories of the land and people. A cast-iron toy, a hand-sewn dress, old photographs, quilled moccasins and a muzzle-loading rifle are but a few mementos that make the past vivid. Memories, stories, yarns and tall tales are also part of that history. They are worth saving. No greater honor can be given to Montana's history than the effort countless Montanans have made to preserve it.

Nationally and statewide, the effort to preserve Montana's past has been given help through the Historic Preservation Program. Created in 1967, and now under the direction of the Montana Historical Society, this effort seeks to assist local groups in preserving all aspects of their past. Fossil deposits, prehistoric man and Indian camp sites, along with significant buildings or monuments can now be preserved. Some items have been removed and saved in museums—like Indian tools and dinosaur bones. In other places buildings have been singled out—the Pierre Wibaux home in Wibaux, the superintendent's house in Granite or the Conrad Mansion in Kalispell are examples. Similar community, state and national action has saved groups of structures. Poplar's Fort Peck Agency and Historic Districts at Fort Benton, Helena and Butte have preserved whole blocks. The entire town of Bannack is now a state park. Under the supervision of the Fish and Game Department it is being restored much as it was during the gold rush era.

Sparked by community pride and in some cases the national Bicentennial celebration, some counties and localities have further preserved their past in written form. Local history groups published and continue to publish history. These volumes provide histories of existing towns and pioneer families. Taken together, these books provide a valuable historical resource, full of photographs and memories that are part of the heritage we all share.

Individual authors have added their words and insights to our study of Montana. It would be impossible to list every book written about the state. It would be equally impossible to list every Montanan who has written a book. Checking closely, we can discover some of both from almost every town and county in the state. Those writers who stand out in our minds have probably said what we like to hear about life and Montana.

Some readers watched a young boy grow up on a fictionalized ranch near Big Sandy and saw themselves. Bertha M. Bower's *Chip of the Flying U* told a very real story in novel form. In time, more than sixty novels came from this author's pen, many of them reflecting life on the cattle ranges of central Montana. Walt Coburn and Bob Fletcher wrote on similar topics. Bob Fletcher also gave tourists a series of quick histories on the state when he wrote the words for many of the historical markers lining the state's highways. "Just turn your fancy loose," he recommended. Range the coulees, gulches, prairies and mountains, Fletcher went on, "and if your imagination isn't hobbled you can people them with picturesque phantoms of the past."

As these and other authors peopled the range with cowpunchers on horseback, two other men brought to life the ways of earlier plains riders. James Willard Schultz wrote *My Life As An Indian* and over thirty other books dealing with Montana's various tribes. By the time he was seventeen he had given up his life in the East, had come to Montana, and was living with the Blackfeet. He married Mutsiawotan Ahki and took for himself the name Apikuni—Far Off White Robe. His stories tell about the early days among Montana's Indians.

Frank B. Linderman came to Montana in 1885, at the age of sixteen. He lived variously in Butte, Helena, Madison County and the Flathead Valley. In the last spot he felt at

James Willard Schultz and Many Tail Feathers of the Blackfeet. Schultz lived with the Blackfeet and wrote nearly forty books about Indian and frontier life.

Frank Bird Linderman wrote stories about Indian life in Montana and biographies of Indian leaders. He was also instrumental in the creation of Rocky Boy's Indian Reservation in 1916.

home. Before his death in 1938, he had written fifteen books, many of them sensitive to traditions and ways of life he observed among Montana Indians. His *Indian Why Stories*, for example, is still read and reread. When bands of landless Indians sought a reservation home in Montana, Linderman worked for the creation of Rocky Boy's Reservation. Dan Cushman's *Stay Away Joe* also deals with the landless Indians in fiction form. His non-fiction *Great North Trail* added further to the study of early Indian movements into Montana.

No author has attempted to cover the entire breadth of Montana's history like A. B. Guthrie, Jr. In a series of five novels, beginning with *The Big Sky* (1947) and ending with *The Last Valley* (1975), Guthrie covered the story of white settlement. His fine attention to detail gives readers the feeling they are there. He earned the Pulitzer Prize for Literature with his second volume in the series, *The Way West*. His novels and short stories have become part of Montana's literary tradition.

Dorothy M. Johnson has given Montanans many volumes of delightful reading.

Where Guthrie took all of Montana as his subject, a young girl fresh out of Butte High School tried to describe just herself and her city. Mary MacLane shocked Montanans when she exposed her innermost thoughts in *The Story of Mary MacLane*, written in 1902. Butte has inspired other writings, including historical studies by C. B. Glasscock (*The War of the Copper Kings*) and C. P. Connolly (*The Devil Learns to Vote*).

Several Montana authors received their start in journalism. Their newspaper columns and stories told Montanans about the past; about those who had crossed the land before them. Among these writers, Ralph Henry and Dorothy Johnson stand out for their books as well as their articles. Henry wrote *High Border Country*, plus numerous newspaper stories, magazine articles, and other books. Dorothy Johnson's works have achieved note in published form as well as in movies. *The Hanging Tree*, *The Man Who Shot Liberty Valance*, and *A Man Called Horse* appeared first as books, then as films. Other works like *Some Went West*, on frontier women, *The Bloody Bozeman*, and *Buffalo Woman* told stories of the men and women who made Montana's history. Any mention of newspapers should also include a word on the photojournalism of Mel Ruder and the *Hungry Horse News* at Columbia Falls. His creativity with camera and typewriter earned the Pulitzer Prize in 1965.

Few deserve as prominent a place in the development of modern Montana literature as does H. G. Merriam. He began teaching English at the University of Montana in 1919. Within a year he founded and began editing *The Frontier*, which became *the* magazine of Montana prose, poetry and history until it ceased publication in 1939. In the classroom, Merriam exposed students to his infectious enthusiasm for writing. On the pages of *The Frontier* (later called *Frontier and Midland*), promising poets and authors got a chance to display the products of their creativity. Merriam also took an important part in the Federal Writers Project during the 1930s, which encouraged good writing at all levels. In 1948, he was one of the leading forces behind the creation of the Montana Institute of the Arts. During more than thirty years of existence, the MIA has encouraged creativity in all of Montana's communities and in a wide variety of mediums from prose and poetry to painting and pottery. Unquestionably, Merriam's influence in Montana has been profound and long-standing.

In addition to the Montana Institute of the Arts, there have been several other groups encouraging Montanans to look creatively at themselves and their traditions. The Work Projects Administration's Federal Writers Project gathered the history of the land and people from all across the state.

They published a state guide book, a history of Butte entitled *Copper Camp*, and stories of the Assiniboine in *Land of Nakoda*. WPA workers inventoried the records of many counties so historians would know what resources were available. They also recorded the memories of many old-timers. Some of the results have survived in the archives of the Montana Historical Society and Montana State University. They tell personal stories of Montanans from all walks of life.

Between 1944 and 1947, the Rockefeller Foundation sponsored the Montana Study. It was a program to encourage local communities to examine the quality of life they offered citizens. Many towns in western Montana modelled their studies after the first one conducted at Lonepine. Under the direction of Baker Brownell and Bert B. Hansen, these projects produced several community pageants and plays. In many ways they set the stage for community studies during the 1960s and 1970s that produced so many local history volumes.

One of the writers in the Montana Study was Joseph Kinsey Howard. He had already given the state a good look at itself and its past in *Montana, High Wide and Handsome*. He did the same thing for the state's literature in his book *Montana Margins*, a collection of many writings about Montana.

Since 1972, yet another organization in the state has encouraged community discussion in such areas as history, philosophy, literature, archeology, politics and the arts. The Montana Committee for the Humanities is an affiliate and receives monies from the National Endowment for the Humanities. It then regrants those funds to many Montana groups.

Programs and conferences held under the committee's sponsorship have promoted dialogue on important public policy issues. Actual topics have been far-reaching in terms of both subject matter and geography. Examples include a seminar on Kootenai Indian heritage in Libby; examination of various ethnic influences, held in Plentywood; and discussions of the different roles women and families have played during recent years, put on in Glendive. The Montana Committee for the Humanities joins the WPA, the Montana Study and Montana's educational system in promoting study and discussion of changing life-styles that are part of Montana's past.

Unmentioned to this point have been Montana's poets. There is something in the sweeping panorama of the plains, or a beautiful sunset, that makes all of us want to capture the inspiration in poetry. Some have succeeded. Many of these poems have been set to music, including songs like J. Campbell Cory's "Take Me Back to Old Montana," and Joe Howard's familiar words "Montana, Montana, Glory of the West"—now the state song. Berton Braley told the story of Butte as a bustling city. He described the mines and minorities, the filth and frivolity of the Richest Hill on Earth in a

Newspaperman, author, lecturer and a great Montana personality, Joseph Kinsey Howard.

series of poems he began writing for local newspapers in 1905. To those who looked at the bustling mining camp and saw only an ugly, bleak series of tailing piles, Braley had a poetic reply: Butte's beauty lay within the community's heart and soul, not on the surface.

Other poets, like Missoula's Richard Hugo, have looked across Montana for its poetry and form. In Hugo's *The Lady in Kicking Horse Reservoir*, he found a variety of inspirations that can serve to direct modern, would-be poets.

Somewhere among writers, novelists and poets of Montana are tucked historians. They have served the state faithfully since J. Allen Hosmer recorded his trip to the states and Thomas Dimsdale told everyone how the vigilantes did in Henry Plummer's bunch. In truth, any and everyone who has attempted to save some part of Montana's past can take the historian's mantle. Many have labored long at the task. Merrill Burlingame of Montana State University began collecting state history about the time H. G. Merriam was gathering up the literary produce. Like Merriam, Burlingame's efforts were ceaseless. Stanley Davison at Western Montana College had also labored long at the task of collecting and recording. In Missoula, Al Partoll and Paul C. Phillips directed their talents in this direction. Charles Bovey of Great Falls preserved Virginia City and reconstructed Nevada City to save this segment of our history. K. Ross Toole added to our understanding of Montana's past through his work as director of the Montana Historical Society in the early 1950s and in his list of publications about a state that he accurately terms an "uncommon land." More recently, Michael Malone and Richard Roeder at Montana State University have added to Montana's historical bibliography.

Not to be omitted in the history effort has been the Montana Historical Society itself. Since its creation in 1865, this agency and its supporters have worked continually to preserve and publish Montana's history. *Contributions* was a series of source books issued between 1876 and 1940. Since 1951 the society's award-winning journal *Montana, the Magazine of Western History* has included articles on a wide variety of topics. The historical society's list of publications is much longer and speaks of the broad interest in history that Montanans share.

H. G. Merriam, editor of *Frontier and Midland*, who encouraged and inspired many Montana authors and poets.—*H. G. Merriam Collection, University of Montana Archives, Missoula, Montana*

Montana has been lucky when it comes to having a record of the territory and state. White settlement came to Montana about the time the camera was being perfected. That meant that while people were building the towns, rounding up cattle, and plowing the land, photographers recorded the events on glass plates and film. Like authors, the list of photographs becomes almost endless, particularly once the "Kodak" or box camera came into the hands of "shutter bugs" everywhere.

Very early, there were some Montana photographers who carted bulky glass plate camera and fully-equipped dark rooms around in wagons or railroad cars. F. J. Haynes, for example, covered the routes of the Northern Pacific in a special railroad car. Later he explored and recorded on film the wonders of Yellowstone Park. In the cattle country, L. A. Huffman not only watched the roundups and cowboys, he preserved them in photographs. He also captured the changing life-styles of Montana's plains Indians. Farther west, Missoula photographer R. H. McKay did the same for the Flathead Indians.

McKay also pointed his lens at city subjects and his photographs give us an idea of what a city was like, fifty years ago and more. Other picture-takers also found worthy subjects in the city. E. H. Train and Les Jorud photographed Helena. C. Owen Smithers documented Butte. Bill Culver watched Maiden and Lewistown grow through his camera lens.

The camera froze in an instant not only its subject, but also the times in which he or she lived. Old photographs tell us about clothing styles, car types and even social values if we look carefully. Every photograph—the one dated 1865 or the one you took yesterday—tells us something about people and the land on which they live.

As certainly as the camera froze a moment in history, Montana's artists have tried to capture life on canvas. In a sense they have also stopped the action. Yet through colors and flowing lines, an artist brings that instant back to life. He relights campfires; stirs up the dust of our imaginations or memories; makes us feel and hear the sound of mountain water. A good painting is magic. It "says" something to the viewer. True, it may not "say" the same thing to everyone who sees it, but in a very real sense, it lives.

Montana's first painters came with the early explorers. Karl Bodmer travelled the Missouri River in 1833 and 1834 with a rich European prince. Just as we take slides and movies of our vacations, the prince took back Bodmer's drawings and paintings. Karl Bodmer's work shows us what the Missouri River looked like without settlements or dams. He gave us paintings of Montana's Indians not long after their first contact with white trappers and traders.

As gold seekers began to crowd native Montanans, a Danish painter toured the mining camps. Brush in hand, Peter Tofft saw Montana from Virginia City to Fort Owen to Fort Benton. His fine paintings show the land when white settlements were few and far between. The roads he travelled and painted had been cut delicately into canyons and hillsides. Tofft gave us another view of early Montana.

In 1877 Edgar S. Paxon came to Montana from Buffalo, New York. As a young man of twenty-five, Paxon lived the life of a scout and frontiersman. All the while his eye recorded the land, the settler and the Indian. Later his brush translated these mental notes to paintings. With a good feel for space and distance, as well as history, Paxon painted. He did landscapes and sensitive portraits of Montanans, Indian and white. Some of his paintings were exhibited at the Chicago World's Fair in 1893. Perhaps his best known work is his portrayal of the Battle of the Little Big Horn. His murals at the State Capitol and the Missoula County Court House also tell graphic stories of Montana's development. Montana and the West lost a great artist when he died in 1919.

About the time Paxon was making a name for himself, a sixteen-year-old kid from Missouri was trying his hand at being a cowboy in the Judith Basin. Charles M. Russell's cowboy days were limited, but his capacity for seeing the world around him was not. When his boss wanted some way of telling the ranch owners how bad the winter of 1886-1887 really was, Russell sketched a starving steer "Waiting for a Chinook." It became one of his best-known pieces. Not long after that, Russell quit making his living throwing a rope and tried his hand at painting and illustrating. *Harper's Weekly* and the vault doors of a Lewistown bank were among his early commissions. He improved. Improvement meant two things. He became a better artist, and his fame and prices increased. His wife Nancy became Russell's business manager, and before long she was peddling his work for what he called "dead man's prices." Montanans, and people all across the country, developed a fondness for Russell and his art. They mourned his death in 1926. On canvas he showed Montanans what they remembered—or wanted to remember—about the land and the past they shared.

Russell had talent and he knew talent. Olaf C. Seltzer came to Great Falls at the age of fourteen in 1892. He worked

Russell watched the young artist. Above the Mint Saloon—one of Russell's hangouts—the two worked together in a makeshift studio. Seltzer's paintings were called "gems of perfection in detail and in color harmony." His subject matter came from the land and the people surrounding him. His Blackfeet and Piegan portraits, his cowboys, gamblers and settlers seemed real. Before his death in 1957, Seltzer painted over 2,500 different works, far more than any other Montana artist.

Saving Montana's heritage on canvas was not something unique to Paxon, Russell and Seltzer. Winold Reiss captured the Blackfeet art and dress. William Standing (Fire Bear), an Assiniboine born at Oswego, Montana, painted the Indian, past and present. His illustrations in *Land of Nakoda* portray the Indian's heritage. His sketches of twentieth century Montana Indians sometimes offer pointed commentary on the modern Indian's circumstances.

Other artists have bridged the gap of the centuries in their work. No one could name them all, but Shorty Shope, Ace Powell and J. K. Ralston have given Montanans many paintings to enjoy. Their brushes have returned the Indian to Montana, before the white man came. They have traced the pioneers through gold camps and cow camps to airplanes and pickup trucks. And art does not stop at the edges of a framed painting. The sculpture of Charlie Russell, Earl Heikka, John Clarke and Bob Scriver make bronze, wax and wood come to life. Horses strain under riders, bear cubs scurry up trees and former Montana residents pause forever in lifelike form. Larger than life, other Montanans have been preserved in the statues of John Weaver. His recreation of Russell in Statuary Hall at the nation's capitol and his Bullwhacker in Helena's downtown mall are examples.

Who can really say what the teacher, author, poet, photographer or artist have done? They help us see ourselves. Each in his or her own way has retraced the trails across the land that we all have followed, sometimes for real, sometimes only in our imaginations.

Montana is land and people. The land is soft and it is harsh. We can feel the state touch us gently in the delicate pink of the bitterroot, or the subtle blue of the plains larkspur. We have also been overpowered in the vastness, ruggedness and savagery that can be the land and its climate.

This photograph of the great Charles Marion Russell was taken at about the time his fame as an artist was growing.

variously for a horse outfit and for the Great Northern Railway. In his spare time he painted, something he had taken up in his native Denmark before the age of twelve.

Olaf C. Seltzer was one of Montana's great western painters. An immigrant from Denmark, Seltzer was a friend of C. M. Russell and lived in Great Falls.

In its many moods Montana is the land—the space—and the freedom to wander it.

Montana is also people. Urban citizens, rural residents, reservation dwellers—we are all Montanans. The problems and challenges the future holds for us will come when we mix the realities of the different places we live. Cities have their needs. Farms and ranches have their own unique requirements. Reservations contain still different problems. From outside the state even other pressures continue to mount.

To the east, south and west, live Americans who see relief from their own problems in Montana. Montana has space into which they can escape. Some will come to visit Glacier and Yellowstone National Parks. Others will ski Big Sky, Big Mountain and a dozen different slopes. Many will visit Montana only to stay and become Montanans themselves. It is a pattern centuries old. At one point or another, every Montana family came from someplace else.

The new settlers in moving vans and rental trucks will change Montana just as surely as did the ones in covered wagons. They will bring many of the values and expectations they thought they were escaping. Indians welcomed horses and rifles. Fur traders imported whiskey and disease. Miners introduced water and air pollution. Yet in the same baggage of change came vaccines, wheat seeds, education, religion and modern machines.

Other people who will never set foot in Montana will change the land and people. They will buy grain and livestock. They will demand more coal, petroleum, electricity, copper and wood. In exchange for each will come money and jobs.

Montanans are faced today with a dilemma older than we are. We have our land. We have our people. What of our resources will we spend? What will we save? Let us do the spending and saving wisely.

STATE OF MONTANA

A Selective Bibliography

by David Walter

This *Selective Bibliography* is designed to assist readers in the further study of Montana history. The listing is organized in two main sections:

> **General Montana History**
> **Local Montana History**
>   Clark Fork Region
>   Upper Missouri Region
>   High Line Region
>   Central Region
>   Yellowstone Region

The first section presents some books of general interest for the Montana history enthusiast. These volumes could comprise a nucleus for any library. For more topical works, however, "Suggested Readings" accompany each chapter of the text.

This first bibliographic section necessarily is limited. Yet one especially useful source of general and specific Montana history information is a series of state subscription histories. These works often contain several volumes and sometimes are called the "mug books," because they routinely include flattering biographies and portraits of prominent state citizens. Nevertheless, these volumes also present historical information available in few other sources. Montana's eight commonly recognized subscription histories are:

Michael A. Leeson, ed. *The History of Montana, 1739-1885.* Chicago, Ill.: Warner, Beers, and Company; 1885.

Joaquin Miller. *An Illustrated History of the State of Montana.* Chicago, Ill.: The Lewis Publishing Company; 1894.

Progressive Men of the State of Montana. Chicago, Ill.: A. W. Bowen and Company; c. 1900.

An Illustrated History of the Yellowstone Valley. Spokane, Wash.: Western Historical Publishing Company; 1907.

Helen Fitzgerald Sanders. *A History of Montana.* 3 vols. New York, N.Y. and Chicago, Ill.: The Lewis Publishing Company; 1913.

Tom Stout, ed. *Montana: Its Story and Biography.* 3 vols. New York, N.Y. and Chicago, Ill.: The American Historical Society Publishing Company; 1921.

Robert G. Raymer. *Montana: The Land and the People.* 3 vols. New York, N.Y. and Chicago, Ill.: The Lewis Publishing Company; 1930.

Merrill G. Burlingame and K. Ross Toole, eds. *A History of Montana.* 3 vols. New York, N.Y.: Lewis Historical Publishing Company; 1957.

The second bibliographic section offers published materials of local history interest. For easy reference, the listing is organized in five geographical divisions, each of which includes several Montana counties.

Selected General Works on Montana History

Abbott, Newton C. *Montana in the Making.* Ed., Adelia M. Price. 13th revised edition. Billings: Gazette Printing Company; 1964.

Bigart, Robert. *Montana: An Assessment for the Future.* Missoula: University of Montana Publications in History; 1978.

Brown, Margery H., and Virginia G. Griffing. *Montana: A Student's Guide to Localized History.* New York, N.Y.: Teachers College Press; 1971.

Burlingame, Merrill G. *The Montana Frontier.* Helena: State Publishing Company; 1942.

———, comp. *Montana Historical Calendar [1978; 1979].* Bozeman: Circle Press; 1977/1978.

Cheney, Roberta Carkeek. *Names on the Face of Montana: The Story of Montana's Place Names.* Missoula: University of Montana Publications in History; 1971.

Farr, William E., and K. Ross Toole. *Montana: Images of the Past.* Boulder, Colo.: Pruett Publishing Company; 1978.

Federal Writers Project, W.P.A. *Montana: A State Guide Book.* New York, N.Y.: Viking Press; 1939/1949. Also— East Lansing, Mich.: Somerset Publishers; 1973.

Hakola, John W., ed. *Frontier Omnibus.* Missoula: University of Montana Press; 1962.

Hamilton, James McClellan. *The History of Montana: From Wilderness to Statehood.* Ed., Merrill G. Burlingame. Portland, Ore.: Binfords and Mort; 1957/1970.

Henry, Ralph C. *Our Land Montana: The Story of Our Treasure State.* Helena: State Publishing Company; 1962/1972.

Howard, Joseph Kinsey. *Montana: High, Wide and Handsome.* New Haven, Conn.: Yale University Press; 1943/1959/1968.

———, ed. *Montana Margins: A State Anthology.* New Haven, Conn.: Yale University Press; 1946/1972.

Johnson, Dorothy M. *Montana.* New York, N.Y.: Coward-McCann Publishers; 1970.

Malone, Michael P., and Richard B. Roeder. *Montana: A History of Two Centuries.* Seattle, Wash.: University of Washington Press; 1976.

———, eds. *The Montana Past: An Anthology.* Missoula: University of Montana Press; 1969.

Miller, Don C. *The Ghost Towns of Montana.* Boulder, Colo.: Pruett Publishing Company; 1974.

Milne, Bruce G., and Herbert T. Hoover. *A Teaching Guide for the Cultural History and Geography of the Western Frontier and Upper Missouri Region.* Vermillion, S.D.: University of South Dakota; 1975.

Montana Advertising Service, and the Montana Press Association. *Newspaper Directory and Rate Book, 1979.* Helena: Montana Advertising Service; 1978.

Montana Historical Society Staff. *Not in Precious Metals Alone: A Manuscript History of Montana.* Helena: Montana Historical Society; 1976.

Montana History Project [Lolo]. *Montana: Two Lane Highway in a Four Lane World.* Missoula: Mountain Press Publishers; 1978.

Myers, Rex C. *The Symbols of Montana.* Helena: Montana Historical Society and the Helena Kiwanis Club; 1976.

Spence, Clark C. *Montana: A Bicentennial History.* New York, N.Y.: W. W. Norton and Company; 1978.

———. *Territorial Politics and Government in Montana, 1864-1889.* Urbana, Ill.: University of Illinois Press; 1975.

Taylor, Robert L., et al. *Montana in Maps, 1974.* Bozeman: Big Sky Books; 1974.

Toole, K. Ross. *Montana: An Uncommon Land.* Norman, Okla.: University of Oklahoma Press; 1959.

———. *Twentieth-Century Montana: A State of Extremes.* Norman, Okla.: University of Oklahoma Press; 1972.

Waldron, Ellis, and Paul Wilson. *An Atlas of Montana Elections, 1889-1976.* Missoula: University of Montana Publications in History; 1978.

Wolle, Muriel. *Montana Pay Dirt: A Guide to the Mining Camps of the Treasure State.* Denver, Colo.: Sage Books; 1963.

Selective Local Histories

This section of the Selective Bibliography presents a listing of published materials with a local history focus. The references are divided in five geographical portions, each of which includes a number of Montana counties.

Clark Fork Region
Upper Missouri Region
High Line Region
Central Region
Yellowstone Region

The counties comprising each region are listed at the beginning of the respective divisions. Every local history reference contains a county annotation; so the researcher need concentrate only on the pertinent county to compile a personal listing for his/her town or locale.

With a personal listing in hand, the most productive places to begin the collection of local history materials are the school library, the public library, the area historical society and the local historical museum. Although local history materials most readily are found in the respective community, a researcher also can rely on the Montana State Library's Inter-Library Loan System for particularly elusive sources. Most public librarians will explain this lending procedure upon request.

The following bibliography is selective: it presents only published works, each of which should be available locally. The listing, for instance, excludes magazine articles and newspaper issues, although these sources can be primary to local history research. Local repositories—especially the town newspaper office—are the best places to find newspaper editions and magazine issues.

The listing also excludes unpublished manuscript materials, for example, diaries, private research papers, reminiscences, business records, scrapbooks and correspondence collections. These resources are referenced in a useful volume:

Brian Cockhill and Dale L. Johnson, comps. and eds.
A Guide to Manuscripts in Montana Repositories.
University of Montana Library; 1973 Missoula.

The three main manuscript repositories in Montana are: (1) the Montana Historical Society Archives in Helena; (2) the University of Montana Archives in Missoula; (3) the Montana State University Archives in Bozeman. Other manuscript materials of local history interest can be found in each town's library and historical society/museum.

The researcher might wish to consult two other, more comprehensive local history bibliographies, each of which includes published and unpublished materials:

Coburn Johnson, et al.
Bibliography of Montana Local Histories
Missoula: Montana Library Association and the
University of Montana Library; 1977.
David A. Walter
"Montana Mosaic: A Teacher's Guide to Montana
Local History Materials"
Montana Historian Magazine, VIII, 2 (May, 1978).

Some of the most stimulating and effective Montana history work involves local resources. The following bibliography of *Selective Local Histories* is provided to assist the initiation of just such community and county projects.

Selective Local Histories of the Clark Fork Region

Including the Counties of:

Deer Lodge	Missoula
Flathead	Powell
Granite	Ravalli
Lake	Sanders
Lincoln	Silver Bow
Mineral	

Allen, Robert Sharon, ed. *Our Fair City* [Articles and Sketches of Butte, Silver Bow County, Montana]. New York, N.Y.: Vanguard Press; 1947.

Anaconda Diamond Jubilee Committee. *Anaconda* [Deer Lodge County, Montana] *Copper Etchings: Diamond Jubilee, 1883-1958.* Butte: McKee Printers; 1958.

Andrew, Berenice M. *Hellgate, 1860: The Beginnings of Missoula* [Missoula County], *Montana.* Missoula: Office of the County Superintendent of Schools; 1957.

Arlee High School American History Class. *A History of Arlee* [Lake County], *Montana.* Missoula: Mountain Press; 1973.

Avon "Get Together Club," comp. *Our Neighborhood: Here and There* [in Powell County, Montana]. Ed., Dorothy Terrence Mannix. Avon: Club; 1977.

———. *Our Neighborhood: Newsy and Nosey* [Powell County, Montana]. Spokane, Wash.: Evergreen Printing; 1949/1950/1971/1975.

Bonner School Bicentennial Committee. *A Grassroots Tribute: The Story of Bonner* [Missoula County], *Montana* [1850-1976]. Missoula: Gateway Printing and Lithography; 1976.

Brothers, Beverly J. *Historic Butte* [Silver Bow County, Montana]: *The Richest Hill on Earth.* A publication of the Committee for the Historic Preservation of Butte and Silver Bow County, Montana. Butte: Artcraft Printers; 1977.

———. *Sketches of Walkerville* [Silver Bow County, Montana]: *The High and the Mighty* [1873-1932]. Butte: Ashton Printing; 1973.

Browman, Audra A., comp. *Nemissoolatakoo Valley, Crossroads of Western Montana: The Early History of Missoula* [Missoula County]. Missoula: author; 1971.

Buchholtz, Curtis W. *Man in Glacier: An Interpretive History of Glacier National Park* [Flathead and Glacier Counties, Montana], *1750-1975*. West Glacier: Glacier Natural History Association; 1975.

Chaffin, Glenn. *The Last Horizon* [Pioneering in the Corvallis-Hamilton Area of the Bitterroot Valley, Ravalli County, Montana; 1864-1970]. Somerset, Calif.: Pine Trail Press; 1971.

Clarke, Debbie. *The History of Victor* [Ravalli County], *Montana* [1840-1968]. Stevensville: Tribune Publishers; 1964/1968.

Cotter, James A. *These Five Valleys . . . The Missoula* [Missoula County], *Montana, Area*. Missoula: Missoulian Publishers; 1976.

Daley, Dennis M., and Jim Mohler. *An Historical Resources Identification and Location Study for National Resource Lands: Garnet Mining District* [Granite County, Montana]. A project of the U.S. Department of the Interior. Missoula: Bureau of Land Management; 1973.

Davis, Evelyn M., Ruth Harlo, Russell R. Ross, et al. *An Article Compilation of the History of Western Montana* [Particularly Sanders County]—*including Places, People, and Institutions*. Comp., Dorothy H. Hunton. Thompson Falls: authors; 1966.

Davis, William Lyle, S. J. *A History of the St. Ignatius Mission* [Lake County]: *An Outpost of Catholic Culture on the Montana Frontier* [1831-1900]. Spokane, Wash.: C. W. Hill Printing; 1954.

Deer Lodge [City] Bicentennial Committee of School District #1, Book Committee. *An Historical Sketch of Deer Lodge* [City, Powell County], *Montana, 1864-1976*. The revision of a 1964 publication, under the direction of the Powell County Museum and Arts Foundation. Deer Lodge: Platen Press; 1976.

Deer Lodge County History Group, coll. and comp. *In the Shadow of Mount Haggin: The Story of Anaconda and Deer Lodge County* [Montana], *1863-1976*. Anaconda: Leader Publishers; 1975.

Dufresne, Lorraine. *A Heritage Remembered: Early and Later Days in the History of Western Sanders County* [Montana]. Thompson Falls: Ledger Publishers; 1976.

Eckelberry, Henry. *Yesterday Was Demersville* [Kalispell, Flathead County, Montana]. Kalispell: Thomas Printing; 1974.

Elwood, Henry, ed. *Somers* [Flathead County], *Montana* [1857-1948]: *The Company Town—including an Album of Photographs of Flathead Lake Steamboats*. Kalispell: Thomas Printing; 1976.

Evans, Lucylle Hartz. *St. Mary's in the Rocky Mountains: A History of the Cradle of Montana's Culture* [Stevensville, Ravalli County]. Stevensville: Montana Creative Consultants; 1976.

Flint, Kedric W., and Nona D. Paul. *The Early History of Bigfork and Surrounding Communities* [Flathead and Lake Counties, Montana]. Bigfork: authors; 1957.

Florian, Martin. *The Story of St. Mary's Mission, in Stevensville* [Ravalli County], *Montana*. Missoula: Missoulian Publishers; 1959.

Frenchtown Historical Society Book Committee. *Frenchtown Valley Footprints* [Western Missoula County, Montana; 1800-1976]. Missoula: Mountain Press; 1976.

Groff, Mr. and Mrs. H. Clay, and Mrs. Adam Hornung. *Some of the History of Victor* [Ravalli County], *in the Bitterroot Valley* [Montana, 1866-1946]. Missoula: University of Montana Press; 1946. Also, a revised and updated version—Victor: Federated Church; 1960.

Group of Persons Interested in Preserving Local History, A. *More Bitterroot Memories, 1930–1976: A Bicentennial Publication of the Florence Community* [Ravalli County, Montana]. Comps., Gladys Ostrom, et al. Hamilton: Republic Publishers; 1976.

———. *Some Bitterroot Memories, 1860–1930: A Homey Account of the Florence Community* [Ravalli County, Montana]. Missoula: Gateway Printing; 1973.

Harrington, Leona, ed. *The History of Apgar* [Flathead County, Montana]—*Compiled by the Pupils of Apgar School and Their Teacher, Mrs. Leona Harrington.* Columbia Falls: School District #6; 1959.

Hill, Ivy Hooper Blood, comp. and ed. *The Flint Creek Valley* [Granite County], *Montana.* Philipsburg: Mail Publishers; 1962.

Hot Springs Historical Society. *Settlers and Sod Busters* [in Lake and Eastern Sanders Counties, Montana; 1900-1975]. St. Ignatius: Mission Valley News Publishers; 1976.

Jacobsen, Hazel, comp. and ed. *A Profile of Early Ovando* [Powell County], *Montana: 1878-1900.* Deer Lodge: Platen Press; 1977.

James, Don. *Butte's Memory Book* [Silver Bow County, Montana; including the Photos of C. Owen Smithers]. Caldwell, Idaho: Caxton Press; 1975.

Johns, Samuel E. *The Pioneers* [of Flathead County, Montana: Ten Scrapbook Histories and an Index Volume, Collected 1945-1954]. Kalispell: Flathead County Carnegie Library; 1962.

Johnson, Olga Weydemeyer. *Early Libby and Troy* [Lincoln County], *Montana* [1808-1920]. Libby: Western News Publishers; 1958.

—————, ed., for the Pioneers of the Tobacco Plains Country. *The Story of the Tobacco Plains Country—The Autobiography of a Community* [Eureka, Lincoln County, Montana; 1860-1948]. Caldwell, Idaho: Caxton Press; 1949/1950.

Koelbel, Lenora. *Missoula* [Missoula County, Montana] *the Way It Was: A Portrait of an Early Western Town.* Missoula: Gateway Printers; 1972.

Kvale, Velma R. *Where the Buffalo Roamed* [Ronan and Lake County, Montana]. Ed., Margaret Sterling Brooke. St. Ignatius: Mission Valley News Publishers; 1976.

Libby Pioneer Society, and the Libby Woman's Club. *Nuggets to Timber: Pioneer Days at Libby* [Lincoln County], *Montana.* Libby: Libby Lithography and Western News Publishers; 1970.

Lolo History Committee. *Lolo Creek Reflections* [Lolo, Woodman, and Lolo Hot Springs, Missoula County, Montana]. Ed., Mary Carpenter. Missoula: Economy Printers; 1976.

McAlear, J. F. *The Fabulous Flathead: The Story of the Development of the Flathead Indian Reservation* [Missoula, Sanders, Flathead, and Lake Counties, Montana; 1700-1960], *As Told to Sharon Bergman.* A publication of [Polson] The Reservation Pioneers, Inc. Polson: Treasure State Publishers; 1962.

McCallum, Ruth, comp. *An Anthology of St. Regis* [Mineral County], *Montana.* Superior: Independent Publishers; 1959.

McCurdy, Edward B. *Wild Horse Island* [in Flathead Lake, Lake County, Montana]—*Yesterday, Today, and Tomorrow.* Polson: Treasure State Publishers; 1975.

Mineral County Jaycees. *A Pictorial History of Mineral County* [Montana]. Missoula: Artcraft Printers; 1970.

Missoula-Hell Gate Centennial Committee. *Missoula-Hell Gate* [Missoula County, Montana] *Centennial, 1860-1960.* Missoula: Missoulian Publishers; 1960.

Montana Federation of Women's Clubs. *A Local Community History of Libby* [Lincoln County], *Montana.* Comp., A. V. Howard. Libby: Western News Publishers; 1926/1940.

Montana Historical Society of Mineral County, and the Mineral County Jaycees. *One Hundred Eighteen Years of History* [1858-1976]: *Mineral County, Montana.* Superior: Independent Publishers; 1976.

Montana Institute of the Arts, Libby's Writers Group. *In the Shadow of the Cabinets: The Early Kootenai* [Valley] *Country* [Lincoln County, Montana]. Libby: Western News Publishers; 1976.

—————. *Times We Remember In and Around Libby* [Lincoln County], *Montana.* Libby: Western News Publishers; 1974.

Montana Study, Greater University of Montana. *Historical Subjects in Dixon* [Sanders County], *Montana—by the Dixon-Agency Study Group.* Missoula: University of Montana; 1946.

—————. *Life in Montana, As Seen in Lonepine, A Small Community* [in Sanders County]. Missoula: University of Montana; 1945.

—————. *The Woodman Community* [Missoula County]—*An Assessment by the Montana Study Group of Lolo, Montana.* Missoula: University of Montana; 1946.

Moss, G. M., and Dorothy M. Johnson. *Whitefish* [Flathead County], *Montana, in 1951*. Whitefish: Pilot Publishers; 1952.

Ostberg, Jacob H., for the Butte Senior Citizens Group. *Sketches of* [Foreign Populations in] *Old Butte* [Silver Bow County, Montana; 1863-1968]. Butte: Senior Citizens Group; 1972.

Partoll, Albert John. *Hell Gate Pass* [Missoula County, Montana]: *River Portal to Adventure, from Hell's Gate to Paradise—A Glimpse of the Past*. Missoula: Missoulian Publishers; 1961.

Rhone, John A., and the Plains Historical Society. *Wild Horse Plains* [Sanders County, Montana; 1870-1910]. Plains: Plainsman Publishers; 1970.

Robinson, Donald H. *Through the Years in Glacier National Park* [Flathead and Glacier Counties, Montana]: *An Administrative History*. Ed., Maynard C. Bowers. West Glacier: Glacier Natural History Association; 1960/1967.

St. Ignatius Senior Citizen Group. *The Heritage of the Mission Valley* [Lake County, Montana; 1854–1960]. Comp. and ed., Olive C. Wehr. St. Ignatius: Mission Valley News Publishers; 1975.

Schafer, Betty, and Mabel Engelter. *Stump Town to Ski Town: The Story of Whitefish* [Flathead County], *Montana* [1880-1973]. A publication of the Whitefish Library Association. Whitefish: Pilot Publishers; 1973.

Shea, Marie Cuffe. *The Early Flathead* [Valley] *and the Tobacco Plains: A Narrative History of* [Flathead and Lincoln Counties] *Northwestern Montana*. Kalispell: Thomas Printing; 1977.

Spritzer, Donald E. *Waters of Wealth: The Story of the Kootenai River* [Lincoln County, Montana], *Prepared for the Libby Dam Visitor Center*. Omaha, Nebra.: U.S. Corps of Army Engineers; 1973.

Stephenson, Garnet. *The Silver Empire* [Philipsburg, the Flint Creek Valley, and Granite County, Montana]. Philipsburg: Mail Publishers; 1966.

———. *The Snows of Echo Lake* [Settlement in Granite County, Montana; 1883-1965]. Philipsburg: Mail Publishers; 1966.

Stevensville Historical Society. *Montana Genesis: A History of the Stevensville Area of the Bitterroot Valley* [Ravalli County, 1805-1970]. Missoula: Mountain Press; 1971.

Trippet, Edgar W. *Historical Information Concerning the Upper Flathead Country* [Flathead County], *Montana*. Kalispell: Trippet Publishers; 1971.

Trippet, Frank H., and Lewis L. Bain, comps. *Historical Highlights of the Flathead Valley* [Lake and Flathead Counties, Montana]; *1800-1956*. 3 vols. [usually bound in one]. A compilation of historical materials from the [Kalispell] *News-Farm Journal;* including the separately published Bigfork, Kalispell, and Whitefish town histories. Kalispell: Trippet Publishers; 1956.

Vallance, May Pierson, comp. *Memories: Fair Play School and Community* [Ravalli County], *in the Bitterroot Valley, Montana*. Hamilton: author; 1974.

Waldo, George B., and C. E. Thomas. *This Is My Valley* [Darby and the Bitterroot Valley, Ravalli County, Montana]. Missoula: Delaney Printing; 1954.

Wehr, Olive C., ed. and comp. *To Live on the* [Flathead Indian] *Reservation* [Missoula, Sanders, Flathead, and Lake Counties, Montana]: *A Bicentennial History, 1854-1976*. St. Ignatius: Mission Valley News Publishers; 1976.

Whitepine Home Makers Extension Club, comp. *Crosscuts and Rails: The History of Alger, Belknap, and Whitepine* [Sanders County, Montana]. Missoula: Delaney Printing; 1975.

Woody, Frank H. *The History of Missoula* [Missoula County], *Montana*. Missoula: Democrat-Messenger Publishers; 1897.

[   ]. *Butte's Diamond Jubilee Portfolio: Seventy-five Years of Progress* [1879-1954; Silver Bow County, Montana]. Butte: Standard Publishers; 1954.

[   ]. *One Hundred Years in the Flathead Valley: The St. Ignatius Mission Centennial* [1854-1954; Lake County, Montana]. Missoula: Missoulian Publishers; 1954.

Selective Local Histories of the Upper Missouri Region

Including the Counties of:

Beaverhead	Jefferson
Broadwater	Lewis and Clark
Cascade	Madison
Gallatin	Meagher

Augusta High School Anniversary Committee. *Then, and Now: A Golden Anniversary History of Augusta High School* [Lewis and Clark County, Montana], *1921-1971*. Helena: Helena Letter Shop; 1971.

Barsness, Larry. *Gold Camp: Alder Gulch and Virginia City* [Madison County], *Montana* [1863-1870]. New York, N.Y.: Hastings House; 1962.

Berthold, Mary Paddock. *Big Hole Journal: Notes and Excerpts* [on Beaverhead County, Montana]. Detroit, Mich.: Harlo Press; 1973.

———. *Turn Here for the Big Hole* [Beaverhead County, Montana; 1884-1960]. Detroit, Mich.: Harlo Press; 1970.

Bertsche, William H. *The Building of a City: Great Falls* [Cascade County], *Montana*. Great Falls: Dufrene Foundation; 1975.

Boulder Valley Bicentennial Group. *Our Yesterdays: Community and Family Histories from the North Boulder Valley* [Jefferson County, Montana; 1860-1976]. Boulder: Group; 1976.

Brammer, Mauck. *The Naming of Clancy, Alias "Clancey"* [Jefferson County], *Montana—including Short Biographical Sketches of Two Judges: Judge William Clancey of Clancy and Judge William Clancy of Butte*. Helena: author; 1976.

Brown, Kimberly Rice. *An Historical Overview of the Dillon District* [Beaverhead County], *Montana* [1862-1967]. A publication of the U.S. Department of the Interior, Bureau of Land Management. Boulder, Colo.: Western Interstate Commission for Higher Education; 1975.

Burlingame, Merrill Gildea. *Gallatin County's Heritage: A Report of* [Montana] *Progress, 1805-1976*. Bozeman: Gallatin County Bicentennial Committee; 1976.

———, and the Gallatin County Centennial Committee. *Gallatin* [County, Montana]: *A Century of Progress* [1864-1964]. Bozeman: Artcraft Printers; 1964.

Dearborn Homemakers Club. *Dearborn Country: A History of the Dearborn, Wolf Creek, and Craig Areas* [Lewis and Clark County, Montana]. Fairfield: Times Publishers; 1976.

Denning, Frances. *Growing Pains:* [A History of] *Three Forks* [Gallatin County], *Montana, 1908-1976*. A Publication of School District #J-24. Bozeman: Color World; 1975.

Eden Area Historical Committee: *A Century in the Foothills* [1876-1976]: *The History of the Eden Area* [Cascade County, Montana]. Fairfield: Times Publishers; 1976.

Eliel, Frank, with Eirene and Lambert Eliel. *The Beaverhead Revisited.* [Beaverhead County, Montana; 1869-1930]. Dillon: Finefrock Publishing; 1969.

Francis, Bertha Agnes Wraton. *The Land of the Big Snows* [The Big Hole Basin, Beaverhead County, Montana; 1804-1910]. Caldwell, Idaho: Caxton Press; 1955.

Gordon, Taylor. *The Man Who Built the Stone Castle* [Byron Roger Sherman; Meagher County, Montana; 1867-1967]. White Sulphur Springs: News Publishers; 1967.

Great Falls Diamond Jubilee, Inc. *Portrait of Progress: The Great Falls* [Cascade County], *Montana, Diamond Jubilee, 1884-1959*. Great Falls: Tribune Publishers; 1959.

Great Falls Public Library. *A History of Great Falls* [Cascade County], *Montana*. Great Falls: Public Library; 1961.

Haines, Aubrey L. *The Yellowstone* [National Park] *Story* [Gallatin and Park Counties, Montana]. 2 vols. A publication of the Yellowstone Library and Museum Association. Boulder, Colo.: University of Colorado Press; 1977-1978.

Harlowton Pioneer History Committee, and the Harlowton Woman's Club. *Yesteryears and Pioneers* [Meagher and Wheatland Counties, Montana; 1880-1972]. Billings: Western Printing and Lithography; 1972.

Hollaway, Grace, ed. *The History of Townsend* [Broadwater County], *Montana*. Townsend: Star Publishers; 1964/1969.

———, et al. *The History of Broadwater County* [Montana]. Townsend: Star Publishers; 1964/1969/1974.

Iverson, Ronald J. *The Princess of the Prairie: A History of Belgrade* [Gallatin County], *Montana* [1862-1965]. A publication of the [Bozeman] McGill Museum. Bozeman: Montana State University; 1965.

Johnson, Lloyd and Mabel, et al., comps., for the Gettel Home Demonstration Club. *We Called Them Back: Montana Homesteaders and Pioneers of the Old Wilson Post Office Country* [Northwestern Cascade County, 1889-1964]. Fairfield: Times Publishers; 1974.

Kuhlman, Fay. *The Ghost of Castle Mountain* [Meagher County, Montana]. Bearcreek: Banner Publishers; 1957.

McBride, Sr. Genevieve, O.S.U. *The Bird Tail* [St. Peter's Mission, Cascade County, Montana]. New York, N.Y.: Vantage Press; 1974.

Madison County History Association, comp. *Pioneer Trails and Trials: A History of Madison County* [Montana], *1863-1920*. Great Falls: Blue Print and Letter Company; 1976.

Malone, Michael Peter. *The Gallatin Canyon* [Gallatin County, Montana] . . . *and the Tides of History*. A publication of the M.S.U./National Science Foundation's Gallatin Canyon Study. Bozeman: Montana State University; 1973.

Meagher County Historical Society, Centennial Pictorial History Committee. *Meagher County: An Early-day Pictorial History* [Wheatland, Fergus, Judith Basin, Broadwater, and Meagher Counties, Montana], *1867-1967*. White Sulphur Springs: News Publishers; 1967/1968/1976.

Montana Institute of the Arts, Great Falls History Group. *The Early History of Great Falls* [Cascade County, Montana]. Great Falls: Great Falls Public Schools; 1963.

———. *Historical Sketches* [of Cascade County, Montana] *by Members of the Great Falls History Group*. Great Falls: Tribune Publishers; 1958. An enlarged, revised edition published in 1965.

Nielsen, Mrs. Sterlin, and Mrs. Paul Wetzel, for the Vaughn Community History Committee. *Vaughn* [Cascade County, Montana] *History*. Vaughn: Committee; 1970.

Ovitt, Mabel. *Golden Treasure* [Stories of early Bannack, Beaverhead County, Montana]. Dillon: Tribune Publishers; 1952. Also—Helena: State Publishing Company; 1954.

Pace, Dick. *Golden Gulch: The Story of Montana's Fabulous Alder Gulch* [Madison County]—*Being a True, Quite Partial, and Somewhat Humorous History* [1863-1962]. Virginia City: Information Center; 1962. Also—Virginia City: Virginia City Trading Company; 1962/1968/1970—and Great Falls: Blue Print and Letter Company; 1974.

Pine Grove Home Demonstration Club. *The Story of Lincoln Gulch* [Lewis and Clark County, Montana], *1805-1905*. Helena: Club; 1973.

Portage Historical Society. *Prairie Pioneers: A Narrative of Montana Homestead Days* (Chouteau and Cascade Counties, 1800-1964]. Great Falls: Blue Print and Letter Company; 1966.

Pound, Edmond O. *Pioneers and Possibilities* [Early Days in the Musselshell River Valley, Montana; 1848-1885]. Vol. I of *A Central Montana* [Meagher, Wheatland, Golden Valley, and Musselshell Counties] *Trilogy*. Harlowton: Times-Clarion Publishers; 1969.

———. *The Years After* [Dryland Farming in the Musselshell River Valley, Montana; 1908-1960]. Vol. III of *A Central Montana* [Meagher, Wheatland, Golden Valley, and Musselshell Counties] *Trilogy*. Harlowton: Times-Clarion Publishers; 1970.

———. *The Years Between* [The Coming of the First Dryland Farmers to the Musselshell River Valley, Montana; 1885-1908]. Vol. II of *A Central Montana* [Meagher, Wheatland, Golden Valley, and Musselshell Counties] *Trilogy*. Harlowton: Times-Clarion Publishers; 1970.

Rennewanz, L. H. *Steam, Grain, and Saw Dust: A History of Farming and Logging in Gallatin County, Montana* [1880-1968]. Bozeman: Tribune Publishers; 1968.

Rowe, Jean Conrad, comp. and coll., for the Cascade Historical Committee. *Mountain and Meadows: A Pioneer History of Cascade, Chestnut Valley, Hardy, St. Peter's Mission and Castner Falls* [Cascade County, Montana], *1805-1925*. Great Falls: Blue Print and Letter Company; 1970.

Sharp, Paul Frederick. *Whoop-Up Country: The Canadian-American West, 1865-1885* [Glacier, Toole, Liberty, Hill, Pondera, Chouteau, Teton, Lewis and Clark, Cascade, Judith Basin, and Meagher Counties, Montana]. Minneapolis, Minn.: University of Minnesota Press; 1955/1957. Also—Helena: Montana Historical Society Press; 1960— and Norman, Okla.: University of Oklahoma Press; 1973.

Spray, James S. *Early Days in the Madison Valley* [Madison and Gallatin Counties, Montana]: *A History Written in Commemoration of Our Honored Pioneers*. Virginia City: Madisonian Publishers; 1949.

Stearns, Harold Joseph. *A History of the Upper Musselshell Valley* [Golden Valley, Wheatland, and Meagher Counties] *of Montana* [1805-1920]. Harlowton/Ryegate: Times-Clarion Publishers; 1966.

Stuwe, Jane Willits. *Valley Ventures: Settlers in the Simms and Fort Shaw Area* [Cascade County] *of Montana* [to 1925]. Great Falls: Herald Publishers; 1967.

Sun River Valley Centennial Committee. *Montana Centennial, 1864-1964: Sun River Valley Histories* [Teton, Lewis and Clark, and Cascade Counties]. Simms: High School Commercial Department; 1964.

Townsend Seventh/Eighth Grade Social Studies Classes, and John Hinton. *Broadwater County* [Montana] *History: People, Places, Events, 1863-1970*. Townsend: School District; 1974-1976.

United States, Federal Works Agency, Works Progress Administration, Federal Writers Project, Montana. *Butte* [Silver Bow County, Montana], *Past and Present: 1864-1936*. New York, N.Y.: Viking Press; 1936.

United States, Federal Works Agency, Works Progress Administration, Federal Writers Project, Montana. *Copper Camp: Stories of the World's Greatest Mining Town—Butte* [Silver Bow County], *Montana* [1856-1941]. New York, N.Y.: Hastings House; 1943/1976.

———. *Great Falls Yesterday: Comprising a Collection of Biographies and Reminiscences of Early Settlers* [Cascade County, Montana]. Ed., Edith R. Maxwell. New York, N.Y.: Hastings House; 1939.

Waite, Susan. *An Historical Inventory of the Marysville Ghost Town* [Lewis and Clark County], *Montana*. A publication of the U.S. Department of the Interior. Missoula: Bureau of Land Management; 1974.

Watson, Arthur H. *Montana Trials and Tribulations* [Settling Meagher County, Montana; 1909-1975]. Billings: Western Printing and Lithography; 1975.

Whitehall High School History Class of 1928, comp. *The History of the Jefferson Valley* [Madison, Jefferson, Gallatin, and Broadwater Counties], *Montana*. Whitehall: Valley News Publishers; 1928.

Williams, Lyle K. *Historically Speaking: Stories of the Men and Women Who Explored and Settled the Missouri River Headwaters* [Three Forks Area: Madison, Jefferson, Gallatin, and Broadwater Counties, Montana]. Three Forks: Herald Publishers; 1975.

Wirtz, Shirley, and Lorene Lovell. *One Man's Dream: The Elkhorn Mine at Coolidge* [Beaverhead County], *Montana*. Butte: Ashton Printing; 1976.

[   ]. *The Cascade County* [Montana] *Golden Jubilee, 1887-1937*. Great Falls: Tribune Publishers; 1937.

[   ]. *East Helena's Diamond Jubilee, 1888-1963* [Lewis and Clark County, Montana]. Helena: Union-News Publishers; 1963.

[   ]. *Helena's Diamond Jubilee* [Lewis and Clark County, Montana], *1864-1939*. Helena: Record-Herald Publishers; 1939.

[   ]. *One Hundred Years of Progress* [in Gallatin County, Montana], *1864-1964*. Bozeman: Chronicle Publishers; 1964.

[   ]. *Tri-County Atlas: Meagher, Sweet Grass, and Carbon* [now also Wheatland, Golden Valley, Stillwater, and Big Horn] *Counties* [Montana—Historical and Biographical]. Big Timber: Henry and Geiger; 1902.

Selective Local Histories of the High Line Region

Including the Counties of:

Blaine	Pondera
Daniels	Roosevelt
Glacier	Sheridan
Hill	Teton
Liberty	Toole
Phillips	Valley

Aasheim, Magnus, comp. and coll., and the Sheridan County Historical Society. *Sheridan's Day Break: A Story of Sheridan County* [Montana] *and Its Pioneers* [1900-1920]. Great Falls: Blue Print and Letter Company; 1970.

Allison, Janet S. *Trial and Triumph: One-Hundred-One Years in North Central Montana* [Hill and Blaine Counties, 1867-1968]. A Publication of the [Chinook] North Central Montana Cow Belles. Chinook: Opinion Publishers; 1968.

Anderson, Josephine Goldman. *Golden Reflections of Bygone Days: Phillips* [and Valley] *County*[ies], *Montana* [1898-1973]. Tumwater, Wash.: H. J. Quality Printing; 1973.

Andreasen, Irving, ed. *The First Fifty Years: Glimpses from the Dagmar Community* [Sheridan County, Montana; 1906-1956]. Cedar Falls, Iowa: Holst Printing Company; 1956.

Barry, Edward E. *The Fort Belknap Indian Reservation* [Blaine and Phillips Counties, Montana]: *The First One Hundred Years, 1855-1955*. A publication of the Montana State University Endowment and Research Foundation. Bozeman: Big Sky Books; 1974.

Berry, Gerald L. *The Whoop-Up Trail: Alberta-Montana Relationships* [Glacier, Toole, Pondera, Teton, and Chouteau Counties]. Edmonton, Alberta: Applied Arts Products, Ltd.; 1953.

Bertins, Belle. *Culbertson's Diamond Jubilee, 1887-1962: Seventy-Five Years of Progress* [Roosevelt County, Montana]. Culbertson: Searchlight Publishers; 1962.

Buchholtz, Curtis W. *Man in Glacier: An Interpretive History of Glacier National Park* [Flathead and Glacier Counties, Montana], *1750-1975*. West Glacier: Glacier Natural History Association; 1975.

Chinook History Interest Group, comp. *Blaine County History to 1964: A Jubilee Centennial Edition*. Chinook: Opinion Publishers; 1964.

Costello, Gladys, and Dorothy Whitcomb Klimper. *Top O' the Mountain: Charley Whitcomb, Mining Man in Zortman* [Blaine and Phillips Counties], *Montana*. Great Falls: Blue Print and Letter Company; 1976.

Cottonwood Home Demonstration Club. *In Years Gone By* [Simpson and Cottonwood, in Northern Hill County, Montana; 1910-1965]. Havre: Herald Publishers; 1965.

Daniels County Bicentennial History Committee. *Daniels County* [Montana] *History, 1902-1976*. Great Falls: Blue Print and Letter Company; 1977.

Dupuyer Centennial Committee. *Bygone Days and Modern Ways: The Dupuyer* [Pondera County, Montana] *Centennial, 1877-1977*. Havre: Griggs Printing; 1977.

Dutton Golden Jubilee Committee. *Dutton's Golden Jubilee* [Teton County, Montana]: *1909-1959*. Ed., Tom Kerin. Great Falls: Leader Publishers; 1959.

Egly Country Club, comp. *Trails, Trials, and Tributes* [Egly, Liberty, and Chouteau Counties, Montana; 1895-1954]. Fort Benton: River Press Publishers; 1954/1958. Also—Chester: Times Publishers; 1974.

Fort Peck Reunion Committee. *Fort Peck Dam* [Valley County, Montana]—*A Job Well Done: October, 1933, to August, 1977*. Ed., Leroy Von Eschen. Glasgow: NeMont Printers; 1977.

Froid Commercial Club. *The Golden Jubilee of Froid* [Roosevelt County], *Montana: 1910-1960*. Williston, N.D.: Reporter Publishers; 1960.

Glasgow "Montana Backgrounds" Extension Course. *Montana Backgrounds: Homestead Days in Northeast Montana* [The Lower Milk River Valley and Valley County]. Havre: Northern Montana College; 1953.

Hagener, Antonia R. *An Index of Newspapers Published in Havre* [Hill County], *Montana, 1893-1953—with an Emphasis on Historic Events.* Havre: author; 1974.

Hamaker, Dorothy M., ed. *Napi's Lookout: The Story of Willow Rounds* [Pondera County, Montana; 1805-1964]—*A History of the Early Settlers in the Winter Hunting Area of the Blackfeet Indians.* Kalispell: Thomas Printing; 1967.

Havre Chamber of Commerce. *Looking Back* [Pioneer Reminiscences from Hill County, Montana]. Havre: Herald Publishers; 1950.

Hill County Bicentennial Commission. *Grit, Guts, and Gusto: A History of Hill County* [Montana, 1805-1976]. Havre: Bear Paw Printers; 1976.

Hingham High School American History Class. *A Study of Hingham* [Hill County, Montana], *Past to Present—by the Class of 1972.* Hingham: School District Office; 1971.

Hinsdale Woman's Club. *They Thought the Land Was Free: The Story of Hinsdale Homesteaders* [Valley County, Montana], *1893-1976.* Glasgow: NeMont Printers; 1976.

History Committee of the Turner Golden Jubilee Celebration. *A Golden Jubilee History of Turner, Blaine County, Montana: 1912-1962.* Chester: Times Publishers; 1962.

Hoye, Leota, ed. *Roosevelt County* [Montana] *Treasured Years: A History, 1800-1976.* Great Falls: Blue Print and Letter Company; 1977.

Liberty County Museum. *Our Heritage in Liberty* [County, Montana; 1900-1976]. Coll. and ed., Iva Kolstad. Chester: Times Publishers; 1976.

MacDonald, Marie Peterson. *After Barbed Wire: A Pictorial History of the Homestead Rush into the Northern Great Plains* [Fallon, Custer, Wibaux, Prairie, Dawson, McCone, Richland, Valley, and Roosevelt Counties, Montana], *1900-1919.* A publication of the [Glendive] Frontier Gateway Museum. Billings: Maynard Stationery; 1963.

Minneota Friendly Home Demonstration Club. *Tumbleweeds and Tar Paper Shacks* [Northeastern Liberty and Northwestern Hill Counties, Montana; 1910-1970]. Iowa Falls, Iowa: General Publishing and Binding; 1971.

Monkman, Olga Wagnild, comp. *Teton County* [Montana] *History* [Reminiscences of Area Pioneers]. Chouteau: Acantha Publishers; 1955.

Montana Federation of Women's Clubs. *A Local Community History of Valley County, Montana* [to 1910]. Comp., Vesta O. Robbins. Glasgow: Courier Publishers; 1925. Reissued in 1976 as a publication of the Valley County Homemakers Council.

Montana Institute of the Arts, Blaine County History Group. *Blaine County* [Montana] *History: A Jubilee Centennial Edition* [1864-1964]. Chinook: Opinion Publishers; 1964.

Montana Institute of the Arts, Havre History Interest Group, and the Havre Chamber of Commerce. *A Business Directory and a Short History of Havre* [Hill County], *Montana.* Havre: Herald Publishers; 1957.

Montana Institute of the Arts, Shelby History Group. *Shelby* (Toole County, Montana] *Backgrounds* [1877-1958]. Shelby: Times Publishers; 1958.

———. *Toole County* [Montana] *Backgrounds* [1877-1958]. Shelby: Times Publishers; 1958.

Montana Study, Greater University of Montana. *A Community Study and a History of Conrad* [Pondera County, Montana]—*by the Conrad Study Group.* Missoula: University of Montana; 1946.

North Valley County Bicentennial Committee. *Homesteading: Our Heritage in Northern Valley County, Montana.* Great Falls: Blue Print and Letter Company; 1978.

O. N. O. Homemakers Club of Brockton, comp. *The Anderson-Biem Communities* [Roosevelt County, Montana]: *A History, 1917-1971.* Brockton: Our-Night-Out Club; 1972.

Paladin, Vivian A., comp. and ed. *From Buffalo Bones to Sonic Boom: Glasgow's Seventy-Fifth Anniversary Souvenir* [Valley County, Montana; 1887-1962]. A publication of the Glasgow Jubilee Committee. Glasgow: Courier Publishers; 1962.

Phillips County Diamond Jubilee Committee. *Railroads to Rockets, 1887-1962: The Diamond Jubilee of Phillips County, Montana.* Malta: News Publishers; 1962.

Ponde-Toole Extension Homemakers Club. *Grime, Grit, and Gumption: The Early History of the South Marias* [Pondera and Toole Counties, Montana]. Shelby: Promoter Publishers; 1976.

Pondera History Association. *Pondera, A County History* [Montana, 1805-1968]. Great Falls: Blue Print and Letter Company; 1968.

Prairie Homemakers Home Extension Club, and the Jayhawker Ridge Home Extension Club, comps. *Echoes from the Prairies: A History of North Toole County* [Montana]. Shelby: Promoter Publishers; 1977.

Richland Community Bicentennial Committee. *Richland [Valley County], Montana: A History* [1926-1976]. Glasgow: NeMont Printers; 1976.

Robinson, Donald H. *Through the Years in Glacier National Park* [Flathead and Glacier Counties, Montana]: *An Administrative History.* Ed., Maynard C. Bowers. West Glacier: Glacier Natural History Association; 1960/1967.

Ruffcorn, Andrea G., comp. *A Historical Sketch, Commemorating the Fiftieth Anniversary (1910/1920-1970) of Homesteading Days of the Baylor Community* [Valley County, Montana], *and Commemorating the Town of Baylor (1911-1937).* Glasgow: NeMont Printers; 1970.

Sampson, Sam. *The Saga of Fort Peck* [Valley County], *Montana.* Portland, Ore.: Binfords and Mort; 1941.

Scobey Community History Group. *An Anniversary Album of the Scobey Community, Daniels County, Montana, 1901-1948: A Picture Story of Its Pioneers, Its Progress, and Its Present.* Scobey: Junior Chamber of Commerce; 1948.

Scobey Eighth Grade Social Studies Class, and the Scobey Boy Scouts. *The History of Scobey* [Daniels County], *Montana.* Scobey: High School Commercial Department; 1937.

Scobey Homesteaders' Golden Jubilee Association. *Daniels County Golden Jubilee, 1913-1963: A Brief Historical Review of Life and Times on the Northeastern Montana Prairies.* Ed., Dorothy Rustebakke. Scobey: Leader Publishers; 1963.

Shane, Ralph M. *A Brief History of the Fort Belknap Indian Reservation* [Blaine and Phillips Counties], *Montana.* Billings: Area Office of the U.S. Bureau of Indian Affairs; 1974.

———. *A Brief History of the Rocky Boy's Indian Reservation* [Chouteau and Phillips Counties], *Montana.* Billings: Area Office of the U.S. Bureau of Indian Affairs; 1974.

Sharp, Paul Frederick. *Whoop-Up Country: The Canadian-American West, 1865-1885* [Glacier, Toole, Liberty, Hill, Pondera, Chouteau, Teton, Lewis and Clark, Cascade, Judith Basin, and Meagher Counties, Montana]. Minneapolis, Minn.: University of Minnesota Press; 1955/1957. Also—Helena: Montana Historical Society Press; 1960— and Norman, Okla.: University of Oklahoma Press; 1973.

Staudinger, Richard, and McLellan Smith. *The Fort Peck Dam and Reservoir* [Garfield, McCone, and Valley Counties, Montana]. Bozeman: Montana State University; 1976.

Sun River Valley Centennial Committee. *Montana Centennial, 1864-1964: Sun River Valley Histories* [Teton, Lewis and Clark, and Cascade Counties]. Simms: High School Commercial Department; 1964.

Toole County Superintendent of Schools. *Homestead Days in Toole County, Montana.* Shelby: Office of the County Superintendent; 1936.

———. *Montana Backgrounds: Toole County History, 1894-1956.* Shelby: Office of the County Superintendent; 1956.

Valley County Homemakers Council. *Since Homesteading Days: The Histories of the Communities of Larslan, Avondale, and Sunnyside* [Valley County], *Montana.* Ed., Lenore Olson. Glasgow: NeMont Printers; 1976.

Wall, O. J., and Arthur H. Fast. *The Lustre-Larslan-Volt Story* [Valley County, Montana]: *1916-1966.* Fraser: Fraser Community Club; 1966.

Wessel, Thomas R. *A History of the Rocky Boy's Indian Reservation* [Chouteau and Hill Counties], *Montana.* Bozeman: author; 1975.

Wolf Point Golden Jubilee History Committee. *A Brief History of the Development and Progress of Wolf Point* [Roosevelt County], *Montana: Golden Jubilee, 1915-1965.* Wolf Point: Herald-News Publishers; 1965.

Wolf Point Public Schools Social Studies Classes. *A Scrapbook History of Wolf Point, Roosevelt County, and Montana, 1870-1970.* Wolf Point: High School District; 1970.

[   ]. *An Anniversary Record* [of Conrad and Pondera County, Montana]: *1919-1969.* Conrad: Independent-Observer Publishers; 1969.

[   ]. *The Early Days: The Glasgow* [Valley County, Montana] *Diamond Jubilee, 1887-1962.* Glasgow: Courier Publishers; 1962.

[   ]. *The Golden Fiftieth Anniversary* [of Cut Bank, Glacier County, Montana], *1909-1959.* Cut Bank: Pioneer Press Publishers; 1959.

[   ]. *North of the Missouri: The History of Hill County and Northern Montana* [1895-1965]. Havre: Herald Publishers; 1954.

[   ]. *Plentywood* [Sheridan County, Montana]: *The Golden Years, 1912-1962.* Plentywood: Herald Publishers; 1962.

Selective Local Histories of the Central Region

Including the Counties of:

Chouteau	McCone
Fergus	Musselshell
Garfield	Petroleum
Golden Valley	Wheatland
Judith Basin	

American Revolution Bicentennial Committee of Golden Valley County. *Bicentennial Golden Valley County* [Montana]: *Heritage '76.* Roundup: Record-Tribune Publishers; 1976.

Anderson, Edna V. *A History of Lewistown* [Fergus County], *Montana.* A publication of the [Lewistown Chapter] American Association of University Women. Lewistown: Argus-Farmer Publishers; 1943.

Barrett, Viola, for the Historical Committee of the Hobson Women's Club. *Hobson* [Judith Basin County, Montana]: *Gateway to the Golden Grain Fields.* Lewistown: Argus Publishers; 1965.

Castor, Jack K. *Carter* [Chouteau County, Montana]: *A New Town Making Good.* San Rafael, Calif.: Castor Publishers; 1975.

Childs, Elsie Forbes, comp. *It Is Good to Remember: A Brief History* [of the Taylor Creek Area of Garfield County, Montana]. Helena: author; 1976.

Circle Homemakers' Clubs, and the Pioneer Historical Circle. *Pioneers and Progress on the Prairie* [Histories from McCone County, Montana]: *1864-1964.* Billings: Gazette Publishers; 1964.

Craig, Ruby Allen, comp. *Paths of the Past on Teton Bench* [Chouteau County, Montana]. Fort Benton: author; 1965.

DeHaas, John N., Jr., ed. *Central Montana Ghost Towns: Kendall, Giltedge, Maiden, and Fort Maginnis* [Fergus County, Montana]. Bozeman: Montana Ghost Town Preservation Society; 1975.

Denton Bicentennial Heritage Committee, comp. *Homestead Fever: The History of Denton, Danvers, and Coffee Creek* [Fergus County], *Montana.* Great Falls: Blue Print and Letter Company; 1977.

Egly Country Club, comp. *Trails, Trials, and Tributes* [Egly, Liberty, and Chouteau Counties, Montana; 1895-1954]. Fort Benton: River Press Publishers; 1954/1958. Also—Chester: Times Publishers; 1974.

Garfield County High School Montana History Classes, 1968-1969. *Garfield County, 1919-1969* [A History]. Comp., Darlyne Dasher. The first volume of a two-volume set: *The Historical Background of Early Settlers* [in Garfield County, Montana]. Miles City: Star Publishers; 1969.

Berry, Gerald L. *The Whoop-Up Trail: Alberta-Montana Relationships* [Glacier, Toole, Pondera, Teton, and Chouteau Counties]. Edmonton, Alberta: Applied Arts Products, Ltd.; 1953.

Brockway Homemakers Club, comp. *As It Was Yesterday* [Brockway and McCone County, Montana; 1910-1976]. Billings: Western Printing and Lithography; 1977.

Byerly, Ken. *Central Montana's Communities* [Wheatland, Golden Valley, Musselshell, Petroleum, Judith Basin, and Fergus Counties]: *Yesterday, Today, and Tomorrow* [Including an Index to Fifty-nine Communities]. Lewistown: Central Montana Publishing Company; 1959.

Geraldine Bicentennial History Committee. *Spokes, Spurs, and Cockleburs* [Chouteau County, Montana; 1876-1976]. Fort Benton: River Press Publishers; 1976.

Gordon, Albie, Margaret Lehfeldt, and Mary Morsanny, comps. *Dawn in Golden Valley, A County in Montana* [1879-1970]. Ryegate: Golden Valley Press; 1971.

Harber, Nora E. *Our Fort Benton, "The Birthplace of Montana": A Collection of Stories and Pictures of Early-Day and Modern Fort Benton* [Chouteau County, Montana]. Fort Benton: River Press Publishers; 1937.

Harlowton Pioneer History Committee, and the Harlowton Woman's Club. *Yesteryears and Pioneers* [Meagher and Wheatland Counties, Montana; 1880-1972]. Billings: Western Printing and Lithography; 1972.

Highland, Geneva. *Big Dry Country* [Garfield, Prairie, and McCone Counties, Montana; 1865-1920]. Billings: Billings Printing Company; 1960.

Highwood Woman's Club. *Highwood* [Chouteau County], *Montana: Trails and Tales of the Highwoods* [1876-1960]. Great Falls: Tribune Publishers; 1961/1964.

Jackson, Dorman, for the Moore Woman's Club. *The History of Moore* [Fergus County], *Montana, 1904-1964.* Lewistown: Argus Publishers; 1964.

Judith Basin Bicentennial Committee. *Furrows and Trails in the Judith Basin* [Fergus and Judith Basin Counties], *Montana*. Stanford: Basin Press Publishers; 1976.

Lawrence, Lou. *Pioneer Days at Big Sandy* [Chouteau County], *Montana* [1879-1919]. Big Sandy: Mountaineer Publishers; 1963/1970.

MacDonald, Marie Peterson. *After Barbed Wire: A Pictorial History of the Homestead Rush into the Northern Great Plains* [Fallon, Custer, Wibaux, Prairie, Dawson, McCone, Richland, Valley, and Roosevelt Counties, Montana], *1900-1919*. A publication of the [Glendive] Frontier Gateway Museum. Billings: Maynard Stationery; 1963.

McKenna, George. *Merino* [Harlowton, Wheatland County], *Montana: 1880-1900*. Harlowton: Clarion Publishers; 1930.

Meagher County Historical Society, Centennial Pictorial History Committee. *Meagher County: An Early-day Pictorial History* [Wheatland, Fergus, Judith Basin, Broadwater, and Meagher Counties, Montana], *1867-1967*. White Sulphur Springs: News Publishers; 1967/1968/-1976.

Moore Woman's Club. *Snowy Mountain Roundup: A History of Moore* [Fergus County], *Montana*. Lewistown: News-Argus Publishers; 1976.

Murray, Henry Thomas. *Judith Basin Pioneers: A Story of Early Days in Central Montana* [Fergus and Judith Basin Counties]. Lewistown: Argus Publishers; 1965.

Musselshell Valley Historical Museum Research Committee, comp. *Roundup on the Musselshell: Pieces of the Past* [Musselshell County, Montana; 1880-1920]. Billings: Reporter Printing; 1974.

Musselshell Valley Pioneer Club, Musselshell Valley History Committee, comp. *Horizons O'er the Musselshell* [Musselshell County, Montana; 1882-1974]. Roundup: Record-Tribune Publishers; 1974.

Overholser, Joel F. *A Centenary History of Fort Benton* [Chouteau County], *Montana, 1846-1946*. A publication of the Fort Benton Centennial Association. Fort Benton: River Press Publishers; 1946.

———. *A Souvenir History of Fort Benton* [Chouteau County]: *"Birthplace of Montana."* Fort Benton: River Press Publishers; 1958.

Penkake, Judy, ed. *In the Shadow of the Twin Sisters: Ubet, Garneill, Straw, and Buffalo* [Fergus, Wheatland, and Judith Basin Counties], *Montana* [1890-1973]. Lewistown: Montana Business Services; 1973.

Pleasant Valley Home Demonstration Club. *Footprints through the Valley* [Chouteau County, Montana; 1910-1955]. Great Falls: Art-Litho Printing and Office Supply Company; 1957. Also—Fort Benton: River Press Publishers; 1957/1972.

Portage Historical Society. *Prairie Pioneers: A Narrative of Montana Homestead Days* [Chouteau and Cascade Counties, 1800-1964]. Great Falls: Blue Print and Letter Company; 1966.

Pound, Edmond O. *Pioneers and Possibilities* [Early Days in the Musselshell River Valley, Montana; 1848-1885]. Vol. I of *A Central Montana* [Meagher, Wheatland, Golden Valley, and Musselshell Counties] *Trilogy*. Harlowton: Times-Clarion Publishers; 1969.

———. *The Years After* [Dryland Farming in the Musselshell River Valley, Montana; 1908-1960]. Vol. III of *A Central Montana* [Meagher, Wheatland, Golden Valley, and Musselshell Counties] *Trilogy*. Harlowton: Times-Clarion Publishers; 1970.

———. *The Years Between* [The Coming of the First Dryland Farmers to the Musselshell River Valley, Montana; 1885-1908]. Vol. II of *A Central Montana* [Meagher, Wheatland, Golden Valley, and Musselshell Counties] *Trilogy*. Harlowton: Times-Clarion Publishers; 1970.

Ronish, Henry G. *Homesteaders in the Judith Basin* [Fergus and Judith Basin Counties, Montana]. Lewistown: Argus Publishers; 1974.

Rossmiller, Genevieve F., and Gladys S. Neyland, comps., for the Triple-F Home Demonstration Club of Chouteau County. *The History of the Knees Community* [Chouteau County, Montana; 1886-1955]. Fort Benton: Club; 1956.

Schillreff, Fern E., and Jessie M. Shawver. *Garfield County* [Montana]: *The Golden Years*. The second volume of a two-volume set: *The Historical Background of Early Settlers* [in Garfield County, Montana]. Jordan: Tribune Publishers; 1969.

Shane, Ralph M. *A Brief History of the Rocky Boy's Indian Reservation* [Chouteau and Hill Counties], *Montana*. Billings: Area Office of the U.S. Bureau of Indian Affairs; 1974.

Sharp, Paul Frederick. *Whoop-Up Country: The Canadian-American West, 1865-1885* [Glacier, Toole, Liberty, Hill, Pondera, Chouteau, Teton, Lewis and Clark, Cascade, Judith Basin, and Meagher Counties, Montana]. Minneapolis, Minn.: University of Minnesota Press; 1955/1957. Also—Helena: Montana Historical Society Press; 1960—and Norman, Okla.: University of Oklahoma Press; 1973.

Shawver, Jessie M. *Jackaroo Saga, 1900-1961* [Illustrated; Jordan and Garfield County, Montana]. Bursett: author; 1961.

Silloway, Perley Milton, comp. and ed. *Silloway's History of Central Montana* [Fergus and Judith Basin Counties]: *A Review of the Development of Montana's Inland Empire*. Lewistown: Democrat Publishers; 1936.

Sparlin, Alberta C., for the Central Montana Historical Association. *The Trail Back: A Bicentennial History of Central Montana* [Fergus and Judith Basin Counties]. A Bicentennial project of the Central Montana Historical Association. Great Falls: Blue Print and Letter Company; 1976.

Staudinger, Richard, and McLellan Smith. *The Fort Peck Dam and Reservoir* [Garfield, McCone, and Valley Counties, Montana]. Bozeman: Montana State University; 1976.

Stearns, Harold Joseph. *A History of the Upper Musselshell Valley* [Golden Valley, Wheatland, and Meagher Counties] *of Montana* [1805-1920]. Harlowton/Ryegate: Times-Clarion Publishers; 1966.

Utica Historical Society Committee. *Utica* [Judith Basin County], *Montana* [1890-1965]. Stanford: Press Publishers; 1968.

Wangen, Mary, et al. *The Historical Background of McCone County, Montana*. Circle: Banner Publishers; 1956.

Wessel, Thomas R. *A History of the Rocky Boy's Indian Reservation* [Chouteau and Hill Counties], *Montana*. Bozeman: author; 1975.

Willson, Virgil A., and the San Souci Home Demonstration Club. *Chouteau County* [Montana: A Descriptive History]. Fort Benton: River Press Publishers; 1963.

Winifred Golden Committee, and the North Fergus County Civic Club. *Winifred's Golden Jubilee* [Fergus County, Montana]: *1913-1963*. Lewistown: News Publishers; 1963.

[   ]. *Big Sandy* [Chouteau County], *Montana: A Community History* [to 1940]. Big Sandy: Mountaineer Publishers; 1956/1957.

[   ]. *Tri-County Atlas: Meagher, Sweet Grass, and Carbon* [now also Wheatland, Golden Valley, Stillwater, and Big Horn] *Counties* [Montana—Historical and Biographical]. Big Timber: Henry and Geiger; 1902.

Selective Local Histories of the Yellowstone Region

Including the Counties of:

Big Horn	Prairie
Carbon	Richland
Carter	Rosebud
Custer	Stillwater
Dawson	Sweet Grass
Fallon	Treasure
Park	Wibaux
Powder River	Yellowstone

Annin, James T. *Eighty Years of Memories on the Banks of the Yellowstone* [River; Stillwater County, Montana; 1895-1975]. Billings: Artcraft Printers; 1976.

———. *They Gazed on the Beartooths* [Stillwater County, Montana, Histories; 1873-1960]. 3 vols. Billings: Reporter Printing; 1964.

Baker Chamber of Commerce. *Baker's Golden Jubilee, 1908-1958* [Fallon County, Montana]. Baker: Times Publishers; 1958.

Barnhart, Esther. *We Went West—Ho, Ho, Ho: The Epsie Community, Powder River County, Montana.* Broadus: Examiner Publishers; 1976.

Big Horn County Heritage Committee, comp. *Grass, Tipis, and Black Gold* [Big Horn County, Montana]. Billings: Artcraft Printers; 1976.

Big Horn County Historical Society Bicentennial Committee. *Lookin' Back: Big Horn County* [Montana, 1870-1976]. Hardin: Herald Publishers; 1976.

Big Horn County Home Demonstration Clubs. *Crow Country* [Big Horn County, Montana]. Hardin: Herald Publishers; 1955.

Breuchaud, Irene Gibbs. *Memoirs of Montana, 1882: Coulson/Billings* [Yellowstone County]. New York, N.Y.: Anderson Printers; 1959.

Brown, Mark Herbert. *The Plainsmen of the Yellowstone: A History of the Yellowstone Basin* [Montana, 1806-1898]. New York, N.Y.: G. P. Putnam's Sons; 1961. Also—Lincoln, Nebra.: University of Nebraska Press; 1976.

Carrington, Ruth, and Edna Mackley, eds. *Tales of Treasure County* [Historical Essays by Residents of Treasure County, Montana]. A publication of the Treasure County Bicentennial Commission. Billings: Times Publishers; 1976.

Clarke, William B. *Dusting Off the Old Ones* [Reminiscences of Miles City, Custer County, Montana; 1883-1959]. Miles City: Star Publishers; 1954-1959/1963.

Fromberg Service Club. *Fromberg: The Fruit Basket of Carbon County* [Montana, 1900-1976]. Billings: Empire Printing; 1976.

Fulmer, Genie Philbrick. *Cabins and Campfires in Southeastern Montana* [Forsyth and Rosebud County, Montana; 1876-1910]. Worland, Wyo.: Press Publishers; 1973.

Glendive Woman's Club. *From Glendive Creek to Gate City: A Pictorial History of the Glendive Area of Dawson County, Montana.* A publication of the Dawson County Bicentennial Committee. Glendive: Ranger-Review Publishers; 1976.

Glidden, Ralph. *Exploring the Yellowstone High Country: A History of the Cooke City Area* [Park County, Montana]. Livingston: Enterprise Publishers; 1976.

Haines, Aubrey L. *The Yellowstone* [National Park] *Story* [Gallatin and Park Counties, Montana]. 2 vols. A publication of the Yellowstone Library and Museum Association. Boulder, Colo.: University of Colorado Press; 1977-1978.

Hansen, Virginia, and Al Funderburk. *The Fabulous Past of Cooke City* [Park County, Montana; 1865-1940]. Billings: Billings Printing Company; 1962.

Higgins, James T., comp. *The City of Red Lodge* [Carbon County, Montana]. Billings: Montana National Bank; 1975.

Highland, Geneva. *Big Dry Country* [Garfield, Prairie, and McCone Counties, Montana; 1865-1920]. Billings: Billings Printing Company; 1960.

Hoffman, Emmett, O.F.M. Cap. *The Saint Labre Indian Mission* [Ashland, Rosebud County, Montana], *1893-1957, in the Light of the Franciscan Apostolate.* Ashland: Mission School; 1958.

Huntley Project History Committee. *Sod 'N Seed 'N Tumbleweed: A History of the Huntley Project, Yellowstone County, Montana.* Ed., R. H. Scherger. Billings: Frontier Press; 1977.

Hysham High School Social Studies Classes, 1962-1963. *An American Community: Hysham and Treasure County, Montana.* Hysham: High School District; 1963.

Jones, Agnes L. Schock. *Crow Country: Historical Notes on the Yellowstone Valley of Montana.* Billings: Rocky Mountain College Print Shop; 1959.

Jones, Irene James. *Trails along Beaver Creek: A Chronicle of Wibaux County, Montana* [1500-1976]. Wibaux: Pioneer-Gazette Publishers; 1976.

Kuhlman, Fay. *Bearcreek* [Carbon County], *Montana.* Bearcreek: Banner Publishers; 1972/1973.

Kurkowski, George. *Custer's Country: A Historical Atlas of Custer County, Montana.* A publication of the Custer County Bicentennial Commission. Miles City: Star Printing Company; 1976.

Lloyd, David. *A History of Early Rosebud* [County, Montana; 1806-1931]. Forsyth: Times-Journal Publishers; 1931.

Lodgegrass Public School Students. *A History of the Crow Indians, Based on Written Sources—Book I: From the Roaming Days to the Reservation* [Big Horn and Yellowstone Counties, Montana]. Ed., Charles C. Bradley. Lodgegrass: Public School District; 1971.

MacDonald, Marie Peterson. *After Barbed Wire: A Pictorial History of the Homestead Rush into the Northern Great Plains* [Fallon, Custer, Wibaux, Prairie, Dawson, McCone, Richland, Valley, and Roosevelt Counties, Montana], *1900-1919.* A publication of the [Glendive] Frontier Gateway Museum. Billings: Maynard Stationery; 1963.

———. *Glendive* [Dawson County, 1880-1968]: *The History of a Montana Town.* Glendive: Gateway Press; 1968.

Miles City Corral of Range Riders, Inc., and the Range Riders Reps of Custer County. *Fanning the Embers* [Miles City, Custer County, and the Yellowstone Valley, Montana, to 1910]. Billings: Gazette Printing and Lithography; 1971.

Mon-Dak Historical and Arts Society. *Courage Enough: Mon-Dak Family Histories* [Richland County, Montana; 1880-1975]. Ed., Gilda Buxbaum. Bismarck, N.D.: Tribune Publishers; 1975

O'Fallon Historical Society of Baker. *O'Fallon Flashbacks* [A History of Baker and Fallon County, Montana]. Billings: Western Printing and Lithography; 1975.

Oliver, George A. *Joliet* [Carbon County, Montana]: *Its Pioneers and Early Days.* Huntsville, Ala.: Monroe Printing; 1973.

Parsons, Henry L. *Stillwater County* [Montana]: *A General Study of Historical Information Relating to Stillwater County.* Bozeman: Montana State University; 1956.

Pioneer Society of Sweet Grass County. *Pioneer Memories* [Biographies and a History of Sweet Grass County, Montana; 1864-1926]. Bozeman: Bozeman Business Services; 1960.

Place, Marian Templeton. *Buckskins and Buffalo: The Story of the Yellowstone River* [Valley, 1800-1872]. New York, N.Y.: Holt, Rinehart; 1864.

Powder River County Extension Homemakers Council. *Echoing Footsteps: A Powder River County* [Montana] *History* [1850-1967]. Butte: Ashton Printing; 1967.

Powder River Portraits Committee of Broadus, comp. and ed. *Powder River Portraits: A Pictorial History* [Powder River County, Montana]. Miles City: H&T Quality Printing; 1977.

Prairie County Historical Society, comp. *Wheels Across Montana's Prairie* [County, 1880-1974]. Includes a supplementary insert: *More Wheels Across Montana's Prairie.* Billings: Western Printing and Lithography; 1974.

Pryor Public School Students. *A History of the Pryor Community* [Big Horn County, Montana], *and the Clan System of Crow Indians.* Pryor: School District; 1973.

Utterback, Gretchen, and Isabella Murphy. *The Pioneers of Old Dawson County, Montana* [Reminiscences, Photographs, and News Items: 1878-1965]. A publication of the Glendive Chamber of Commerce. Glendive: Review Publishers; 1965.

Veraldi, Marion, Betty Sweeney, and Clara Doles. *The Cavill School* [Yellowstone County, Montana] *Golden Anniversary: Fifty Years, More or Less, 1912-1964.* Billings: Frontier Press; 1964.

Welch, Charles A. *The History of the Big Horn Basin* [Carbon, Big Horn, Yellowstone, and Treasure Counties], *Montana: With Stories of Early Days, Sketches of Pioneers, and Writings of the Author.* Salt Lake City, Utah: Deseret News Press; 1940.

Whithorn, Bill and Doris. *A Photo History of Aldridge* [Park County, Montana]: *Coal Camp that Died A-bornin'* [1895-1910]. Minneapolis, Minn.: Acme Printing and Stationery; 1965/1966.

———. *A Photo History of Chico Lodge, Early Resort Area* [1864-1968]: *A County Doctor* [Townsend] *and the Oldest Town in Park County* [Emigrant, Montana]. Livingston: Enterprise Publishers; 1968.

———. *A Photo History of Gardiner, Jardine, and Crevasse* [Park County, Montana; 1870-1967]: *The Entrance to the Yellowstone National Park Wonderland.* Livingston: News Publishers; 1968/1972.

———. *A Photo History of Livingston* [Park County], *Montana* [1882-1966]. Livingston: News Publishers; 1966/1967.

———. *A Photo History of the Livingston-Bozeman Coal Country* [Park and Gallatin Counties, Montana; 1880-1976]: *Cokedale, Timberline, Chestnut, Storrs, Hoffman, and Maxey Lived on Coal.* Livingston: Enterprise Publishers; 1976.

———. *A Photo History of the Shields Valley* [Park County, Montana; 1870-1969]: *An Eden of Rich Grass and Deep Loam, A Land of Prize Crops and Unsurpassed Beauty.* Livingston: News Publishers; 1969/1970.

———. *Sixty Miles of Photo History: The Upper Yellowstone* [River] *Valley* [Park County, Montana; 1871-1965]. Livingston: News Publishers; 1965/1966/1969.

Wibaux Golden Jubilee Committees. *Wibaux's* [1911-1961] *Golden Jubilee* [History; Wibaux County, Montana; 1892-1961]. Wibaux: Gazette Publishers; 1961.

Wright, Kathryn Hutchinson. *Billings* [Yellowstone County, Montana]: *The Magic City and How It Grew* [1876-1919]. Billings: Reporter Printing; 1953/1954.

[   ]. *Aldridge* [Park County, Montana], *As It Was Then* [1896-1910] *and Now.* Livingston: News Publishers; 1962.

[   ]. *A Brief History of Rosebud County, Montana.* Forsyth: Independent Publishers; 1975.

[   ]. *Dawson County* [Montana] *History and Pioneer Stories.* Glendive: Monitor Publishers; 1927.

[   ]. *The Early History of Billings* [Yellowstone County, Montana], *As First Published in the* [Billings] *Gazette-Journal's Thirtieth Anniversary Edition* [1914]. Billings: Gazette Publishers; 1932.

[   ]. *The Founding of Custer County* [Montana, 1877]. Helena: Rocky Mountain Publishers; 1900.

[   ]. *A History of Miles City, Forsyth, Ekalaka, and Wibaux* [Custer, Rosebud, Carter, and Wibaux Counties], *Montana: 1876-1900.* A facsimile reproduction of a historical supplement first published by the [Miles City] *Yellowstone Journal* in 1900. Miles City: Star Publishers; 1976.

[   ]. *The Tarpoleon: Cowboy Country from the Time of Custer to the Time of Quemoy* [1875-1960; Carter County, Montana]. Ekalaka: Eagle Publishers; 1960.

[   ]. *Tri-County Atlas: Meagher, Sweet Grass, and Carbon* [now also Wheatland, Golden Valley, Stillwater, and Big Horn] *Counties* [Montana—Historical and Biographical]. Big Timber: Henry and Geiger; 1902.

Index

Abbott, E. C. "Teddy Blue," 88
Adolph (Flathead), 71
Agricultural Adjustment Administration, 211
Agriculture, 21, 85-93, 103, 144, 164-73, 191, 194, 196-201, 204-06, 209, 211
Airmail, 133
Airplane travel, 133-34, map, 135
Alder Gulch, 8, 34, 40-44, 45, 51
Alice mine, 37
Allen, B. F., 148
Alone, 128
Aluminum refining, 152
Amalgamated Copper Company, 158, 182-83, 185, 186, 190
American Fur Company, 18, 24-26, 127, 149
American Smelting and Refining Company, 152
Amsterdam, 113
AMTRAK, 131
Anaconda, 38, 131, 132, 135, 151-52, 181, 189
Anaconda Copper Mining Company, 152, 153, 154, 158, 181-83, 185, 199-200, 202-04, 211, 221, 222
Anaconda mine, 38
Anderson, Bertha, 113
Anderson, Forrest, 215
Anderson, Leroy H., 213
Apex clause, mining, 182
Arastra, 151
Archaic people, 5
Argenta, 9, 37, 46
Arlee (Flathead), 71
Armells Creek, 86
Aronson, J. Hugo, 214
Artists, 233-34
Ashley, James M., 51, 53-54, 57, 113
Ashley, William, 18, 24
Assiniboine Indians, 6-7, 65, 67, 71, 87, 231
Astor, John Jacob, 18, 24-25
Atlatl, 5

Atsina Indians (also called Gros Ventre), 6, 17, 19, 65, 67, 68, 71, 77, 87
Automobile, 132-33, 156
Ayers, Roy E., 210

Babcock, Tim, 214, 215
Baker, E. M., 68, 81
Baker, I. G., 80
Baker Massacre, 53, 68, 81
Ball, J. P., Jr., 115
Banking, 46-48, 148-49, 168-69, 171, 180, 197-99
Bannack, 7, 8, 33-35, 45, 46, 51, 54, 103, 108, 228
Bannock Indians, 7
Basement rocks, 3
Bass, J. B., 115
Baucus, Max, 213
Beadwork, 77-78
Bear Paw Mountains, 70
Beaver, 17-19, 23-26
Beaverhead Valley, 7, 33, 35, 86
Belly River, 1
Benteen, Frederick, 69
Benton Transportation Company, 128, 138
Berkeley Pit, 158, 211
Berthold, Bartholomew, 23
Bicentennial celebration, 228
Bielenberg, John, 81, 86, 97
Big Hole Battlefield, 81, 98, 189
Big Horn, 127
Big Horn Mountains, 15
Big Horn River, 17, 18, 29
Big Timber, 150, 151
Billings, 103, 104, 106, 128, 132, 150, 160, 212
Billings Polytechnic Institute, 110
Billings Water Power Company, 154
Bishop, J. F., 87
Bison, see buffalo
Bissell, G. G., 40
Bitterroot, 6, 85
Bitterroot Valley, 6, 19, 20-23, 27, 28, 33, 70, 85-86, 153, 212

Black Eagle Dam, 154
Black Robes, see Jesuits
Blackfeet Indian Reservation, 71, 87, 172
Blackfeet Indians, 6, 17, 22, 28-29, 53, 65, 67-68, 75-78, 80, 81, 228, 234
Blackfoot City, 106
Blackfoot Milling and Manufacturing Company, 153
Blackfoot War, 68
Blacks, see Negroes
Blake, A. Sterne, 45
Blood Indians, 6, 65, 68
Board of Regents, 227
Boardman, J. M., 174
Boardman, John M., 99
Bodmer, Karl, 233
Bonner, John, 214
Book publishing, 108
Boston and Montana Copper Company, 39, 152, 154, 182
Botkin, Alexander, 61
Boulder River School, 110
Bourquin, George M., 192-93
Bovey, Charles M., 44, 232
Bow and arrow, 5, 65, 75-76
Bowdoin gas field, 9
Bower, Bertha M., 228
Box Elder Creek, 86
Bozeman, 132, 135
Bozeman Pass, 29, 78
Bozeman Road, 53, 67, 78, 125, map, 14
Braley, Berton, 231-32
Bridger, Jim, 18, 24, 125, 155
Bridger Mountains, 29
Brisbin, James S., 88
Broadwater, Charles A., 47, 48, 54, 58, 59-60, 142-43, 188
Brownell, Baker, 231
Buffalo, 5, 10-13, 16, 27, 66, 74-78
Bullboats, 127
Burlington Northern Railroad, 131, 141
Bus transportation, 132-33
Butte, 8-9, 37-39, 103, 106, 111, 119-21, 132, 135, 142, 151-52, 154, 155, 157-59, 185-87, 189, 199, 211, 220-21, 231-32
Butte, Anaconda and Pacific Railroad, 131
Butte Daily Post, 186

Butte Fire Department, 119-21
Butte Hardware Company, 120-21
Butte Miners Union, 111, 157-59, 186
Butte Reveille, 182
Byam, Don, 43

Callaway, James E., 56, 59
Camp Cooke, 53, 68, 78
Camp Disappointment, 28
Campbell, Hardy Webster, 165-66, 168
Canyon Ferry Dam, 155
Capital location, 54, 180-81, 189
Carey Land Act (1894), 165
Carpenter, B. Platt, 55, 56
Carpenter, David, 165
Carroll College, 110, 227
Carroll Trail, 127, map, 14
Carter, Thomas H., 55, 179, 181, 189, 202-03
Carter County, 4
Cat Creek oil field, 9
Cataract Milling Company, 149
Catholic church, 42, 108, 110, see also Jesuits
Cattle raising, 55, 81, 84-99, 211
Cavanaugh, James, 53
Cenozoic Era, 4
Charbonneau, Baptiste, 29
Charbonneau, Toussaint, 16
Charlot (Flathead), 23, 71
Cheyenne Indians, see Northern Cheyenne Indians
Chicago, Burlington and Quincy Railroad, 130, 143, 165, 166
Chicago, Milwaukee and St. Paul Railroad, 131, 164, 165, 167, 171
Chinese, 41, 42, 56, 98, 108, 109, 114-15
Chinook, 4
Chinook, wind, 1, 95, 96
Chippewa, 127
Chippewa Falls, 128
Chippewa Indians, 7, 72-73
Choteau, Auguste and Pierre, Sr., 17
Chouteau, Natawista Ixsana and son Charles, 25
Chouteau, Pierre, Jr., 18, 23-26
Christianity, see religion and names of individual denominations

255

Civil War, 45, 52, 57, 59, 142
Civilian Conservation Corps, 210
Claessens, William, 21
Clagett, William, 58, 59
Clancy, William, 182-83
Clark, William, 16-17, 20, 26-29
Clark, William A., 37, 48, 55, 56, 121, 151, 153, 158, 179, 181-83, 188-91
Clark, William P., 72
Clark Fork River, 1, 5
Clarke, Helen Piotopowaka, 109
Clarke, John, 234
Clarke, Malcolm, 68, 81
Coal, 4, 9-10, 103, 142, 143, 167-68, 199, 211, 215
College of Great Falls, 110, 227
College of Montana, 110
Colonel McLeod, 127
Colstrip, 9, 199, 215
Colstrip generating plants, 154, 215
Colter, John, 19
Columbia Fur Company, 18, 24
Commissioner of Higher Education, 227
Communism, 158, 199, 212
ConAgra, 160
Confederate Gulch, 35
Congress of Industrial Organizations, 158
Conley, Frank, 204
Connolly, C. P., 230
Conrad, 172
Constitutional conventions, 55-56, 99, 179, 189, 213-14
Continental Divide, 1, 2, 16
Cooney, Frank H., 210
Copper, 8-9, 37-39, 103, 151-52, 182-83, 188-91, 199, 211
Corbin, Daniel C., 47
Corrine-Virginia City Road, 86, 125, 126, map, 14
Cory, J. Campbell, 231
Coulson, Martin, 140
County-busting, 168, 174-76, map, 171
Cover, Tom, 40, 149
Cow Island, 127-28, 136
Cowan, Thomas "John," 34-35
Cowan, William, 205
Cowboys, 84-99
Coxey, Jacob S., 180
Crab, John, 34-35

Crane, 174-75
Crazy Horse (Sioux), 67, 69
Cree Indians, 6, 72-73, 95
Cretaceous Period, 9
Croatian stonemasons, 114
Crook, George, 69, 81
Crosby, John Schuyler, 54-55
Crow Indians, 6, 15, 17, 19, 22, 29, 40, 65, 71, 75-78, 87, 110
Cruse, Thomas, 36-37
Cruzatte, Pete, 29
Culbertson, Alexander, 18, 25
Culver, Bill, 233
Cushman, Dan, 229
Custer, George A., 7, 68-69, 81, see also, Little Big Horn Battlefield
Custer Battle, see Little Big Horn Battlefield
Custer County, 94
Cut Bank Creek, 17, 27, 143

DHS Ranch, 47, 88, 94, 95, 98-99
Dairy industry, 150
Dakotah, 137
Daly, Marcus, 37-38, 48, 55, 131, 150, 151, 157, 158, 181-83, 188-91
Dance, Walter, 42, 45
Daniels, James, 106
Darling, Lucia, 35, 108, 227
Davis, Andrew J., 47, 98
Davison, Stanley, 232
Dawes Act (1887), 71, 72, 73
Dawson County, 94, 174-76
Dawson Community College, 227-28
Daylight Creek, 40, 42
Decker, 9
Deer Lodge, 188-89, see also, Penitentiary
Deer Lodge Valley, 33, 86, 97-99, 135
Deidesheimer, Philip, 46
Democratic party, see politics
de Mores, Marquis, 88
Depression (1929-1940), 209-11, 216-19
Desert Land Act (1877), 85, 165
DeSmet, Pierre Jean, 19, 20-23
de Trobriand, Philippe, 81
Dexter Mill, 37
Diamond City, 91, 93
Dillingham, D. B., 35

Dillon, 103
Dimsdale, Thomas J., 43, 97, 106, 108, 227, 232
Dinosaurs, 4
Dixon, Cromwell, 133
Dixon, Caroline Worden, 184, 202
Dixon, Joseph M., 165, 183, 184, 193, 199-200, 201-04, 221
Dog Soldiers, 7
Drought, 169-70, 194, 197, 201, 205, 209-11
Drumlummon mine, 35, 36-37
Dry farming, see agriculture
Dude ranches, 156
Dull Knife (N. Cheyenne), 72
Dun and Company, R. G., 147-48
Duncan, Hugh, 108
Duncan, Lewis, 158
Dunkirk, 172
Durston, John H., 107

E6 Ranch, 96
Earthquakes, 4
East Helena, 39
Eastern Montana College, 100, 227
Eastern State Prison, 106
Eddy, Hammond and Company, 152
Edgar, Henry, 34, 40
Edgerton, Sidney, 43, 46, 51-52
Education, see schools and names of individual units of higher education
Electrical power, 48, 154-55, 217
Elkhorn, 9
Emilie, 45
English exploration in Montana, 15-18, 26
Enid, 174-75
Enlarged Homestead Act (1909), 165, 172, 174
Environmental concern, 215
Episcopal church, 42, 108
Erickson, John E., 200, 209, 210
Erickson, Leif, 223
Ethnic groups, 38, 41, 79, 113-16, see also, Chinese
Evans, John B., 202
Executive reorganization, 213, 215

Fair Trials Bill, 183
Fairview, 174-75

Fairway Farms Project, 197, 201, 209
Fairweather, Bill, 34, 40
Far West, 69, 128, 140
Farlin, William L., 37
Farming, see agriculture
Federal aid to Montana, 209-11, 216-19
Federal Emergency Relief Administration, 210
Federal Writers Project, 230-31
Fergus, James, 40, 86
Ferries, 126
Festival of Nations, 114
Fetterman, William J., 67
Finlay, Francois "Benetsee," 33
Finntown, 113
Fires, 106, 117, 119-21
First National Bank of Bozeman, 149
First National Bank of Butte, 47
First National Bank of Deer Lodge, 149
First National Bank of Helena, 46-47, 149
First National Bank of Missoula, 149
Fisk, Elizabeth Chester, 116-19
Fisk, Robert E., 53, 54, 57-60, 107, 108, 115, 116-19
Fisk Expeditions, 35
Fitzpatrick, Thomas, 24
Flathead Indians, 6, 17, 19, 20-23, 28, 53, 65, 66, 71, 165
Flathead Lake, 128
Flathead Valley Community College, 227-28
Fletcher, Robert, 156
Flour milling, 21, 149, 159-61
Flour riots, 44, 147
Ford, Robert, 81
Ford, Sam C., 193, 214
Foreign investments in cattle industry, 88
Forest fires, 154
Forest Reserve Act (1891), 153
Forsyth, 181
Fort Abraham Lincoln, 68
Fort Assinniboine, 60, 73, 135
Fort Belknap Indian Reservation, 71
Fort Benton (Big Horn River), 18
Fort Benton (Missouri River), 18, 25, 33, 35, 45, 53, 79, 85, 103,

104, 127-28, 136, 140
Fort Benton National Bank, 47
Fort C. F. Smith, 67, 78
Fort Clatsop, 16, 28
Fort Custer, 60, 73
Fort Ellis, 53, 67, 78, 80
Fort Fetterman, 67, 69
Fort Fizzle, 70
Fort Keogh, 60, 72, 103, 135
Fort Laramie, treaties and meetings at, 66-67
Fort McKenzie, 18, 25, 127
Fort Maginnis, 60, 73, 86, 98
Fort Missoula, 60, 73
Fort Owen, 22, 33, 85, 103
Fort Peck Dam, 128, 210, 216-19, 222
Fort Peck Indian Reservation, 71
Fort Phil Kearny, 67
Fort Piegan, 18
Fort Shaw, 53, 67, 68, 69, 78-81, 85
Fort Union, 18, 25-26, 128
Fort William Henry Harrison, 73
Fossils, 4
Four Georgians, 34-35
Fox Lake, 174-75
Free Masons, 35, 189
Freighting, 42, 126-27, see also, individual types of transportation
French exploration in Montana, 15-17, 26
Frenchtown, 113
Frissell, M. A., 174-75
Frontier Airlines, 134
Frontier and Midland, 230
Fruit processing, 150
Fur trade in Montana, 17-19, 23-26, 66, 85, 147

Gall (Sioux), 69
Gallatin Valley, 28, 78, 86
Garfield County, 4
Gates of the Mountains, 28
General Mills, 160-61
Geology, 3-5, 8-10
German ethnic groups in Montana, 107, 113, 193
Gibbon, John, 69, 80, 81, 85, 189
Gibson, Paris, 142-44, 149, 181-82, 190
Giorda, Joseph, 23, 40
Girard, 174, 175

Glacial Lake Missoula, 5
Glacier National Park, 1, 71, 128, 156, 212, 223
Glasgow, 210, 216-19
Glass, Hugh, 18, 19
Glasscock, C. B., 230
Glendive, 1, 96, 129, 174-76
Glendive Commercial Club, 175
Glidden Auto Tours, 132
Gneiss, 3
Gold, 8-9, 19, 33-48, 67, 103-04, 147
Gold Creek, 8, 33, 45, 129
Good Templars, 93
Goodnight-Loving Trail, 88
Gore, Sir George, 155
Grangers, see Patrons of Husbandry
Granite, 9
Granite Peak, 1
Grant, Johnny, 86, 97
Grant, Quarra, 97
Grant-Kohrs Ranch National Historic Site, 86, 97-99
Grasshopper Creek, 33
Great American Desert, 1, 168
Great Falls, 39, 96, 103, 104, 132, 142, 149, 152, 154, 160
Great Falls Land Office, 167
Great Falls of the Missouri River, 16, 28, 142
Great Falls Tribune, 136, 144, 185
Great North Trail, 5
Great Northern Railroad, 114, 128, 130-31, 141-44, 152, 165, 166-67, 172-73, 234
Great Spirit, 75, 77
Grizzly bear, 16, 19, 27
Gros Ventre Indians, see Atsina Indians
Guthrie, A. B., 1, 229

Haggin, James Ben Ali, 38
Hall, Vess, 192-93
Handgame, 75
Hansen, Bert B., 231
Harlowton, 131
Harney, Edward, 182-83
Harrison, Russell B., 96
Haskell, Ella Knowles, 180, 184
Hauser, Samuel T., 37, 45-48, 51, 54, 55, 58, 59-62, 98, 149, 155, 188
Hauser Dam, 48

Havre, 204, 206
Haynes, F. J., 233
Hearst, George, 38
Heavy Runner (Piegan), 68, 81
Hedges, Cornelius, 61, 109, 115
Heikka, Earl, 234
Heinze, F. Augustus, 158, 182-83
Helena, 34-35, 46-48, 54, 103, 105, 106, 116-19, 132, 135, 142, 154, 155, 165, 181, 189
Helena earthquake (1935), 4
Helena Herald, 55, 59
Helena Independent, 59
Helena and Livingston Smelting and Reduction Co., 39, 47
Helena Mining and Reduction Company, 47
Hell Gate River, 33
Henry, Ralph, 230
Higgins, Christopher P., 33, 45, 47, 149
Highways, 132-33, map, 133
Hill, James J., 47, 130-31, 141-44, 166
Hill, Mary Theresa Mehegan, 142
Hill County, 141
Historic Preservation Program, 228
Hogan, William, 180-81
Holt, Elmer, 210
Holter, A. M., 47, 148, 151
Holter Dam, 48
Homestead Act (1862), 85, 165
Homesteading, 104, 164-77, 197
Honyockers, see homesteading
Hooban, Tom, 97
Hope Mining Company, 46
Hornblende, 3
Horses, 5-6, 17, 28, 29, 65, 86, 98, 150, 205
Hosmer, J. Allen, 108, 232
Hot springs resorts, 155-56
Hough, A. M., 42, 108
Howard, Joe, 231
Howard, Joseph Kinsey, 1, 231
Howard, Oliver O., 70, 81
Howie, Neil, 44
Hudson's Bay Company, 18, 25, 33
Huet, Charles, 21
Huffman, L. A., 233
Hughes, Barney, 40
Hugo, Richard, 232
Hump (Sioux), 67

Huntley Irrigation Project, 165

Ice ages, 4-5
Ignace (Big Ignace, Young Ignace, Ignace La Mouse), 20
Indians, 5-7, 10-13, 20-23, 53, 58, 65-78, 234, map of distribution, 7, map of reservations, 82, see also, individual tribes
Industrial Workers of the World (IWW), 154, 185-87, 191-93, 203
Initiative, 183
Insects, 170, 205
Intermountain Union College, 110
International Typographical Union, 157
Interstate highways, 132-33
Irrigation, 85, 165, 205, 211
Ives, George, 35-36, 43

J. Neils Lumber Company, 153-54
Jackson, David, 24
Jefferson, Thomas, 15-17, 26-29
Jesuit missionaries, 19, 20-23, 87, 108, 110
Jewish religion, 111
Jocko Reservation, 67, 71, see also, Flathead Indians
Johnson, Dorothy, 230
Jorud, Les, 233
Joseph (Nez Perce), 70, 81
Judge, Thomas L., 215
Judith Basin, 27, 47, 86, 96, 167, 233
Jurassic Period, 9

KDYS (radio station), 136
KOOK-TV, 136
Kalispel Indians, 6, 19, 65
Kalispell, 4
Kaufman and Stadler Cattle Company, 95-96
Keelboats, 127
Kemmis, Walter D., 174
Kennedy, Will, 180
Kenyon-Connell Hardware Company, 119-21
Ketcham, Harry G., 174-75
Key West, 127
Kimball, G. G., 87
Kipp, James, 18, 24
Kleinschmidt, Theodore H., 46
Knights of Labor, 111, 157

257

Knowles, Hiram, 62
Kohrs, Augusta, 97-99
Kohrs, Conrad, 47, 81, 86, 96, 97-99, 149
Kootenai River, 1, 17, 128
Kutenai Indians, 6, 17, 65-66, 71

LaBarge, Joseph, 128
Labor unions, 111, 154, 157-59, 185-87, 191
LaFollette, Robert M., 222
Lambert, 174-76
Landless Indians, 7, 72-73
Langford, Nathaniel P., 46, 51, 53
Langrishe, Jack, 42
Larabie, S. E., 188-89
Last Chance Gulch, 34-35
La Verendrye, Louis and Francois, 15
Lead, 8-9, 37
Leavitt, Erasmus D., 61
Leeson, Michael A., 108
Legislative Council, 213
Leighton Act (1911), 168, 174
Leslie, Preston, 55
Lewis, Meriwether, 16-17, 26-29
Lewis and Clark Expedition, 5, 16-17, 26-29, 65, 66, 125, map, 14
Lewis and Clark Pass, 28
Lewistown, 114
Libby, 17
Libraries, 111, 118
Linderman, Frank B., 73, 228-29
Linfield, F. B., 166
Liquor trade, 18-19, 25
Lisa, Manuel, 17-18
Little, Frank, 158, 186, 192, 193
Little Big Horn Battlefield, 4, 7, 69, 81, 128, 135
Little Wolf (N. Cheyenne), 72
Livestock, see cattle, horses and sheep
Livingston, 106
Lolo Pass, 16, 28
Looking Glass (Nez Perce), 70
Louisiana Purchase, 15-16, 23
Lower Yellowstone Irrigation Project, 165
Loyal Legion of Loggers and Lumbermen, 154
Luce, Timothy, 42
Lumbering, 103, 104, 152-54, 211-12

McAdow, P. W., 149
McCone County, 176
McGlynn, Mickey, 193
McHaffie Site, 5
McKay, Dan, 168, 174-75
McKay, R. H., 233
McKenzie, Kenneth, 18, 24-25
McLane, Mary, 230
McLean, Samuel, 53
McLeod the hewer, 97
Madison County, 52
Madison River Earthquake (1959), 4
Maginnis, Martin, 54-55, 56, 58-62, 142-43, 179
Makoshika State Park, 5
Malone, Michael, 232
Mandan, 128
Mandan Indians, 16, 26-27, 29, 66
Mansfield, Mike, 212
Mantle, Lee, 181, 190
Marias Pass, 130, 143
Marias River, 17, 18, 27-28
Maroney, T. T., 133
Mars, J. C., 133
Marsh, Grant, 128, 140
Marysville, 35, 36-37
Matador Cattle Company, 88
Meader, Charles A., 151
Meadowlark, 5, 92
Meagher, Thomas Francis, 52-53, 55, 68, 78
Meagher County, 92-93
Meat packing, 149-50
Medicine, 21
Medicine Lake, 1
Medicine Rocks, 5
Melcher, John, 213
Mengarini, Gregory, 19, 20-23
Merchandising in mining camps, 34, 42, 147-48, 188
Merriam, H. G., 230, 232
Mesozoic Era, 4, 8, 9
Metcalf, Jim, 174-75
Metcalf, Lee, 212-13
Methodist church, 42, 108, 110
Metis, 7, 95, 114
Mexican-Americans, 113
Mica, 3
Miles, Nelson A., 70, 72
Miles City, 88, 103, 106, 149, 193
Miles Community College, 227-28
Military District of Montana, 78
Milk River, 27

Milk River Irrigation Project, 165
Millard, J. H., 148
Miller, D. J., 34-35
Mills, James H., 107
Mine, Mill and Smelter Workers Union, 158
Minerals, 8-10
Miners courts, 35, 43
Ming, John, 42
Mining, 33-48, 55, 103-04, 113, 182-83, see also, individual types of ore
Minneapolis, St. Paul, and Sault St. Marie Railroad, 131
Minnesota Wagon Road, 35
Minnetaree Indians, 27, 28
Minnie Healy mine, 182
Missionaries, 19, 20-23, 85, 110, see also, Jesuits and individual denominations
Missoula, 103, 106, 132, 135, 184, 200, 203, 212
Missoula National Bank, 47
Missoulian, 200, 203
Missouri Fur Company, 17-18
Missouri River, 1, 4, 16-19, 26-29, 33, 48, 86, 91, 210, 216-19, 233, see also, riverboats
Missouri Valley Authority, 212
Monida Pass, 129
Montana Aeronautics Commission, 134
Montana Agricultural Experiment Station, 144, 150, 166, 167, 169, 173, 197, 201, 204-06
Montana Board of Education, 227
Montana Central Railroad, 142-43, 152
Montana College of Mineral Science and Technology, 110, 227
Montana Committee for the Humanities, 231
Montana Company, Ltd., 37
Montana Council of Defense, 187, 192-94, 214, 221
Montana-Dakota Utilities, 154, 155
Montana Deaf and Dumb School, 110
Montana Education Association, 227
Montana Federation of Teachers, 227
Montana Highway Department, 132, 156
Montana Historical Society, 35, 231, 232
Montana Improvement Company, 152-53
Montana Institute of the Arts, 230
Montana Legislative Assembly, 179, see also, politics
Montana Lumber Manufacturers Association, 154
Montana National Guard, 134, 158
Montana Orphans' Home, 110
Montana Post (Virginia City), 43, 157, see also, Thomas Dimsdale
Montana Power Company, 155, 215
Montana Public Service Commission, 184
Montana Railroad Commission, 184
Montana Reform School, 110
Montana State College, see Montana State University
Montana State University (Bozeman), 110, 227, 231, see also, Montana Agricultural Experiment Station
Montana Stockgrowers Association, 47, 88, 96
Montana Study, 231
Montana Union Railroad, 98
Montana University (Helena), 110
Montana Wilderness Society, 215
Mountain Chief (Piegan), 68, 81
Mountain men, 17, 19, 23-26
Mountain ranges, map, 3
Moyle, 128
Mullan Road, 33, 35, 45, 67, 78, 86, 125, map, 14
Murray, James E., 210-11, 212
Murray and Freund Hospital, 121
Museums, 228
Music, 42, 80, 118
Musselshell River, 27, 167
Myers, Henry L., 193, 200

National Park Airways, 134
Natural gas, 4, 9-10
Negroes, 111, 115-16
Nellie Peck, 140
Nevada City, 34, 40, 232
New Deal, 209-11, 216-19

Newlands Reclamation Act (1902), 165
Newspapers, 107-08, see also, names of individual newspapers
Nez Perce Indians, 7, 17, 21, 28, 70, 81, 189
Non-Partisan League, 192, 193, 203
North West Company, 17-18
Northern Cheyenne Indians, 7, 19, 65, 67, 69, 71-72, 81, 86, 110
Northern Montana College, 110, 227
Northern Montana Forestry Association, 154
Northern Pacific Railroad, 37, 47, 58, 68, 71, 80, 86, 88, 92, 129-31, 142, 152, 165, 167, 199, 215, 221, 233
Northern Plains Resource Council, 215
Northern Securities Company, 130, 143
Northwest Orient Airlines, 134
Northwest Passage, 26
Nutter, Donald G., 214

O'Connell, Jerry, 211
O'Donnell, I. D., 150
Oil, see Petroleum
Olsen, Arnold, 213
O'Neill, Hugh, 42
Orem, Con, 42
Oro y Plata, 8
Orr, William C., 86
Owen, John, 19, 22, 149, see also, Fort Owen
Oxarart, Michel, 97-98

Pacific Power and Light Company, 155
Paddlefish, 4
Paleozoic Era, 4, 9
Pambrun, Alexander, 97
Panic of 1893, 39, 180
Partoll, Al, 232
Patrons of Husbandry, 85, 91-93
Paxon, Edgar S., 233
Peavy, 160-61
Pemmican, 76
Pend d'Oreille Indians, 6, 17, 19, 65-66, 71
Penitentiary, 61, 99, 106, 204
People's Power League, 183

Petrified wood, 4
Petroleum, 4, 9-10, 103, 152, 199, 211, 212
Pfouts, Paris, 44
Philipsburg, 46
Phillips, Paul C., 232
Photography, 232-33
Pictograph Cave, 5
Piegan Indians, 6, 17, 19, 25, 65, 68, 234
Pierre's Hole, 20
Pine Hill School for Boys, see Montana Reform School
Pioneer, 99
Pioneer Cattle Company, 47, 98-99
Piskun, 5, 10-13
Pleistocene Epoch, 9
Plentywood, 199
Plummer, Henry, 35-36, 43, 46
Poetry, 231-32
Poindexter, Philip, 86, 87
Point, Nicholas, 20, 22
Politics, 43, 47-48, 51-61, 174-76, 178-95, 199-204, 220-23
Pollution, air and water, 106
Pompey's Pillar, 29, 128
Populist party, 180-81, see also, politics
Potts, Benjamin Franklin, 54, 57-59, 115, 189
Powder River, 67, 68
Powder River Cattle Company, 88
Powell, Ace, 234
Power, T. C., 60, 80, 179
Pratte, Chouteau and Company, 25
Precambrian Era, 3, 9
Preemption Act (1841), 85
Presbyterian church, 110, 118
Primary elections, 183
Prison, see penitentiary
Progressive Era, 183-85
Public Works Administration, 210, 216-19
Pulitzer Prize, 229, 230

Quartz, 3
Quillwork, 77

Racetrack Creek, 98
Radio broadcasting, 136
Railroad transportation, 47, 58, 92, 103, 113, 125, 128-31, 141-44, 156, map, 130, see also, names of individual railroads
Ralston, J. K., 234
Rankin, Jeannette, 178, 183, 184, 192, 193, 212
Rarus mine, 182
Ravalli, Anthony, 19, 21-23, 85, 149, 152, 160
Ravalli County Bank, 149
Raymond, Sarah, 109
Recreation, 103, see also, Tourism
Red Cloud (Sioux), 67
Red Cross, 192, 193, 209, 216
Red Lodge, 9, 103, 104, 215
Reeve, Moise, 149
Referendum, 183
Reiss, Winold, 234
Religion, 6, 77, see also, individual denominations
Rendezvous, 18, 24-25
Reno, Marcus, 69
Republican party, see politics
Reynolds, Richard, 87
Richland County, 174-76
Rickards, John E., 179
Riel, Louis, 7, 72-73, 114
Riverboats, 35, 127-28, 136-40
Rock Creek, 10
Rocky Boy Indian Reservation, 7, 72-73, 229
Rocky Mountain College, 110, 227
Rocky Mountain Fur Company, 18, 24-25
Rocky Mountain Husbandman, 85, 91-93, 94
Rodgers, Harry, 40
Roeder, Richard, 232
Romney, Miles, 183
Ronan, Peter, 42, 73
Roosevelt, Franklin D., 209-11, 212, 216-19, 222
Roosevelt, Theodore, 96, 153, 184, 190, 203
Ross, Kenneth, 154
Ross' Hole, 20, 28
Roundup, 9, 103, 104, 215
Ruder, Mel, 230
Rural Electrification Administration, 155, 211
Russell, Charles M., 20, 95-96, 233-34
Rustling cards, 158, 186
Ryan, John D., 155

Sacagawea, 16, 27-28
St. Ignatius, 19, 23, 149
St. Labre School, 110
St. Louis and Montana Mining Company, 46
St. Mary's Lake, 128
St. Mary's Mission, 19, 20-23, 149, 152
St. Paul, Minneapolis and Manitoba Railroad, see Great Northern Railroad
St. Peter's Mission, 87
St. Xavier School, 110
Saleesh House, 17
Sand Coulee, 143
Sanders, Wilbur F., 35-36, 43, 46, 51, 53, 54, 57-58, 61, 179
Sapphires, 10
Saskatchewan River, 1
Savage, 174
Sawmills, 21, 152-54
Scannon, 28
Schist, 3
Schneider, Simon, 193
School Foundation Program, 213
Schools, 35, 92, 108-09, 110, 227-28
Schultz, James Willard, 228
Schultz, Mutsiawotan Ahki, 228
Scissorbills, see homesteading
Scott, Joseph, 96
Scriver, Bob, 234
Sculpture, 234
Sedition Act (1918), 187, 193
Seltzer, Olaf C., 233-34
Senators, direct election, 182, 183
Shaw, Thomas, 166-67, 168, 173
Sheehan, Mollie, 41-42, 44
Sheep, 86, 87-88
Sheepeater Indians, 7
Sheridan, Philip, 81
Sheridan County, 1, 199
Sherman Silver Purchase Act, 180
Shonkin Pool, 88
Shope, Shorty, 234
Shoshoni Indians, 5-6, 7, 16, 28
Shoup, Richard, 213
Sidney, 174-76
Sieben, Henry, 87
Silver, 8-9, 37, 46, 48, 103, 180
Silver Bow Trades and Labor Assembly, 157
Simmons, Lew, 40
Sioux Indians, 6, 7, 65, 67-69, 75-

259

78, 80, 81, 86
Sioux Pass, 174
Sitting Bull (Sioux), 69
Smallpox, 6, 7, 21
Smelting, 151-52, see also, separate ore types
Smith, Green Clay, 53
Smith, Jedediah, 18, 24
Smith, Robert B., 180, 183, 190
Smithers, C. Owen, 233
Smokejumpers, 134
Socialists, 158, 199
Soil, 1
Spanish exploration, 15, 26
Specht, Joseph, 21
Speculator mine, 186
Spokan Indians, 7, 19
Spriggs, A. E., 190
Stagecoach travel, 126
Standard Oil Company, 182
Standing, William, 234
Stanley, Reginald "Bob," 34-35
Starch, Elmer, 209
Stauffer Chemical Company, 152
Steamboats, see riverboats
Steele, William, 40
Steitz, August, 46
Stevens, Isaac I., 33, 66-67, 125
Stevens, John F., 143
Stevensville, 23
Stewart, Samuel V., 192
Stimson, Katherine, 133
Story, Nelson, 86, 96
Street railways, 111, 131-32
Strip mining, 199, 215
Stuart, Granville, 33, 45, 47, 86, 88, 94, 98
Stuart, James, 33, 34, 37, 40, 42, 45
Sublette, Milton, 18
Sugar beets, 21, 113, 150
Sun Dance, 77
Sun River Irrigation Project, 165
Sun River Valley, 6, 79, 81, 86, 97, 135
Superintendent of Public Instruction, 227
Sutherlin, Robert N., 91-93
Sutherlin, William, 91-93
Swan River Cattle Company, 88
Sweeney, Mike, 40

Tanning hides, 12-13
Taxation, 56, 92, 203-04

Taylor, Charles E., 199
Tbalt, Nicholas, 35, 43
Teapot Dome Scandal, 200-01, 222
Telegraph, 80, 134-35
Telephones, 111, 135
Television broadcasting, 136
Terry, Alfred H., 68-69, 81
Tertiary Period, 4, 8, 9-10
Teton County, 172-73
Tevis, Lloyd, 38
Texas cattle, 86, 88, 94
Theater, 42, 80
Thomas, George, 149
Thompson, David, 17, 125
Thompson, Francis M., 85, 86, 90, 113
Thompson Falls, 17
Three Forks, 17, 28
3-7-77, 36
Three Year Homestead Act (1912), 165
Threshing, 205-06
Tilton, D. W., 108
Timber Culture Act (1873), 85
Timber and Stone Act (1878), 85
Tipis, 10, 76-77
Toft, Peter, 233
Toll roads, 126
Tongue River, 7, 72
Toohoolhoolzote (Nez Perce), 70
Toole, Joseph K., 56, 62, 179, 183
Toole, K. Ross, 1, 232
Tourism, 132, 155-56, 212
Townsend, 59, 91, 103
Train, E. H., 233
Transportation, 125-45, see also, individual types
Trask Hall, 110
Traveler's Rest, 17
Travis, Lee, 108
Travona mine, 37
Triple Divide Peak, 1
Trolleys, see Street railways
Truck transportation, 132-33
Tufts, James, 53
Turkey Track Ranch, 96
Tuttle, Daniel S., 42, 108
Two Moons (N. Cheyenne), 69

Unemployment, 180
Union Pacific Railroad, 125, 131, see also, Utah and Northern Railroad

U. S. Army, 65-74, 78-81
U. S. Army Corps of Engineers, 128, 216
United Steelworkers of America, 158
University of Montana, 110, 227
Upper Missouri Outfit, 18, 24-26
Utah and Northern Railroad, 47, 58, 86, 97, 129-30, 152

Valley County, 216-19
Valley Mercantile and Lumber Company, 175-76
Van Orsdel, William W., 108
Varina, 34, 40
Vegetable processing, 150
Vigilantes (1863-64), 35-36, 43-44, 51
Vigilantes (1884), 47, 88
Vigilantes (Helena), 106, 118
The Vigilantes of Montana, 43, 106, 108
Villard, Henry, 129
Virginia City, 8, 34-35, 40-44, 51, 54, 103, 104-05, 109, 134-35, 148-49, 157, 188, 232
The Virginian, 90
Vocational and technical centers, 227
Volcanic activity, 4, 8

Wagon trains, 34
Walker Brothers, 37, 157
Walsh, Thomas J., 183, 185, 200-01, 203, 210, 221-22
War of the Copper Kings, 181-83, 188-91, see also, William A. Clark and Marcus Daly
Warren, Conrad and Nell, 99
Washoe Smelter, 151
Water, 1, map, 2
Water Conservation Board, 211
Weaver, John, 234
Wellcome, John B., 190
Western Airlines, 134
Western Energy Company, 215
Western Federation of Miners, 158, 186
Western Lumber Company, 153
Western Montana College, 110, 227
Western Trail, 88
Wheat, 21, 159-61, 168-70, 173, 191, 194, 197, 204-06, 211

Wheeler, Burton K., 183, 185-86, 192-93, 199, 203, 210, 212, 216, 220-23
Wheeler, Lulu White, 220
Wheeler, William F., 81
Wheeler-Howard Act (1934), 222
White, Benjamin F., 55
White, John, 33
White Bird (Nez Perce), 70
White buffalo, 11-13
White Sulphur Springs, 93
Whiteside, Fred, 181, 190
Whitetail, 131
Whoop-Up Trail, map, 14
Wibaux, Pierre, 88
Wickes, 47
Widmyer, J. R., 175
Wilderness Act (1964), 213, 215
Wilderness areas, 215
Williams, James, 43
Wilson, M. L., 197, 201, 204-06, 209
Winter of 1886-87, 55, 88, 94-96, 98
Wister, Owen, 90
Women's suffrage, 56, 118, 183-84
Woody, Frank H., 202
Woolen mills, 151
Worden, Frank L., 33, 149, 184
Workmen's Compensation Law (1915), 184
Works Progress Administration, 210, 230-31
World War I, 168, 170, 185-87, 191-94, 197-98, 221
World War II, 211-12, 222-23
Wright, Joseph, 107
Wright, W. D., 107

Yeager, Red, 43
Yellowstone, 18, 25
Yellowstone Journal and Live Stock Reporter (Miles City), 95
Yellowstone National Park, 1, 4, 19, 47, 70, 98, 155, 212
Yellowstone River, 1, 4, 6, 17, 27, 71, 80, 128, see also, riverboats
Yellowstone Trail, 132
Yogo, 10

Zinc, 8-9